GAMING REPRESENTATION

DIGITAL GAME STUDIES

Robert Alan Brookey and
David J. Gunkel, editors

GAMING REPRESENTATION

Race, Gender, and Sexuality in Video Games

EDITED BY **JENNIFER MALKOWSKI** AND **TREAANDREA M. RUSSWORM**

INDIANA UNIVERSITY PRESS

This book is a publication of

Indiana University Press
Office of Scholarly Publishing
Herman B Wells Library 350
1320 East 10th Street
Bloomington, Indiana 47405 USA

iupress.indiana.edu

∞ The paper used in this publication meets the minimum requirements of the American National Standard for Information Sciences—Permanence of Paper for Printed Library Materials, ANSI Z39.48-1992.

Manufactured in the United States of America

Cataloging information is available from the Library of Congress.

ISBN 978-0-253-02573-9 (cloth)
ISBN 978-0-253-02647-7 (paperback)
ISBN 978-0-253-02660-6 (ebook)

1 2 3 4 5 22 21 20 19 18 17

For Kim Malkowski and Armandé Millender,
our siblings and most formative gaming
partners and rivals

CONTENTS

Foreword | Anna Everett ix
Acknowledgments xvii

Introduction: Identity, Representation, and Video Game Studies beyond the Politics of the Image | Jennifer Malkowski and TreaAndrea M. Russworm 1

PART I. GENDER, BODIES, SPACES

one "I Turned Out to Be Such a Damsel in Distress": Noir Games and the Unrealized Femme Fatale | Jennifer Malkowski 19

two No Time to Dream: Killing Time, Casual Games, and Gender | Braxton Soderman 38

three "Aw Fuck, I Got a Bitch on My Team!": Women and the Exclusionary Cultures of the Computer Game Complex | Jennifer deWinter and Carly A. Kocurek 57

four Attention Whores and Ugly Nerds: Gender and Cosplay at the Game Con | Nina B. Huntemann 74

five Video Game Parodies: Appropriating Video Games to Criticize Gender Norms | Gabrielle Trépanier-Jobin 90

PART II. RACE, IDENTITY, NATION

six Dystopian Blackness and the Limits of Racial Empathy in *The Walking Dead* and *The Last of Us* | TreaAndrea M. Russworm 109

seven *Journey* into the Techno-primitive Desert | Irene Chien 129 *eight* The Rubble and the Ruin: Race, Gender, and Sites of Inglorious Conflict in *Spec Ops: The Line* | Soraya Murray 147

nine Representing Race and Disability: *Grand Theft Auto: San Andreas* as a Whole Text | Rachael Hutchinson 164

ten Entering the Picture: Digital Portraiture and the Aesthetics of Video Game Representation | Lisa Patti 179

PART III. QUEERNESS, PLAY, SUBVERSION

eleven Playing to Lose: The Queer Art of Failing at Video Games | Bonnie Ruberg 197

twelve Romancing an Empire, Becoming Isaac: The Queer Possibilities of *Jade Empire* and *The Binding of Isaac* | Jordan Wood 212

thirteen A Game Chooses, a Player Obeys: *BioShock*, Posthumanism, and the Limits of Queerness | Edmond Y. Chang 227

Afterword: Racism, Sexism, and Gaming's Cruel Optimism | Lisa Nakamura 245

Index 251

FOREWORD

NOW IS AN OPPORTUNE MOMENT FOR VISIONARY THINKING ABOUT THE gaming industrial complex (GIC) vis-à-vis the intersectionality of gender, sexuality, race, and the ludic imagination, especially as we look toward the third decade of the twenty-first century. Since the remarkable rebound of the video game industry in the 1990s following its near total collapse in the early 1980s, there have been phenomenal transformations in the business, technology, and culture of gaming. Among gaming's more notable paradigmatic shifts are theoretical debates about the primacy of narratology versus ludology in games' meaningful play and procedural rhetorics; interrogations of gaming's structures of play and affective engagement on- and off-line; the rise of professional gaming; and, most recently and interestingly, the neo-formalist tech turn to platform, software, and code studies. Moreover, humanities disciplines finally joined the social/behavioral/cognitive and computing sciences in recognizing video games and the GIC as legitimate objects of study. Subsequently, the humanities fields have incorporated vibrant academic gaming studies programs, especially and fittingly in film and media studies. Most pertinent for my consideration here is the fact that humanities and cultural studies' qualitative analytics and critical discourse methodologies have crafted particularly insightful analyses for understanding and deconstructing race, gender, class, sexuality, and disability matters in society and culture. And yet there apparently is a notable retrenchment from addressing critical theories of identity politics in gaming, if it ever was fully embraced.

Nonetheless, a sign of our millennial times is how willing gaming journalists are to raise concerns about race, gender, and sexuality discourses in gaming culture and in the GIC. Additionally, today's moral panics reflect heightened concerns about society's increased aggression, violence, misogyny, and racism (to a lesser degree) often attributed to so-called addictive gaming. Consequently, perpetrators of school shootings and even the Gamergate controversy, for example, signify to the public "addictive" gaming's inevitable dark side. Moreover, the explosive rise in critical discourse analyses of games and gaming cultures in the academy with a concomitant mushrooming in multiplatform gaming journalism—that rightly tracks with the global economic juggernaut that is the GIC—have engendered a robust and ever-evolving gaming media ecology of developers, gamers-users-fans, critics, and industries. Exemplary here is popular gamer, citizen (games) journalist, and YouTuber Satchell "Satchbag" Drakes, who exposes his audience to advanced game analysis concepts like ludonarrative dissonance, a tension that arises between some games' competing imperatives of story arcs and play mechanics.

Thus, it seems safe to say that *Gaming Representation: Race, Gender, and Sexuality in Video Games* enters this incredibly important and fractured discursive fray with prescient, timely, and forward-looking treatises on gaming that push gaming scholarship to new levels of inquiry, theorizing, cognition, speculation, imagination, and creativity. In fact, when Jennifer Malkowski and TreaAndrea M. Russworm invited me to contribute remarks reflecting on my scholarly writing on race and video games as a foreword to this volume, I was honored and delighted. I realized immediately the potential impact and import of *Gaming Representation* to the evolving critical terrain of media studies focusing on gaming, identity, and society. Equally significant, I see this volume as fulfilling my and other scholars' hopes for and expectations that new research and scholarship will recognize, build on, and move well beyond our own early contributions. *Gaming Representation* represents, for me, just such an important undertaking. After all, gaming has evolved and is characterized now by new levels of cultural complexity and technological sophistication that demand new voices and insights.

There are several developments in gaming that strike me as necessary to probe (if briefly) before any honest assessment can proceed regarding just how gaming has evolved in the years since my essay "Serious Play: Playing with Race in Contemporary Gaming Culture" was first published in 2005 in the MIT Press collection *Handbook of Computer Game Studies*. First, gaming's persistent racial, gender, and sexuality problematics seem particularly disarticulated from our so-called postracial, postfeminist, and post-civil-rights existential imaginary, also known as the Age of Obama. Second, the population of gamers in the United States continues to climb, with 63 percent of US households currently boasting at least one invested gamer.[1] Third, news flash! Adult women far outnumber teenage boys in gaming, and this fact complicates perceptions of the Gamergate debacle (more about this later). Also, African American and Latino American gamers still play more video games than other demographic groups. Fourth, wide-ranging as well as sophisticated critical discourses online that address gender, race, and sexuality in gaming have increased exponentially in the years since I penned my own interventionist writing on race and gaming at the beginning of this new millennium.

These four key developments provide a useful lead-in to my retrospective gaze on conducting research about gaming and identity in the early years of game studies. In this conversation I consider the stakes involved then and now. Starting with development number one, the fact is that society was not then in the throes of a "postracial" or color-blind societal imaginary. When I began studying gaming in the late 1990s, Toni Morrison, apparently, unleashed a controversy that mythologized Bill Clinton as America's first black president. With Senator Barack Obama elected as America's actual first black president in 2008, the racial discourse in the nation reached a fever pitch, toggling back and forth between racial tolerance and progressivity, on the one hand, and racial polarization and intolerance in American civil society, on the other hand. Millennials, that group of people born roughly between 1980 and the early 2000s, were formidable in the election and reelection of President Obama, and they embraced the idea that their group's political power helped to usher in a postracial, post-civil-rights American society. While there is some truth in the changing attitudes around race in the new millennium when compared to the 1950s and 1960s, there was also a significant backlash against America's first black president. Gaming, gamers, and the GIC were not impervious to the new normal discourses of race that the 2008 historic political moment instantiated. In fact, far from developing narratives and gameplay protocols along race-neutral or gender-neutral lines, gaming was following many of the racist and sexist practices of the film, TV, and music industries in its evolution toward cinema-like photorealist visual aesthetics, familiar genre norms, and gangsta rap music lyrics.

When "Serious Play" was published in 2005, it reflected my scholarship on the topic dating back nearly a decade prior. And in fact, my decision to study games emerged from my own return to gameplay as a graduate student at the same time that Rockstar Games' *Grand Theft Auto* (*GTA*) franchise and gaming journalism were blowing up. But, my impetus for writing critically about gaming and race was a segment in the early 2000s on *Good Morning America* (*GMA*) about *GTA 3*'s unprecedented levels of violence and the game's effects on children. I was incredulous because the black reporter Michelle Norris introduced an all-white panel of so-called experts whose commentary essentialized black youth gamers as special dupes from the ghetto incapable of separating reality from the stylized hyperviolence of gameplay, unlike the sophistication of white youth gamers who could tell the difference. I was shocked that, in one fell swoop, *GMA*'s brand of moral panic condemned Rockstar Games' then-latest iteration of the highly profitable *GTA* franchise and labeled young black gamers as dumb and criminal! From that moment, I began paying attention to the public discourse about race and gaming. That was my wake-up call. For me, it was important to tackle, at once, race as both discourse and gameplay praxis.

Moving on to gaming's shifting demographics, statistics bear out the fact that by 2014 the average age of gamers had risen to thirty-one years. Unquestionably, video games are no longer mere child's play. Additionally, the game industry in the United States saw sales reach upward of $21 billion, a clear indication of the influence, power, and scope of the GIC and gaming's ever-broadening fan base.[2] Early on, my gaming analyses and writings centered primarily on race even though I was acutely aware of the emerging GIC's replication of the film and TV industries' white male hegemony, notably its enduring ethos of sexism. Since scholarship and research into gaming's gender problematic far outpaced work on race, I opted to focus primarily on race, while simultaneously attending to video games' unique brand of double oppression: demeaning and victimizing women of color (WOC), especially in gaming's action narratives, and excluding WOC designers from the games' development process altogether. I feel confident making this observation because surely no women gamers of color pitched creating the hordes of "hos" and cannibalistic zombie chicks in the *GTA* and *Resident Evil* (1996–, Capcom) franchises, for example.

In my 2014 essay "Race," for *The Routledge Companion to Video Game Studies*, I was cognizant of the full decade that had elapsed, and I addressed some of the notable changes occurring in the GIC on the race and gender fronts. Of course, due to the intersectionality of race and gender, the percentage of women gamers has reached an all-time high, with a few diversity-minded game developers constructing game worlds around "sheroes" to augment the popular Lara Croft, D'arci Stern, Princess Peach, and Zelda female character icons. In "Race," I delved into efforts occurring in some of gaming's most successful titles and franchises to feature a range of black male must-play characters (MPCs) and optional play characters (OPCs) beyond *Grand Theft Auto: San Andreas*'s original African American MPC, CJ.

Here, I examined the slow pace of the game industry's capitulation to making black females playable characters (PCs), finally. In the essay's subsection "At Last, Black Women Are PCs," I critique this historic move where Capcom and Ubisoft follow the UK's Mucky Foot in featuring a black woman MPC. D'arci Stern, the shero in *Urban Chaos* (1999, Mucky Foot Productions) was conceived as an alternative or companion type to Lara Croft. With *Resident Evil 5*'s PC Sheva Alomar, and Aveline de Grandpré (of African French origins), the MPC of *Assassin's Creed 3: Liberation* (2012, Ubisoft), developers increased the black female lead characters in gaming by 200 percent! That the addition of only two characters represents a 200 percent representational jump is telling. Gaming's epic gender problem became hyperreal with the global controversy erupting around the Gamergate debacle of 2014.

If the Gamergate controversy has had any lasting benefits, it is clearly the ability to disabuse many of the perceived truths associated with "post" imaginary: postfeminist, postracial, and other post- post-isms and imaginings becoming endemic to the new millennium. When Gamergate happened, gamers around the globe learned what feminist gamer-scholars, gamer-critics, and gamer-journalists had been observing and communicating all along—an inconvenient truth about gender and gaming aptly summed up in this headline from the *Guardian*: "52% of gamers are women—but the industry doesn't know it."[3] It seems hardly surprising that gaming and mainstream journalists' tracking and touting of women's increasing numbers as gamers, games enthusiasts, and independent games developers, Anita Sarkeesian's unanticipated Kickstarter crowdfunding success in 2011 with her Feminist Frequency video series critiquing gender in gaming, and Zoë Quinn's 2013 release of her indie game *Depression Quest* all converged in the social media lane of the internet to blow up #Gamergate and its subsequent cultural maelstrom. When Malkowski and Russworm encouraged me to reflect on whether the need for scholarly critical discourse analysis of gaming and identity politics is still as urgent and relevant today as I have argued it is for more than a decade now, the fact and reach of Gamergate pushes me to respond, unequivocally, "Hell yeah!"

In fact, my deeply affective response to the Gamergate phenomenon was exacerbated when I happened to catch an inevitable ripped-from-the-headlines episode of *Law and Order: SVU* while writing these remarks. That *SVU* episode, titled "Intimidation Game," was inspired by Gamergate and follows the case of a female video game developer, Raina, who is harassed and ultimately kidnapped, beaten, and raped by a group of violently misogynistic male gamers. It aired in February 2015, and it did not disappoint—certainly not as a familiar *SVU* sexploitation text, with a twist. While "Intimidation Game" did forego the usual sensationalized sexual violence and pedophilic depravity narratives typical of *SVU*, it did follow other video game and crime story lines that the *Law and Order* brand has treated over the decades of the franchise's popular programming, including hyperbolic stories inspired by *Second Life*, and other real-life video game stories covered in gaming journalism.

What *SVU* could exploit about Gamergate that fit its story arcs perfectly was the real-life gender violence and intrigue of the relative obscurity of the indie games movement juxtaposed to the high-profile cosplay conventions, gaming IPO launches, technology, and Electronic Entertainment Expo (E3) convention-style mega-events revolving around this actual big news story. Briefly, Gamergate occurred in late 2014 as a particularly virulent form of online harassment by a number of angry activist male gamers targeting several high-profile women in gaming under the guise of challenging bad games journalism. More specifically, the Gamergate incident revolved around the bitter breakup between Quinn and her gamer ex-boyfriend and subsequent claims that she traded sexual favors to get her interactive casual game, *Depression Quest*, developed and released. With her critique of gaming's endemic sexism, Sarkeesian was ensnared prominently in Gamergate, as was game developer Brianna Wu. These women were condemned as not true gamers and were subjected to death threats and incessant bullying and harassment on social media.

The must-have narrative twist of *SVU*'s "Intimidation Game" is evident in the show's visual enactments of some of Gamergate's more notorious verbal threats and "slut shaming" leveled against Quinn, Sarkeesian, and other high-profile women in gaming. *SVU*'s Gamergate performativity included the conflation of these two women gamers in one composite character named Raina, enactments of violent abductions of and attacks on female gamers, an inexplicable visual reference to Islamic State terrorism with online screenings of beheadings, and, of course, first-person-shooter game iconography. With dialogue such as "That slut Raina deserves all the pain that's coming to her. Her game is derivative, mind-numbing garbage. . . . If she and her social justice warriors don't leave gaming now, we will make them," apparently *SVU* also rips from misogynist YouTubers' hate-filled rants to score cheap points to appear timely and in-group familiar.

As this brief sketch of "Intimidation Game" suggests, the episode was a hot mess and generated a flurry of damning reviews, tweets, and Facebook posts across social media platforms, mainstream journalism, and gaming journalism alike. All told, it is difficult to avert one's gaze from this show, since *SVU*'s disturbing "Intimidation Game" is symptomatic of gaming's deep-seated gender troubles, to extrapolate from Judith Butler's highly relevant interventionist criticism to this context.[4] And yet most problematic was the episode's plot resolution, predicated on game developer Raina's complete surrender of her entrepreneurial dreams following her violent abduction. When asked by the *SVU* rescuers if she would continue the feminist fight and deny the intimidators' efforts to run women out of gaming, Raina responds dejectedly, "They already won." Thus, the female game developer is imagined as doing exactly what her attackers wanted: learning her place. This sad ending sees Gamergate as a self-fulfilling prophesy. Clearly, Gamergate and *SVU*'s "Intimidation Game" are highly teachable moments. And they seem fitting as I wrap up my remarks and reflections, in eager anticipation of the exciting research and scholarship contained in the following chapters.

Regarding the fourth and final development on my list, there has been an amazing proliferation and increasing sophistication of gaming journalism centering on gaming's identity matters since 2004. Let me offer a little earworm on this topic: Sweden, the home of *Minecraft* and other global games titles, is encouraging its game industry trade group to consider adding a rating for sexism alongside its rating system of age and content. What a concept! How about we push to add ratings for racism and homophobia too?

It is indicative of a paradigm shift in gaming journalism that the Public Broadcasting System's Digital Studios began engaging with games with its online *PBS Game/Show* and a dizzying array of sophisticated gaming blogs and websites have mushroomed, including a few of my favorites—Feminist Frequency's Tropes vs. Women, Blacks in Gaming, and Satchbag's Goods. They remind me of my early influences. It was October 1999 that saw the first mainstream newspaper feature article on race and gaming, titled "Blood, Gore, Sex and Now: Race," written by Michel Marriott for the *New York Times*. Marriott informed not only my "Serious Play" article but my subsequent essays as well, including my cowritten book chapter, "The Power of Play: The Portrayal and Performance of Race in Video Games" (with Craig Watkins in 2008), and two separate encyclopedia entries on race in *The Encyclopedia of Video Games* and in *The Routledge Companion to Video Game Studies*, in 2012 and 2014, respectively. Over the years, of course, a number of scholarly articles and books have been published forming an important corpus of work constitutive of the emergent field of race, gender, sexuality, and disability studies in gaming.

Finally, my present collaboration with this new generation of gaming scholars further inspires me to remain critically engaged with evolving and next-gen games and gaming cultures.

Anna Everett
Santa Barbara, CA
April 2015

ANNA EVERETT is Professor of Film, Television, and New Media Studies at the University of California, Santa Barbara. Her publications include *Returning the Gaze: A Genealogy of Black Film Criticism, 1909–1949*; *Learning Race and Ethnicity: Youth and Digital Media*; and *Digital Diaspora: A Race for Cyberspace.*

Notes

1. Entertainment Software Association, "2016 Sales, Demographic and Usage Data: Essential Facts about the Computer Video Game Industry," 2016, http://www.isfe.eu/sites/isfe.eu/files/attachments/esa_ef_2016.pdf.
2. Ibid.
3. Meg Jayanth, "52% of Gamers Are Women—but the Industry Doesn't Know It," *The Guardian*, September 18, 2014, https://www.theguardian.com/commentisfree/2014/sep/18/52-percent-people-playing-games-women-industry-doesnt-know.
4. See Judith Butler, *Gender Trouble* (New York: Routledge, 1990).

ACKNOWLEDGMENTS

THE EDITORS ARE GRATEFUL FOR THE MANY LEVELS OF SUPPORT WE HAVE received throughout this process. At Indiana University Press, we appreciate the time Janice Frisch has devoted to the book (as well as her predecessor, Raina Polivka, with whom we initially worked). We also thank series editor Robert Brookey and an anonymous reader for their helpful and timely comments on our manuscript. Additionally, many of our colleagues from the Society for Cinema and Media Studies Video Games Studies Scholarly Interest Group have provided encouragement, feedback, and promotion, especially the group's board members: Harrison Gish, Felan Parker, Diana Pozo, and John R. Vanderhoef II.

Some of our inspiration for working together began in 2012, when we partnered to codesign a Mellon grant–supported digital humanities course administered by the Five Colleges Women's Studies Research Center and Five Colleges Incorporated. We thank Maria San Filippo for her collaboration on that course, as well as Karen Remmler and Nayiree Roubinian for administrative support.

Most of all, we are indebted to our contributors, whose incredible ideas kept us excited about this book during the long process of its creation—and who were unfailingly patient throughout that process! We extend special thanks to Anna Everett and Lisa Nakamura, who have been inspirations to so many of us in this field, for lending their (rightfully in-demand) voices to the book in the foreword and afterword.

Jennifer's acknowledgments: I thank Ron Becker, Damon Blanchette, Richard Campbell, Kerry Hegarty, Alex Keller, Kim Malkowski, Rick Malkowski, Kate Mason, and Hilary Pople for support of many different types during the completion of this book. TreaAndrea has been an amazing partner in this project every step of the way and has been gracious about putting up with her control-freak coeditor. Academic collaboration has truly never been this much fun—and not just because the subject is video games. For me, the research for this book emerged from and was nurtured in the classroom, most directly in my course Linking Film and New Media. I am grateful to my students in that course—first at Smith

College in 2012 and then at Miami University in 2015—for sharing with me their insights about, romance with, anger at, and hope for the medium of video games.

TreaAndrea's acknowledgments: I thank Ron'na Lytle, Mark James, Tracy Harkless, Armandé Millender, and my writing partners and friends: Laura Furlan, Laura Kalba, Gulru Calmak, Gina Valesquez, K. C. Nat Turner, Florence Sullivan, and Priscilla Page. Special thanks go to my gaming colleagues and friends: Michael Forbes, Jordy Rosenberg, Hoang Phan, and Ruth Jennison. I am especially grateful to see some of my professional and personal interests in video games flourish into this rich work. Playing and analyzing dystopian games over the years with sharp and equally passionate students from my Dystopian Games, Comics, and Media seminars at the University of Massachusetts, Amherst, has been a treasured career highlight that has also contributed to how I write and think about games. Similarly, it has been immeasurably rewarding to play and write with Jen, and I am relieved that the process of editing a collection has only strengthened our friendship. Finally, shout-outs to God for transformations big and small—for all the things!

GAMING REPRESENTATION

INTRODUCTION

Identity, Representation, and Video Game Studies beyond the Politics of the Image

JENNIFER MALKOWSKI AND TREAANDREA M. RUSSWORM

OF WHAT SIGNIFICANCE ARE QUESTIONS ABOUT IDENTITY (ESPECIALLY RACE, gender, and sexuality) to the evolution of video game studies? Has the trend toward code analysis and platform studies inadvertently worked to silence, marginalize, or dismiss representational analysis in the field? Are there ways in which the often-violent protection of video games as a masculine playspace has affected academic approaches to games—particularly when some voices are taken for granted as natural experts on the medium while others are decentered and naturalized as less proficient in the assumed boys' club of gaming? More pointedly, are we at a moment when "representation," "diversity," and "identity" have become dirty words in game studies? These are just a few of the questions that animate *Gaming Representation: Race, Gender, and Sexuality in Video Games,* a collaboration born from and nurtured by a new energy around questions of identity and representation that has been building in game studies over the past few years.

The discipline itself has grown rapidly, with an ever more significant presence in the programs of various disciplinary conferences, outlets for article publication in places like *Games and Culture* and *Game Studies,* and the enthusiastic support of academic presses releasing dozens of new books on the medium annually. Yet for most of game studies' history, conversations about identity have only ever happened on the margins—a dynamic that became particularly apparent to us because of our backgrounds in fields in which such conversations have secured more prominence (film and media studies, queer studies, feminist studies, literary studies, and African American studies). To make a comparison to the disciplinary history of film studies, for example, where is this field's Laura Mulvey moment?[1] Film studies enjoyed a long post-Mulvey period when explicitly feminist topics and methodologies were not just accepted but dominant—when, to hear our senior colleagues tell it, work that neglected to account for gender, where relevant, struggled for acceptance for the first time. In game studies, a selection of publications has productively adapted theories of identity, politics, and representation from the broader world of visual culture studies or—in the most exciting cases—has used games to challenge and reshape those theories. But, until very recently, there has not been sustained or prominent attention to these subjects in the discipline's mainstream. There has not been a critical mass of scholars asking the kinds of questions we and our contributors found ourselves asking of the medium. That critical mass has finally emerged with a new wave of scholarship that we are grateful to be part of—one that might just guide questions of identity and representation into the central current of game studies.

We return to both the existing and new work in these areas ahead, but we first want to address this question: Why *has* game studies, until this recent flourishing, pursued questions of identity and representation so infrequently and incompletely?[2] Given academics' penchant for critique, the endless supply of "bad objects" that video games offer in relation to identity makes it even more surprising that scholars have not explored this terrain more fully; as Adrienne Shaw puts it, "In many ways, digital games seem to be the least progressive form of media representation, despite being one of the newest mediated forms."[3] Coming to prominence, for the most part, during and after the successes of the civil rights movement, second-wave feminism, and the gay liberation movement, the video game industry has nevertheless been less willing, overall, than other media industries to pursue meaningful diversity or refrain from egregious stereotyping. And yet there exists only sparse academic scholarship that addresses either the medium's long history of failures in this area or its sparks of progress that have appeared more recently.

Some reasons for this neglect may stem from the particulars of game studies' formative years. Anna Everett well summarizes in the foreword that analyses of identity in video games were effectively displaced in the narratology-versus-ludology debates, the focus on procedural rhetorics and "interrogations of gaming's structures of play and affective engagement," and, more recently, "the neoformalist tech turn to platform, software, and code studies." A casualty of these ideological battles and shifts in game studies' affections, representation has been treated, as Braxton Soderman asserts in chapter 2, like "the casual element ('casual' here defined as the contingent) while the mechanics became the hard-core essence of the game form." Viewed in this way, representational analysis becomes the less rigorous, less medium-specific way to approach video games, compared to a focus on "hard-core" elements.

But these attitudes misunderstand both the nature and importance of representation in the medium. It is both possible and essential to study representation productively in video games, even as this pursuit might initially seem poorly aligned with the ontology of video games (built as they are on processes and actions) or with disciplinary trends toward areas like code and platform studies.

Throughout this collection, we and our contributors are guided by three central beliefs about representation and game studies. First, representation is not fully separate from the implicitly hard-core elements of games: it is achieved through and dependent on player and machine actions, on code, and on hardware, not just on surface-level images and sounds. Second, games still prominently include images and sounds (and plot, characters, language, etc.); having code underlying these elements does not negate their existence or impact, and game studies should be comprehensive enough to welcome their analysis. And third, the field would prove itself dangerously out of touch if it did not attend meaningfully to representation in this moment when representation, identity, and their intertwined relationship in games and game culture have become (or, rather, have been revealed as) such high-stakes matters. The social, political, and cultural context of the #Gamergate era, the #BlackLivesMatter movement, and fan-created campaigns like #INeedDiverseGames make this a unique and urgent time for game studies to develop better critical proficiencies for representational and identity-based analyses.

With these three premises in mind, we assert that there is much to say about representation and identity in games and gaming culture that goes beyond flat assessments of good and bad objects, code versus image, and form versus content. In fact, it is our understanding that a focus on race, gender, and sexuality need not exclude other factors of production, and we believe that such analysis must be accountable to the medium-specificity of video games. Representation and identity have often been sidelined in game studies with the implicit justification that the discipline should focus instead on the richer objects of code and of game platforms as complex systems—not audiovisual surfaces. Yet, as we argue throughout *Gaming Representation*, representation and identity are similarly complex systems that are always relevant to the ways in which games, codes, platforms—indeed, all technologies—are constructed. Representation in game studies must be viewed as a system that functions as akin to—rather than as a distraction from—the discipline's more celebrated, hard-core objects of study.

Our thinking on representation here is inspired by cultural studies theorist Stuart Hall's meditations on the various politics of representation. Hall conceives of the politics of representation as a way of approaching media analysis that pushes beyond the politics of the image or a focus on the distance between and image and reality. He argues that "the 'machineries' and regimes of representation in a culture do play a *constitutive*, and not merely a reflective, after-the-event, role. This gives questions of culture and ideology, and the scenarios of representation—subjectivity, identity, politics—a formative, not merely expressive, place in the constitution of social and political life."[4] Hall continues, "Representation is possible only because enunciation is always produced within codes which have a history, a position within the discursive formations of a particular space and time."[5] Although Hall never wrote about video games during his prolific career, we find more than a passing significance for the present collection's aims in his reference to the "machineries" of representation and its "codes." For there exists in the realm of games not just one kind of code; alongside computational code, there is representational code. And as much as game software creates complex systems of play, so too is identity itself a complex system—one whose potential ontological affinities with the medium of video games have not yet been fully grasped by academics in this field. This book imagines a critical blueprint for what it might mean to treat representation as "a formative, not merely expressive" system in game studies.

* * *

In our preceding speculations on the lack of prominent, sustained work on identity in the history of video game studies, we do not want to imply that our collection is charting wholly unexplored territory, neglect the authors who produced excellent scholarship in these areas in the discipline's earliest years, or underestimate those who have quite recently added their voices. As it turns out, in embarking on this project when we did, we were adding our energies to a powerful wave of scholarship on identity and games that was beginning to take shape. The volume of submissions we received in that initial call, combined later with enthusiastic interest in the collection from many presses, evinces one way issues of identity in games has built up more and more momentum during the years of our manuscript's formation. This new scholarly enthusiasm certainly owes thanks to those outside of academia—journalists, bloggers, vloggers, podcasters, and the like—who for years have been attending to this intersection of identity and games and proving why it matters. Their efforts have inspired many of us to help game studies catch up with and build on what has already been written online and in the popular press (indeed, some of their work figures prominently in the chapters that follow). But within academia, too, we have been keenly aware of the growing number of scholars who have worked to make identity and representation relevant to game studies—a community that includes, to name just a few, Aubrey Anable; Samantha Blackmon; André Brock; Derek Burrill; Justine Cassell and Henry Jenkins; Shira Chess; Mia Consalvo; Anna Everett; Kishonna Gray; D. Fox Harrell; Tanner Higgin; Yasmin B. Kafai, Carrie Heeter, Jill Denner, and Jennifer Y. Sun; Alex Layne; David J. Leonard; Lisa Nakamura; Laine Nooney; Adrienne Shaw; T. L. Taylor; S. Craig Watkins; and, of course, the fourteen scholars contributing chapters to this book.

Of the growing list of inspirational approaches to games and identity, we delve into only a few here that have particularly shaped our own thinking and our approach to *Gaming Representation*. Anna Everett and Lisa Nakamura, who have contributed the foreword and afterword, respectively, are two pioneering voices in this area—particularly in the fairly recent practice of writing about race and gaming.[6] Everett's *Digital Diaspora: A Race for Cyberspace* (2009) has been instrumental in disrupting the commonly held notions of a digital divide, where minority communities have been erroneously perceived as lagging behind white (usually male) early adopters in technological use and innovation.[7] Her work on games evolved concomitant with her written histories of black participation in online communities, a history that has become essential to understanding some of the many complexities of community participation and racial representation in video game culture. In "Serious Play," while exploring various "representational casualties" of the medium, including the persistence of "high-tech blackface" and "black skins" in games like *Ready 2 Rumble: Round 2* (2000, Midway), Everett also offers close textual analysis of the racist ideologies and representational codes that inform video game strategy guides and user manuals.[8] Her groundbreaking work on race and games has sought to both expose and problematize "the still unbearable whiteness of being in mainstream media's . . . vision and . . . conceptualization of new media technologies and gaming cultures' increasing cultural power and much-lamented societal influences."[9] Additionally, her theorization of the terms "Afrogeek" and the "black cyberflaneur," which stress agency, radical cooptation, and uplift remain useful for thinking about minority gaming communities' formative—and continued—active engagement with the medium.

Likewise, in *Cybertypes: Race, Ethnicity, and Identity on the Internet* (2002) and *Digitizing Race: Visual Cultures of the Internet* (2008), Lisa Nakamura's broader interventions in internet studies and digital culture has had an early and lasting impact on how we have come to think about video games. By dispelling the notion that race, ethnicity, and other aspects of identity, like gender and nationality, do not matter in online and digital spaces, Nakamura's equally transformative contributions to cyber-cultural studies established the conceptual precedent for her later work on identity and games. In bringing a cultural studies critical approach to environments that were being taken for granted as "race-neutral," Nakamura argued that race is "cybertyped" in digital culture, as ideology that is both reconceptualized and decontextualized, and importantly, that "digital systems . . . operationalize and instrumentalize race."[10] Not only do race and ethnicity matter when it comes to studying digital systems, argues Nakamura, but the digital and media formats are themselves "bumpy, layered, and pitted with the imprint of contact with other cultures; none avoid the mark of imperialist power relations."[11]

Although Nakamura was writing about digital culture more broadly when she discussed "cybertyping" as a more applicable term than "stereotyping" to thinking about the "'cultural layer' or ideologies regarding race" that are evident in the complex relays between people and machines, the concept retains promising potential for moving the discursive focus on representation in video games beyond the surface politics of the image.[12] Since these contributions to digital cultural studies, Nakamura has worked on games and identity in a variety of contexts, from the labor practices in *World of Warcraft* (2004–2014, Blizzard) to the gender politics of *The Sims* (2000–2015, Maxis), and she has written passionately about the need for film and media scholars to both play and write about video games in ways that explicitly prioritize close readings of image and aesthetics.[13]

During this same period (2003–2009), work from S. Craig Watkins on minority youth and gaming communities, David J. Leonard on politicized racial representations in games, and Jo Bryce and Jason Rutter on the complexities of gendered game spaces complemented Everett's and Nakamura's work and further established some early precedent for studying identity and representation in games.[14] For example, Leonard persuasively argues that popular discussions on games like *Grand Theft Auto: San Andreas* reactivate US racial ideologies that pathologize blackness. Leonard specifically calls for prioritizing a "complex level of media literacy" within game studies that might serve as "part of an antiracist praxis and ideological formation."[15] Meanwhile, Bryce and Rutter contributed early work on gaming culture that debunks the myth of the average gamer as white, antisocial, and male. Their research argues against "fetishizing gaming texts or technologies" as they remind us that game worlds "are created within and incorporate specific cultural values but these values are open to resistance, negotiation, rereading, ironicising, reproduction or valorization only through their use."[16]

Mia Consalvo has also been a consistent voice in these areas since the early years, with a particular (though not exclusive) focus on gender. Often grounded in social science methodologies (both quantitative and qualitative), her scholarship on games tackles large-scale questions, such as whether women and men behave in the same ways as game players and how the game industry can attract and retain female developers. Although it represents only one thread of work in her prolific career, Consalvo's published work on identity and games dates back to 2003 with her contribution to *The Video Game Theory Reader*, "Hot Dates and Fairy-Tale Romances: Studying Sexuality in Video Games." Several of her coauthored articles have productively investigated the gendered actions and attitudes of players—especially female players—in online games, including "Women and Games: Technologies of the Gendered Self" (2007), "Looking for Gender: Gender Roles and Behaviors among Online Gamers" (2009), "The Sexi(e)st of All: Avatars, Gender, and Online Games" (2009), and "The Strategic Female: Gender Switching and Player Behavior in Online Games" (2014). Her coauthored article "The Virtual Census: Representations of Gender, Race and Age in Video Games" (2009) has been especially useful to researchers working on identity and games, as it performs a broad and well-structured content analysis of recent games to meaningfully determine which demographic groups are under- and overrepresented in video games (spoiler alert! males, whites, and adults are systematically overrepresented). But what particularly distinguishes Consalvo's work is its breadth, contributing research on identity and gamer behavior, textual analysis of identity in games themselves, gender issues in game industry employment (2008's "Crunched by Passion: Women Game Developers and Workplace Challenges"), and big-picture perspectives on sexism in game culture (2012's "Confronting Toxic Gamer Culture: A Challenge for Feminist Game Studies Scholars").

Most recently, we have been influenced by two important books that have expanded the discourse about identity, representation, and games: D. Fox Harrell's *Phantasmal Media: An Approach to Imagination, Computation, and Expression* (2013) and Adrienne Shaw's *Gaming at the Edge: Sexuality and Gender at the*

Margins of Gamer Culture (2014). Through an invigorating discursive shift, Harrell argues that computer technology is inherently culturally biased because it is informed by cultural "phantasms": elements of human imaginative cognition that include understandings of self, other, social ills, everyday experiences, and "narrative imagining" or human poetic thought.[17] In an approach to games that blends cognitive science with social theory, Harrell argues persuasively that gaming and computing technologies necessarily include "polymorphic poetics—an expressive set of possibilities centered upon the contingency and imaginative nature of even the most entrenched social identities, such as those of gender and race."[18] It is the lack of "critical computing," says Harrell, that "has resulted in software that at best ignores opportunities for empowerment, and at worst results in perpetuating longstanding social ills of discrimination and disenfranchisement."[19] We find Harrell's work instructive not only for theorizing representation as a system but also for imagining critical bridges between humanities, social science, and computer science approaches to games analysis and development.

Following several years of influential article publication on sexuality and games, Shaw's *Gaming at the Edge* became the first book-length study of that topic (among other topics) in 2014.[20] Using an ethnographic approach to study "those placed at the margins of the constructed center of gaming," Shaw unfurls a nuanced reading of how and why representation matters to marginalized gamers.[21] By observing that issues of identity and representation were much more complicated for queer gamers than just wanting to be able to play as queer characters, she also challenges game developers and game studies scholars alike to rethink the goals of better representation. In addition, Shaw calls for an understanding of diversity founded on "hybridity, intersectionality, and coalitional politics" rather than more traditional identity politics.[22] And in one of her sharpest insights, she recognizes the neoliberal attitude game studios have largely taken to increasing diversity in their titles by allowing players to choose the gender, race, and sexuality of their characters: "Players are made responsible for making their game characters go against male, heterosexual norms in game representation . . . put[ting] responsibility for diversity onto audiences. If the player needs to push a 'gay button,' as game designer Anna Anthropy has termed it, to see same-sex relationships in games, then anyone who doesn't know . . . that the button exists can continue to consume the heteronormative-dominated texts."[23]

* * *

The important work on identity and representation in digital culture and games that we have sampled in the previous section demonstrates not only that there is a cresting interest in these areas but also that there are vibrant discursive communities in place to receive work like this. Yet, since we have always intentionally sought out these perspectives, we are also aware of the extent to which our training and research interests place us in the proverbial choir. That is, we have known where to look to have the conversations about games that bring humanist discourses prioritizing representational analysis to game studies—critical approaches that necessarily obliterate a computational-representational divide. But we are much less sure that there are obvious go-to places for other scholars—and, indeed, engaged video game developers and fans—to find the discursive threads in game studies about identity and representation.

Gaming Representation centralizes some such perspectives in a single volume. The chapters collected here are interdisciplinary by design, as our contributors have backgrounds in African American studies, American studies, art history, communication, comparative literature, digital art, digital humanities, digital media studies, English, film studies, gender and sexuality studies, Japanese studies, journalism, media studies, television studies, and women's studies.

A note about the games analyzed in the chapters that follow: at the time of publication, many of these are newer while a few others date back to the mid-2000s (*Max Payne 2*, *Grand Theft Auto: San Andreas*, *Jade Empire*). With this collection, we want to attend to influential or notable representations of identity from an extended span of recent game history and resist the temptation to write about only the newest games (a tricky proposition, anyway, given the speed of academic publishing and what we hope will be a long lifespan for the book).

Because technologies change so quickly, one might assume a game developed several years ago would be outdated in terms of its representations of race, gender, and sexuality. But we know that representations actually change slowly in digital media, just as they have in more traditional forms of media. Further, individual games used to be subject to a rapid cycle of mainstream obsolescence as soon as their consoles were replaced by the next generation. Today, this dynamic has changed through rampant porting and remastering of old games for current consoles (as with *The Last of Us* and *Grand Theft Auto: San Andreas*), and heightened nostalgia for the titles of yesteryear. Streaming services that bundle and sell games in flash sales at significantly reduced prices—like the services PlayStation Now, Steam, and Amazon Games—have also ensured that popular titles from each platform generation will remain relevant to new and old gaming audiences alike. While streaming and subscription services continue to flourish as the Netflixes of the gaming world, players can access ever-expanding archives of "old" games to revisit or play for the first time. The same can be said for the way both YouTube and Twitch have capitalized on the spectatorial pleasures of watching other people play. Some of the most popular YouTube content creators and Twitch streamers often select games based on audience recommendations and feature play-throughs of retro games as part of contests, challenges, and completionist fan agendas. Finally, the developers and franchises of some of the oldest games we analyze here—BioWare, Rockstar, *Grand Theft Auto*, *BioShock*—remain highly relevant to current gaming culture, as do our contributors' insights about them.

We have organized this book into three parts that connect in some way to the broad categories of "race," "gender," and "sexuality." Although we are mindful of the fact that organizing the book as such may seem to discourage intersectionality, we have done so for two main reasons. First, although these identity categorizations are certainly not comprehensive and are at times rightly problematized, we have used them here as an organizational rubric because the terms make it possible for readers to establish a quick sense of topics, games, and issues the book covers at the chapter level. Second, we felt comfortable organizing the book around these particular categories because our contributors' multi- and transdisciplinary training meant that connections and intersections between and among multiple aspects of identity were already hardwired into the individual chapters.

Gaming Representation's opening part, "Gender, Bodies, Spaces," is its broadest, acknowledging what a pervasive—in addition to explosive—topic gender has been within video game culture in recent years. The authors in this part explore many corners of the medium's universe, writing about gender in game genres, casual games, industry employment, game culture online, cosplay, conventions, and paratexts. While each chapter assumes a deep misogyny present in the medium's culture as a premise, these authors also push beyond simply identifying and condemning this gender trouble. Instead, they trace it back to its cultural and historical roots and/or imagine ways forward for video games and their fraught relationship with gender.

Jennifer Malkowski opens this part with "'I Turned Out to Be Such a Damsel in Distress': Noir Games and the Unrealized Femme Fatale," positing the ludic femme fatale character as one potential salve for the industry's inflamed gender relations. Despite this character's long-standing popularity in film and her promise for adaptation to an action-based medium, Malkowski observes that among video games' remediations of film noir, the femme fatale rarely occupies a meaningful role and is even more rarely a playable character. Through close readings of the two games that have most fully rendered playable femmes fatales—*Max Payne 2* (2003, Remedy Entertainment) and *Heavy Rain* (2010, Quantic Dream)—Malkowski argues that these iterations of the character are ultimately disempowered through regressive strategies from the classic film noir period. "Too *fatale* to let live—too *fatale*, even, to be simply killed," each woman "must reveal her essential, feminized, emotional weakness and be undone by it." An analog for contemporary game culture's paranoid fantasy of the "fake geek girl"—"conning her way into male spaces through deception and sex appeal"—the femme fatale, unfortunately, proves too threatening in today's cultural climate to manifest in games in a truly empowered form.

Like Malkowski, Braxton Soderman also relies on close reading, but turns this collection's attention to casual games in "No Time to Dream: Killing Time, Casual Games, and Gender." Soderman examines the temporality of casual games—both within their texts and externally, in terms of how players fit them into their daily schedules—through analysis of *Diner Dash* (2003, Gamelab), "an urtext . . . [whose] gameplay mechanics and design fundamentally model and self-reflexively interrogate [the] idea of interruptibility" that is so central to casual games. He links *Diner Dash*'s themes of the temporal demands on women and the fragmentation of their time with broader issues about the quality of women's leisure and the anxious, hostile, gendered devaluation of casual games by a vocal subset of self-identified hard-core male gamers. Seeking in part to redeem casual games and acknowledge their potential ideological richness, Soderman also historicizes the gendered hostility toward them as simply a new chapter in a long modernist history of the aggressive safeguarding of men's leisure time at the expense of women's.

Continuing Soderman's theme of women's marginalization and video games, Jennifer deWinter and Carly A. Kocurek perform a broad analysis of this marginalization within the medium's culture and industry in "'Aw Fuck, I Got a Bitch on My Team!': Women and the Exclusionary Cultures of the Computer Game Complex." The authors begin by challenging the assumption that women are underrepresented in the game industry primarily because girls never get interested in this masculine medium and because of a gendered education gap in the required fields. DeWinter and Kocurek demonstrate instead that "antifemale policing in video game culture"—grounded in harassment, isolation, and the threat of rape—"create[s] an aggressively exclusionary culture of gaming with no space for women, their participation, or their voices, as players or as makers." The authors document and analyze this misogynist hostility in both game culture and the game industry, noting that its toxicity sadly leaks into video game studies, as well, in a different form: as women game scholars, "producing these records and doing the work of these interventions becomes demoralizing, a job that we clock into instead of the safe magic circle of play."

Narrowing down from deWinter and Kocurek's overview of women's marginalization in game culture, Nina Huntemann examines a single site of this marginalization in "Attention Whores and Ugly Nerds: Gender and Cosplay at the Game Con." Huntemann explains that for many women who have felt unwelcome in the gaming community, cosplay has represented "an alternative path . . . [that is] often the difference between public participation in game culture and playing alone." As that culture shifts closer to the mainstream and greater gender inclusivity, though, highly visible women cosplayers have become prime targets for harassment, ridicule, and dismissal at game conventions and beyond in what Huntemann identifies as an attempt to use women's bodies "to reinstate male dominance in video games." Huntemann focuses on the twin accusations that cosplayers are either attention whores or ugly nerds: "Women whose bodies most closely resemble the bodies of video game characters may meet the industry's beauty norms, but because they are attractive, they are suspected of faking their fandom. Women whose bodies do not measure up are rejected regardless of their knowledge or devotion to games." This double bind, Huntemann argues, creates a hostile environment where legitimacy within the dominant game culture may elude any woman cosplayer because of her body's—not her costume's—appearance.

Concluding this part, Gabrielle Trépanier-Jobin's "Video Game Parodies: Appropriating Video Games to Criticize Gender Norms" turns this book's attention to game paratexts, in the form of internet video parodies. While accounting for the different affordances of basic machinima and animations that use more complex modeling software, Trépanier-Jobin analyzes video paratexts of *Super Mario Bros.* (1985–2013, Nintendo) and *World of Warcraft* (2004–2014, Blizzard Entertainment) that engage with gender in these games. She finds, though, that despite the subversive potential of their format, these game parodies remain largely "surface-level efforts to modernize the damsel in distress figure" or denounce conventional beauty standards for avatars "without being entirely progressive." Trépanier-Jobin advocates for parody producers to signal their gender critiques more strongly—using interpretive clues, direct criticisms, and reflexive devices—lest they end up reproducing sexist tropes for audiences already primed to accept these by an often-misogynist game culture.

Each of the authors in the book's second part, "Race, Identity, Nation," discusses images of racial identity in video games in ways that dynamically situate those images in conversation with the codes and systems inherent in other ideologies, social practices, and cultural histories. Fittingly perhaps, many of the games analyzed in this part are of a dystopian, apocalyptic, or anti-utopian nature. Examining these, our contributors take various cultural-studies-inspired approaches in exploring the degree to which the games are reflexive about their objects of critique—whether tropes of blackness, white masculinity, or the subordinated status of women and children. The part's final chapter problematizes the very notion of identification (self-identification through racialized avatars) as something we might take for granted.

TreaAndrea M. Russworm's "Dystopian Blackness and the Limits of Racial Empathy in *The Walking Dead* and *The Last of Us*" begins the part by challenging the game industry to do better than simply populating virtual worlds with racially diverse characters. She uses the explosively popular genre of dystopian games—with their tremendous potential to function both as objects of catharsis and critique—to argue that even as the medium moves toward including more black characters, it is largely still failing to do so imaginatively or progressively. Most often, video games instead fall back on an established pattern of "conflating black identity with the pathos of sacrifice and suffering." Using the tools of postmodern theory and film and media criticism, Russworm reveals how *The Last of Us* (2013, Naughty Dog) uses blackness "to shore up white character agency" and how *The Walking Dead: Season One* (2012–2013, Telltale Games) limits the player's control in embodying a black character, forcing the narrative toward sentimentalism, empathy, and—again—obligatory sacrificial blackness. Russworm calls for game designers to develop an awareness of the historical tropes of blackness and, with that, use a "dialogic process . . . not just a procedural or algorithmic [one]" as they integrate blackness into dystopian games—an awareness she believes could help fulfill the considerable promise of what she theorizes as "critical racial dystopias" in video games.

With Irene Chien's "*Journey* into the Techno-primitive Desert," the collection shifts from dystopian rubble to an adjacent space of the primitive, postapocalyptic desert and the way its metaphor constructs ethnicity and nationality. Using literary history, cultural theory, and games criticism, Chien provides a cultural and historical framework for understanding how the art game *Journey* (2012, thatgamecompany) evokes the strong emotional responsiveness for which it has been so widely praised. Chien frames *Journey* as a "techno-primitive" racialized fantasy set in an implicitly Middle Eastern desert's open landscape, whose literary associations as a site of spiritual regeneration contrast with its video game associations as a chaotic, terrorist-ridden wasteland and common backdrop for first-person shooters. Exposing a tension in *Journey* between the desert as a primordial blank slate, on the one hand, and a reservoir of "soft" feminized technologies and exotic resources, on the other, Chien's skilled reading of the game, its mechanics, and cultural contexts encourages us not to take *Journey*'s departure from the way other games have depicted the Middle East as confirmation that the work is entirely progressive or resistant. Rather, "the desire for the desert apocalypse is therefore also a racialized, imperial desire" that provides an imaginary space for "the besieged white Western male subject" to problematically "recover from the corruptions of modern technologized existence."

Soraya Murray expands on the theme of besieged, beleaguered, and dysphoric white masculinities adrift in a Middle Eastern topography with "The Rubble and the Ruin: Race, Gender, and Sites of Inglorious Conflict in *Spec Ops: The Line*." Set in a fictitious Dubai's ecological apocalypse, *Spec Ops: The Line* (2012, Yager Development) graphically renders the emotional consequences of military conquest and humanitarian missions. Murray's method of analysis—a fusion of postcolonial, psychoanalytic, and cultural studies modes of critique—prioritizes the game's proximity to cinematic and literary history, putting *The Line* in conversation with existing touchstone texts about the emotional toll of military occupation such as *Heart of Darkness* (1899, Joseph Conrad) and *Apocalypse Now* (1979, Francis Ford Coppola). Though the game is deliberate about representing a destabilized white masculinity, in Murray's eloquent assessment, it is much less critical about its subordination of women and children or its nihilistic portrayal of Dubai, since both are needed to service the game's depiction of wounded American men. "The pleasure in the game," argues Murray, "comes from tapping into a deeper American cultural imaginary of the Arab world as regressing into calamity and mired in extreme poverty, reinforced through continual media representation." The chapter concludes with an open reflection on how games might create works that are geopolitically significant without also succumbing to nationalist rhetoric and propaganda.

In "Representing Race and Disability: *Grand Theft Auto: San Andreas* as a Whole Text," Rachael Hutchinson encourages gaming scholars to consider racial tropes and stereotypes in relation to a game's entire narrative and overall investment in social satire. Using cultural studies methods, Hutchinson asserts that the fantasy of the racial other as we get to know it in *Grand Theft Auto: San Andreas* (2004, Rockstar North) through CJ, the lead black character, is indeed stereotypical. But moving beyond that, her chapter demonstrates that characters like CJ are best understood through a nuanced analysis of how player-character interaction, embodiment, and identification function across the full story campaign and also in the free-roaming play of the game's vast "sandbox." Hutchinson's reading concludes that the black and Latino characters in the game actually "negotiate racial prejudice and overcome biased attitudes" in complex ways. Yet the overlooked aspects of the game's racial politics converge around the Orientalist portrayal of Wu Zi Mu, an important secondary character, and his physical disability. By more deeply exploring some of the ways in which "narrative, representation, and gameplay dynamics are intertwined and interdependent," the chapter offers a critical approach to representation in video games that transcends white-black racial binaries.

Lisa Patti's contribution, "Entering the Picture: Digital Portraiture and the Aesthetics of Video Game Representation," concludes this part by tracing themes of diversity in video games beyond the borders of individual games or even the main currents of game culture and analyzing its manifestation in the art world's digital portraiture. Patti examines three projects that create portraits of gamers and/or their avatars: *Alter Ego* (2007, Robbie Cooper), *13 Most Beautiful Avatars* (2006, Eva and Franco Mattes), and *Immersion* (2008– , Robbie Cooper). Reading these comparatively alongside Andy Warhol's *Thirteen Most Beautiful* (1964–1966) screen tests, Patti reveals how, for example, *13 Most Beautiful Avatars* explores the notion of beauty in virtual space and the way avatar embodiment can "simultaneously resist and reassert social realities," or how the video portrait of Drew Hugh—a child who cries when he plays video games—challenges assumptions about the relationship between black masculinity and the medium's frequently violent content. Through analysis of these portraiture projects that "establish a new census of representation" for video games, Patti contends that "the virtual world is neither a utopian space where the expression of different gendered and racial identities can proceed free from scrutiny or harassment nor an industrially codified sphere that neatly replicates off-line structures of power."

Finally, our third part, "Queerness, Play, Subversion," turns to sexuality. Its three chapters are linked not only by this shared focus but also by their mutual challenge to the notion that queerness in games is primarily about seeing LGBT characters on-screen. The authors here avoid performing "'straight' queer reading[s]" of games and simply "bird-watching for queer characters," as Edmond Y. Chang puts it. Instead, they establish new frameworks for thinking about what "queer" means to video games as a medium—how it combines with the notion of play and exists meaningfully beyond the realm of representation.

Bonnie Ruberg's "Playing to Lose: The Queer Art of Failing at Video Games" leads off this part with a theoretical approach. Putting two recent works of game studies and queer theory into conversation, Ruberg mines the intersection of

Jesper Juul's *The Art of Failure: An Essay on the Pain of Playing Video Games* and Jack Halberstam's *The Queer Art of Failure* to establish a foundation for her own notion of queer failure in video games. Challenging the assumption that failing in games is always undesirable—an unpleasant obstacle on the path to success—Ruberg posits that "failure might be its own success, its own pleasure, its own art," and a queer art, at that: "a spectacular, masochistic mode of resistance that disassembles normative expectations in and out of the game world." Through readings of "straight" fighting and racing games—most prominently, *Burnout: Revenge* (2005, Criterion Games)—Ruberg explores the queer practice of failing "for failure's sake," develops a dichotomy of failing either toward or against the game system, and untangles the paradoxes that queer failure generates (e.g., how do you fail at a game that positions failure as success?). Her wonderfully incendiary aim in unearthing the queerness of failure is to claim all games as queer: "to the extent that no game can exist without failure, no game can exist without queerness."

Jordan Wood's approach to finding queerness in video games is similarly broad in "Romancing an Empire, Becoming Isaac: The Queer Possibilities of *Jade Empire* and *The Binding of Isaac*." His essay concentrates on the meaningful affinity between queer theory's notions of time and space and video games, "a medium that works by generating a sense of alternate embodiment and temporality via simulation . . . [and] can reject linearity, contain multiple unresolved narratives, and offer a space-time that rejects reproductive norms." Games and queer space-time share a ludic core, and Wood teases out the potential of this shared playfulness through Jack Halberstam's theory of the archive, as well as a Deleuzian ethic of becoming. Finally, Wood applies these ideas and flips conventional styles of analyzing identity and games by exposing the underlying ideological conservatism of *Jade Empire* (2005, BioWare)—generous as it is in its inclusion of LGBT characters and romances—and celebrating the more radical queerness of *The Binding of Isaac* (2011, Valve), which features no explicit LGBT content.

Edmond Y. Chang completes this trio of chapters with a focused analysis of one game's queer potentials and shortcomings that reflects on the broader potentials and shortcomings of the medium itself for "queergaming," with its "ways of playing against the grain, against normative design, and ways of designing gamic experiences that foreground not only alternative narrative opportunities but ludic ones as well." In "A Game Chooses, a Player Obeys: *BioShock*, Posthumanism, and the Limits of Queerness," Chang contemplates video games' "technonormative matrix," asserting that "the tyranny of the binary, of the Boolean, of the matrix" makes the medium technologically and fundamentally conservative and ill-suited to the creation of truly queer texts, which require an embrace of uncertainty and ambivalence. In performing a close reading of *BioShock* (2007, Irrational Games), Chang reveals a game whose potentially substantial queerness—through its posthuman themes, character of Sander Cohen, and seeming critique of the medium's rhetoric of player agency—is subverted by its underlying reliance on the binary logics so ingrained in video games. Despite his disillusionment with *BioShock*, though, Chang does use it to imagine the medium's largely unrealized capacity to queerly embrace "the gaps and glitches, the overlaps and undertexts, and the dissonances and resonances of play, player, and program."

Lisa Nakamura closes *Gaming Representation* with an afterword, "Racism, Sexism, and Gaming's Cruel Optimism." Here, she identifies and critiques the common belief that gaming can solve its inequality problems through the mechanisms of "procedural meritocracy," wherein players outside the dominant straight, white, male culture can "create habitable spaces for themselves by displays of superior skill . . . proving their worth by dominating other players." Nakamura reads this belief against two recent disruptions of meritocracy in relation to difference in the United States: the game-specific case of the misogynist crusade against developer Zoë Quinn, and the more general case of Michael Brown's death at the hands of police.

* * *

Gaming Representation, to return to the metaphor of the choir, is about moving the choir out from behind the pulpit—or moving perspectives on race, gender, and sexuality from the margins of game studies to the center of an emergent canon. The book represents an attempt to bring together voices from multiple fields into one volume and demonstrate that the discussions about women and masculinity, racial and national identities, sexuality and queerness are not only relevant to other ways of studying games (like the focus on platforms and systems) but can also make the study of games more relevant and accessible to other fields and broader audiences.

JENNIFER MALKOWSKI is Assistant Professor of Film and Media Studies at Smith College. Her research areas include digital media; documentary; race, gender, and sexuality in media; and death and dying. She is the author of *Dying in Full Detail: Mortality and Digital Documentary*.

TREAANDREA M. RUSSWORM is Associate Professor of English at the University of Massachusetts, Amherst, where she teaches classes on digital media, race, and popular culture. She is coeditor of *From Madea to Media Mogul: Theorizing Tyler Perry* and author of *Blackness Is Burning: Civil Rights, Popular Culture, and the Problem of Recognition*.

Notes

1. Laura Mulvey's "Visual Pleasure and Narrative Cinema," published by *Screen* in 1975, made a tremendous impact in the young discipline of film studies, ushered in an era of robust feminist film scholarship, and became one of the discipline's most cited and most taught essays.

2. We previously discussed some of the following ideas about representation as maligned in game studies with the online discussion group empyre, in a week on games and representation convened by *Gaming Representation* contributor Soraya Murray. See "Welcome to Week 2 on empyre: Games and Representation," April 8–15, 2015, http://empyre.library.cornell.edu/phpBB2/viewtopic.php?t=829.

3. Adrienne Shaw, *Gaming at the Edge: Sexuality and Gender at the Margins of Gamer Culture* (Minneapolis: University of Minnesota Press, 2014), 6.

4. Stuart Hall, *Stuart Hall: Critical Dialogues in Cultural Studies*, ed. David Morley and Kuan-Hsing Chen (London: Routledge, 1996), 443 (emphasis in original).

5. Ibid., 446.

6. The practice spans only about as far back as 2002, and book publishing on race and games is an even newer development, less than a decade old. Early approaches to race and games were typically only peripherally about games, as most of these were internet/cyberspace studies. See, for example, Lisa Nakamura, Beth Kolko, and Gilbert Rodman, *Race in Cyberspace* (New York: Routledge, 2000); and Anna Everett, "The Revolution Will Be Digitized: Afrocentricity and the Digital Public Sphere," *Social Text* 20, no. 2 (2002): 125–146.

7. See Anna Everett, *Digital Diaspora: A Race for Cyberspace* (New York: State University of New York Press, 2009).

8. Ibid., 109–146.

9. Ibid., 142.

10. Lisa Nakamura, *Digitizing Race: Visual Cultures of the Internet* (Minneapolis: University of Minnesota Press, 2008), 209.

11. Ibid., 92.

12. Lisa Nakamura, *Cybertypes: Race, Ethnicity, and Identity on the Internet* (New York: Routledge, 2002), 3.

13. See Lisa Nakamura, "Don't Hate the Player, Hate the Game: The Racialization of Labor in *World of Warcraft*," *Critical Studies in Media Communication* 26, no. 2 (2009): 128–144. See also Lisa Nakamura, "Digital Media in *Cinema Journal*, 1995–2008," *Cinema Journal* 49, no. 1 (2009): 154–160.

14. S. Craig Watkins, *The Young and the Digital* (Boston: Beacon Press, 2009).

15. David Leonard, "Young, Black (and Brown) and Don't Give a Fuck: Virtual Gangstas in the Era of State Violence," *Cultural Studies ↔ Critical Methodologies* 9, no. 2 (2009): 252. Also see David J. Leonard, "'Live in Your World, Play in Ours': Race, Video Games, and Consuming the Other," *Studies in Media and Information Literacy Education* 3, no. 4 (2003): 1–9.

16. Jo Bryce and Jason Rutter, "Killing Like a Girl: Gendered Gaming and Girl Gamers' Visibility," in *Computer Games and Digital Cultures Conference Proceedings*, ed. Frans Mäyrä (Tampere, Finland: Tampere University Press, 2002), 253.

17. D. Fox Harrell, *Phantasmal Media: An Approach to Imagination, Computation, and Expression* (Cambridge, MA: MIT Press, 2013).

18. D. Fox Harrell, "Toward a Theory of Critical Computing: The Case of Social Identity Representation in Digital Media Applications," *CTheory*, May 13, 2010, http://www.ctheory.net/articles.aspx?id=641.

19. Ibid.

20. See, for example, "Putting the Gay in Games: Cultural Production and LGBT Content in Video Games," *Games and Culture* 4, no. 3 (2009): 228–253; and "Do You Identify as a Gamer? Gender, Race, Sexuality, and Gamer Identity," *New Media and Society* 14, no. 1 (2012): 25–41.

21. Shaw, *Gaming at the Edge*, 38.

22. Ibid., 5–6.

23. Ibid., 33–34.

Part I

GENDER, BODIES, SPACES

chapter one

"I TURNED OUT TO BE SUCH A DAMSEL IN DISTRESS"

Noir Games and the Unrealized Femme Fatale

JENNIFER MALKOWSKI

ONCE UPON A TIME IN MEDIA HISTORY, A CHARACTER TYPE CALLED THE femme fatale accomplished a minor miracle: she infused the products of a deeply misogynistic industry, US cinema in the 1940s, with a spark of interest for its female consumers while simultaneously adding strong appeal for its male consumers. A statement like this one requires a long list of qualifiers, as bold proclamations come less easily to academics than to the denizens of films noir.[1] But the basic story here holds. Hollywood in the immediate pre-noir years created dynamic female characters only rarely, and these were often ghettoized into genres like the aptly titled "woman's picture."[2] Women (and viewers of any other gender) going to the movies hoping to see such characters were typically greeted, instead, by the bland female love interest. She was there in a dual role as visual spectacle for the male viewer and to support or motivate the male protagonist while making as little other narrative impact as possible, it seemed.[3] Enter, then, the femme fatale, who both amplified visual spectacle with her intense sexuality and took control of film narratives in new ways and on her own behalf. Avoiding the domesticity to which so many on-screen women were constrained, she had smarts, sex appeal, ambition, and—most importantly—power of her own in a man's world of crime and violence. Though she could never win in the end, thanks to the Motion Picture Production Code, the femme fatale's temporary empowerment in films noir made an indelible mark on the medium.[4]

It's hard to imagine a media industry that needs what the femme fatale character provided to cinema more than the contemporary video game industry. With, sadly, just as much misogyny seeming to course through its veins as 1940s Hollywood, this industry is under much greater pressure to reform its relationship with women on multiple fronts. It is tenaciously courting female customers, but its representation of women within its products—again, with notable exceptions—tends to range from neglectful to insulting. It is apparently courting female employees, but overwhelmingly remains a boys' club.[5] And a highly vocal minority of its most devoted male customers has made game culture feel hostile and unsafe for many women.[6] From getting groped at conventions to being aggressively disrespected in multiplayer environments to receiving death and rape threats via social media, women wanting to get involved in game culture have a long list of disincentives to do so. Obviously, creating games that feature femmes fatales will not dismantle this formidable web of gender trouble in the video game industry. But many who are working to alleviate these problems do advocate for increasing the number of nuanced, powerful, and playable female characters in games as one core strategy.[7]

The noir femme fatale offers an especially promising template here, in that it strikes a bargain between industry and feminist priorities: sexualized enough to give a presumed hetero-male audience its presumed desire for women in games, the femme fatale also exudes the strength and complexity of character that many players (hetero male and otherwise) probably care about more. By design, the femme fatale neither alienates men nor demeans and bores women. She is an erotic object but also an active subject—in fact, one of the most active female character types in film that could be translated into the action-based medium of video games. And with today's game industry unencumbered by the production code, the moralizing narrative constraints that held back classic femmes fatales would not be a problem; the femme fatale could win in contemporary games the way she never could in film noir's classic cycle. Continuing a long, successful tradition of games remediating elements from cinema, noir video games could create memorable femmes fatales that would help sell games profitably and snag some good PR for an industry increasingly vulnerable to accusations of sexism and gendered exclusions.[8]

Surprisingly, then, while studios have been making noir games since the 1980s, very few of these include playable femmes fatales. Even in non-player character (NPC) roles, the femme fatale is often missing from these games, or relegated to small roles in specific missions. Keeping in mind this puzzling absence as I analyze the two most prominent efforts to create playable femmes fatales, in *Max Payne 2* (2003, Remedy Entertainment) and *Heavy Rain* (2010, Quantic Dream), I argue that video games have yet to unlock this character's considerable representational and ludic potential. Further, when the femme fatale does emerge as a playable character, her power is subverted—either gradually throughout the game or acutely at the end—through an exposure of her underlying and essential feminine weakness. This resolution of the femme fatale's narrative directly mirrors the bleakest variety of her fate in film noir's classic cycle. Neo-noir films began vigorously challenging this regressive 1940s convention decades ago. But video games seem, thus far, content to replicate it, despite their eagerness to update other aspects of classic film noir by adding the sex, violence, and adult themes that the midcentury films had to minimize.

But why *do* games ignore the femme fatale or include her in disempowered forms? One could surmise that because the femme fatale's power is generally social rather than physical—in other words, she deceives an enemy more often than she shoots him—her character would be difficult to adapt to the medium, as violence-based actions are so central to video games. As I illustrate later, though, this is a red herring in the case of the missing femme fatale. The more convincing explanation comes back to game culture rather than game mechanics: to the perceived threat of women's incursion into the contemporary gaming world.

The Appeal of the Filmic Femme Fatale

Film noir's femme fatale emerges in the classic period as a study in contrasts: her overt sexuality prompts erotic links to others in the narrative, but her fierce independence propels her toward autonomy; she is highly feminine in appearance, but often exercises her agency in masculinized ways (e.g., deftly wielding a gun); and, as previously noted, she is simultaneously an object to be looked at and an active subject. Aligning with these tensions, the femme fatale's primary trait, beyond even her sexuality, is her status as an enigma, as Mary Ann Doane explains: "Her most striking characteristic, perhaps, is the fact that she never really is what she seems to be. She harbors a threat which is not entirely legible, predictable, or manageable. In thus transforming the threat of the woman into a secret, something which must be aggressively revealed, unmasked, discovered, the figure is fully compatible with the epistemological drive of the narrative."[9] Thus, woman in these noir stories is "an epistemological trouble"—a walking, talking question mark put in the path of the investigator-protagonist and located within a narrative whose central thrust is about uncovering truths from a morass of mystery and deception.[10]

This figure of woman as simultaneously powerful and unknowable could not, in the classic noir era, be permitted to triumph—not only because of the blunt prescriptions of the production code, but because of her more penetrating threat to the midcentury patriarchal order. And so "the *femme fatale* propelled the action, but her narrative options were numbered: she either died, reformed, or turned out not to be a *femme fatale* at all."[11] To that list, add that her story could also end with imprisonment and that her "reformation" was often signified by romantic coupling with the protagonist.[12] In film after film, then, this cathartic cycle repeats: the deadly woman emerges forcefully, poses a seductive threat to one or more men in the film, and has her power contained in the last reel. As Janey Place articulates in her formative essay on the subject, the societal threat posed by the figure of the aggressive, independent, and sexual woman is in film noir "allowed sensuous expression" but then destroyed, "and by its limited expression, ending in defeat, that unacceptable element is controlled."[13]

While the power of every femme fatale is undermined by her ultimate failure to secure the independence, money, or "great whatsit" she is seeking, there is one special ending scenario in noir through which women's power is most insidiously and effectively snuffed out. Appearing in films like *The Strange Love of Martha*

Ivers (1946, Lewis Milestone) and *Pursued* (1947, Raoul Walsh), this outcome was made iconic in one of the most beloved films noir of all time: *Double Indemnity* (1944, Billy Wilder).[14] By the time this climactic scene begins, femme fatale Phyllis Dietrichson has murdered a woman to marry her husband (most likely), convinced protagonist Walter Neff to murder that husband so that she can profit from his life insurance, and seduced a new male pawn whom she may maneuver into murdering Walter. When Walter arrives at her home to confront and kill her, Phyllis acts first and shoots him in the shoulder. Wounded, he approaches, goading her to finish him off. In this moment, the ultimate neutralization of the femme fatale's threat is born, as Phyllis's wrist goes limp and she allows Walter to take her gun. Leaning in close, she tearfully explains, "I never loved you, Walter, not you or anybody else . . . until a minute ago, when I couldn't fire that second shot." This is no final act of deception. Phyllis means it, and she begs Walter to hold her. He obliges for a moment and then sticks a gun into her midsection and fires twice, killing her.

For the femme fatale to be killed is no surprise and would not necessarily even contain her captivating power in the minds and memories of viewers. In most films noir, as Place asserts, "it is her strength and sensual visual texture that is inevitably printed on our memory, not her ultimate destruction."[15] But in *Double Indemnity*, the badass femme fatale's legacy is forever marred not by her death but by her textual reduction to a faltering, lovesick dupe just before it. Abandoning so many key traits of the femme fatale, Phyllis now becomes honest, transparent, sentimental; her emotions govern her actions, and she reorients her decisions and ambitions to revolve around a man (who, by contrast, keeps his composure). A woman who has been previously characterized in the film as decisive, manipulative, and a master of her own and others' emotions now has those layers peeled back to reveal, underneath, her essential and feminine weakness. The implication that *Double Indemnity* introduces—which would be seized on by other films and eventually by games noir—is that the femme fatale can't win not because of favored noir forces like fate or luck or karma or even the production code but because women, by nature, just aren't cut out for this kind of thing.

At this juncture, it seems appropriate to return to a broad question. Given all the complications and caveats of her empowerment, why is the femme fatale a character feminists might want to see adapted into video games? Her original incarnation in 1940s and 1950s films has not been wholly embraced by feminist film scholars, who have pointed out that her character associates female sexuality with danger and death, is far from a progressive role model, and is "not the subject of feminism but a symptom of male fears about feminism."[16] Indeed, the figure of the femme fatale emerges and reemerges in US cinema during periods when "male fears about feminism" rise as women make sharp gains in social and/or economic power: initially in the 1940s as women joined the workforce during wartime and then again with the character's resurgence in the 1980s, in the wake of second-wave feminism and with the escalating "threat" of the career woman.[17]

At the same time, though, there is a reason that feminist film scholars, despite their misgivings about the femme fatale, are fixated on her (as evidenced by the abundance of research on this character). As much as her inevitable defeat may cathartically soothe antifeminist fears, her embodiment and actions throughout the rest of the film may even more cathartically satisfy feminist frustrations—both with the general state of gender equality and with their treatment by the film industry, in particular. Describing these pleasures, Place notes that noir provides "one of the few periods of film in which women are active, not static symbols, are intelligent and powerful, if destructively so, and derive power, not weakness, from their sexuality."[18] Thus, the femme fatale represents something of a compromise between competing audience desires—and the game industry is certainly in need of these—though one I believe slants favorably in the feminist direction. In the classic noir era, providing visual pleasure and being defeated in the end allowed the femme fatale to get away with a tremendous transgression: having true power.

Further, the femme fatale is not frozen in her midcentury form; she can be updated for our current cultural moment. Game designers need not do all this work themselves, as neo-noir filmmakers have been evolving the classic character since the 1970s. During this period, femmes fatales generally have gotten smarter, stronger, richer, more ambitious (especially in relation to their careers), and more independent—even as neo-noir's male protagonist has evolved to be less competent and confident. Some neo femmes fatales have used sex for pleasure as well as power, and many have embraced queer sexualities. Most importantly, the neo femme fatale—freed from the production code—can "*avoid textual suppression*, to win on her own terms," as Kate Stables writes; "this seems to utterly subvert the classic noir procedure with the fatale in which the power of the strong sexual woman is first displayed, then destroyed, in order to demonstrate the necessity of its control."[19] While the neo-noir evolution of the femme fatale is not wholly driven by feminist goals, many of the changes have made the character more promising in this regard and could be readily implemented in a ludic femme fatale.

Within the context of video games, one might counter: But hasn't what the femme fatale offers already been delivered outside of noir through often-maligned figures like Lara Croft and Bayonetta? It's true that these are female characters who are highly sexualized and highly powerful. While I don't necessarily find them disempowering or offensive, the difference between them and the femme fatale is that their sexualized portrayal runs counter to their narrative situations: the shortest shorts ever fabricated aren't what anyone would wear to raid tombs, for example, nor does it seem wise to brawl with supernatural foes completely naked.[20] Thus, these inclusions of female sexuality in powerful, playable characters may feel like pandering excesses rather than satisfying dimensions of said characters. A well-designed femme fatale within a noir game would allow for a narratively justified expression of female sexuality, which gamers of any gender and sexual orientation may appreciate and enjoy, for a variety of reasons including and beyond titillation. Draining women's representations of all sexuality is, after all, not a feminist ideal.

This truth may become more clear if a decline in egregious depictions of female sexuality (and here I am not referring to the likes of Lara Croft or even Bayonetta) ever gives feminists a break from having to constantly critique these.

But how to translate the filmic femme fatale into the medium of games, grounded as it is in player and machine *actions*?[21] The two games I now examine attempt this translation, creating playable femmes fatales within noir environments. While each finds at least some success in aligning game mechanics with the femme fatale's core attributes, both fail the character at narrative and ideological levels in ways that mirror classic film noir at its most misogynistic.

The Too-*Fatale* Ludic Femme Fatale: *Max Payne 2*

Video games' first attempt to create a playable femme fatale arrives in one of its most self-referentially noir series, the popular third-person shooter *Max Payne*. The title character is our protagonist, a maverick cop (and, briefly, DEA agent) who in each of the first two games is drawn into investigating complicated criminal conspiracies. Max is initially motivated by the murder of his wife and daughter—a plot point that also leaves him free to pursue a volatile romance with the series' femme fatale, Mona Sax. Their intense relationship stems from a typical noir setup: "a man whose experience of life has left him sanguine and often bitter meets a non-innocent woman of similar outlook to whom he is sexually and fatally attracted."[22]

This non-innocent woman is introduced as such in the narrative cutscenes of the original *Max Payne* (2001, Remedy Entertainment). These take the form of comic-book-style illustrated panels accompanied by Max's brooding, retrospective voice-over narration (another staple of noir). Training a notably oversized handgun on Max when they first meet, Mona supports his voice-over assessment that she is "a knockout femme fatale" in the way that she identifies herself (as the sister of a woman he is investigating): "Mona Sax, Lisa's evil twin. . . . Lisa's the damsel in distress. I'm the professional. I'd blow you away without batting an eye." Given Mona's transparency, it initially seems as if *Max Payne* has mislabeled her as a femme fatale, but she quickly engages in an act of seductive deception to earn the title, convincing Max to accept a drugged whiskey (to keep him out of her way). When she returns later in the game, Mona violates her avowed professionalism as a contract killer and promise to "blow [Max] away" without hesitation, instead demonstrating a soft spot for this unstable head case she barely knows. Ordered to kill him by her employer, Mona smiles and tells Max to relax: she doesn't kill "nice guys." Seconds later, shots ring out and she pushes Max out of the line of fire, taking a bullet in the head herself instead. Lamenting her death, Max reassesses: "She was a nice girl, not really a stone-cold killer." Thus, *Max Payne* replicates—in an extremely abbreviated form—the *Double Indemnity* trajectory of the femme fatale: a seductive woman demonstrates that she is highly dangerous, appears to be calculating and self-interested, and then abruptly sacrifices her own plans and ultimately her life based on her sentimental attachment to the male protagonist. Since it confines its femme fatale to the narrative comic book panels, though, this first installment does not actually adapt the character to video games' ludic environment.

Without explanation, Mona survives her presumably fatal headshot in the first game and reappears as a major and playable character in *Max Payne 2: The Fall of Max Payne*. This sequel features Mona and Max on the cover, embracing with their guns drawn under the tagline, "a film noir love story." Here, Max reencounters Mona as they are both killing some goons (Max as a cop, Mona as a hired gun), and they are pushed together when a powerful secret society puts hits out on each of them for knowing too much. Forging an uneasy alliance to take out their mutual enemies, Max and Mona grow closer—or, at least, Max becomes increasingly obsessed with Mona and with "solving" the mystery of the enigmatic femme fatale. He muses frequently about her motives with frustration ("I couldn't crack her. I had to crack the case"), sees mirages of her on billboards and bus stop ads, and has a vivid, playable dream in which he's running through a maze of hallways following the sound of Mona orgasming. Mona seems markedly less interested in Max; she does save him from a burning building, but at other points in the game she abandons him to danger when it suits her self-interest.

Their relationship also becomes sexual outside Max's dreams. When Max finds Mona at her hideout and interrupts her showering, the consummate femme fatale asks him to hand her a towel and slowly slinks into the next room to get dressed. Max, ever the self-aware noir protagonist, reflects, "The way she was acting, I was the only one in danger here." At a later encounter, Mona pulls Max into a steamy kiss, which quickly escalates into a make-out session that would have made a production code censor blush (had "underboob" entered the lexicon yet in the 1940s?). Thus, throughout these comic book cutscenes (and the in-game cutscenes that supplement them), Mona's gendered deadliness is consistently presented and intertwined with her intense sexuality. Bringing the femme fatale archetype back to its biblical roots, Mona even finds a spare moment at Max's apartment to take a single, seductive bite out of an apple.

Max Payne 2 builds a developed, engaging femme fatale in these cutscenes, but its real innovation is to make her a playable character. The player must take control of Mona for four of the game's twenty-four chapters. In analyzing how its designers translate the femme fatale's traits into game actions, *Max Payne 2*'s third-person shooter format does not seem promising for accommodating a character type whose power is not traditionally defined by physical violence. Further, it initially seems as if Mona "is simply a female 'skinned' version of the male protagonist" (a common shortcut for creating playable women in games): there is no meaningful shift in how your avatar moves or attacks when you transition from controlling Max to controlling Mona (other than some purely ornamental acrobatics in her movements).[23]

Despite these hindrances, *Max Payne 2*'s industry-first attempt at a playable femme fatale is—for most of the game—more successful than it seems, in both clear and subtle ways. Mona's overpowering talent with firearms gives the femme fatale a refreshing level of competence in a crucial skill set for noir's violent environments and puts her (at least) on par with the male protagonist. Proficiency at violence, rather than relying on men to take physical action for her, is one of the amplified talents of the neo-noir femme fatale but also has precedents in the classic era—most memorably, *Gun Crazy*'s (1950, Joseph H. Lewis) ruthless sharpshooter, Annie Laurie Star. Indeed, much has been made of the phallic significance of the gun-wielding woman in noir, and Mona maximizes that empowered (and threatening) symbolism throughout the gameplay, cutscenes, and even advertisements for *Max Payne 2*. In Mona's first playable chapter, "Routing Her Synapses," an aerial view swoops dramatically downward and encircles the player's new avatar, Mona, who stands confidently posed with an almost comically oversized Dragunov sniper rifle whose length seems to surpass her height (figure 1.1). And in Max and Mona's signature tableau for cutscenes and advertisements, intimately holding guns to each other's heads, Mona is always portrayed with a larger handgun than Max, despite the fact that a large handgun is seldom the optimal weapon for Mona during gameplay and Max frequently uses large weapons.

Beyond the empowerment of her weaponry and skilled shooting, though, this femme fatale's unique playability derives not from the actions she is afforded but from the distinct scenarios programmed for her. Where Max's chapters rarely make his sniper rifle an efficient option for the player, Mona's practically demand

Figure 1.1. Mona with her signature sniper rifle (*Max Payne 2* game still)

significant use of this weapon by repeatedly placing her high above distant enemies who are distracted by another target (Max). These game scenarios associate Mona with a sneakier variety of action than Max despite their identical programmed abilities. Rather than charging headlong into a tangle of opponents, she kills from cover—unseen and unknown—in a way that resonates with the femme fatale's character attributes. The game's creators thus overcome the constraints of its third-person shooter mechanics to more subtly translate the femme fatale's propensity for covert maneuvering into the actual gameplay of a third-person shooter. Further, *Max Payne 2* scenarios reverse typical gendered scenes of rescue, placing Max more frequently in the damsel-in-distress role and casting a playable Mona as his savior.

For players who lost interest in *Max Payne 2* before its concluding chapters, Mona Sax may still live on as a creative and empowering ludic take on the femme fatale. The rest of us, though, would see this carefully crafted neo femme fatale shamefully unraveled in later cutscenes that had been foreshadowed by the game's opening line: "God! I turned out to be such a damsel in distress." Mona, we can intuit, is careening toward that self-articulated sorry outcome even as she deftly takes down dozens of midgame enemies. It arrives when Max (again the playable character) and Mona are climactically pursuing their main enemy, Vlad, through an ally's sprawling manor. A cutscene shows Mona blindside Max with a blow to the head and then aim her gun straight at him, explaining that she's been hired "to clear up this mess and you're a part of it." After a multiple-panel hesitation, during which Max narrates about the meaning of true love, Mona admits—just like *Double Indemnity*'s Phyllis Dietrichson—"I can't do it." Dropping her gun without seeing Vlad behind her, Mona is promptly shot. Max is pulled away from this scene for a while, but returns to the wounded Mona in time to hear her quavering last words: the game's opening line, now placed in a legible continuity, "God! I turned out to be such a damsel in distress" (figure 1.2). In a final parting shot, *Max Payne 2* reinscribes Mona as a mere accessory to Max's character development as he reflects, "Because of her, I had solved the case. My case, all of it. Who I am." Caressing her lifeless face, he later adds, "Now, like all my loves, she is mine forever." Once an elusive mystery, the femme fatale, emotionally exposed and then killed, can now be known and possessed by the male protagonist.

Improbably, then, the *Max Payne* series manages to demean, declaw, and kill its femme fatale *twice*, repeating this ending to her story in both of the first two games.[24] Mona, it seems, could only be unleashed as such a threateningly powerful, big-gunned woman ("She's worse than him!" we overhear an NPC henchman remark) in the world of *Max Payne* if that power would be fully contained by the game's end. Mona's fate as a femme fatale aligns with so many from the classic noir era; within those films, "[the femme fatale's] ritualized death reveals her status as a mirror of deep male fears that extend beyond sexual inadequacy and the limits of social law, and thus require deeper purgation."[25] Mona proves too *fatale* to let live—too *fatale*, even, to be simply killed. Instead, *Max Payne 2* reverses

Figure 1.2. Mona's death scene (*Max Payne 2* game still)

course on its embrace of neo-noir elements and regresses to classic noir's most underhanded method of disempowering a femme fatale. Following this *Double Indemnity* model, she must reveal her essential, feminized, emotional weakness and be undone by it. This revelation occurs not just through Mona's inability to "blow [Max] away without batting an eye"—as she claimed she could in her first series appearance—but also through her vocalized acceptance of the maligned damsel-in-distress role, to which women in video games have historically been consigned. So strong is the game creators' desire to code Mona this way before she dies that they write this line for her in contradiction to its narrative context. Mona is not, in fact, the damsel in distress stereotype here, since she's beyond rescue. She's just a more refined, and more insulting, stereotype: the once-strong femme fatale brought low by her own inherent emotional weakness. As Max summarized way back when Mona "died" the first time, "She was a nice girl, not really a stone-cold killer."

Getting inside the Ludic Femme Fatale's Head: *Heavy Rain*

Before giving a great femme fatale a terrible ending, *Max Payne 2*'s Remedy Entertainment found moderate success adapting this character to fit the quite-limited game mechanics of a third-person shooter. In 2010, Quantic Dream's noir game *Heavy Rain* presented a new opportunity for the ludic femme fatale, freed from the constraints of the shooter. With a control scheme based on quick time events

(QTEs), this "interactive drama" (as Quantic Dream's marketing material often calls it) offered greater narrative and gameplay flexibility. Through QTEs, the player's action of pressing X, for example, isn't forever mapped onto the character's action of jumping but might be used at different junctures in the game to have that character catch a falling object, duck under a wire, or call out to someone—all depending on context. QTE control schemes are not beloved by gamers but nevertheless give *Heavy Rain*'s designers tremendous freedom, allowing them to incorporate many different kinds of human actions beyond video game standards like running, jumping, and attacking. Actions in this game range from making origami, tying a necktie, and feeding an infant to driving into oncoming traffic, escaping a submerged vehicle, and severing your own finger. QTEs, thus, have good potential for adapting the filmic femme fatale into video games because they make room on the controller for the femme fatale's complex social, intellectual, and erotic powers to become game actions. *Heavy Rain* does indeed feature a playable femme fatale that capitalizes on some of the QTE affordances, but as in *Max Payne 2*, this character is ultimately disempowered—this time more through her continual undermining during the game than through a sudden narrative shift at the end.

Set in a drab version of Philadelphia, *Heavy Rain*'s noir narrative begins with a mild-mannered father, Ethan Mars, who loses one of his young sons to a fatal traffic accident and, soon, another to abduction by the Origami Killer. While Ethan subjects himself to this serial killer's gruesome challenges to earn information on where his son, Shaun, is being held, three other playable investigators simultaneously attempt to identify the Origami Killer: FBI agent Norman Jayden, PI Scott Shelby, and insomniac Madison Paige, our femme fatale. I identify Madison initially only as an insomniac because—consistent with her overall status as the least developed of these four characters—Madison is given no clear connection to the Origami case when she is introduced. Her apparent motivation for getting involved is her instant attachment to Ethan, whom she meets at a cheap motel.

Though she fits the character type less cleanly than does Mona Sax, Madison is a femme fatale because she deceives multiple men during the game, sometimes by seducing them, in order—at least initially—to pursue her own ambitious goals.[26] Unbeknownst to either Ethan or the player until very late in the game, she is actually a journalist who contrived to meet Ethan "by chance" to pursue a career-making story about his son's abduction and the Origami Killer. Indeed, *Heavy Rain*'s downloadable prequel, *The Taxidermist*, would reveal that the ambitious Madison had been on the trail of the Origami Killer for some time already.[27]

Madison's actions have, on paper, empowering overtones (if the player performs well). She courageously pursues leads to Shaun's location in dangerous situations, uses both her wits and her self-defense skills to survive these, and is never positioned as the damsel in distress who needs to be rescued. Depending on the player's performance and choices, she may contribute to saving Shaun and besting the Origami Killer in physical combat at the game's end—or even accomplish both of these on her own without help from any of the other playable characters. But along the way to these potential outcomes, *Heavy Rain* undercuts Madison's power in two major ways: by repeatedly placing her in sexual danger and by exposing her inner fears and insecurities to the player.

While the femme fatale in noir is a highly sexualized character, it is less the simple presence of sexuality that defines her than her control of sexuality—her ability to perfectly calibrate her own sexuality for deception and to play on the desires of her targets. In *Heavy Rain*, though, Madison's ability to mobilize her powers of seduction is overshadowed by the constant rape threats she encounters and vocally fears. She is physically assaulted in five of her nine playable chapters (far more often than any male investigator) and three of these five assaults are directly or implicitly sexual.

In her introductory chapter, she is brutally attacked in her apartment in the middle of the night by three masked male intruders; the player controls her as she alternates between trying desperately to fend them off and fleeing in terror. Even though this event is later revealed to be a dream, the player still experiences the disturbing sexual peril of embodying a weaponless woman in a tank top and panties as she is, for example, violently thrown onto her bed and then mounted by her knife-wielding male attacker. In another Madison chapter, she gets knocked out by a crooked doctor whom she is investigating at his home. He ties her to an operating table in his basement, revs up a power drill, and begins lowering it toward her crotch. Even with a perfect string of QTE inputs, the ensuing fight will end with Madison collapsing forward onto the operating table to play dead and the doctor salaciously groping her ass before she springs up and strikes a fatal blow. There is thus no way for Madison to escape this basement without being sexually assaulted and debased, and if the player loses her fight with the doctor, Madison will indeed be murdered in an eroticized manner and will be lost as a playable character.[28]

If she survives, later that same day Madison will again face the threat of sexual violence when she follows her new lead to the Blue Lagoon nightclub and its seedy proprietor, Paco, from whom she must also extract information. Dancing erotically within view of Paco's VIP lounge, Madison soon succeeds in using her seductive abilities to get his attention and he leads her to his private room. Her plan is to pull her gun and let that convince him to talk, but Paco quickly takes her purse, pulls his own gun, and commands her to start stripping for him (figure 1.3). In what can be an extremely long scene of fearful degradation—depending on how quickly the player maneuvers Madison into hitting Paco over the head with a nearby lamp—the weaponless Madison will be forced to dance and remove items of clothing, potentially until she is down to just her panties with her breasts fully exposed to Paco and the player. During this striptease, low angle close-ups provide clear and lingering views of Madison's swaying crotch and ass, encouraging

Figure 1.3. Madison is forced to strip for Paco (*Heavy Rain* game still)

the player to enjoy her as an abject erotic object more so than identify with her as a frightened subject. Once again, the player has no agency—regardless of skill or choices—to spare the femme fatale from sexual violation. Adrienne Shaw's observation about a controversial assault scene in 2013's *Tomb Raider* applies equally well here: "The choice to include the threat of sexual assault . . . demonstrates an assumption that players of the game have never feared or been the targets of sexualized violence"—or, in *Heavy Rain*'s case, it demonstrates at least a lack of concern for how playing through multiple, brutal, sexualized attacks might affect such players.[29]

Introduced as a woman who has nightmares about being sexually assaulted and who then *is* sexually assaulted multiple times as she pursues her goals, Madison becomes a femme fatale whose sex appeal makes her vulnerable more often than it makes her strong or effective. Unlike her filmic predecessors, this femme fatale's sexual environment is very much out of her control. Madison's constant exposure to rape threats, in fact, highlights how seldom filmic femmes fatales face them, even in the neo-noir era when this adult theme could be explicitly portrayed. Perhaps the seeming invulnerability to rape of the highly sexual femme fatale has been one of the character's long-standing appeals to female audiences—the fantasy of being able to deploy and enjoy your sexuality without the (realistic, all too familiar) fear of it being turned against you. This is an appeal *Heavy Rain* denies Madison and her player.

The second way in which *Heavy Rain* disempowers its femme fatale is through the unique feature of allowing players to hear each character's thoughts throughout their investigations, echoing film noir's fondness for first-person narration (figure 1.4). As a player is commanding Madison to follow Paco up to his private

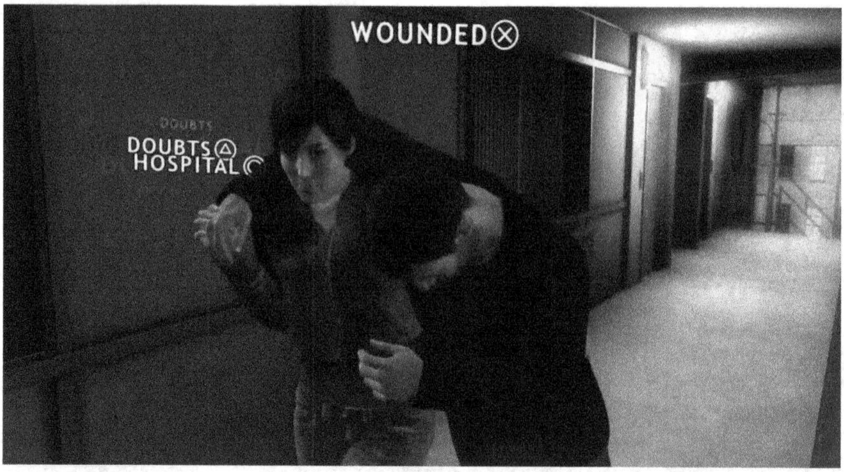

Figure 1.4. The player can choose which of Madison's thoughts to hear (*Heavy Rain* game still)

room, for example, she can hold down a button to see three or four topics Madison is pondering and choose whichever ones she'd like to hear Madison's thoughts about. Allowing access to the usually enigmatic femme fatale's thoughts is, in principle, a promising accompaniment to making her a playable character—potentially reinforcing her subjecthood, strengthening her bonds with the player, and giving this female game character a rich inner life. Film audiences, alongside protagonists, may often wonder what the femme fatale is thinking as she so calmly and expertly maneuvers through noir scenarios, and *Heavy Rain* offers a window into that mysterious mind. What we see here, though, is not a cool and collected seductress but rather an uncertain and frequently panicked individual who feels overwhelmed by her circumstances.

When Madison senses that there may be an intruder in her apartment, she engages in a cycle of fear and self-doubt typical to her character, thinking, "How on earth did the fridge door get open like that? Get it together, girl. You probably just left it open by accident" and "Girl, get a grip. The door is locked tight, and you're home alone." When she finds Ethan at his motel room injured after one of the Origami Killer's challenges, her thoughts are panicked and excessively emotional (considering that this is a man she's just met and is using professionally for a story). And even at the juncture when her encounter with Paco is going totally according to plan, before he takes her gun, Madison's thoughts reveal a severe crisis of confidence: "This is no time to get squeamish, even if my legs do feel like they're about to give way" and "Shit. You're making the biggest mistake of your life, Madison." Getting inside Madison's head, then, reveals that while she may seem powerful and in control externally, the femme fatale is racked with insecurity and fear. Newly disempowered in the eyes of the audience, she now seems perpetually just one wrong move away from being physically overpowered and/or psychologically undone.

Ultimately, the extent to which Madison fulfills the femme fatale role in *Heavy Rain* and her fate within that role will depend on the player's choices. It is possible to play Madison as a more pure and somewhat more empowered femme fatale than I have described. This requires a complicated series of choices that one would have to map out in advance with the express goal of willing a decent femme fatale into this noir game. A few key steps in this process would be to, as Madison, play poorly when twice helping Ethan escape the cops and allow him to be jailed to keep him out of your way, choose not to call any of the other investigators once you have Shaun's location, and then save Shaun and defeat the Origami Killer on your own to get your scoop as a reporter. This elaborate method of rigging the game to provide a better femme fatale also requires the player to fail challenges as other investigators (to prevent them from arriving at the final showdown) and to avoid listening to Madison's undermining thoughts, but it will not prevent Madison from suffering the disempowering indignities of her many sexual assaults. Further, as much as *Heavy Rain*'s programming gives the player a chance to consciously empower its femme fatale through the preceding actions, it also creates a parallel chance to consciously disempower her. Just as the committed feminist player can forge a slightly better femme fatale than the game's default, so, too, can the committed misogynist player debase and defeat the femme fatale beyond the game's default. Players could, for example, miss QTE inputs to see Madison get stabbed a few times in addition to having her throat slit during her intruder nightmare; they could have Ethan reject her when she leans in to kiss him; they could purposefully lengthen Madison's striptease and make sure she is maximally humiliated; or they could simply let her die, permanently and horribly (drilled to death by the doctor, burned alive in an apartment fire, strangled by the Origami Killer, etc.), to spare themselves from playing a female character for any longer than necessary.

Because *Heavy Rain*'s unusually flexible narrative allows the femme fatale's story to end in several different ways, her threat cannot be reliably contained through a disempowering ending alone, as Mona Sax's is. The "happy" ending the game most incentivizes through trophies, though, positions Madison as the redeemed femme fatale in classic noir's taxonomy. In this scenario, she regains Ethan's trust, after deceiving him about her career, by racing to help him save Shaun in the game's climax. When the epilogue cutscenes roll (somewhat customized to the player's choices throughout the game), Madison is shown moving into a stylish loft with Ethan and his rescued son. Subsumed into (implied) marriage, family, and domesticity, the once-ambitious and enigmatic Madison is now fully transparent and talks only about the chance to "lead a normal life" and "be happy." In most scenarios, then, Madison will not conclude *Heavy Rain* as a victorious and unapologetic femme fatale. But the ending here will be an afterthought, regardless, as the game reverses the impression left by classic noir's femme fatale. In those films, "it is her strength and sensual visual texture that is inevitably printed on our memory, not her ultimate destruction."[30] The opposite is true of *Heavy Rain*. No matter how Madison's story ends, it is her persistent underconfidence and debasement that is "inevitably printed on our memory."

Conclusion: "Destroyers of Male Strength"

For some time now, the film industry has been dreaming up and showcasing dynamic femmes fatales who conclude their stories victorious and uncompromised in a way their 1940s and 1950s predecessors never could. *Body Heat* ends with Matty enjoying her ill-gotten fortune on a tropical beach; *Bound* shows Violet riding off into the sunset in a shiny new truck with her butch lesbian partner in crime (and in bed); and *The Last Seduction*, the ultimate "admiring symphony that sings the praises of the bitch-goddess," reveals a self-satisfied Bridget burning up the last piece of evidence that could incriminate her in a profitable murder instead of her duped male lover.[31] Noir games have never come anywhere near "sing[ing] the praises of the bitch-goddess." They have mostly discarded the fascinating femme fatale character and occasionally—as in *Max Payne 2* and *Heavy Rain*—have put her into players' hands only to thoroughly undermine her threatening power in a revival of 1940s-style gender anxiety.

Perhaps I should be less surprised that the video game industry, with its unbearably fraught gender relations, has not chosen to capitalize on the neo femme fatale's potential. After all, this strong female character who invaded men's homosocial playground of guns and power in the 1940s crime film sounds remarkably like the female bogeymen whom Gamergaters and misogynists of their ilk imagine invading contemporary game culture. Like these monstrous women today, femmes fatales in classic noir were framed as "amoral destroyers of male strength," and their routine on-screen summoning and suppression pointed to "a mass market demand to see these demonstratively ambitious and thus dangerous women put back in their domestic 'place.'"[32] These sentiments will sound familiar to any gamer who has been viciously targeted in a multiplayer shooter just for being identifiably female, or who has been told by a male player to get back in the kitchen and make him a sandwich. The femme fatale in her time played the role of today's paranoid fantasy, the "fake geek girl"—conning her way into male spaces through deception and sex appeal. In midcentury films, as Place explains, and, as I would add, in today's dominant game culture, figures like the fictional femme fatale and the actual female gamer create anxiety through their failure to be "defined in relation to men. . . . The primary crime the 'liberated' woman is guilty of is refusing to be defined in such a way, and this refusal can be perversely seen (in art, or in life) as an attack on men's very existence."[33]

When game studios imagine a presumed male, presumed antifeminist game buyer, the femme fatale must seem like too clear and present a danger to be allowed to manifest in games in her most empowered forms. Little wonder, then, that the most satisfying (if, necessarily, small-scale) playable femme fatale I have encountered comes from an indie mobile game and, thus, a branch of this industry that caters less to presumed male, presumed antifeminist consumers. In *Framed* (2014, Loveshack), the player often controls a nameless, stylishly silhouetted woman whose femme fatale traits shape not just *Framed*'s style and narrative but its mechanics too. In this touch screen noir game about rearranging comic-book-style panels to change level outcomes, her playable portion begins by introducing a new ability: the power to rotate panels in addition to changing their order, established by rotating one that depicts a little bottle of sedative to have the femme fatale tip it into the male protagonist's coffee and knock him out. The femme fatale's game-specific playability is thus associated with her long-established character traits from film and literature: guile, deception, and the power to turn the story and the protagonist's best-laid plans upside down, here literalized in her power to turn game panels upside down. *Framed*'s femme fatale uses charm, violence, stealth, and smarts to best two playable male rivals and finish the game in possession of its coveted great whatsit, a mysterious briefcase. As little developed as a character in a short and narratively minimal mobile game can be, she is the rare example of a truly neo femme fatale in a medium that has otherwise refused to update this particular noir element.

Back in the wider game industry, what may have felt like enough of a step forward in 1940s cinema—the creation of the classic femme fatale whose strength would rise and fall within the course of a film—feels like a step backward today. Disempowered ludic femmes fatales like Mona and Madison, created in the classic noir mold, may function as pressure valves to release antifeminist gamers' anxieties. But, unfortunately, those gamers already have plenty of places to see their worldviews reflected back at them—both in games themselves and in their surrounding culture. What we need instead are ludic femmes fatales who will concentrate rather than dissipate this character's power, unleashing its wicked pleasures in games the way they already have been in film—and this time, in playable form.

JENNIFER MALKOWSKI is Assistant Professor of Film and Media Studies at Smith College. Her research areas include digital media; documentary; race, gender, and sexuality in media; and death and dying. She is the author of *Dying in Full Detail: Mortality and Digital Documentary.*

Notes

1. Not all women liked film noir; nor did all men. Factoring in the sexual orientation of audience members—as the studios never did in that era—complicates this summary of the femme fatale's appeal. And while the misogyny of the industry was formidable, it was not all-consuming; women did work in Hollywood at that time in important capacities, and the studios did design some films and genres to appeal to women.

2. The madcap, fast-talking leading woman of the 1930s screwball comedies provides another notable exception to this trend. Like later femmes fatales, these independent women were often tamed by the end of the film.

3. Laura Mulvey famously articulates the woman's obligation to remain passive and provide visual pleasure within classical Hollywood cinema in "Visual Pleasure and Narrative Cinema," *Screen* 16, no. 4 (1975): 6–18.

4. During film noir's classic cycle (from the early 1940s through the mid-1950s), US cinema was governed by the Motion Picture Production Code and its system of industry self-censorship. Because the code forbade the depiction of crime in a sympathetic light, screenwriters could not allow femmes fatales (or any other antagonists of film noir) to get away with their crimes and deceptions cleanly. The code specified, for example, that "the treatment of crimes against the law must not . . . inspire potential criminals with a desire for imitation [or] make criminals seem heroic and justified." Leonard J. Leff and Jerold L. Simmons, *The Dame in the Kimono: Hollywood, Censorship, and the Production Code*, rev. ed. (Lexington: University of Kentucky Press, 2001), 298.

5. Jennifer deWinter and Carly Kocurek, "#1reasonwhy Women in the Gaming Industry Matters," *Flow* 17 (2013), http://flowtv.org/2013/02/1-reason-why-women-in-the-gaming-industry-matters/. See also chapter 3.

6. See chapter 3 and Mia Consalvo, "Confronting Toxic Gamer Culture: A Challenge for Feminist Game Studies Scholars," *Ada: A Journal of Gender, New Media, and Technology*, no. 1 (2012), http://adanewmedia.org/2012/11/issue1-consalvo.

7. Most prominently, this is the call often sounded by Anita Sarkeesian's website, Feminist Frequency. Game studies scholarship on playable female characters—which this chapter continues—extends back to early and influential work on *Tomb Raider*'s Lara Croft and includes Helen W. Kennedy, "Lara Croft: Feminist Icon or Cyberbimbo? On the Limits of Textual Analysis," *Game Studies* 2, no. 2 (2002), http://www.gamestudies.org/0202/kennedy/; Maja Mikula, "Gender and Videogames: The Political Valency of Lara Croft," *Continuum* 17, no. 1 (2003): 79–87; Anne-Marie Schleiner, "Does Lara Croft Wear Fake Polygons? Gender and Gender-Role Subversion in Computer Adventure Games," *Leonardo* 34, no. 3 (2001): 221–226.

8. In fact, these remediations of film noir are already second- or third-hand, as the classic noir cycle adapted much of its content from literature and theater.

9. Mary Ann Doane, *Femmes Fatales: Feminism, Film Theory, Psychoanalysis* (New York: Routledge, 1991), 1.

10. Ibid., 103; Yvonne Tasker, "'New Hollywood,' New *Film Noir*, and the *Femme Fatale*," in *Working Girls: Gender and Sexuality in Popular Cinema* (New York: Routledge, 1998), 120.

11. Chris Straayer, "*Femme Fatale* or Lesbian Femme: *Bound* in Sexual *Différance*," in *Women in Film Noir*, ed. E. Ann Kaplan, rev. ed. (London: BFI, 1998), 153.

12. To offer some examples from each category: Femmes fatales who die are by far the most numerous, including *Detour*'s Vera, *Gun Crazy*'s Laurie, *The Killing*'s Sherry, *The Lady from Shanghai*'s Elsa, *Murder, My Sweet*'s Helen, *Out of the Past*'s Kathie, *The Postman Always Rings Twice*'s Cora, and *Scarlet Street*'s Kitty. Those on their way to jail at the end of their films include *The Killers*' Kitty, *The Maltese Falcon*'s Brigid, *Mildred Pierce*'s Veda, *Pitfall*'s Mona, and *Sunset Boulevard*'s Norma. The smaller cohort of "reformed" femmes fatales features *Gilda*'s title character, *The Lady in the Lake*'s Adrienne, and *Pickup on South Street*'s Candy.

13. Janey Place, "Women in *Film Noir*," in Kaplan, *Women in Film Noir*, 48.

14. In *Pursued*, the character in question only assumes the femme fatale role briefly.

15. Place, "Women in *Film Noir*," 63.

16. Doane, *Femmes Fatales*, 2–3; see also Place, "Women in *Film Noir*," 47.

17. Tasker, "'New Hollywood,'" 120.

18. Place, "Women in *Film Noir*," 47.

19. Kate Stables, "The Postmodern Always Rings Twice: Constructing the *Femme Fatale* in 90s Cinema," in Kaplan, *Women in Film Noir*, 171 (emphasis in original). For examples of the femme

fatale evolution I mention, see, especially, *Body Heat*, *Basic Instinct*, *The Last Seduction*, *Bound*, and *Mulholland Drive*.

20. Lara's short shorts do not, thankfully, appear in 2013's *Tomb Raider* reboot, where the heroine wears more practical adventuring clothes. In the highly stylized *Bayonetta* series, the title character's long, magical hair forms her outfit, so when she needs her hair to activate special attacks, she becomes nude until the hair can go back into service as clothes (perhaps wearing some protective clothing or armor would save the hair this need to multitask). Fans of Bayonetta's hypersexuality, though, are numerous and are not only hetero men; see Leigh Alexander, "Bayonetta: Empowering or Exploitative?" *GamePro*, January 6, 2010, http://web.archive.org/web/20110607152912/http://www.gamepro.com/article/features/213466/bayonetta-empowering-or-exploitative/; and Gavin Greene, "Bayonetta: The Great Exception?" *GayGamer*, October 6, 2014, https://web.archive.org/web/20141014060750/http://gaygamer.net/2014/10/bayonetta-the-great-exception.

21. For a helpful overview of video games' basis in actions, see Alexander Galloway, "Gamic Action, Four Moments," in *Gaming: Essays on Algorithmic Culture* (Minneapolis: University of Minnesota Press, 2006), 1–38.

22. James Damico, "*Film Noir:* A Modest Proposal," *Film Reader* 3 (1978): 54.

23. Alex Layne and Samantha Blackmon, "Self-Saving Princess: Feminism and Post-play Narrative Modding," *Ada: A Journal of Gender, New Media, and Technology*, no. 2 (2013), http://adanewmedia.org/2013/06/issue2-layne-blackmon.

24. Players can unlock an alternate ending in which Mona survives her wound by beating the game on its hardest difficulty level. This ending, though, is limited-access and seems to be noncanonical, given her absence from *Max Payne 3*'s story mode.

25. Jack Boozer, "The Lethal *Femme Fatale* in the Noir Tradition," *Journal of Film and Video* 51, no. 3 (1999–2000): 23.

26. In some ways, Madison combines traits of multiple noir characters: the femme fatale, the investigator, and the nurturing woman, usually cast as a foil to the femme fatale. Place, "Women in *Film Noir*," 60–66.

27. In *The Taxidermist*, Madison is more slasher horror's "final girl" than noir's femme fatale, but the prequel remains consistent with *Heavy Rain* by focusing on her eroticized peril and letting the player decide whether she will prove capable enough to survive or will be slaughtered by a homicidal misogynist.

28. There is one unlikely scenario in which the player can avoid the basement scene, by refraining from investigating any of the house's back rooms after finding the necessary clue.

29. Adrienne Shaw, *Gaming at the Edge: Sexuality and Gender at the Margins of Gamer Culture* (Minneapolis: University of Minnesota Press, 2015), 60.

30. Place, "Women in *Film Noir*," 63.

31. Tasker, "'New Hollywood,'" 130.

32. Foster Hirsch, *The Dark Side of the Screen: Film Noir* (Cambridge, MA: Da Capo Press, 1981), 21; Boozer, "Lethal *Femme Fatale*," 22.

33. Place, "Women in *Film Noir*," 47.

chapter two

NO TIME TO DREAM

Killing Time, Casual Games, and Gender

BRAXTON SODERMAN

IN HIS POSTHUMOUSLY PUBLISHED *PARIS SPLEEN* FROM 1869, CHARLES Baudelaire penned a fascinating prose poem imbued with both the rhetoric of play and gender. Within the poem, "The Gallant Marksman," a husband and wife pause at a shooting gallery to kill time during a carriage journey through the woods. I quote the poem in its entirety:

> As the carriage was going through the woods, he had it stop near a shooting gallery, saying that it would be pleasant to take a shot or two to kill Time. And is not killing that monster the most ordinary and legitimate occupation of all of us? Gallantly, then, he held out his hand to his dear, delectable, and execrable wife, to the mysterious woman to whom he owed so many pleasures and so many pains, and perhaps a large part of his genius as well.
>
> Several shots went wide of the mark; one even buried itself in the ceiling; and as the charming creature began to laugh hilariously, twitting her husband on his want of dexterity, he turned toward her brusquely and said: "You see that doll over there to the right, with its nose in the air and its haughty mien? Well, now, my dear angel, I am going to imagine it is you." And he closed his eyes and fired. The doll was neatly decapitated.
>
> Then bowing to his dear, delectable and execrable wife, his inevitable and pitiless Muse, and respectfully kissing her hand, he added: "Ah, dear angel, thank you so much for my dexterity."[1]

The poem's narrative reveals a moment of casual play, a brief interruption of what must be a laborious voyage. While the marksman desires to kill time in the colloquial sense, he also elevates his leisure to a more transcendent occupation, to kill Time with a capital T. The marksman becomes a figure for the artist, the poet, playfully engaging with the written word in order to make his mark and create a "timeless" artwork. Yet such high hopes are clearly not attainable for the marksman's shots continually miss, a failure met with the mocking laughter of the wife who ridicules her husband's lack of prowess, his impotency and embarrassing misfire, indeed, his inability to make his mark. Faced with his inadequacies and the feminine laughter that threatens his masculine dominance, the marksman shifts his aim toward a doll he imagines as his wife, and thus the metaphor shifts its target as well: time is now associated with the wife, with the marksman's "Muse." Ultimately, the marksman only accomplishes his objective to kill Time through a substitution, metaphorically silencing the mocking laughter of his wife (i.e., decapitating the doll) and the voice that threatens to distract him from his goal.

The marksman's task is fulfilled—his leisurely act of killing time consummated—only through the destruction of a traditional, childhood object of feminine play: the doll. His aggressive, violent shooting disfigures a figure for another kind of play represented by the passive doll, a foreign, feminine object in his masculine gallery of active entertainment. Moreover, the husband literally turns a blind eye to this doll as he closes his eyes to fire, refusing to see it, refusing to consider a different form of play, only imagining it as placeholder for his wife's threatening superiority ("with its nose in the air and its haughty mien"). If the doll is a marked object of gendered play, then its decapitation could be read as a silencing of women's ludic culture. The silencing is accomplished by a masculine aggression that is blind to the significance of this other culture, perceived only as an inarticulate threat to the privileged sphere of masculine play.

What I want to suggest is that Baudelaire's prose poem allegorizes a gendered dynamic where a privileged sphere of masculine art and leisure is established only by aggressively defending and policing its bounds. When the "other" of such a sphere becomes too visible or vocal—for example, through playful genres that might be directed toward the concerns, pleasures, and desires of others, here figured as the doll/wife—then the hard-core marksman of cultural policing closes his eyes to the present and blindly lashes out in order to reestablish the significance of his own play. Moreover, Baudelaire's poem depicts a gendered scenario of leisure and play where the masculine actor consumes his leisure time while the wife waits and watches. It is his time for active leisure, not hers. If the doll in Baudelaire's poem is a figure for gendered play and Time itself, and the fulfillment of the marksman's leisure time occurs through the literal fragmentation of the doll, then metaphorically the potential time for feminine play is killed and fragmented as well. Simply put, man's leisure time must not be interrupted, and his uninterrupted, privileged time for leisure is achieved through the fragmentation of women's leisure time.

Baudelaire's "The Gallant Marksman" provides a poignant allegory for contemporary issues concerning the gendered divide between hard-core and casual gaming. I begin with the poem to introduce this chapter's two intertwined aims. First, I assert that the current divide between hard-core and casual gaming repeats a standard dynamic in modernism whereby a privileged sphere of masculine culture (e.g., hard-core games) establishes its significance and continuation through the aggressive devaluation and feminization of other forms of popular culture (e.g., casual games). Confronted with the "threatening" rise of casual gaming, the hard-core gaming community blindly lashes out against this perceived peril. Its devaluation and feminization of casual games is simply a rhetorical ruse, attempting to protect hard-core gaming and elevate it into a transcendent sphere of play. Hard-core games are not inherently more significant, aesthetically valuable, or formally interesting than casual games, but the discourse that devalues casual games labors to sustain this illusion.

Second, I argue that casual games are formally structured to inhabit contemporary experiences of fragmented leisure, a fragmentation that largely affects the everyday lives of many women. Through a close reading of one of the urtexts of casual games, *Diner Dash* (2003, Gamelab), the desire for more uninterrupted leisure time appears simultaneously with a game that habituates women to constant interruption. If one is to break the cycle where modernism repeats abusive, gendered divides between supposedly high, elite, masculine culture and low, popular, feminine culture, then structural problems concerning the unequal *quality* of leisure time will need to be overcome as well.

Hard-Core versus Casual: The Feminization of Mass Gaming

The difference between hard-core and casual games (and players) has become a divisive topic producing passionate arguments in gamer forums concerning the meaning (or meaninglessness) of these designations. Hard-core games are stereotypically defined as difficult games with violent themes that require considerable dedication and time to complete, and which appeal to the traditional demographic of gamers cultivated by the game industry in the 1990s—that is, young white males with a lot of time on their hands. Casual games are stereotypically defined as easier pastimes with less negative themes, that take less dedication and time to play, and which appeal to a wider demographic of potential players such as non-identifying gamers, women, young children, older players, or former players who now do not have adequate time or money to commit to more expensive and temporally demanding hard-core games (e.g., because they have started families).

In 2007, the Casual Games Association (CGA) produced an influential market report explaining that "casual games are video games developed for the mass consumer."[2] The report also helped dislodge a stereotype that casual games are predominantly played by women, showing a near even split where 51 percent of casual players identified as women and 49 percent as men (a Nielsen report from 2009 suggested that 58 percent of casual gamers identified as female). Yet CGA's report also found that women typically pay for these games at a much higher rate than men, 74 percent versus 26 percent.[3] Thus, while the numbers show a relatively balanced distribution of casual play in terms of gender, the industry consistently describes casual gamers in terms of stereotypical gendered discourse, often feminizing casual play.[4] For example, an article explains that in the UK 52 percent of gamers identified as women in 2014 but then goes on to claim, "It goes without saying that mobile and casual gaming has contributed to the steady rise in female gaming," even though it quickly adds that "56% of female gamers have played on a console and 68% have played online."[5]

The persistence and ubiquity of gendered discourse surrounding casual and hard-core games cannot be ignored, as it is often severe and extends beyond industry discourse into the heart of video game culture. For example, video game critic Rowan Kaiser blatantly exposes the gendered subtext of the casual versus hard-core divide in an attempt to progress beyond their connotations and simply call gamers "gamers":

> Let's cut through the crap, shall we? . . . For gamers, terms like "hardcore" and "casual" are a code with clear meanings. So let's be real, and call a spade a spade: "Hardcore" means dick. Or rod. Or johnson. Or, for the critical analysis fans out there, the phallus. "Hardcore" equals masculine. "Casual" equals feminine. It's just that simple, and all the marketing-speak about "core" gamers won't change that.[6]

While Kaiser suggests that the connotations of these terms are hidden, within the popular press (and in blog posts and comments from the public) the casual game market is often explicitly feminized and simultaneously denigrated. While some manifestations might contain seemingly innocuous mentions of casual games as "chick friendly," as the choice of "bored housewives," or as titles for "grannies, girlfriends and non-gamers," others take the form of vitriolic sexist rants.[7] Further, the rhetoric can become embedded in actual games themselves. For example, a downloadable character in *Borderlands 2* (2012, Gearbox Software) called Gaige contains a "Best Friends Forever" skill tree that lead designer John Hemingway supposedly referred to as "girlfriend mode," designed for people who "suck at first-person shooters" but wish to play casually and support another player (presumably, the boyfriend).[8] The tree contains a skill called "Close Enough" where bullets have a chance to ricochet off walls and deal half damage to nearby enemies: "Can't aim? That's not a problem," Hemingway quipped.[9] While Gearbox attempted to downplay the sexist gaff and explained that "Best Friends Forever" was intended for novices and "newbies" no matter their gender, briefly scanning the skill tree reveals content that consistently evokes (usually negative) gender stereotypes for women: for example, "Fancy Mathematics," "Cooking Up Trouble," "Potent as a Pony," or even "The Better Half."

In other articles and blog posts, the gendered rhetoric appears as images of women playing "casual consoles" such as the Wii or the handheld Nintendo DS. One such image retrieved from an online article, "Are 'Casuals' Killing Gaming?" depicts a middle-aged "Mom" grasping a Wii controller in the background while a young white male occupies the foreground of the image, holding a PS3 controller up toward the camera, his face contorted in an intense scream. Such an image displays an appropriation of the cultural (gamic) phallus by the Wii-wielding woman—a threatening image of feminization that must be visually contained through the hyperbolic excess of "hard-core" masculinity displayed predominantly in the center of the image.[10]

The rise of casual games and their concurrent gendering as feminine has ignited a palpable anxiety in (masculine) hard-core culture where these gamers—once the darlings of the industry—worry that the mass consumer and the casual gamer will kill or overrun the hard-core.[11] The hard-core gamer frets that games will be dumbed down and increasingly simplified, a process that supposedly will not ignore titles traditionally viewed as hard-core, as these too will absorb principles of casual gaming in order to increase their audience and distribution. This anxiety marks the reappearance of a supposedly outdated rhetoric where the autonomous sphere of (white, masculine) high culture expresses worry that the masses (in this case, figured as the others of this privileged male position—women, children, the elderly, gaymers, etc.) will eventually overwhelm and destroy it. As Lynne Joyrich has argued—in reference to the medium of television—"the use of feminine imagery to describe our 'lowest' cultural form (in opposition to whatever is held up as more respectable and 'masculine'—print or film) has not faded away with the passing of modernism."[12] Now the "respectable and masculine" form is solidifying around the hard-core game versus the "lowest cultural form" of the feminized casual game. "The introduction of a feminized, popular category of video game to gaming culture," writes John Vanderhoef, "might be seen as undermining the fragile masculinity that has had to continuously defend its cultural position for several decades."[13] As women gamers and women's game genres become more visible (often in relation to casual games) masculine gaming culture responds with discourses of threat, anxiety, and containment—the latter accomplished by the continued degradation of casual games as simple, insignificant, and reductive of hard-core aesthetics.

How does one combat this rhetorical degradation that sustains a gaming culture feminists are increasingly referring to as a "toxic" environment for women, an environment evidenced by the sexist and misogynistic Gamergate culture war?[14] Within game studies, theorists investigating gender issues are critiquing sexism in mass culture and gaming, advocating for the increased presence of women in the game industry, combating forces of exclusion within that industry, and elevating the visibility of women developers, past and present. Others argue for speaking out in the face of harassment, documenting online harassment (for present and future analysis), exposing marketing strategies and developer comments that perpetuate sexism in the culture, analyzing networks that diffuse sexist and racist comments, continuing to critique hypersexualized representation of female avatars, resisting exploitation and harassment at game cons, and so on.[15] In terms of casual games, since the dynamic of devaluation often spills over into overt sexism, scholars must employ an additional strategy: critically engaging with the recovery of the significance and depth of casual games in order to combat their gendered dismissal.[16]

While these interventions are all laudable pursuits, the preceding analysis also reveals a vertiginous repetition where culture perpetually returns to these abusive gendered divides—as evidenced in Baudelaire's prose poem, Joyrich's analysis of the feminization of television, feminist analyses of other devalued women's media forms such as romance novels and soap operas, and now the dismissal of casual games, couched in aggressively gendered rhetoric. Feminist scholars must also interrogate and critique these larger historical repetitions, exposing the structural elements that generate these recurring problems in the hopes of actively resisting them. Baudelaire's prose poem, for example, clearly indicates that there is blindness toward women's genres of leisure and also an active, aggressive dismantling of their importance, particularly when they threaten masculine forms of leisure. Yet the poem also revolves around time, killing time, and the threat of interrupting the time for man's leisure. One of the structural problems that game theorists must address in relation to the casual versus hard-core rhetoric concerns the gendered category of leisure time itself—for it is truly women's leisure time that is fragmented and "killed" in contemporary society while the forms of entertainment that emerge within this fragmented temporality (such as some genres of casual games) are devalued and even ridiculed. In the following section I turn to a close analysis of *Diner Dash*—an influential casual game with a complex relationship to time, women's leisure, and casual play itself.[17]

Casual Games and the Flo of Everyday Life

Mizuko Ito and Matteo Bittanti recently highlighted "killing time" as a "genre of practice" in video gaming, suggesting that "games are often used while waiting for relevant things to happen, as fillers between more structured events."[18] While Ito and Bittanti stress that any type of game can serve this function, in the popular imagination killing time in gaming tends to be associated with casual gaming and women gamers who are allegedly, writes game journalist Mikel Reparaz, "more interested in killing time than in killing monsters."[19] Reparaz cites *Diner Dash* and *Cake Mania* (2006, Sandlot) as examples of killing time, which is intriguing because both fall into the casual genre of time management games that are largely marketed to women players. It is important to keep in mind that games in the *Diner Dash* franchise are not entirely played by women, though its publisher claims that its "core audience is older women."[20] In fact, porting the franchise to Facebook increased its demographic reach: "We've got about 20 percent male [players], when historically we've been 90 percent female."[21] Yet, given that the core remains heavily female, the following analysis is geared toward the female audience largely courted, and imagined, by the game's publisher.

In *Diner Dash*—a game that has spawned myriad sequels and also clones such as *Delicious* (2006, Zylom), *Fashion Boutique* (2008, Total Eclipse), *Diaper Dash* (2009, Zemnott), *School House Shuffle* (2008, Sarbakan), and so on—the player assumes the role of Flo, a woman who has left the frantic business world in order to pursue an entrepreneurial career managing various restaurants. Yet *Diner Dash* is not a restaurant simulation that explores the intricacies of managing an actual diner; its gameplay instead emphasizes the "dash" as Flo becomes the sole waitress serving an onslaught of customers. The player has two game options. In the story mode of the game, "Flo's Career," there are five restaurants that Flo must manage, each with ten levels or discrete "shifts." As the player progresses through these shifts, Flo earns money with which she automatically upgrades, restores, and repairs the restaurant. The second mode, "Endless Shift," offers a single, interminable shift where Flo must please as many customers as possible and accrue the highest score. In either mode, the gameplay produces a frenzied, arcade dynamic that partially simulates the hectic working life of a multitasking waitress at the height of a rush.

When a shift begins, the player drags waiting clusters of customers onto tables in order to seat them—attempting to match the color of a customer with a similarly colored seat to score bonus points (figure 2.1). Once customers have been seated, the player directs Flo to complete a series of tasks by clicking on various screen locations, providing an itinerary that Flo will follow: taking customers' orders, delivering entrées, providing the check, and clearing the table. Flo can only carry a limited number of objects at a time (orders, dirty dishes, etc.), requiring her to make extra trips (and the player to make extra clicks) while seating and serving customers. Each group of customers is accompanied by a "timer" represented as a row of small hearts beside them. If the player fails to serve the

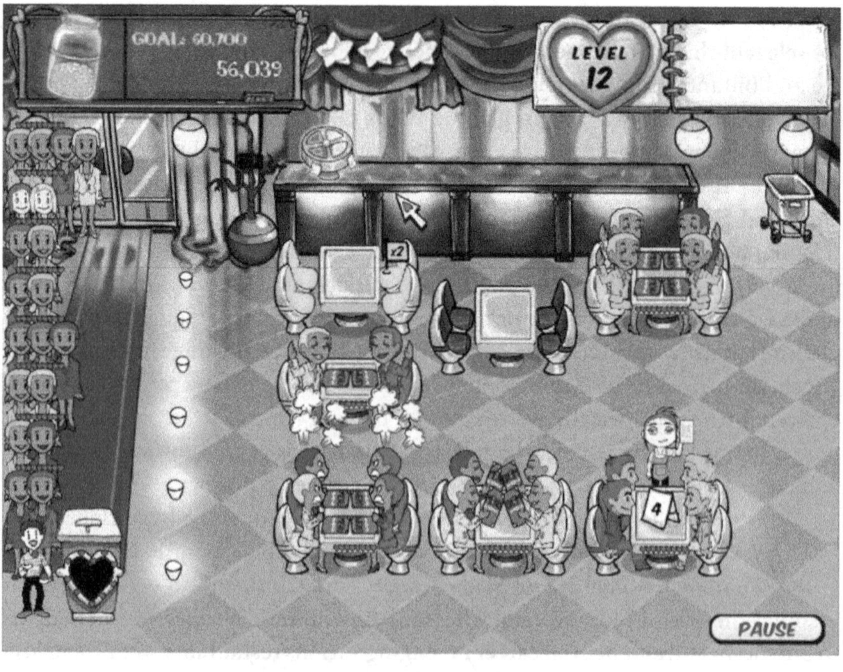

Figure 2.1. Flo waits tables (*Diner Dash* game still)

customers in a timely manner, their hearts deplete and the angry customers disappear, penalizing the player's score. If the player does not reach a certain score, he or she must repeat the shift. Thus, the gameplay mechanics of *Diner Dash* concern temporal pressure, multitasking, and the extraction of order from chaos, again and again, shift after shift.

If casual games are often used in everyday life situations of waiting, the kind of "waiting" performed within the game of *Diner Dash* (and *wait*ressing in general) is hardly one of killing time, but the sheer, intensive experience of managing many relevant things that are all happening simultaneously. As Aubrey Anable writes, "Games [like *Diner Dash*] offer a rhythm that addresses a desire for flow in a digital landscape that is defined more by distraction and interruption."[22] Indeed, the gameplay structure of time management games—multitasking, distraction, and interruption—brings to mind a key design element of casual games. As game theorist Jesper Juul puts it, casual games allow for "flexibility" in how they are played: one can play for a short period of time or sit down for a few hours of relatively uninterrupted play.[23] If a game is interrupted—say by one's boss appearing or a child waking from a nap—the design does not punish the player harshly (e.g., forcing her to surrender significant progress that must be repeated). Hard-core games, though, are inflexible, meaning that they often require longer, uninterrupted spans of time where significant progress might be lost if the gamer interrupts a play session or it would seriously impact other players' progress in social gaming situations (e.g., a raid in *World of Warcraft* [2004, Blizzard]).

Diner Dash is an urtext of casual games because its gameplay mechanics and design fundamentally model and self-reflexively interrogate this idea of interruptibility. Within the game Flo exists in a near constant state of interruption, and the player must manage this distracted state in order to progress. While some may say that women players are killing time with casual games such as *Diner Dash*, in fact, the truth is that many women hardly have time to kill at all, often working a first shift (outside the home), then a second shift (when housework and child care call), and then a third shift (where the brief segments of time that women can truly call their own are killed by "working-through" the anxieties caused by the negotiation of the first and second shifts).[24] As author and entrepreneurial coach Michele Bolton writes:

> If it's de rigueur in your set to be a crazed working woman, up at five to exercise, checking voice mail messages at six, dropping off kids at eight, and careening into your first staff meeting a half-hour later, there's a certain adrenaline charge that accompanies the start of each day. Your life is endless movement, running from one thing to the next, multitasking your head off.... [W]omen today take great pride in their ability to manage multiple roles.[25]

This quotation warns that simply denouncing the multitasking intensity of women's daily lives masks the potential pleasure and/or pride that managing produces.

Indeed, there is immense pleasure in *Diner Dash* when the chaos is returned to order and one succeeds in managing the demands of all the customers. Nevertheless, moving beyond this pleasure, one must also understand how *Diner Dash* fits into the temporal structure of contemporary leisure.

While the leisure gap between genders persists, with recent studies showing that men enjoy five more hours of leisure a week than women, the quality of this leisure also differs.[26] In a recent quantitative study, Michael Bittman and Judy Wajcman found that women's quality of leisure time is significantly different from men's, tending to be more "fragmentary," "harried," and "interrupted."[27] Drawing on a number of feminist studies of time, Valerie Bryson writes that women "often have to force a number of activities into the same period," and that their "leisure time cannot be planned in advance, but can only be snatched in unpredictable fragments (15 minutes here if the baby doesn't wake; half an hour there if the children don't get bored in the garden)."[28] Thus, the frenzied, multitasking gameplay in *Diner Dash* might be quite familiar to many women, and the game's structure—as a series of relatively short, discrete shifts in story mode—would also allow for short bursts of play that could fit into the fragments of free time "snatched" from the day.[29] As Shira Chess points out in her reading of *Diner Dash* and time management games, "in-game work stresses re-enact stresses that many women experience in the real world."[30]

One way to understand how casual games such as *Diner Dash* align with the fragmented temporal realities of many women's everyday lives is through the distinction that the positive psychologist Mihaly Csikszentmihalyi draws between experiential states of flow and microflow. Flow activities—such as games and play—are designed to produce pleasurable experiences where one is completely absorbed in a task. Csikszentmihalyi is primarily interested in what he calls "deep flow," or an experience where the complex challenges of a task align with an individual's skills, and thus the actor enters a concentrated zone of action for extended periods of time. Taking a cue from the truncation of Flo's name, casual games also embody what Csikszentmihalyi calls microflow activities—quasi truncations of flow experiences. These activities produce flow states "at a lower level of complexity," "fill the gaps in daily routine," and "make reality manageable."[31] Examples include fidgeting, chewing gum, daydreaming, doodling, smoking, and even watching television.[32] The differences between deep flow—which requires longer, uninterrupted spans of time—and the reduced complexity of microflow could be used to distinguish hard-core and casual games. Yet, more importantly, what do microflow activities tell us about the function of casual games, particularly in relation to women's experience?

Microflow activities—by structuring daily life and "making reality manageable"—are potential ways to cope with what has become known as the "third shift," a term describing the interstitial moments in women's everyday life where negotiations between work and home are mulled over. Bolton writes, "A first shift at work and a 'second shift' at home can be physically tiring, but the third shift is psychologically relentless; it ranges over professional anxiety about workplace assignments and self-perceived derelictions on the home front. In essence, every day is lived at least twice, like a videotaped instant replay that won't shut off."[33] The third shift is the product of anxiety experienced throughout the day in those "private, quiet times" snatched from the demands of the first and second shifts. Casual games such as *Diner Dash* could be understood as external activities that substitute the pleasurable anxiety of multitasking play for the psychological anxiety generated by the third shift. Yet Bolton argues that while the third shift is potentially debilitating, it is also a positive opportunity for meaningful self-reflection and awareness.[34] A woman's free time (even in snatched moments) might be a location for reflecting on her social condition and what causes the fragmentation of women's leisure in general—unequal domestic responsibilities for men and women socially inscribed in a patriarchal society, extended work hours in late capitalism fueled by the blurring boundaries of work and leisure, the office and home, and so on—and even for reflecting on how to transform this social condition. Thus, casual games such as *Diner Dash* become contradictory: they positively replace the anxiety that can occur in the third shift with the pleasurable anxiety of play but simultaneously consume the time needed to think through how to transform the social conditions that create the anxieties of the third shift in the first place.

The situation where a particular media form fits snuggly with the social situation of women is hardly new. Tania Modleski once argued that soap opera narratives also reflected the social reality of women's lives: "Thus the narrative, by placing ever more complex obstacles between desire and its fulfillment, makes anticipation of an end an end in itself. Soap operas invest exquisite pleasure in the central condition of a woman's life: waiting—whether for her phone to ring, for the baby to take its nap, or for the family to be reunited shortly after the day's final soap opera has left its family still struggling against dissolution."[35] The soap opera creates pleasure through the expectation of a final, familial resolution that never actually comes, not even in real life because the ultimate unity of the (heterosexual) family is an ideological illusion sustained by the social norms of dominant society. In *Diner Dash* the expectation of fulfillment does not stem from family unity—Flo is a single entrepreneur whose "family" is only presented allegorically in terms of the customers—but from the desire to finish one's work in an efficient manner, perhaps in order to open the possibility for a leisurely time without interruption. In the multitasking lives of many women today—particularly those who also work a first shift outside the home—the "exquisite pleasure" of waiting has more in common with the intense activity of waiting tables and the successful management of time (not killing time). But, like the soap opera that constantly moves from the hope of resolution to dissolution, after *Diner Dash*'s initial narrative scene Flo (and the player) has to "wait" through forty shifts of gameplay before the next narrative cutscene, constantly returning order to chaos in hopes of closure. While the gameplay mechanics are central to *Diner Dash*, analysis of its narrative and visual representations remains essential, particularly for interpreting what hope or wish the player is "waiting" for (in both senses of the verb).

Representation as the Management of Gameplay

All too often in game studies the narrative and visual elements of video games are devalued while gameplay mechanics are upheld as the defining characteristic of the medium. This was one outcome of the famed narratology versus ludology debates, where representation might be termed the casual element ("casual" here defined as the contingent) while the mechanics became the hard-core essence of the game form. This devaluation of the significance of representation is also accompanied by gendered rhetoric, from the use of terms such as "cosmetics" and "eye-candy" to refer to a game's graphical elements to more subtle erasures of the importance of gender such as Espen Aarseth's claim that the visual aspects of Lara Croft are "irrelevant" to the player. He writes, "When I play, I don't even see her body, but see through it and past it."[36] While Aarseth posits that literary and film theorists have "analyzed [Lara Croft] to death," arguably Aarseth annihilated her iconic status as an important, contemporary "representative" of gender issues in video games.[37] Ignoring the visual and narrative representations in games simply truncates a close analysis of a particular gamic text. While the narrative and visual elements of *Diner Dash* are indeed minimal, they function as a significant representational frame that focuses a close interpretation of the game. Indeed, looking past Flo and ignoring how she is represented would be a serious error of exegesis. Viewed from a representational perspective, *Diner Dash* quickly becomes a complex text bubbling with contradictions, subtle commentary, and a dose of self-reflexivity often cleverly integrated into the gameplay itself.

The comic-style introduction to *Diner Dash*'s story mode provides a brief backstory for the protagonist Flo—a woman who literally flees a stressful, dreary office job (figure 2.2) and stumbles on the idea to open her own restaurant. Flo's decision to leave the corporate environment is subtly connected to gender as well. For example, as Flo flees from her coworkers into the city's streets she exclaims, "I gotta lose these guys!!" and "Man! There's GOT to be something better than THIS!!" One is tempted to read this last expression not only in its colloquial sense, but where the "THIS" obliquely refers to the designation "Man!" as if offering the possibility of something better than "man" himself or at least a more rewarding experience than life within a corporate environment traditionally inscribed as man's home away from home. Yet, while the liberating move to self-employment and entrepreneurship is framed as a literal escape from aggressive, "masculine" demands, one might interpret the response of opening a restaurant as a regressive, safe return to an occupation traditionally associated with women's labor, particularly when gameplay in *Diner Dash* concerns the semirepetitive work of a waitress, not the detailed management of a restaurant. In the final segment of the introductory narrative, Flo has escaped down an alley and turns to see a boarded-up diner with a sale sign. She declares, "Of course!! My own restaurant!!" Yet her revelation

Figure 2.2. The first narrative frame shows Flo fleeing the corporate world (*Diner Dash* game still)

to open her own restaurant is also subtly coded as a return to domesticity, to the familiar, where the representation of the dilapidated restaurant Flo encounters looks more like a small home surrounded by nature (a grassy lawn, trees, etc.) rather than a diner with surrounding buildings, streets, and a parking lot.

Moreover, an intriguing symmetry exists between the representation of the occupation that Flo abandons and the eventual form of gameplay that *Diner Dash* embodies. Namely, in the opening narrative sequence Flo is inundated with disembodied hands that present her with tasks or "orders" in the form of reports that she must examine. Yet taking orders and answering the frantic demands of multiple customers (also represented in the gameplay by extended hands calling the player's attention) is precisely how *Diner Dash* represents Flo's newly chosen occupation. This representational symmetry suggests that while Flo flounders under the pressures of the corporate workplace, such pressures are potentially manageable within the historically feminine environment of restaurant service (or even the home). Even the customer types—the young girls, the college age boys, the adult male hot shots, the seniors, and the businesswomen—begin to operate as familial surrogates (children, boyfriend/husband, grandparent, friend) who, day in and day out, must be tended to emotionally, especially when they gather together in a single space for mealtime.

During actual gameplay, the representations also harbor significance. For example, Flo directly addresses the player when she waits for input, looking languidly out from the screen with half-closed eyes, slightly tussled hair, and her mouth awry in a coy, ironic grin. Her expression remains strangely ambiguous. Is she happy or sad or somewhere in between? Is she exhausted, bored, indifferent? In the rare moments when the player has nothing to do and waits for customers' demands, Flo will automatically perform miniature, discrete animation sequences: brushing something off her sleeve, putting her hands on her hips and swaying, or finally, yawning massively. These animations are akin to Flo's moments of microflow, automatic gestures structuring her workday within the interstices of her activity. In these moments of waiting, Flo directly addresses the player, gazing out into the play situation and doubling it; that is, if the gamer plays *Diner Dash* in states of boredom or fatigue after a day at work, then Flo reflects these characteristics. The representations of Flo killing time as she waits parallel the real-life activity of playing *Diner Dash* as the player supposedly kills time while casually gaming. Interestingly, as one's skill at *Diner Dash* increases, these representations disappear, and the player—always looking ahead of Flo toward her next destination—never focuses on the images of Flo's boredom or fatigue that solicit reflective interpretation, even self-reflection: is this harried running around (in the game and in life) worth it?

While Flo's in-game looks remain ambiguous, the long-awaited narrative sequences near the end offer material for a clearer interpretation of the unfulfilled wish that percolates the game. After the fortieth shift, the game rewards the player with a surprise comic-style cutscene. Flo is astonished by the manifestation of a goddess with six arms, sitting on a cloud and holding a knife, spoon, fork, and menu. The goddess tells Flo that one test remains "to fulfill your destiny" and "*finally* be my equal." She then transforms Flo into an image of herself, where Flo is given another pair of arms and also rests on a cloud. Transformed in such a way, Flo can now carry four items instead of two. When the game resumes, Flo is in a restaurant serving Indian cuisine, poised with her eyes closed, floating on a cloud with her legs crossed and seemingly in a state of intense calm or nirvana (figure 2.3). Yet, in terms of the gameplay, Flo's transformation shifts play only slightly. Having more hands would seem to allow one to finish work more quickly than before, but it means more things to balance simultaneously, an intensification of multitasking.[38]

The manifestation of the goddess, Flo's transformation into an otherworldly being, the fantasy restaurant where the chairs become hands and the tabletops depict peaceful faces, Flo's closed eyes—all these elements suggest a dream scene. After playing ten intensive shifts in this restaurant, the player is offered a final cutscene suggesting that the goddess is actually Flo herself. On congratulating Flo, the goddess's watch alarm goes off, and she winks at Flo (and the player) saying, "Oh, I have to get going! Gotta get back to MY restaurant." If Flo and the goddess are one and the same, then the alarm itself is a wake-up call where work calls (again),

Figure 2.3. A representation of Flo after her transformation by the goddess (*Diner Dash* game still)

awakening Flo from her dream and the player from his or her casual slumber, indicating that it is time for the dream (game) to end and for the player to get back to work. If Flo is indeed dreaming in these final ten stages of play, what is the dream-wish involved? Within the actual game, what the doubling of Flo's arms represents in terms of a wish is ambiguous. On the one hand, Flo wants to become an equal of the goddess, a superhuman entity who can accomplish twice the work and manage a hectic restaurant. Recalling the point from Bolton, women take "great pride" in successfully managing multiple roles and tasks. Moreover, in the final stages Flo is hyperbolically represented in a state of complete, relaxed fulfillment. The animations of microflow and the representations of Flo as tired and bored have disappeared. She has been completed, no longer simply "Flo" but experiencing "flow" as Csikszentmihalyi would term it, a state of intense enjoyment.

On the other hand, gaining more appendages cannot be separated from the popular wish to have the means to more efficiently complete one's work in order to experience a less fragmented and interrupted leisure time. In terms of the actual situation of the gamer playing *Diner Dash,* this wish might indeed be fulfilled. Within the game, the duration of each shift increases as the player progresses, thus moving from shorter segments to longer spans of play that cannot be easily interrupted. Before the final shift players are warned, "this is going to be the *longest shift* that we have ever seen." Indeed, the final shift and those that immediately precede it require far more time commitment than those in the previous parts of the game. The game subtly progresses from being easily interruptible to less interruptible, from flexible to inflexible (as Juul might term it), from casual to hard-core. The extension of uninterrupted gameplay—in the real life of the player—suggests that a wish for more leisure time has been, in a sense, granted.

Nevertheless, the irony is that the desire for more time—symbolized through the addition of appendages with which to complete the tasks at hand—is met only with intensified multitasking, more demanding customers and longer shifts, more work to be done. The extra means for the fulfillment of the wish only pushes its true fulfillment further away. Even if the gamer is experiencing a longer duration of uninterrupted play at the end, this suggests that the process of habituation to interruption and distraction (within the game) has succeeded. Flo's meditative state suggests that she can now do this with her eyes closed, literally. She is at peace with her harried multitasking, although it also suggests that she is closing her eyes to the doubling of labor that now demands her attention.

In the final narrative segment, time itself interrupts Flo from attaining the "Destiny" that was promised to her. The alarm on the goddess's watch sounds, and the word "Destiny" itself is truncated simply to "Dest-." Flo's fate, then, is to awake from her dream (of uninterrupted time) into more of the same (fragmented time), destined to wrest order from chaos, again and again, toward the horizon of an endless shift. Yet this is how her destiny (and the player's) will be fulfilled, forging bravely into the many *Diner Dash* sequels that follow, forever managing the multiple interruptions and demands of time, forever "waiting."

Time to Dream

Redeeming casual games and highlighting their complexity—as the previous reading of *Diner Dash* has attempted—is essential but will not repair the "toxic" environment for women gamers that the vitriolic gendering and devaluation of casual games has helped create and maintain. As previously mentioned, myriad interventions are needed to transform this environment. Yet, given that the devaluation of casual games is tied to larger historical processes that repeatedly feminize mass, popular culture, this larger historical trajectory must be recognized, analyzed, critiqued, and dismantled—not only to create a more equitable gaming community in the present but also to make possible a future where divisions in mediated culture are not animated by aggressive and dismissive gendered rhetoric.

Why does this monster continually respawn even though it has been exposed in various guises and ostensibly slain before? In the opening poem from Baudelaire, the mocking laughter of the wife threatened to interrupt the marksman's leisure, catalyzing his aggressive turn to metaphorically silence both the wife and her leisure through the decapitation of the doll. Indeed, the wife's fun was ultimately interrupted in order to fulfill the "timelessness" of the marksman's leisure. Current research shows that women's free time is being interrupted, fragmented, and snatched in states of multitasking. What if the inequality of the quality of leisure was overcome? What if uninterrupted leisure time was shared among all? This is the threat, based on gendered inequality, that animates the hard-core gaming community's anxiety and that causes it to lash out aggressively against the perceived feminization of casual games. If casual games are fundamentally characterized by flexibility—interruptible and allowing for varying degrees of time commitment—then casual games and gaming are constant reminders of a fragmented leisure time that threatens the accumulation of time that hard-core gamers experience. A vocal faction of male hard-core gamers mock casual games as simple means for killing time because they fear a more equal future in which their leisure time will wane and even be interrupted and killed.

To confront the inequalities that leave Flo's dream unfulfilled, one must travel far beyond the realm of gamer culture itself, toward difficult structural problems animated by capitalism and patriarchy. Arlie Hochschild's call for a "time movement" near the end of her book *The Time Bind: When Work Becomes Home and Home Becomes Work* begins to indicate the kind of thinking needed to address these problems.[39] As Hochschild argues, just as labor movements in the nineteenth and twentieth centuries fought to reduce hours of work, in the contemporary world where the boundaries between work and home break down, issues of reducing work-time press against society once again. Such a time movement would certainly need to include issues of gender inequality in the quality of leisure.

The magnitude of the task is immense, but not insurmountable. In E. P. Thompson's influential 1967 article, "Time, Work-Discipline, and Industrial Capitalism," he briefly turns to consider the relationship of time to the labor of women, quoting from Mary Collier's poem "The Woman's Labour" from 1739:

We must make haste, for when we Home are come,
Alas ! we find our Work but just begun;
So many Things for our Attendance call,
Had we ten Hands, we could employ them all.
Our Children put to Bed, with greatest Care
We all Things for your coming Home prepare:
You sup, and go to Bed without delay,
And rest yourselves till the ensuing Day;
While we, alas ! but little Sleep can have,
Because our froward Children cry and rave;
. . .
In ev'ry Work to take our proper Share;
And from the Time that Harvest doth begin,
Until the Corn be cut and carry'd in,
Our Toil and Labour's daily so extreme,
That we have hardly ever *Time to dream*.[40]

Time to dream for all will not come through the addition of appendages, no matter how many, but only in a world where free time is both quantitatively and qualitatively equal for all—the world whose temporal equality feels like such a threat to certain hard-core gamers. Such a world is worth the wait.

BRAXTON SODERMAN is Assistant Professor in the Department of Film and Media Studies at the University of California, Irvine. He researches digital media, video games, new media aesthetics, the history of technology, and critical theory, and has published in the *Journal of Visual Culture, Space and Culture, differences: A Journal of Feminist Cultural Studies, Dichtung Digital: A Journal of Art and Culture in Digital Media,* and elsewhere.

Notes

1. Charles Baudelaire, "The Gallant Marksman," in *The Paris Spleen* (New York: New Directions, 1970), 90.
2. Casual Games Association, "Casual Games Market Report 2007: Business and Art of Games for Everyone," 2007, p. 3, https://www.yumpu.com/en/document/view/24638051/download-casual-games-market-report-2007.
3. Ibid., 5.
4. Shira Chess, "Youthful White Male Industry Seeks 'Fun'-Loving Middle-Aged Women for Video Games—No Strings Attached," in *The Routledge Companion to Media and Gender*, ed. Cynthia Carter, Linda Steiner, and Lisa McLaughlin (New York: Routledge, 2014), 171–172. See also John Vanderhoef, "Casual Threats: The Feminization of Casual Video Games," *Ada: A Journal of Gender, New Media, and Technology*, no. 2 (2013), http://adanewmedia.org/2013/06/issue2-vanderhoef; and Wade Tinney, "Understanding the Casual Gamer," *IGDA Online Games Quarterly* 1, no. 2 (2005), http://web.archive.org/web/20130315153356/http://www.igda.org/online/quarterly/1_2/casual.php.
5. Krista Lofgren, "2015 Video Game Statistic and Trends: Who's Playing What and Why?" *Big Fish*, March 3, 2015, http://www.bigfishgames.com/blog/2015-global-video-game-stats-whos-playing-what-and-why/.
6. Rowan Kaiser, "Hardcore Maleness," *The Escapist*, June 1, 2010, http://www.escapistmagazine.com/articles/view/video-games/issues/issue_256/7622-Hardcore-Maleness.
7. Chris Jager, "Has Nintendo Killed Hardcore Gaming?" *PC World*, April 23, 2009, http://www.pcworld.idg.com.au/article/300491/has_nintendo_killed_hardcore_gaming_/; "Net Games Lure 'Bored Housewives,'" *BBC News*, June 10, 2004, http://news.bbc.co.uk/2/hi/technology/3791983.stm; Clive Thompson, "Getting Lucky: Hard-Core Gamers Penetrate *Peggle*'s Physics," *Wired*, March 9, 2009, http://archive.wired.com/gaming/gamingreviews/commentary/games/2009/03/gamesfrontiers_0309. While Thompson's article does not explicitly address gender, his discussion of casual and hard-core gamers implicitly equates hard-core attitudes with an active, potent sexuality at the expense of casual gamers. See also Ben Croshaw, "Zero Punctuation: Peggle," *The Escapist*, September 26, 2007, http://www.escapistmagazine.com/videos/view/zero-punctuation/7-Peggle.
8. Wesley Yin-Poole, "Borderlands 2: Gearbox Reveals the Mechromancer's 'Girlfriend Mode,'" *Eurogamer.net*, August 13, 2012, http://www.eurogamer.net/articles/2012-08-13-borderlands-2-gearbox-reveals-the-mechromancers-girlfriend-mode.

9. Ibid.

10. Clint McCredie, "Are 'Casuals' Killing Gaming?" *GamePlayer*, April 17, 2008. See also Joe Paulding, "Casual vs Hardcore Games," *G4*, February 23, 2008, http://www.g4tv.com/ttackoftheshow/blog/post/683070/casual-vs-hardcore-games/?page=3; and Lynne Joyrich, *Re-viewing Reception: Television, Gender, and Postmodern Culture* (Bloomington: Indiana University Press), 74.

11. Vanderhoef, "Casual Threats."

12. Joyrich, *Re-viewing Reception*, 74.

13. Vanderhoef, "Casual Threats."

14. Mia Consalvo, "Confronting Toxic Gamer Culture: A Challenge for Feminist Game Studies Scholars," *Ada: A Journal of Gender, New Media, and Technology*, no. 1 (2012), http://adanewmedia.org/2012/11/issue1-consalvo. See also Anita Sarkeesian, "Image Based Harassment and Visual Misogyny," *Feminist Frequency*, July 1, 2012, https://feministfrequency.com/2012/07/01/image-based-harassment-and-visual-misogyny; and chapters 3 and 4.

15. Consalvo, "Confronting Toxic Gamer Culture." See also Leigh Alexander, "In the Sexism Discussion, Let's Look at Game Culture," *Gamasutra*, July 16, 2012, http://www.gamasutra.com/view/news/174145/Opinion_In_the_sexism_discussion_lets_look_at_game_culture.php.

16. Consalvo, "Confronting Toxic Gamer Culture"; Shira Chess, "Going with the Flo: *Diner Dash* and Feminism," *Feminist Media Studies* 12, no. 1 (2012): 96.

17. Although *Diner Dash* has garnered excellent attention from scholars such as Shira Chess and Aubrey Anable, its rich and influential combination of narrative and gameplay provides a depth of multiple interpretations. See Chess, "Going with the Flo"; and Aubrey Anable, "Casual Games, Time Management, and the Work of Affect," *Ada: A Journal of Gender, New Media, and Technology*, no. 2 (2013), http://adanewmedia.org/2013/06/issue2-anable/.

18. Mizuko Ito and Matteo Bittanti, "Gaming," in *Hanging Out, Messing Around, and Geeking Out* (Cambridge, MA: MIT Press, 2010), 202.

19. Mikel Reparaz, "The Death of Hardcore Gaming?" *GamesRadar*, August 30, 2007, http://www.gamesradar.com/the-death-of-hardcore-gaming.

20. A. J. Glasser, "PlayFirst Sunsets Chocolatier as Diner Dash Ramps Up Monetization, Social Features," *Social Times*, April 20, 2011, http://www.adweek.com/socialtimes/playfirst-sunsets-chocolatier-as-diner-dash-ramps-up-monetization-social-features/583018.

21. Ibid.

22. Anable, "Casual Games."

23. Jesper Juul, *A Casual Revolution: Reinventing Video Games and Their Players* (Cambridge, MA: MIT Press, 2012), 36.

24. Arlie Hochschild, *The Second Shift* (New York: Penguin Books, 1989); Arlie Hochschild, *The Time Bind: When Work Becomes Home and Home Becomes Work* (New York: Henry Holt, 2001).

25. Michele Bolton, *The Third Shift: Managing Hard Choices in Our Careers, Homes, and Lives as Women* (San Francisco: Jossey Bass, 2000), 148.

26. Bruce Drake, "Another Gender Gap: Men Spend More Time in Leisure Activities," Pew Research Center, June 10, 2013, http://www.pewresearch.org/fact-tank/2013/06/10/another-gender-gap-men-spend-more-time-in-leisure-activities/. Also see Chess, "Going with the Flo," 3.

27. Michael Bittman and Judy Wajcman, "The Rush Hour: The Quality of Leisure Time and Gender Equity," in *Family Time: The Social Organization of Care*, ed. Nancy Folbre and Michael Bittman (London: Routledge, 2004), 188–189.

28. Valerie Bryson, *Gender and the Politics of Time* (Bristol, UK: Policy Press, 2007), 147.

29. While men certainly play casual games and experience the fragmentation of multitasking in contemporary culture, they "have many more hours of pure leisure" than women that is uninterrupted and continuous. Bittman and Wajcman, "Rush Hour," 189.

30. Chess, "Going with the Flo," 9.

31. Mihaly Csikszentmihalyi, *Beyond Boredom and Anxiety: The Experience of Play in Work and Games* (San Francisco: Jossey-Bass, 1975), 141, 159, 160.

32. Ibid, 141.

33. Bolton, *Third Shift*, 1.

34. Chess, "Going with the Flo," 7–10. Chess also highlights that "*Diner Dash* games can be understood as a 'third shift'" but that placing Flo at work negates the ideal use of a third shift to negotiate and reflect on the first and second shifts. Moreover, I believe it is not just the fact that play becomes work in *Diner Dash* but that the structure of the short, interruptible gameplay—common in many time management games—creates a form of play and leisure that negates the positive space within the third shift for working through and transforming the gendered inequalities of contemporary leisure time.

35. Tania Modleski, "The Search for Tomorrow in Today's Soap Operas: Notes on a Feminine Narrative Form," *Film Quarterly* 33, no. 1 (1979): 12.

36. Espen Aarseth, "Genre Trouble," *Electronic Book Review*, May 21, 2004, http://www.electronicbookreview.com/thread/firstperson/vigilant.

37. Ibid.

38. Flo's transformation into a goddess, serving Indian food in an exotic restaurant, with her skin tone changing to yellow opens intriguing representational questions concerning race. Donna Haraway famously quipped, "I would rather be a cyborg than a goddess" in order to undermine the feminist figure of the goddess as a return to a natural essentialism that tended to exclude difference and the feminist perspectives of women of color; thus Flo's transformation also reveals *Diner Dash*'s essential privileging of white women's labor. Moreover, the change of her skin color invokes traditional racialized imaginaries while also enacting a cultural appropriation where the state of enjoyment Flo expresses only elides serious questions concerning the differences between work and leisure temporalities among white women and women of color. See Chess, "Youthful White Male Industry," 173.

39. Hochschild, *The Time Bind*, 245–246.

40. E. P. Thompson, "Time, Work-Discipline, and Industrial Capitalism," *Past and Present* 38, no. 1 (1967): 79.

chapter three

"AW FUCK, I GOT A BITCH ON MY TEAM!"

Women and the Exclusionary Cultures of the Computer Game Complex

JENNIFER DEWINTER AND CARLY A. KOCUREK

AS THE QUOTATION USED IN OUR TITLE MAKES CLEAR, WOMEN IN GAMING culture face more than a little hostility from outspoken male gamers.[1] The video game industry currently faces scrutiny from industry professionals, players, and cultural critics who deplore the lack of women and diversity in the production of games. A popular argument around this gender disparity is that games are for boys, and if we made games for girls, more women would enter the field. The numbers, however, do not support this claim: 45 percent of US game players are women of all ages, and the number hovers around 50 percent women players in other countries, as well.[2] Yet women make up only 14 percent of the production side of the industry, with 11 percent working in art and design and the other 3 percent in programming. The problem does not stem from educational disparities, we argue; women complete academic training in computer science, art, and design, and they are going on to careers that use these skills in demanding industries. Women make up 60 percent of workers in graphic design and 20 percent in computer industries—industries that use the same technologies and programs that are common in game production.[3] This points to a problem of culture, not of education, access, or even interest. And this culture was highlighted in November 2012, when Luke Crane casually tweeted, "Why are there so few lady game creators?" In response, hundreds of people who worked in the game industry, primarily women, started the #1reasonwhy hashtag, through which they cataloged the egregious harassment heaped on women in the industry.

In this chapter, we demonstrate that the participatory cultures of gaming aggressively resist feminist critiques of games and that these forms of male-dominated resistance continue to marginalize women in gaming industries and cultures. These discursive practices can be seen in the interactions between men and women in online gaming spaces, from gaming magazine editorial content to YouTube comments. Also, we consider the ways in which women who apply feminist critiques to the industry are verbally and psychologically abused—as in the backlash to Anita Sarkeesian's Kickstarter, horrifyingly illuminated by the "Beat Up Anita Sarkeesian" mini game (2012, Ben Spurr). And finally, we look to the ways in which women game industry professionals and women gamers are harassed in an anachronistic parody of 1950s works culture as cataloged under Twitter's #1reasonwhy.

In what follows, we chronicle this significant and often violent circling of the wagons and also theorize why this type of resistance occurs in a way that is absent from the discourse surrounding most popular media, such as books, television, or film. We interrogate what is at stake for those who police the boundaries of video games, protecting the parapets from the slow incursion of female gamers into the rarified male space of hard-core gamer and game maker. We consider here a large amount of gender-relevant data from across different areas of game culture, suggesting that the discourse around gender and the game industry is Foucauldian in that it is diffused broadly and implicates numerous actors across multiple institutions and cultural practices in policing borders. Within this, we argue that the antifemale policing in video game culture is an expression of sex and violence that depends on the rhetoric of isolation and rape. Further, these actions, intentionally or unintentionally, accomplish what antiwomen gamers want: they create an aggressively exclusionary culture of gaming with no space for women, their participation, or their voices, as players or as makers.

"Someone Explain to Me Why 50% of the World Population Is a 'Niche' Market": Hard-Core Gamers, Technological Play, and Male Spaces

Demographic numbers consistently prove that men and women tend to play games approximately equally, yet the foundational definition of gamer remains masculine.[4] Indeed, the very use of the term "hard core" not only brings to mind a dedicated male gamer but also the pornography industry. Pornography scholar Linda Williams develops the idea of pornotopia, which juxtaposes abundance and energy against scarcity and opposition to provide audiences with arousal within the dominant power structures of capitalism and patriarchy.[5] Pornography, then, provides abundance and energy and then spends itself in its play. So, too, is the promise made to the hard-core gamer: more games, more gameplay, more energy put into the game in a (porno-) utopia of play—and just to be clear here, more masculine. Both pornography and game culture—including the game industry as producer and workplace—offer the lure of a cultural form that caters to and seeks to satisfy male desires, promising an abundance of masculinist delights for those eager to indulge in such.

A number of scholars have examined this concept of hard-core gamer in an attempt to account for the many types of players who play games.[6] According to Aphra Kerr, the very designation of hard-core gamer is a construction of the game industry in an attempt to define a dedicated market.[7] And this definition, according to Mia Consalvo, does not account for other types of players who take their games equally seriously and spend significant time playing those games.[8] Yet this expanding of the demographic market does little to disrupt what Janine Fron and her collaborators define as the core market of hard-core gamers: "It is characterized by an adolescent male sensibility that transcends physical age and embraces highly stylized graphical violence, male fantasies of power and domination, hyper-sexualized, objectified depictions of women, and rampant racial stereotyping and discrimination."[9] However, as these authors point out, gamers are not necessarily a demographic defined by the industry, or at least not only defined by the industry. Rather, people self-select into this (often exclusionary) identity.

Even within the community, the definition and very existence of the hard-core gamer identity is problematized and questioned. According to Adrienne Shaw, even the apparently apolitical designation of "gamer" is fraught, as people who play video games do not necessarily identify nor want to identify themselves as gamers. She found in her ethnographic study that male participants were more willing to identify as "gamers," suggesting that the category as a whole is gendered.[10] This disparity has a very real precedent both in the history of video gaming and in the history of the underlying technologies. Computing in particular has been historically associated with men in cultural narratives, an association that effaces the real contributions of women computer researchers and programmers and serves to masculinize the field.

Critiques of gaming's gender trouble are nothing new; however, as the critiques mount, voices from the gamer community have come out strongly in defense of the hard-core gamer and the gamer in general, which exclude casual and female gamers. On the *Men Going Their Own Way* forum, which is a men's separatist space for men's rights activists, one discussion, posted under the title "WTF is with empowered women in video games now," demonstrates how even men who do not self-identify as hard-core gamers feel entitled to police women's participation and representation in video games:

> I am starting this thread because I see a new trend in the video/computer game world and that is the increase in strong playable female characters. . . . I call bullshit on this subject. *Video games are the last place for guys to hang out and now women are taking over.* Why not just save us the trouble and instead of eliminating our fantasy world just throw us in work camp to provide for their bastard children (literally speaking) while they shit all over us . . . wait they already do that.[11]

The extremists of the *Men Going Their Own Way* forum envision the reseparation of the sexes as a solution to their perceived marginalization. However, their rage at women's trespass into gaming culture is echoed across the web, ranging from *Yahoo! Answers* to the *Steam* forums. The widely read gaming site *Kotaku* became infamous for its commenters' use of aggression to police participation not only in the site's discussion but in gaming culture more broadly.[12] The site became so unpleasant—particularly for women—that a browser extension named "Commentless Kotaku" was created to do nothing but hide *Kotaku* comments from view. While as late as January 2012, *Kotaku* was defending the discourse of its comments, the site has more recently changed its tune, expanding comment moderation to facilitate more discussion and reduce the brutality.[13]

Further, threats to women in gaming and in the game industry often deploy sex or the threat of sexual violence as a weapon. Many women, notably including *Depression Quest* (2013, Independent) designer Zoë Quinn, have been threatened with death and rape by raging male gamers, an event that is often identified as one of the flashpoints that started the #Gamergate hashtag. Quinn's ultimately successful efforts to have her game approved by the community-moderated Steam Greenlight earned her a cornucopia of on- and off-line harassment because she'd dared to make a game about depression; most harassment, however, came in the form of misogynistic insults. How, after all, dare she? At one point, she had received so many obscene and threatening phone calls that she stopped answering her phone—men would call to shout obscenities, to threaten rape, or to masturbate. Because of this, she only learned several days after the fact that her father was in the intensive care unit.[14] Following this, an ex-boyfriend decided to defame Quinn in a blog post, discrediting her work by claiming that she slept with games journalists to get positive reviews. This post started what would infamously be known as Gamergate, a movement of misogyny and harassment against feminism in general and individual women designers and scholars in particular. Likewise, Sarkeesian was treated to drawings and doctored fake photographs of her own sexual violation and explicitly threatened with rape and death and even had to cancel an invited talk at Utah State University because of a bomb threat.[15] At least one female game developer reported being sexually harassed by a games journalist during an interview; the developer went on to say that the incident was one of many that had led her to consider leaving the industry.[16]

The idea that gaming should be a rarified environment for men hearkens backward to Victorian-era ideas of separate spheres that placed women squarely outside of public culture. This ideology facilitates the treatment of women gamers as an aberration, as transgressors, as interlopers. Women belong in a different space, separate from the presumably masculine space provided by video games. While this resonates with a Victorian sensibility—the home as feminized space—we see even more in evidence a spatial segregation more akin to 1950s America. Some male gamers embrace gaming as a last bastion of homosocial male space, fighting to protect it from a slow creeping integration of gender. For these men, women's presence in games—as players, producers, or even characters—taints the form.

"Because 'Rape Is Historically Accurate,' Said the Half-Elven Wizard": Performing Sexual Aggression in Games, Performing Sexual Aggression in Life

That games are a bastion of sexual aggression is well documented.[17] Violent misogyny in game narratives is often defended as historically accurate or true to the narrative. While these claims are sometimes bizarre—as in the assertion, mocked in this section's title, that rape is a historically accurate part of a fantasy game—even cases where such a claim could be viewed as credible are frequently accompanied by real player aggression toward real women. Frank critique of sexism and misogyny in games, even when brief, often attracts outrage in two forms: attacks on the person (particularly if that person is a woman) who has highlighted the problem, or defenses of misogyny or harassment as key components of gaming culture. For example, in a review of *Grand Theft Auto V* (2013, Rockstar Games) produced for *GameSpot*, Carolyn Petit briefly described the game as "politically muddled and profoundly misogynistic" and made reference to "its serious issues with women." Overall, Petit rated the game with a 9 out of 10, a high score that indicates an excellent, if imperfect, game.[18] However, because Petit noted the game's problematic gender politics, the review attracted a cavalcade of abusive comments. An online petition calling for Petit's firing was begun and was later removed.[19] Moderation at *GameSpot* restrained some of the vitriol, but the comments elsewhere provide an archive of misogynistic and transmisogynistic abuse. Over a month after Petit's review posted to YouTube, it continued to garner comments like "Fuck this incomplet abomination freak, fuck you carolyn your a freak," and "Get this feminist fired."[20]

Petit's own gender identity—she is, in fact, a transgender woman—may mean that gaming's aggro cultural gatekeepers see her as a particularly deserving target, as they often deploy transmisogynistic jokes and remarks. But Petit is not alone among women reviewers and critics in attracting gendered attacks. Patricia Hernandez, a games journalist best known as a writer for *Kotaku,* was subject to the *IGN* thread titled "Is there a worse internet blogger than Patricia Hernandez at *Kotaku*?" This includes such gems as, "All the feminist bloggers on *Kotaku* are fucking awful," and "We should round up all the people like her in the world and exterminate them."[21] In one of a number of forum threads criticizing games journalist Leigh Alexander on *Giant Bomb,* a commenter said, "Ask me, and she sounds like one of those girls that plays video games solely to attract guys that do nothing but play video games because it's the only thing she can do to get any attention."[22] The idea that anyone might have built a career out of playing video games "to attract guys" would be laughable if it didn't echo routine efforts to expunge women from gaming.

Recently, women gamers and cultural critics have attended to sexual aggression in video games through the simple yet powerful act of archiving these interactions. In 2010, Jenny Haniver created an installation of the male and female gamer experiences in which she collected and displayed comments that she had received while playing *Call of Duty* (2003, Activision) online. This was the first step in her archiving project, now maintained on her website Not in the Kitchen Anymore. Comments recorded here threaten rape, express sexual desire, and dismiss Haniver's abilities based on weight or age.[23] Likewise, the website Fat, Ugly or Slutty is an aggregate website in which people submit evidence of their harassment, offering a means of public shaming. The site's "About" page explains, "If having these messages posted online makes someone think twice about writing and sending a detailed description of their genitals, great!"[24]

A number of popular and academic sources attribute this type of action to anonymity; however, the atmosphere of in-person gaming communities complicates this argument.[25] Filamena tweeted on #1reasonwhy, "Because conventions, where designers are celebrated, are unsafe places for me. Really. I've been groped," which received a number of corroborating tweets about similar experiences.[26] This type of behavior at conventions marginalizes women as industry professionals.[27] Video game conventions often host what is commonly referred to as "booth babes": beautiful models who sell a pixilated story with the same tactics used to sell sports cars and speed boats.[28] This practice has recently come under scrutiny, with Penny Arcade Expo and Eurogamer Expo banning the use of booth babes. Yet publishers get around these rules by hiring "girl gamers" who just happen to be beautiful and scantily clad.[29] Worse yet, at the 2013 RTX convention, a male attendee appropriated satirical "fake geek girl" bumper stickers, sticking them onto the butts and backs of women at the conference.[30] RTX responded immediately, enforcing its no harassment policy and expelling this perpetrator. However, what this man had done was not completely out of line within the observable actions of convention communities. Any quick search for news items about sexual harassment and assault at conventions turns up a disturbing number of hits, such as Olajide Olatunji's YouTube video in which he records himself both harassing women at Eurogamer Expo and outright assaulting booth babes at the same event.[31]

The observations that Tracy Dietz makes about gender and violence within video games themselves could easily be extended to make sense of gamer culture in the material world. She argues that US culture eroticizes male dominance, which puts women in a subordinate position and increases acceptance of rape and sexual aggression.[32] This form of masculinity, especially as it plays out in video games, has real implications for people's tolerance of and even actions in support of sexual aggression toward women. For example, Karen Dill and her collaborators asked 120 females and 61 males (a mean age of 18.82) to view images from video games to determine how these images affected sexual harassment judgments and rape-supportive attitudes. They found that "the males who were exposed to the objectified female video game characters were the most tolerant of any of the groups towards sexual harassment."[33] Further, the longer that people are exposed to these types of images and attitudes the more they develop rape-supportive attitudes.[34]

A subgroup of gamers defend their alleged right to say egregious things and act in worse-than-juvenile ways under the banner of freedom of speech, which protects their "right" to be verbally and psychologically abusive. The most notable contemporary example is *Penny Arcade*'s Dickwolves debacle. In 2010, *Penny Arcade* posted a web comic that poked fun at the strange ethics and practices of games like *World of Warcraft* (2004, Blizzard Entertainment) that, during an in-game rescue scenario, would not allow players to save more slaves or hostages than the requisite number. In the comic, a remaining character asked to be saved because every night, he and his fellows "are raped to sleep by the dickwolves."[35] Following the publication of this strip, a number of readers, mostly women and some rape survivors, expressed their discomfort with the comic's use of rape as a punch line. Instead of recognizing the reception in a meaningful way, Mike Krahulik of *Penny Arcade* and forum participants mocked critics. Krahulik drew a flippant response in the following week's web comic, published a Dickwolf illustration, and began selling "Team Dickwolves" shirts and pennants. Eventually, *Penny Arcade* was pressured into removing the merchandise (to the dismay of some fans), which allowed the controversy to die down. However, at the 2013 PAX Prime convention, in a room packed with thousands of attendees, Krahulik said he regretted pulling the Dickwolves merchandise. The audience cheered. Those who spoke out against this ultimate defense and celebration of Dickwolves received a slew of rape and death threats from the site's loyal defenders.[36]

It is easy to read the Dickwolves defense as a form of hypermasculinity in the guise of free speech. That masculinity is often connected to technological mastery is well documented.[37] Further, masculinity is often defined in opposition to or as the inverse of femininity; thus, the implied syllogism suggests that women are not good at technology—technology is in the domain of the male.[38] We see here, in the performance of rape culture, not just a rearticulation of the masculine/feminine binary, but an extension of the separate spaces for male and female actions, which are guarded with threats of physical and sexual violence.

Rape and rape culture have always been ways of policing women and demarcating spaces where women are permitted. Women who are sexually assaulted are frequently chastised for their choices—clothes, location, relationships, alcoholic consumption, and the like—a phenomenon called "victim blaming." Amy Grubb and Emily Turner found that those who adhere to more traditional gender roles are more likely to blame victims because those female victims deviated from their expected roles.[39] Further research from Jesse Fox and collaborators shows that sexualized avatars in video games may even convince women and men to objectify the female body, which makes them more likely to support rape-myth attitudes.[40] More disturbing, according to these authors, is another finding: "It appears that users of sexualized avatars may be at risk for developing negative attitudes towards women and the self outside of the virtual environment."[41] Avatar representation matters. The more sexualized the avatar, the more likely women and men are to objectify women and subordinate women to the rape myth.

The rape myth in action requires both a sense of segregated space (women should not have been there to begin with) as well as cultural attitudes and practices that enable the objectification of women. In extreme examples of this, women are not seen as gamers; gamers are active participants in a broader sociocultural framework. Rather, women are for consumption as avatars and NPCs in male-centric story lines. When real women enter gaming spaces and ask for equal participatory power, the framework can be mobilized to deny them agency. In other words, if women come into gaming spaces, they are asking for it. The trajectory of the Dickwolves controversy makes a sick sense in this ideological formation: if a space is uncomfortable for women because of male behavior, that means that women should not go there, not that men should behave differently. This reasoning is not unique to online and fan spaces; it can be found in the workplace as well.

"But She Doesn't DRAW Like a GIRL": Feminized Skills, Glass Ceilings, and Locked Doors

The industry says that it wants more women working on developing games.[42] David Mullich's featured *Gamasutra* post "Wanted: More Female Game Developers" argues for this effort strongly after seeing the complete absence of women in his program.[43] Programs such as Girls Who Code, Black Girls Code, and the incubator Pixelles in Montreal attempt to target young women and provide them access to the skills needed to develop digital environments and games. And with women comprising almost half of the gaming population, one would expect that access and experience would translate into a desire to create. Yet Electronic Arts' chief talent officer, Gabrielle Toledano, argues that EA wants to hire more women but cannot find women who have the necessary skills.[44] However, even women who exhibit exceptional skill at either developing or playing games are often devalued or dismissed. It is easy to look at the #1reasonwhy tweet that makes up the title for this section to see the devaluing of skills based on gender. Thus, programs that teach advanced computer skills to girls and young women often ignore the earlier entrance points for this career trajectory, in this case, gaming.

Even when women are skilled gamers, their skills are quickly dismissed. For example, in a post to *Yahoo! Answers*, a user is frustrated that women "want credit" for beating him in-game and asks, "Why are women allowed to play video games?" He writes, "They ruin it. They know by being female people will go easier on them, team with them, give them things, etc. It's pathetic. And they'll pick 'hot' looking characters to have an advantage. It's just like real life without the battling. They use their looks to their advantage. It's annoying. Then if they beat you they try to take credit for it, as if they didn't get all these advantages first."[45] Hell hath no fury like a sore loser, perhaps, but this sentiment has been expressed elsewhere, often in spite of and over women's evidence of the harassment they face in gaming culture. Matthew Inman, who produces web comics as "The Oatmeal," posted a comic of a girl gamer who made a mistake that ruined the team's chances and was told everything was okay in condescending tones used for children. The artist wrote, "I was implying two things: [1] When girls play, often times no one takes them seriously. [2] If they screw up, often times the room is filled with lonely dudes who say things like 'LOL that's okay! Will you marry me?' If I screw up I get eviscerated."[46] He ignored, at least initially, readers' angry responses, which pointed out both that his comic is an example of someone not taking women seriously as gamers and that women are rarely let off so easily in-game. Rather, women's in-game failure is often ascribed to gender, and their successes are ascribed to some man—a boyfriend, a brother—who played on their account or to men who have gone easy on them. These attitudes transfer to the workplace, where some men dismiss women's work, undermine their success, and isolate them from networks that would allow them to succeed.

This idea that women who succeed as gamers have either been propped up by adoring men blinded by their sexual attraction or have succeeded in spite of their inferior skills resonates between game culture and the game industry. We have conducted a series of interviews with women who work in gaming that, alongside online chronicles of similar experiences, evidence the prevalence of this myth. For example, TransformEnt tweeted on #1reasonwhy, "After being told she was hired to 'look pretty & make the guys happy', my old boss got him to repeat this in an email to HR."[47] The woman in the room becomes yet another sexualized object in the room, deskilled and vapid. And as indicated, Human Resources probably has policies against this, so this sexism is not necessarily institutionalized in the company; rather, it is institutionalized in the game complex as a whole.

Systemically, too, the industry discourages women from entering game development in a number of ways. First, according to *Game Developer Magazine*'s 2013 salary survey, the gendered disparity in salary is significant in all areas of game employment except programming and engineering (which is 96 percent male) (table 3.1).[48] The gender wage gap in the video game industry suggests that women

Table 3.1 Figures from *Game Developer Magazine's* 2013 salary survey

Occupation	Gender	Representation (%)	Average salary ($)
Artist/animator	Male	84	77,791
	Female	16	60,238
Game designer	Male	89	76,646
	Female	11	61,983
Producer	Male	77	85,591
	Female	23	78,989
Audio professional	Male	96	82,944
	Female	4	50,000
QA tester	Male	93	49,196
	Female	7	39,375
Business and legal	Male	82	108,571
	Female	18	82,292

are not provided economic incentive (or equal access) to step into a culture that actively mobilizes against them. Further, we see in these numbers a delineation of appropriate avenues for women, one that gets repeated in #1reasonwhy: "The worst sexism is the 'harmless' assumptions. I'm sick of being told art is the only appropriate career for a woman in games."[49] Some of this may be accounted for by Robin Potanin's designated "I" design methodology, which places men at the center of the design process: men make games that they want to play, which attracts more men into the game industry.[50] Looking at the male and female percentages in each of the creative domains suggests that, indeed, the "I" methodology continues to skew masculine.

When women do enter the industry, they are often in the minority, as low as 4 percent in their work pool. This leads, unsurprisingly, to feelings of isolation and anger. For example, in her blog *Dead Reckon*, Whitney Hills spins a story of her years in the video game industry: "You feel that the things that hurt you would never have happened if you weren't female, and on a certain level, you feel that you deserve it."[51] The feelings outlined in this posting are taken up in Ciara Byrne's article "The Loneliness of the Female Coder." She tells the story of a developer who was leaving her company: "At the end of our final status meeting, he launched into a description of a dream he had about me in which I was wearing Uma Thurman's *Kill Bill* catsuit and laying waste to some baddies with a sword. . . . How do you manage a team which is simultaneously picturing you in a yellow catsuit?"[52]

We see two terrible factors in place in these stories. First, the isolation: according to *The Athena Factor: Reversing the Brain Drain in Science, Engineering, and Technology*, isolation leads women to drop out of technical fields because of its emotional toll and the inability to see a trajectory or career that accounts for all the stresses that women feel.[53] The second and more disturbing factor is the sense of "deserving it." The slow psychological violence—because that's what isolation is—turns the victim into the responsible agent. Here is the quieter and more conditional form of the rape myth: the woman in the male space, who is too young and too pretty, who would be included as an equal if she just weren't a woman. Indeed, acceptance of the rape myth, according to Martha Burt, correlates to an acceptance of interpersonal violence.[54] This violence can be extreme, such as the case of a Japanese woman who worked at Capcom and tried to commit suicide after prolonged bullying.[55] Further, with Gamergate organization, player communities are now aggressively harassing and bullying women in the workforce, often with terrible professional consequences.[56] The gamer culture in play is the gamer culture in work.

The feelings of loneliness and isolation lead to another significant problem in game production: silencing women's voices. Byrne speaks to this: "Although I was like them in many respects, I looked at things from a different angle, one which my colleagues often didn't recognize or adapt to. Why should they? I felt like the lone voice in the wilderness."[57] David Gaider writes about a similar phenomenon in discussing a peer review session for a plot in *Dragon Age* (2009, Bioware). After the men provided feedback about what went well and what could be changed, one of the female writers spoke, and according to Gaider, "she brought up an issue. A big issue. It had to do with a sexual situation in the plot, which she explained could easily be interpreted as a form of rape," which the other women on the team also saw.[58] The writer was mortified, and the plot was revised. But Gaider's point has more to do with gender diversity in game development. Had no women been on the team, this scene would have gone into the game. Further, Gaider questions:

> Had that female writer been the lone woman, would her view have been disregarded as an over-reaction? A lone outlier? How often does that happen on game development teams, ones made up of otherwise intelligent and liberal guys who are then shocked to find out that they inadvertently offended a group that is quickly approaching *half of the gaming audience*?[59]

In other words, limited numbers of women are just as bad as no women if women are isolated and silenced in the workforce. Only through a critical mass can gender diversity effect positive change in a reportedly toxic environment. Yet, as Julie Prescott and Jan Bogg argue, the danger of bringing more women into the gaming industry is that they may be segregated and concentrated in female-dominated fields and subfields.[60] The salary survey points to this very phenomenon happening, with more women artists than programmers. And even then, the numbers are shockingly low.

The danger and isolation women feel doesn't have to do with whether women are good at their jobs; it has to do with whether they are in the workplace at all. Their presence is at best an anomaly, leading to isolation, or is interpreted as an invasion, requiring forceful defense. The forceful defense of game culture is publicly discussed and strategized over. ShrineNI's YouTube series "How to Gank a Girl Gamer," for example, outlines his strategies for harassing, or ganking, girl gamers. He introduces his second video thusly: "It's not just about balling in there, you know, ganking. There's actually tactics involved for this sort of thing." He outlines his tactics, and then, after literally teaching people how to drive women gamers out, he says quite explicitly, "I'm not a hero, I'm a silent guardian. A watchful protector."[61] According to gamers like ShrineNI, feminism is the blight. Women are manipulative and sadistic. Oh, and they are weaker both in-game and out of game.

"Who Decided It's Macho, Manly, and Cool to Disrespect and Hate Women?": Pushing Back and Moving Forward

When we first began writing about game culture gone rancid in 2012, we, too, were struck by isolation and depression because, as women game scholars, we subject ourselves to this culture daily.[62] But like others who stick it out, we continue to do it because we love games, the social aspects of play, the challenge of sport, the ability to design—or explore—worlds and narratives. What we see here and elsewhere is a call for a change in discourse. It's not just that we need more girl gamers; we already have them. It's not just that we need more women in the game industry;

women enter and are driven away. It's not just that we need more women writing and speaking up about this; they are, and they are attacked. It's that all these maneuvers must be reflected and protected by policies that shape the discourse of games, and those policies should be strict. Since that first draft of this chapter, we have seen the outcome of these issues at their extreme. The #Gamergate campaign, which organized itself around "ethics in games journalism," has maintained a disturbing momentum in organizing non-point-specific harassment of women and minorities in game culture writ large. If bomb, death, and rape threats were not enough, Gamergaters have also researched and posted home addresses, phone numbers, social security numbers, and credit card numbers of their victims. At their most pernicious, exclusionary cultures produce this: the violent policing of culture marked by threatened and real danger. In their landmark essay, "The Culture Industry: Enlightenment as Mass Deception," Theodor Adorno and Max Horkheimer persuasively make the case that homogenous cultural production can and does produce fascism.[63] This cycle is unfolding in games culture as we watch.

Nevertheless, we cannot and should not throw up our hands in despair. Interventions are possible and can be effective. Already, we have seen the positive impact of nondiscrimination policies. *Kotaku* acknowledged its community responsibility and now has a very clear policy concerning inclusiveness—attack comments will be blocked—changing the tone of the site significantly. This success story points to the dual components of change in institutionalized spaces: policy and enforcement. For example, Penny Arcade Expo has pro-women policies—they famously banned the use of booth babes—but those policies are inconsistently enforced. Hence, Dickwolves. Online play, too, has seen a shift in policy enforcement, thanks in part to the tireless work of Haniver and others who carefully record, report, and publicly expose harassment. For those policies to work, we need people like Haniver, recording horrific transcripts of play; like Tanya DePass, who founded I Need Diverse Games and advocates tirelessly for diversity both in on-screen representation and in the teams that produce games; like Sarkeesian, continuing her cultural criticism in the face of hostility; and like Quinn, who not only continues to make games but founded Crash Override Network to help others subjected to online harassment. And we assure our readers, producing these records and doing the work of these interventions becomes demoralizing, a job that we clock into instead of the safe magic circle of play. As Haniver has noted, even following the appropriate channels to report harassment does not always effect immediate change.[64] How many of us wouldn't just walk away? We know that in the process of writing this chapter, we often wanted to.

Underneath these positive actions is the constant threat that we cannot ignore. Gaming is gender segregated. Spaces and boundaries exist. Underlying the cultures of gaming is a darker culture of gendered segregation in the home, in the workplace, and in our play. While there are positive steps that we can and do take to attend to the boundaries, we will likely always struggle against the conditional rhetorics of sexism. These ideological constructions are not limited to gaming; we see similar attrition in other technical and engineering fields. The problem is pervasive, and the violence and exclusion is performed over a lifetime of exposure. For example, as we read about isolation and attrition in the Harvard Business Review's *The Athena Factor*, we naturally felt sympathetic and angry about the reported cases that these professional women face. But there are untold numbers of people participating in video game culture, from young children to retired adults. And we know that exposure to this psychological violence will start far earlier for children playing games than it should, and that exposure will remain constant throughout their lives, training them to recognize the spaces and opportunities that they will and will not have access to. Should any doubt the lifetime conditioning that women are subjected to in gaming culture, we end with this quotation from one of our interviewees:

> My 8 year old loves minecraft [2011, Mojang]. . . . Occasionally we let her play in multi-player if one of us is nearby. One day she was [playing] around and she said, "someone said they want to have sex with me." I looked at the computer and sure enough, someone had written, "(her name), I want to have sex with you." I got on the keyboard and wrote, "She's 8. Say that again." They then disconnected.[65]

JENNIFER DEWINTER is Associate Professor of Rhetoric and Director of the Interactive Media and Game Development Program at Worcester Polytechnic Institute. She is coeditor of the books *Video Game Policy* and *Computer Games and Technical Communication* and author of *Shigeru Miyamoto: Super Mario Bros., Donkey Kong, The Legend of Zelda.*

CARLY A. KOCUREK is Assistant Professor of Digital Humanities and Media Studies at the Illinois Institute of Technology. She is author of *Coin-Operated Americans: Rebooting Boyhood at the Video Game Arcade* and *Brenda Laurel: Pioneering Games for Girls*, and she develops games for serious and educational purposes.

Notes

1. Jenny Haniver, "Aw Fuck, I Got an Idiot on My Team," *Not in the Kitchen Anymore* (blog), May 6, 2013, http://www.notinthekitchenanymore.com/aw-fuck-i-got-an-idiot-on-my-team.

2. Entertainment Software Association, *Essential Facts about the Computer and Video Game Industry* (Washington, DC: Entertainment Software Association, 2013), 3.

3. Jennifer deWinter and Carly Kocurek, "#1reasonwhy Women in the Gaming Industry Matters," *Flow* 17, no. 7 (2012), http://flowtv.org/2013/02/1-reason-why-women-in-the-gaming-industry-matters/.

4. The quotation in this section's title comes from Ian Schreiber, #1reasonwhy post, *Twitter*, November 27, 2012, 8:20 p.m., https://twitter.com/IanSchreiber.

5. Linda Williams, *Hard Core: Power, Pleasure, and the "Frenzy of the Visible"* (Berkley: University of California Press, 1989), 155.

6. For more on hard-core gaming, see chapter 2.

7. Aphra Kerr, *The Business and Culture of Digital Games: Gamework and Gameplay* (London: Sage, 2006), 97.

8. Mia Consalvo, "Hardcore Casual: Game Culture *Return(s) to Ravenhearst*," paper presented at 4th International Conference on Foundations of Digital Games, Port Canaveral, FL, April 26–30, 2009.

9. Janine Fron, Tracy Fullerton, Jacquelyn Ford Morie, and Celia Pearce, "The Hegemony of Play," in *Situated Play: Proceedings of Digital Games Research Association 2007 Conference* (Tokyo, Japan: DIGRA, 2007), 7.

10. Adrienne Shaw, "Do You Identify as a Gamer? Gender, Race, Sexuality, and Gamer Identity," *New Media and Society* 14, no. 1 (2012): 35.

11. Quoth the OP, "WTF Is with Empowered Women in Video Games Now," *Men Going Their Own Way Forums*, 2013 (emphasis added). The original forum is now blocked, but it was captured on Jess's *STFU, Conservatives* blog in 2013, at http://stfuconservatives.tumblr.com/post/15737396521.

12. Stephen Totilo, "A Note about 'Brutal' Comments and a *Kotaku* for Everyone," *Kotaku*, June 26, 2013, http://kotaku.com/a-note-about-brutal-comments-and-a-kotaku-for-everyon-589637991.

13. Kirk Hamilton, "*Kotaku* Commenters Do Not Suck," *Kotaku*, January 13, 2012, http://kotaku.com/5875949/kotaku-commenters-do-not-suck.

14. Zack Kotzer, "The Sexist BS Women Who Make Video Games Have to Deal With," *Vice*, January 24, 2014, http://www.vice.com/read/female-game-designers-are-being-threatened-with-rape.

15. Ralitsa Vassileva, "Online Trolls Attack Feminist Media Critic," *CNN*, April 18, 2013, https://www.youtube.com/watch?v=wNyxq-gqFNU.

16. Cassandra Khaw, "Game Developer Speaks about Journalist Who Sexually Harassed Her," *Daily Dot*, February 3, 2014, http://www.dailydot.com/gaming/game-developer-sexual-harassment-journalist/.

17. See, for example, Justine Cassell and Henry Jenkins, eds., *From Barbie to Mortal Kombat: Gender and Computer Games* (Cambridge, MA: MIT Press, 2000); and Yasmin B. Kafai, Carrie Heeter, Jill Denner, and Jennifer Y. Sun, eds., *Beyond Barbie and Mortal Kombat: New Perspectives on Gender and Gaming* (Cambridge, MA: MIT Press, 2011). The quotation in this section's title comes from @GeekGirlsRule, #1reasonwhy post, *Twitter*, December 6, 2012, 7:27 a.m., https://twitter.com/GeekGirlsRule.

18. Carolyn Petit, "GameSpot Reviews: *Grand Theft Auto V*," *YouTube*, September 16, 2013, http://www.youtube.com/watch?v=ABiPHyaKgTw.

19. Willy, "Report: GameSpot Reviewer Gives *GTA V* a Generous Score, Readers Want Her Fired," *SystemWars Magazine*, September 16, 2013, https://systemwarsmonthly.wordpress.com/2013/09/16/report-gamespot-reviewer-gives-gta-v-a-generous-score-readers-want-her-fired.

20. Petit, "GameSpot Reviews."

21. "Is There a Worse Internet Blogger than Patricia Hernandez at *Kotaku*?" *IGN*, May 9, 2013, http://www.ign.com/boards/threads/is-there-a-worse-internet-blogger-than-patricia-hernandez-at-kotaku.453010535/.

22. "So Does Leigh Alexander Do Nothing but Criticize People?" *Giant Bomb*, 2012, http://www.giantbomb.com/forums/off-topic-31/so-does-leigh-alexander-do-nothing-but-criticize-p-537308/.

23. See Jenny Haniver, *Not in the Kitchen Anymore*, http://www.notinthekitchenanymore.com.

24. "About," *Fat, Ugly or Slutty*, http://fatuglyorslutty.com/about (accessed December 7, 2016).

25. See, for example, Kirk R. Williams and Nancy G. Guerra, "Prevalence and Predictors of Internet Bullying," *Journal of Adolescent Health* 41, no. 6 (2007): S14–S21; Julie Zhuo, "Where Anonymity Breeds Contempt," *New York Times*, November 30, 2010, p. A27; and *Penny Arcade*, "Green Blackboards (and Other Anomalies)," March 19, 2004, http://www.penny-arcade.com/comic/2004/03/19/.

26. @filamena, #1reasonwhy post, *Twitter*, November 26, 2012, 3:45 p.m., https://twitter.com/filamena.

27. Marc J. Natale, "The Effect of a Male-Oriented Computer Gaming Culture on Careers in the Computer Industry," *ACM SIGCAC Computers and Society* 32, no. 2 (2002): 24–31.

28. For more on booth babe controversies, see chapter 4.

29. Kate Cox, "Eurogamer Expo Begins Booth Babe Ban Next Fall," *Kotaku*, October 3, 2012, http://kotaku.com/5948759/eurogamer-expo-begins-booth-babe-ban-next-fall; Junglist, "So Why Were There Booth Babes at PAX Aus?" *Kotaku*, July 24, 2013, http://www.kotaku.com.au/2013/07/so-why-were-there-booth-babes-at-pax-aus/; Ben Kuchera, "Penny Arcade Expo Fans Come Out against Booth Babes," *Ars Technica*, June 7, 2010, http://arstechnica.com/gaming/2010/06/penny-arcade-expo-fans-come-out-against-booth-babes/.

30. "Fake geek girls" is a new construction that presupposes that all girls and women are not invested in the fan community and the objects of that community, in this case video games. Rather, these fake geek girls are only interested in going to these events to have access to the men who are in attendance.

31. Wesley Copeland, "Sexually Assaulting Women (Verbally or Otherwise) at Gaming Conventions Is Not OK," *Gameranx*, October 5, 2012, http://www.gameranx.com/features/id/9838/article/sexually-assaulting-women-at-gaming-conventions-is-not-ok/.

32. Tracy L. Dietz, "An Examination of Violence and Gender Role Portrayals in Video Games: Implications for Gender Socialization and Aggressive Behavior," *Sex Roles* 38, no. 5 (1998): 430.

33. Karen E. Dill, Brian P. Brown, and Michael A. Collins, "Effects of Exposure to Sex-Stereotyped Video Game Characters on Tolerance of Sexual Harassment," *Journal of Experimental Social Psychology* 44, no. 5 (2008): 1406.

34. Ibid.

35. Mike Krahulik and Jerry Holkins, "The Sixth Slave," *Penny Arcade*, August 11, 2010, http://www.penny-arcade.com/comic/2010/08/11.

36. See, for example, Rachel Edidin, "Why I'm Never Going Back to Penny Arcade Expo," *Wired*, September 5, 2013, http://www.wired.com/underwire/2013/09/penny-arcade-expo-dickwolves/; and Elizabeth Sampat, "Quit Fucking Going to PAX Already, What Is Wrong with You," http://elizabethsampat.com/quit-fucking-going-to-pax-already-what-is-wrong-with-you/ (accessed December 7, 2016).

37. See, for example, Christina Dunbar-Hester, "Geeks, Meta-Geeks, and Gender Trouble: Activism, Identity, and Low-power FM Radio," *Social Studies of Science* 38, no. 2 (2008): 201–232.

38. Ricard A. Lippa, *Gender, Nature, and Nurture* (Mahwah, NJ: Lawrence Erlbaum Associates, 2005).

39. Amy Grubb and Emily Turner, "Attribution of Blame in Rape Cases: A Review of the Impact of Rape Myth Acceptance, Gender Role Conformity and Substance Use on Victim Blaming," *Aggression and Violent Behavior* 17, no. 5 (2012): 449–450.

40. Jesse Fox, Jeremy N. Bailenson, and Liz Tricase, "The Embodiment of Sexualized Virtual Selves: The Proteus Effect and Experiences of Self-Objectification via Avatars," *Computers in Human Behavior* 29 (2013): 932.

41. Ibid., 935.

42. The quotation in this section's title comes from Fryda Wolff, #1reasonwhy post, *Twitter*, November 28, 2012, 3:20 p.m., https://twitter.com/FrydaWolff.

43. David Mullich, "Wanted: More Female Game Developers," *Gamasutra*, August 20, 2013, http://www.gamasutra.com/blogs/DavidMullich/20130820/198618/Wanted_More_Female_Game_Developers.php.

44. Gabrielle Toledano, "Women and Video Gaming's Dirty Little Secrets," *Forbes*, January 18, 2013, http://www.forbes.com/sites/forbeswomanfiles/2013/01/18/women-and-video-gamings-dirty-little-secrets/.

45. N, "Why Are Women Allowed to Play Video Games?" *Yahoo! Answers*, 2013, http://answers.yahoo.com/question/index?qid=20130630232317AAWsLFs.

46. See Alice Marie, "Really, the Oatmeal? REALLY?" *Geekquality*, April 18, 2012, http://www.geekquality.com/really-the-oatmeal-really.

47. TransformEnt, #1reasonwhy post, *Twitter*, November 27, 2012, 1:24 a.m., https://twitter.com/Transform_Ent.

48. Patrick Miller, "Industry in Flux: The 12th Annual *GD* Magazine Salary Survey," *Game Developer*, April 2013, pp. 015–021, http://twvideo01.ubm-us.net/o1/vault/GD_Mag_Archives/GDM_April_2013.pdf.

49. Anthea Smith, #1reasonwhy post, *Twitter*, November 27, 2012, 12:23 a.m., https://twitter.com/AntheaCreative.

50. Robin Potanin, "Forces in Play: The Business and Culture of Video Game Production," in *Fun and Games '10: Proceedings of the 3rd International Conference on Fun and Games* (New York: ACM Press, 2010), 135–143.

51. Whitney Hills, "Girls! Games! Onions!" *Dead Reckon* (blog), 2013, http://www.dead-reckon.com/post/60762312852/games-girls-onions.

52. Ciara Byrne, "The Loneliness of the Female Coder," *Fast Company*, September 11, 2013, http://www.fastcolabs.com/3008216/tracking/minding-gap-how-your-company-can-woo-female-coders.

53. Sylvia Ann Hewlett, Carolyn Buck Luce, Lisa J. Servon, Laura Sherbin, Peggy Shiller, Eytan Sosnovich, and Karen Sumberg, *The Athena Factor: Reversing the Brain Drain in Science, Engineering, and Technology* (Cambridge, MA: Harvard Business Review, 2008).

54. Martha R. Burt, "Cultural Myths and Supports for Rape," *Journal of Personality and Social Psychology* 38, no. 2 (1980): 229.

55. Brian Ashcraft, "Japanese Game Developer Apparently Harassed So Much, She Attempted Suicide," *Kotaku*, May 18, 2012, http://kotaku.com/5911353/japanese-game-developer-apparently-harassed-so-much-she-attempted-suicide.

56. In 2016, Nintendo employee Alison Rapp became a target and was bullied by Gamergaters or perhaps by a spin-off group called Revolt; members of these communities sent Nintendo messages, circulated personal defamation accusations online, and directly harassed her. She no longer works for Nintendo. See, for example, Patrick Klepek, "The Ugly New Front in the Neverending Video Game Culture War," *Kotaku*, March 4, 2016, http://kotaku.com/the-ugly-new-front-in-the-neverending-video-game-cultur-1762942381.

57. Byrne, "Loneliness of the Female Coder."

58. David Gaider, "The Female Perspective in Game Development," *Bittersweetest Thing*, 2013, http://the-gaider-archives.tumblr.com/post/108897777603/the-female-perspective-in-game-development.

59. Ibid. (emphasis in original).

60. Julie Prescott and Jan Bogg, "Segregation in a Male-Dominated Industry: Women Working in the Computer Games Industry," *International Journal of Gender, Science and Technology* 3, no. 1 (2011): 220.

61. Ibid.

62. The quotation in this section's title comes from @MissMeltdown, #1reasonwhy post, *Twitter*, October 21, 2013, 12:47 a.m., https://twitter.com/MissMeltdown_.

63. Theodor Adorno and Max Horkheimer, "The Culture Industry: Enlightenment as Mass Deception," in *Stardom and Celebrity: A Reader,* ed. Sean Redmond and Su Holmes (London: Sage, 2007), 34–43.

64. Haniver has noted this on her blog several times, and *Kotaku* picked up one of her stories in Jason Schreier, "Microsoft's Slow Response to Xbox Harassment Leaves One Woman Stunned," *Kotaku,* August 15, 2013, http://kotaku.com/microsofts-slow-response-to-xbox-harassment-leaves-one-1139807887.

65. E-mail interview by the authors, September 2013.

chapter four

ATTENTION WHORES AND UGLY NERDS

Gender and Cosplay at the Game Con

NINA B. HUNTEMANN

COSPLAY, A PORTMANTEAU OF "COSTUME" AND "PLAY," IS A POPULAR SOCIAL practice at fan conventions whereby attendees create costumes and role-play as characters from the fictional worlds of comic books, films, television shows, anime, manga, and video games. Cosplayers often attend entire conventions in costume and may also compete in organized costume contests. Costuming at fan conventions originated in 1939 at the first World Science Fiction Convention (WorldCon) held in New York City. Science fiction memorabilia collector and writer Forrest "Forry" Ackerman and his companion and fanzine editor Myrtle "Morojo" Douglas appeared at the convention wearing "futuristicostumes" designed and constructed by Douglas.[1] The number of participants wearing costumes to annual WorldCon events grew, and the practice soon spread to other fan gatherings. In the 1980s, costuming was widely adopted in Japan at conventions across multiple genres, and is particularly popular at doujinshi (self-published comics) events. The term "cosplay" is attributed to Japanese media producer Nobuyuki Takahashi, who attended WorldCon in Los Angeles in 1984. Upon his return, Takahashi praised the costumed fans he saw, calling them *kosupure* (コスプレ), in several of Japan's widely read science fiction magazines, popularizing the term and the practice among Japanese fans.[2]

Today, cosplay is not only a principal activity at fan conventions but has also become widely known in mainstream popular discourse, referenced in Hollywood films and television programs not necessarily related to cosplay or geek/nerd culture. These depictions of cosplay are often negative and, like portrayals of fandom in general, frequently characterize cosplayers as obsessed fans who cannot distinguish between fiction and reality. However, as sectors of so-called geek/nerd culture have proven lucrative for the entertainment industries—namely, comic book superhero movies and video game franchises—cosplay has received positive media coverage that does not frame cosplayers as deranged, deviant, or disaffected fans. One example of this representational shift worth mentioning is the docu-series *Heroes of Cosplay*, which first aired in August 2013 on the US cable channel Syfy. While the show adheres to the typical reality television formula, exaggerating the interpersonal drama between cast members and fabricating high-tension scenarios, the series also devotes a significant amount of screen time to the process of creating cosplay. Each episode showcases the skills, hours, and dedication required to design complicated costumes, to transport elaborate props to faraway conventions, and the courage required to walk on stage to be judged by fellow fans.

With this positive and increased attention to cosplay from the mainstream, there has been backlash from within geek/nerd culture. Comic book and video game spaces that otherwise welcome and celebrate expressions of fandom for these historically marginalized media forms have participated in the dismissive and abusive harassment of cosplayers—particularly female cosplayers—who identify as members of the same fan community. This chapter explores this backlash from within video game culture specifically, arguing that the harassment of cosplayers documented in the following sections reveals tensions in game culture that are a result of games moving from a male-dominated subculture to a mainstream media phenomenon. These tensions illustrate the gendered discourses that have undergirded video games for decades but are now faltering as the consumer base for games widens and online networks expand and fragment game communities. This chapter considers how women's bodies are used to, as Suzanne Scott notes, "maintain 'authenticity' and to socially police subcultural boundaries" in an attempt to reinstate male dominance in video games.[3]

Theorizing Cosplay

While scholarship about digital game culture is growing, research about game conventions, and cosplay and cosplayers specifically, is limited. There has been some ethnographic work about cosplay communities and attempts to theorize cosplay on various grounds. Often this scholarship is found in game studies, media studies, and fan studies where cosplay is regularly characterized as a participatory mode of fandom. For example, Theresa Winge's account of the origins and social practices of cosplay describes a cosplayer as "anyone who expresses his or her fandom and passion for a character by dressing and acting similarly to that character."[4] As such, Henry Jenkins's concept of participatory culture provides a useful framework for theorizing cosplay.[5] From this perspective, cosplay stands alongside fan practices like filking, fan fiction, and fan-made art as evidence of consumers "transform[ing] the experience of media consumption into the production of new texts, indeed of a new culture and a new community."[6]

Larissa Hjorth draws from Jenkins's participatory culture and Alvin Toffler's notion of "prosumer" (a portmanteau of "producer" and "consumer") in her exploration of Australian female cosplayers.[7] She writes about cosplay as one of the "emerging forms of creativity and expression within contemporary networked media," that "highlights that the boundaries between fans, players and creative producers are blurring and transforming mainstream culture."[8] She further suggests that engagement in cosplay provides a pathway from player to producer that may empower young women, in particular, to pursue careers in the male-dominated game industry.

In addition to Jenkins's participatory culture framework, cosplay has also been conceptualized in terms of Judith Butler's work on identity and gender performativity. Where Hjorth explores fan identity through cosplay in relation to the industry, Nicolle Lamerichs uses Butler to explore fan identity as a relationship between the fictional text and the fan body. She compares Butler's account of drag in *Gender Trouble* with the performative practices of cosplay.[9] Lamerichs writes, "Cosplayers use their bodies explicitly to display their affection for certain narratives" and that, like drag, "cosplay is not only a practice related to bodies and dress, but also an embodied practice. Both the dress and the body and behavior of the player are important."[10] Here, she is referring not only to the costume, makeup, and accessories that accompany cosplay but also the poses, posture, gestures, and other aesthetic aspects of the character that the cosplayer is attempting to mimic. However, authenticity for the cosplayers in Lamerichs's community is not defined by strict adherence to the fictional character. She reports that "most cosplayers do not wish to exactly duplicate the character they portray; rather, they want to bring something of their own, such as elements of their own appearance, into the cosplay."[11]

It is through the interplay of self and fiction that Lamerichs argues cosplay is transformative. It offers a mode of ludic identity construction similar to Butler's discussion of "iterability" in *Bodies That Matter*: "Identifications are never fully and finally made; they are incessantly reconstituted and, as such are subject to the volatile logic of iterability."[12] In these moments of iterability, Lamerichs finds the transformative potential of cosplay. She concludes, "Cosplay can be seen as an imitation or recitation that is based on a fiction that subjects explicitly enact. It is within these spaces between reality and fiction, and among these pluralities of meanings attached to a text, that subjects experiment with who they can be."[13]

The transformative potential of cosplay that Lamerichs outlines, or the self-empowered and professional potential of Hjorth's account, are significantly limited by the places where cosplay is performed—namely, the game or comic convention. When cosplayers are physically groped, verbally assaulted, or otherwise made to feel threatened while attending a convention, the magic circle of playful participation is broken and the mode of ludic identity construction perhaps offered by cosplay is shut down. These violations are not, as play metaphors might suggest, fleeting or trivial. To the contrary, the gendered harassment and ridicule documented in what follows is, in Butler's terms, an exclusionary force. It acts as a form of repudiation that signifies "that which is strictly foreclosed."[14]

To this end, I consider not only the practices of cosplay but also the politics of the space where cosplay is performed and, because cosplay is ultimately a performance meant for an audience, the actions and reactions of cosplay spectators both at conventions and online.

The Legacy of Morojo

Myrtle Rebecca Douglas, better known to the American midcentury science fiction fan community by her Esperanto name Morojo, is often remembered as Forry Ackerman's girlfriend and "feminine sidekick."[15] As previously mentioned, she was also the first female cosplayer. A year after she appeared with Ackerman in their "futuristicostumes" in New York, they attended the second WorldCon in Chicago in 1940. Ackerman reports that the pair donned their costumes again and "put on a skit based on some dialog from [the H. G. Wells's film] *Things to Come*, and won some kind of prize."[16] This account is the first record of a convention costume contest, which, along with the masquerade ball, has become the largest and most popular event during many contemporary fan conventions.

In most accounts of Forry and Morojo's cosplay, no mention is made of who created the costumes. But, following Douglas's death in 1964, Ackerman wrote in a remembrance, "She designed and executed the famous 'futuristicostume.'"[17] He also recalls Douglas's 1941 WorldCon "frog face" mask and 1946 "snake mother" costume, both of which were modeled after characters from author A. Merritt's fantasy novels. For his role in pioneering the practice of convention costumes, in 1994 Ackerman was named the "Father of Convention Costuming" by the International Costumers' Guild, but no recognition was awarded to Douglas.

As the history of WorldCon demonstrates, even though attendance was overwhelmingly male, especially in the early years, women have always been present at fan conventions, though often not acknowledged.[18] As the themes of fan conventions have expanded to include traditionally feminine genres, like romance, and as the female audience for science fiction, comic books, and video games has grown, the attendance of women at fan conventions has also increased. Comic-Con in San Diego, which attracted 130,000 attendees in 2013, claims that 40 percent of the registered ticket holders were female.[19]

Like other fan-oriented conventions, game conventions provide an opportunity for fans to share their admiration for games. While each convention varies, a common program includes keynote speeches, organized panels, game tournaments; an exposition area (expo) populated by game companies and their wares; free play areas for table-top, console, and PC games; music and comedic acts; merchandise booths; food courts; and masquerade and costume contests.

Even though female attendance at video game conventions has steadily increased, white male journalists, critics, game designers, and industry personnel continue to dominate the list of speakers, presenters, and expo floor representatives. More often than not, a panel that has a majority of women or people of color as panelists is dedicated to gender, race, or sexuality topics. For example, at PAX Prime in 2013 on the four panels that had "gender" in the title or abstract, fourteen of the twenty-five panelists were female-identified. This 56 percent majority female representation on gender-specific panels is far greater than the panel demographics for the entire convention, approximately 23 percent female panelists.

Outside of gender-specific panels, one place where women are in equal, if not larger, attendance than men is at cosplay events. For example, at BlizzCon in 2013, the panel "Epic Cosplay and You" was the only event at the convention with an all-female panel. At PAX East in 2013, a highly technical panel on curing chemicals for costume molds featured the all-female members of Cerberus Productions, a costuming company.

The significant presence of women in and at cosplay events during a convention reflects a widely accepted and often repeated assumption about this fan practice: most cosplayers are female. It is difficult to determine the veracity of this assumption since cosplay exists across multiple physical and digital locales (e.g., conventions, meet-ups, contests, social network sites, photo galleries, community forums), covers a wide range of genres and media, and is practiced in public and in private spaces. What is evident, however, is that within video game and comic book culture, women are more visible as active participants in cosplay than in any other fan practice. Furthermore, it is the visibility of women cosplayers, not male cosplayers, that has drawn attention, comment, and harassment from within geek/nerd culture and beyond.

Women report being drawn to cosplay, in part, because it is related to traditional feminine interests—namely, fashion, dress-up, and crafting. It is the convergence of these feminine domains with the male-dominated cultures of gaming, comic books, anime, and manga that makes the practice of cosplay a particularly rich place to explore how gender is articulated in popular culture, and how men and women negotiate conflicting gender expectations in these overlapping domains.

Cosplay Craft and Women's Work

The central activity that occupies a cosplayer between conventions is costume construction. Cosplayers who attend annual events report working on the next costume as soon as a convention ends, devoting hundreds of dollars and hundreds of hours to creating a new outfit.[20] This process involves deciding which character or characters to cosplay, researching how to best execute the costume, gathering materials, learning new crafting skills, constructing the costume, making alterations, and practicing the performance. For multiday events, cosplayers may prepare several costumes, one for each day of the convention.

The range of techniques employed for creating costumes varies widely. Depending on the needs of a particular costume and the aptitude of the creator, making a costume from scratch can require a broad range of skills such as working with adhesives, manipulating metal, shaping molds, jewelry making, woodworking, textile dyeing, beaded appliqué, and wig construction. Even a simple costume requires, at a minimum, sewing skills and often the application of face and body cosmetics—skills that are traditionally associated with feminine activities. Indeed, professional costume design for television and film production is a field traditionally dominated by women and the skills that define the work are associated with women's domestic activities—namely, sewing and shopping. Production studies scholar Miranda Banks writes that the gendering of costume design in Hollywood has contributed to the marginalization of women's below-the-line labor. Costume design is "underappreciated, undercompensated" and relatively invisible, in contrast to the male-dominated field of fashion design, which is elevated by its association with the visual arts and the upper class.[21]

In part, it is because costuming and crafting are associated with feminine activities that, in the traditionally male-dominated subcultures of comic books and video games, significant numbers of women in those subcultures cosplay. Cosplayers report coming to cosplay with some basic skills at costuming such as sewing and cosmetic application, which were acquired through non-fannish activities. Those who approach cosplay with no previous costuming skills report spending significant amounts of time learning new skills in order to express their fandom through cosplay. In either case, cosplayers describe mastering skills that are not directly related to consuming media as taking their engagement with a media text to a new level.

Following Jenkins and Hjorth, cosplayers are redefining what it means to be a fan, or in terms of video games, a gamer. We might see this activity as expanding fandom from industrially defined modes of media consumption and into fannish modes of media production—alongside practices such as writing fan fiction and creating fan art. In contrast to the marginalization of professional costume designers described by Banks, cosplayers and their skills are revered at fan conventions. Masquerade balls and costume contests are often the main or culminating event, and audiences for these events can be the largest of the convention. Because craftsmanship is a key judging category of a cosplay contest—along with characterization and stage performance—the skills associated with creating award-winning costumes are admired in the community and skill sharing is a main activity at conventions and between conventions, online.

Networking Cosplay

Communities of cosplay creators thrive in multiple spaces online, including YouTube, social network sites focused on do-it-yourself (DIY) culture, photography and art spaces like DeviantArt, discussion forums, blogs, Pinterest boards, and so on. There is an abundance of information about patterns, materials, costuming techniques, and tips on how to construct, wear, and perform specific characters. The DIY culture that populates a significant portion of online social communities like YouTube frequently overlaps with cosplay. As such, the content a cosplayer might reference for costume creation is cross-posted from theatrical, crafting, beauty, reenactment, and live action role-playing (LARPing) sites.

This highly networked configuration of cosplay-related information, communities, and social spaces makes it difficult to draw boundaries around what is part of a distinct cosplay community. However, it is clear from even a cursory search on YouTube, DeviantArt, Pinterest, and the hundreds of links on the popular cosplay site Cosplay Tutorial (cosplaytutorial.com), that the creators of both cosplay-specific content and cosplay-related content are overwhelmingly women. The significant presence of women in cosplay, both in the virtual networks of cosplay craft and at fan conventions, exists in stark contrast to the geek/nerd culture from which cosplay draws inspiration. Not only is video game content populated by far more male characters than female characters, fan communities and other game-related virtual spaces such as online game servers, blogs and message boards, and magazines and review sites, are overwhelmingly populated by men. Cosplay sutures game culture with craft culture, creating a space for participation that challenges the masculine gamer stereotype and recasts fandom through traditionally feminine activities. This form of participatory fan culture is not only on display for others to see but also constitutes a lot of convention attendees' conversations, photographs, interactions, and memories, and thus influences the game con experience for non-cosplay fans as well.

As one overhears cosplay conversations and witnesses group photos, the influence of cosplayers at the game con is unmistakable and, quite literally if you are standing in line among cosplayers, unavoidable. A fan that just plays games is confronted with an additional form of fandom that involves skills beyond mastery of a console controller. Women cosplayers report that when attending game cons not in costume, fellow conference goers often assume they are the nongame-playing significant other, sister, or friend of a male gamer. Once donning a game character costume, however, women report a noticeable difference in the reception of male attendees to their presence at game cons. They are taken more seriously as, or at least assumed to be, gamers themselves and not the reluctant girlfriend of a game-playing boyfriend. Because there is such an emphasis on knowing the character one cosplays, women (and men) can build legitimacy as fans and gamers through their public cosplay performance. As one young female cosplayer and PAX East attendee reports about her fellow convention goers: "I have to cosplay or wear something nerdy [e.g., a T-shirt with a video game reference]; otherwise no one will think I'm into it."[22] This display of legitimacy comes at a potential cost for this female gamer who noted that when she chooses not to cosplay, she avoids "the oglers" and potential harassers but also feels invisible.

Fake Gamer Girls

The increased presence of women at fan conventions, both as cosplayers and uncostumed attendees, has garnered attention from the mainstream and trade press, comic and video game publishers, and industry representatives. Since 2009, when the first *Twilight* film was promoted at San Diego Comic-Con, the phenomenon of more women at the convention and in geek/nerd culture has become a recurrent headline. However, the acceptance of female cosplayers at comic book and game cons is precarious. The persistent male-orientation of both of these media subcultures continues to insist that women do not belong.

The "fake geek girl" (also known as the "idiot nerd girl") meme that reached a peak of circulation in 2012 and 2013, exemplifies how women's playful participation in male-defined spaces is regulated and calls into question the legitimacy that female fans have gained. The fake geek girl is an image meme featuring a young woman wearing glasses with the word "nerd" written on her open palm. Above her head is a reference to geek/nerd culture, and below her torso is an incorrect, ignorant, or naïve statement about the above reference (e.g., "I love PC gaming" or "I play *Farmville* all day."). The meme is a comment on girls and women who pretend to know about geek/nerd culture to garner male attention. The discursive effect of the meme is to frame female participation in geek/nerd culture as always suspect.

The threat posed by women's encroachment into video games—as players, designers, and characters—has encouraged a suspicion that many female players are not real gamers and thus can be rightfully kicked out and dismissed. The "fake gamer girl" is a version of the fake geek/idiot nerd girl trope used to expose women who want the social acceptance and recognition that geek/nerd culture has finally garnered but who do not possess the credibility to claim membership in this community. On CNN's *Geek Out* blog, writer Joe Peacock describes the interloper as "an attention addict trying to satisfy her ego and feel pretty by infiltrating a community to seek the attention of guys she wouldn't give the time of day to on the street."[23] The fake geek/gamer girl concept became attached to cosplay when comic artist Tony Harris posted a tirade on Facebook in November 2012 exclaiming his exhaustion at "cosplay-chicks," who he asserts "don't know shit about comics, beyond whatever Google image search [they] did to get ref [reference] on the most mainstream character with the most revealing costume ever."[24]

Knowledge of comics (or games) is the currency required for entrance into geekdom, but in both Peacock's and Harris's rants about women who do not belong, they focus on the physical attractiveness of these possible fakes, suggesting that any pretty woman at a fan convention is probably faking it. The depth to which a female cosplayer knows the full backstory and every iteration of a character she chooses to cosplay is irrelevant to the power of the "fake" accusation. Her illegitimacy is determined by her gender, not the veracity of the claim. As such, rhetorically, "fake geek girl" applies to all women attendees at fan conventions, especially the attractive ones.

This focus on the body is key to understating the exclusionary force of the fake geek girl label, particularly as a method for regulating female participation in cosplay. Cosplay is an embodied practice requiring the manipulation of one's appearance to represent a fictional character. The demonstration of one's adoration for the character is literally worn on the body. The validation of one's adoration and commitment is achieved only when others behold the manipulation. Dressing to be looked at is the raison d'être of public cosplay events. Condemning female cosplayers for wanting to be looked at (attention whores) removes the spaces at conventions and online where women have gained significant visibility and recognition, both for their interest in geek/nerd culture and for their talents in costuming.

Attention Whores and Ugly Nerds

The characterization of female cosplayers as attention whores must be contextualized within the representational practices of the industries from which cosplay is largely drawn. There are far fewer female characters than male characters in video games and comic books. When present, the representation of the female body adheres to stereotypical images of idealized Western feminine beauty. Women are drawn and animated with long legs, large breasts, small waists; typically light skinned and dressed in clothing that draws attention to the bosom and rear end. The "revealing costumes" that Harris scolds female cosplayers for wearing are representative of the video game and comic book characters from which fans model their cosplay creations.

Because cosplay values authenticity as reflected in the accurate mimicry of the original text, body manipulation is a common aspect of costume creation: tinted contact lenses to change eye color, chest binding or padding to change bust size, corsets and body-shaping garments, hair dye, and temporary tattoos are among the techniques employed to look more like a character. The relationship between a cosplayer's physical features and the character she chooses to cosplay is a controversial topic within some cosplay communities. Strict constitutionalists argue that a cosplayer must consider her body as much a part of the costume as clothing and props. If a character does not wear glasses, a spectacled cosplayer is encouraged to use contact lenses. A more inclusive position supports cosplayers making the character their own by taking liberties with the original text when designing a costume.

One way female cosplayers respond to the lack of female avatar options in video games (and comics and anime/manga) is to crossplay a character. Crossplay is a form of cosplay whereby the performer either alters her appearance to match the gender of the character or changes the character to match her gender. For some cosplayers, feminizing, or fem-ing, characters is a purposefully subversive act aimed at highlighting the lack of female representation, while for others it simply opens the canon of characters from which women can cosplay.

Perhaps most controversial in the cosplay community is the issue of skin color: whether it is appropriate for pale-skinned people to darken their skin in order to cosplay, evoking the racist legacy of blackface. Likewise, lightening one's skin is often discussed as reverse racism. Black cosplayer Chaka Cumberbatch reported in *XOJane* that the advice most often given to people of color is to cosplay "within your range" meaning, keep close to your natural skin tone.[25] Given the representational practices of comic book and video games, which continue to marginalize characters of color, this advice creates a limited and racialized boundary around the characters that are available to nonwhite cosplayers. Since most female video game, comic book, and anime/manga characters are thin, cosplayers with larger physiques confront a body size boundary.

Cosplayers who cross these boundaries often become targets of public body shaming when their photos circulate online. When *League of Legends* (*LoL*) developer Riot Games attended PAX East in 2012, company representatives took photos of cosplayers posing in front of the *LoL* booth. These images were then posted to the *LoL* Facebook page, which has been "liked" by over nine million Facebook users. While most of the user comments were encouraging and complimentary, a common joke was to ask "who fed" the character of the cosplay. This comment is a play on the term "to feed" used in *LoL*, which refers to how players amass gold in the game by killing other players. A skilled player who has collected a lot of kills is recognized as "well fed." However, the term as applied to the photos posted on the *LoL* Facebook page referred to cosplayers whose bodies did not match the proportions of the fictional heroes (called champions) of the game. One of the cosplayers whose photo was ridiculed responded, posting to the official *LoL* online forums: "I'm a normal girl. Normal girls don't weigh 90 lbs and have abs of steel. THAT DOES NOT MEAN WE'RE FAT. Seriously, please GET REAL." She was then accused of being an attention whore for responding to the "fed" comments.[26]

Another internet meme used to socially police the boundaries of media subcultures and associated with the public ridicule of cosplayers is "cosplay fail." Online spaces at Tumblr, FAIL Blog, and Facebook feature cosplay photographs with captions and tags mocking the cosplayers. Common tags include cosplay fail, trying2hard, fat, fugly, 2much tit, and wheres ur tits. The images on these sites share a few characteristics: the targets of ridicule are overwhelming larger-sized cosplayers—particularly women who are wearing small costumes relative to their body size—and hefty, hairy men in crossplay. A comedy feature for the online game magazine *Heavy* exemplifies how cosplay fail censures participation: "The 20 Worst Cosplay Photos" with captions added to the images, such as "The pink wig really warms up your skin flabs" and "This girl looks like the Stay-Puff Marshmallow Man got in a car accident."[27] The effect of these comments is to shame cosplayers whose appearances do not conform to mainstream beauty norms for "having the audacity to go in public dressed as a sexy video game character."[28] The debate within cosplay about playing to one's body type becomes a hostile repudiation of nonconforming (ugly nerd) bodies.

As images of cosplayers' bodies circulate from cosplay communities to wider fans' spaces online, the discourses that accompany these digital artifacts demonstrate little tolerance for physical deviation, even by "normal girls." Furthermore, female cosplayers who publicly defend their fan practice and challenge media representations are scorned. "Attention whore" is a gendered insult that specifically regulates the visibility of women and girls in geek/nerd culture.

Taken together, "attention whore" and "ugly nerd" demonstrate the double bind that censures women from participating in game culture. Conventionally attractive women whose bodies most closely resemble the bodies of video game characters may meet the industry's beauty norms, but because they are attractive, they are suspected of faking their fandom. Women whose bodies do not measure up are rejected regardless of their knowledge or devotion to games. The two rhetorics of authenticity and conformity make it possible to attack almost any woman cosplaying, thus creating a potentially hostile environment for all female cosplayers.

Professionalizing Cosplay

The pejorative "attention whore" must also be contextualized within the controversial marketing practice of using promotional models to sell merchandise at a convention. A promotional model—known colloquially as the booth babe—is hired to stand at product booths in the expo hall and encourage face-to-face interaction with convention attendees. Posing for photos with promotional models is a common scene on the expo floor, and images of booth babes are among the most popular stories that emerge from convention coverage, particularly on game press and industry blogs. However, the practice is widely criticized as sexist, inappropriate, and pandering to a fanboy stereotype that the industry is trying to shed. Some fan conventions have banned the presence of paid promotional models from product booths, but the legacy of booth babes persists.

In 2010, PAX banned booth babes from the expo floor, making the distinction that company representatives had to be "educated about the product" and dress professionally.[29] The policy, which emphasizes the value that fans place on cultural knowledge, has been popular with convention attendees and industry spokespeople. However, the policies—both formal and informal—about promotional models at trade shows and game conventions have exceptions for costumed representatives. If the model is dressed as a character from the promoted game or modeled in some way after the game, the ban may not apply. This gray area was illustrated at PAX East in 2012, when cosplayer Jessica Nigri was asked to leave the convention floor or change her *Lollipop Chainsaw* (2012, Grasshopper Manufacture) costume.

Nigri is a New Zealand–born gamer, comic book fan, and cosplayer. She vaulted to cosplay fame when she attended San Diego Comic-Con in 2009 dressed as the popular Pokémon character Pikachu. At PAX East, Nigri was employed by Warner Bros. to cosplay as Juliet Starling, the lead character from *Lollipop Chainsaw,* and entertain attendees at the game booth. She was asked by PAX East officials to change her outfit, cover more skin, or leave the booth area. She put on a black sweatshirt and continued to work the booth. The difficulty with the PAX booth babe ban is that the majority of female video game characters are dressed (or, more accurately, not dressed) in a manner that would violate policies banning revealing clothing. Furthermore, the dress code does not apply to nonprofessional cosplayers who are often wearing far less than paid promotional models.

The difference between a costumed promotional model or paid cosplayer and the uncompensated fan cosplayer is indiscernible to convention attendees and online audiences. This is evident in trade press and fan photo galleries of conventions that make little to no attempt to accurately identify costumed attendees as promotional models or fans. As a result of this conflation, the contempt for promotional models and the crass commercialism they signify in game culture engulfs the cosplayer, who is often called a booth babe regardless of her relationship to the media text. However, the distinction is critical to female cosplayers who are not ignorant interlopers but have long been members and care deeply about the culture. Like the accusation of being a fake geek girl, the spectacle of the booth babe undermines the legitimacy of the cosplayer. As described by one game convention veteran:

> I'm not a booth babe! Just because I'm pretty or whatever and wearing a costume here doesn't mean I don't know about games. I do, and I could kick their asses. But so many guys assume I don't. Why? Because I have boobs?[30]

The move by publishers to use cosplayers as brand ambassadors recognizes the value these fans offer the media industries. The industrial incorporation of cosplay serves the video game and comic book industry by providing links to communities that are not only highly engaged with media consumption but also represent market segments previously ignored or undervalued. When game developer Red 5 Studios hired well-known cosplayer Crystal Graziano to portray female protagonist Mourningstar from its forthcoming game *Firefall*, a company press release affirmed the importance of its creative fans:

> Developers should embrace these individuals because they add so much to the universe, both in-game and out. This [cosplay sponsorship] program is our way of showing appreciation and support for what they contribute to the game and community.[31]

During production for the highly anticipated sequel *BioShock Infinite* (2013), Irrational Games enlisted Russian cosplayer Anna Moleva to portray female protagonist Elizabeth on the game box and in television ads. A company press release boasted, "We love our *BioShock* cosplayers so much we hired one!"[32]

Hiring cosplayers to embody video game characters at promotional events and in advertisements is a shift from an established practice of using professional models and actresses that was common in the late 1990s and early 2000s. Perhaps the most famous video game character to come to life was Lara Croft from the *Tomb Raider* series. The first model to portray Croft in 1997 was Nathalie Cook, who was followed by eight additional representatives until game developer Crystal Dynamics discontinued the use of professional models in 2008. Like Croft, the protagonists highlighted by the game industry to be represented by cosplaying fans have been female characters. Male characters, which significantly outnumber female characters in video games, are rarely given live bodies. In *BioShock Infinite,* Elizabeth is a secondary NPC who follows Booker DeWitt, the central playable protagonist. However, Irrational did not search for a real-life Booker to accompany cosplayer Moleva.

On the one hand, after decades of male-centric games and marketing campaigns, the industry has started to recognize its female fans, disrupting the privileged position of the fanboy or so-called hard-core gamer. By hiring well-known and respected female cosplayers, companies like Irrational acknowledge the community's disdain for promotional models and spotlight the fandom of women and girl gamers. On the other hand, given the legacy of the booth babe and the history of objectification of women in the media, using female cosplayers as brand ambassadors also reestablishes the male gaze. The invitation to transform her playful participation into a professionalized performance (whether financially compensated or rewarded with privileged access) exchanges the cosplayer's material labor as a designer/creator for aesthetic labor as a live action model. She no longer dresses herself or creates her costumes; the publisher provides these items. Like the booth babe, she fulfills a promotional role for which her passion and knowledge of games legitimizes her presence, but her value to convention attendees, online audiences, and the company ultimately resides in how she looks.

CONsent

The issue of convention harassment experienced by costumed and uncostumed female attendees at fan conventions began drawing increased attention in 2012. Incidents at Readercon, New York Comic Con, PAX East, DragonCon, and GenCon, among others, reached online news sites from *Jezebel* and *The Mary Sue* to *Wired* and *Think Progress.* The reports of harassment varied from sexual comments and verbal insults to uninvited touching and stalking behavior. Female cosplayers describe being questioned by fellow attendees about whether their breasts are real and asked, "can I touch them?" as proof. Women have also reported finding "upskirt" pictures taken of them while walking up stairs or escalators at conventions. As a result of the public accounts of harassment, several convention organizations updated or established antiharassment policies that defined harassing behavior and the consequences to offenders. In July 2013, when well-known American science fiction writer John Scalzi posted on his popular blog *Whatever* that he would not accept invitations to attend any convention that did not have a publicly posted harassment policy, over seven hundred people—including writers, publishers, editors, and convention staff—cosigned his statement.

In addition to organizational changes, a public education campaign called CONsent: The Importance of Treating Cosplayers with Respect was started by Sushi Killer, a writer for the geek culture website *16-bit Sirens.* Killer attended Wondercon in Anaheim, California, in March 2013 and requested that costumed attendees have their picture taken with a sign that read "Cosplay ≠ Consent." The photos were posted on Facebook, Tumblr, and on *16-Bit Sirens,* and gained further visibility via collaborative news blogs like *Metafilter*.[33] The effect of the CONsent campaign on the behavior of attendees at a convention is difficult to measure. Nevertheless, the campaign continues to be used as an effective discursive challenge to assumptions like those held by Harris and Peacock about a cosplayer's desire for attention, particularly sexual attention. The Cosplay ≠ Consent sign asserts that the cosplayer's body is her own, declares that dressing to be looked at does not permit the one looking any additional interaction.

Of course, the exclusionary forces previously described persist at fan conventions and online, pushing back against gains made by new and growing audiences for media subculture texts. Two months after starting the CONsent project, Killer stated that, while the campaign "opened up the community to a dialogue about how to handle" harassment of cosplayers, the photos were a limited intervention. She writes on *16-bit Sirens*, "I now feel the responsibility to move onto the next step, which is less about awareness and more about prevention."[34]

The following comments in a *Kotaku* article about cosplay harassment summarize the tensions occurring, as the audience for games broadens, between enduring assumptions about male-dominated game culture and a redefinition of what it means to participate in game culture. This first comment rationalizes the privileged male consumer and reinforces the male gaze, highlighting industrial practices that for decades have supported the exclusion of women from gaming:

> Most girls DO fake it. Video games and comics are mediums dominated by men. Women play casual games like the Facebook ones, but AAA games are mostly for men, and I have yet to see this proven otherwise. We get so many models that are hired to promote stuff at conventions, what else are we supposed to assume when we see women prancing around in almost nothing? . . . I think most women do this to get attention from lonely nerds. Sure, there are some women that truly like comics and video games, but they're in the vast minority.[35]

The second comment denies the male gaze and privileges making over consuming as evidence of participation in game culture: "Fun fact: hot girls can get guy attention by putting on normal clothes and showing up at a bar, versus spending weeks hot-gluing and hand-sewing and then paying for a three-day pass + hotel room."[36]

For players repeatedly marginalized by game culture, having an alternative path to gaming is often the difference between public participation in game culture and playing alone. Despite the persistence of harassment, through cosplay women (and men) have been able to leverage traditional feminine domains of crafting and costuming in order to gain legitimacy and increase visibility in the male-dominated domains of fan conventions and game culture. More than simply a presence, however, as cosplay has moved into the mainstream, a disruptive discourse has emerged that challenges the exclusionary forces that have long policed the corners of geek/nerd culture, particularly video games and comic books. Outspoken and high-profile female cosplayers have been at the forefront of exposing convention harassment perpetrated by male convention goers, journalists, and industry representatives. Their public testimony and organized actions have provoked members of the industry to respond to criticism about sexism in video game culture. Repudiation is slowly losing ground to greater inclusion as cosplayers change the discourse about who belongs in the gaming community and who the true fans of media texts really are.

NINA B. HUNTEMANN is Director of Academics and Research at edX, an online learning destination and nonprofit Massive Open Online Course (MOOC) provider, and Codirector of Women in Games Boston. She is coeditor of *Joystick Soldiers: The Politics of Play in Military Video Games* and *Gaming Globally: Production, Play and Place.*

Notes

1. Forrest J. Ackerman, "I Remember Morojo," in *Myrtle Rebecca Douglas: An Appreciation*, ed. Elmer Perdue (Los Angeles, 1965), http://efanzines.com/Morojo/Morojo-AnAppreciation-1965.pdf.
2. While named after costume events witnessed in the United States, cosplay has been a more widely adopted and mainstream practice of game and manga culture in Japan. It is worth noting, however, that the events described in this chapter are based on ethnographic reports and interviews at conventions in the United States. As such, this analysis of cosplay is limited to the US context.
3. Suzanne Scott, "Fangirls in Refrigerators: The Politics of (In)Visibility in Comic Book Culture," *Transformative Works and Cultures* 12 (2013), http://journal.transformativeworks.org/index.php/twc /article/view/460/384.
4. Theresa Winge, "Costuming the Imagination: Origins of Anime and Manga Cosplay," *Mechademia* 1 (2006): 68.
5. Henry Jenkins, *Textual Poachers: Television Fans and Participatory Culture* (New York: Routledge, 1992); Henry Jenkins, *Convergence Culture: Where Old and New Media Collide* (New York: New York University Press, 2006).
6. Jenkins, *Textual Poachers*, 46.
7. See Alvin Toffler, *The Third Wave: The Classic Study of Tomorrow* (New York: Bantam, 1980).
8. Larissa Hjorth, "Game Girl: Re-imagining Japanese Gender and Gaming via Melbourne Female Cosplayers," *Intersections: Gender and Sexuality in Asia and the Pacific*, no. 20 (2009): para. 17, para. 15, http://intersections.anu.edu.au/issue20/hjorth.htm.
9. See Judith Butler, *Gender Trouble: Feminism and the Subversion of Identity* (New York: Routledge, 1990).
10. Nicolle Lamerichs, "Stranger than Fiction: Fan Identity in Cosplay," *Transformative Works and Cultures* 7 (2011), http://journal.transformativeworks.org/index.php/twc/article/view/246/230.
11. Ibid.
12. Judith Butler, *Bodies That Matter: On the Discursive Limits of "Sex"* (New York: Routledge, 1993), 105.
13. Lamerichs, "Stranger than Fiction."
14. Butler, *Bodies That Matter*, 188.
15. Frederik Pohl, *The Way the Future Was: A Memoir* (New York: Ballantine, 1978).

16. Ackerman, "I Remember Morojo."

17. Ibid.

18. Dave Kyle, "Sex in Fandom," *Mimosa* 10 (1991), http://www.jophan.org/mimosa/m10/kyle.htm.

19. Toni Fitzgerald, "A Media Buyer's Guide to Comic-Con," *Medialife Magazine*, July 12, 2013, http://www.medialifemagazine.com/a-media-buyers-guide-to-comic-con/.

20. Robin S. Rosenberg and Andrea M. Letamendi, "Expressions of Fandom: Findings from a Psychological Survey of Cosplay and Costume Wear," *Intensities: The Journal of Cult Media* 5 (Spring–Summer 2013), http://intensitiescultmedia.files.wordpress.com/2013/07/expressions-of-fandom-findings-from-a-psychological-survey-of-cosplay-and-costume-wear-robin-s-rosenberg-and-andrea-m-letamendi.pdf.

21. Miranda J. Banks, "Gender Below-the-Line: Defining Feminist Production Studies," in *Production Studies: Cultural Studies of Media Industries*, ed. Vicki Mayer, Miranda J. Banks, and John T. Caldwell (New York: Routledge, 2009), 87–98.

22. PAX East attendee "Jessica," interview by the author, March 22, 2013.

23. Joe Peacock, "Booth Babes Need Not Apply," *Geek Out!* (blog), July 24, 2012, http://geekout.blogs.cnn.com/2012/07/24/booth-babes-need-not-apply.

24. Aja Romano, "Sexist Rants against 'Fake Geek Girls' Hit New Low," *Daily Dot*, November 13, 2012, http://www.dailydot.com/news/tony-harris-peacock-fake-geek-girls-cosplayers.

25. Chaka Cumberbatch, "I'm a Black Female Cosplayer and Some People Hate It," *XOJane*, February 4, 2013, http://www.xojane.com/issues/mad-back-cosplayer-chaka-cumberbatch.

26. ButterflyKisses1, comment in "'FED NIDALEE' srsly just read this" thread, *League of Legends General Discussion Forum*, April 10, 2012, http://forums.na.leagueoflegends.com/board/showthread.php?p=23052933.

27. K. Thor Jensen, "The 20 Worst Cosplay Photos," *Heavy*, March 24, 2010, http://heavy.com/comedy/2010/03/the-20-worst-cosplay-photos/.

28. Caitlin Seida, "My Embarrassing Picture Went Viral," *Salon*, October 2, 2013, http://www.salon.com/2013/10/02/my_embarrassing_picture_went_viral/.

29. Ben Kuchera, "Penny Arcade Expo Fans Come Out against Booth Babes," *Ars Technica*, June 7, 2010, http://arstechnica.com/gaming/2010/06/penny-arcade-expo-fans-come-out-against-booth-babes/.

30. PAX East attendee "Katie," interview by the author, March 22, 2013.

31. Red 5 Studios, "Red 5 Studios Launches Cosplay Sponsorship Program," December 15, 2011, http://www.red5studios.com/2011/12/red-5-studios-launches-cosplay-sponsorship-program/.

32. Irrational Games, "We Love Our *BioShock* Cosplayers So Much We Hired One!" *Insider*, December 2, 2012, http://irrationalgames.com/insider/we-love-our-bioshock-cosplayers-so-much-we-hired-one/.

33. Sushi Killer, "The Beginnings of CONsent," *16-bit Sirens*, April 3, 2013, previously available at http://www.16bitsirens.com/consent.

34. Sushi Killer, "The End of CONsent and The Next Step," *16-bit Sirens*, May 30, 2013, previously available at http://www.16bitsirens.com/consentnext/.

35. MrVince, January 11, 2013, 11:39 a.m. and 12:10 p.m., comments on Patricia Hernandez, "Cosplayers Are Passionate, Talented Folks, but There's a Darker Side to This Community, Too," *Kotaku*, January 11, 2013, http://kotaku.com/5975038/cosplayers-are-passionate-talented-folks-but-theres-a-darker-side-to-this-community-too.

36. Queen of the Imps, January 11, 2013, 12:39 p.m., comment on Hernandez, "Cosplayers Are Passionate, Talented Folks."

chapter five

VIDEO GAME PARODIES

Appropriating Video Games to Criticize Gender Norms

GABRIELLE TRÉPANIER-JOBIN

OVER THE PAST FEW YEARS, GAME SCHOLARS HAVE SHOWN THAT GENDER norms are embedded into video games' stories, design, and codes.[1] Narratives of platform video games often mirror the conventional division of roles between the sexes, and avatars' bodies in role-playing games frequently conform to Western beauty standards. Most video games can therefore be considered as "technologies of gender," which contribute to reproducing, reinforcing, and naturalizing pre-existing beliefs about men and women.[2] Like any other media form, video games play an important role in the construction of gender identities, which are not—according to a constructivist approach—bound to biological features, but socially established through the repetition of similar behaviors, bodily practices, and discourses.[3]

Many players have found creative strategies for overcoming the limited affordances of video games such as hacking their codes or using them in unexpected ways.[4] One of the most promising, but hazardous, ways to increase our agency regarding video games' stereotypes is the production of a video game parody—the term "parody" referring to a comical, ironic, or critical reworking of media material that is generating difference rather than similarity with the use of techniques such as exaggeration, inversion, literalization, extraneous inclusion, and misdirection.[5] However, it would be naïve to believe that all parodies are equally subversive.

In this chapter, I explore the avenues opened up by video game parodies and see how comical imitations and transformations of video games' narratives, design, and characters can call their gender stereotypes into question. I also make clear the limitations of parodies as subversive tools and identify what elements can theoretically compromise their disruptive potential. To do so, I conduct qualitative content analyses of two emblematic examples: the regressive damsel in distress trope in the *Super Mario* core series (1985–2015, Nintendo) and its animation parodies, as well as the sexy Blood Elf avatars in *World of Warcraft* (2004–2016, Blizzard Entertainment) and their machinima parodies (animated films produced in real-time with video game engines).[6] These analyses show how parodic techniques can be used to deconstruct video game stereotypes and how machinima can serve as an empowering tool for those who do not have the technical skills or the financial resources to create an animated film. As I make clear, however, the subversive potential of most video game parodies that can be found on YouTube remains underrealized. What is sorely needed are animation films in which parodic techniques are mobilized in service of a feminist agenda, and in which different strategies are used to clarify their underlying criticism.

Debates around the Subversive Potential of Parody

The subversive potential of parody is an important subject of debate among literature and media theorists. Some believe that parody is childish buffoonery (Carrière), a powerless genre (Sartres) that reinforces what it pretends to overcome (Barthes), a parasitic type of discourse (Madière) based on intellectual property burglary (Voltaire), or an elitist type of discourse whose underlying message remains inaccessible to most audiences. Other theorists consider that parody plays an important role in the modernization of genre conventions (Tomashevsky, Bakhtin), in raising consciousness on the constructed nature of fiction (Rose, Hannosh), and in criticizing stereotypes inherent to some representations (Hutcheon).[7] According to Dan Harries, modern parodies are, however, losing their subversive dimension and evolving toward a standardized form of entertainment that can be considered a "conservative transgression."[8] For my part, I agree with Linda Hutcheon that parody has always been a fundamentally ambivalent form, and its critical potential has always varied from one production to another, depending on whether the parody attacks the ideologies of its target or only mocks its superficial elements.[9] There is an important difference between a sexist parody and parody of sexism, even if each targets a sexist game. While the former trivializes gender issues, the latter disrupts the status quo and undermines backward ideas about men and women. Humor can serve as a vehicle through which gender inequality is maintained and established when jokes serve as a pretext to repeat sexist representations, but humor can also function as a powerful tool for breaking down deeply rooted preconceptions of men and women when it is carefully used.[10]

Because parodies can lead to misunderstandings when their target is not identified or when their irony is not perceived, using them as a means to criticize gender stereotypes and to raise consciousness is always a risky undertaking. Some elements, however, theoretically minimize the risks of confusion such as explicit interpretative clues, direct criticisms, and reflexive devices that raise awareness of the media-making process (mise en abyme, actor's gaze into the camera, display of the filming device, direct address to the viewer, etc.).[11]

The Regressive Damsel in Distress Trope in the *Super Mario* Core Series

First released in 1985 by Nintendo, the platform video game *Super Mario Bros.* revolves around the kidnapping of Princess Peach by a turtle-like monster, Bowser, who wishes to conquer the Mushroom Kingdom. A pudgy Italian plumber named Mario has to pass multiple levels connected by enormous pipes and defeat Bowser in order to rescue this non-playable female character and to save the kingdom.[12] As Nina B. Huntemann and Anita Sarkeesian each point out, this princess-rescue plot device perpetuates the old stereotype of a helpless, passive, and gorgeous damsel in distress saved from a perilous situation by a masculine hero.[13] This millennia-old archetype can be traced back to ancient Greek legends such as Andromeda's, as well as to seventeenth- and eighteenth-century folktales such as *Snow White, Sleeping Beauty,* and *Cinderella,* which were adapted for the screen by Walt Disney during the twentieth century. As with Disney's animated princess movies, *Super Mario* games perpetuate a timeless representation of women that is "detached from social progress" and anachronistically bound to the patriarchal, male-dominated system.[14] Like most of Disney's princesses, who are reduced to "helpless ornaments in need of protection," Peach appears as a weak and passive victim who is waiting for a man to change her situation.[15] Just like the princess figure mentioned by Teresa de Lauretis, she is featured "in someone else's story" instead of being the heroine of her own adventure; she is reduced to a marker of "positions—places and topoi—through which the hero and his story move to their destination."[16] Princess Peach plays a minor role in *Super Mario Bros.* and ultimately serves as a motivation for the hero to accomplish his quest and for the player to complete the game. She is absent from most of the narrative but reappears in the final scene to serve as a reward for the hero who completed his mission and for the players who finished the game.[17]

For all these reasons, *Super Mario* games reinforce the reductionist conception of women as vulnerable and fragile beings who are incapable of engineering their own destiny, in addition to sending the underlying message that women are more desirable when they are dependent and powerless.[18] The fact that Princess Peach is kidnapped and rescued by men who wish to conquer or save the Mushroom Kingdom also perpetuates the old conception of women as spoils of war and as men's properties that can be exchanged in order to cement or break alliances. According to Luce Irigaray, the patriarchy is based on a trading system where men play the role of traders and women, the role of merchandise.[19] As objects of transaction between men, women's value relies on their beauty and on their reproductive capacity but also—most importantly—on men's specific needs and desires. Within this trading system, women are therefore dispossessed of their own bodies, deprived of their specific value, and reduced to objects of competition that circulate from one man to another. As Huntemann explains, the fact that Princess

Peach kisses and hugs Mario at the end of *Super Mario Bros.* sends the underlying message that women are "indebted to the heroes who rescue them."[20] Because of her ability to bear children, the princess also represents the future of the kingdom, the source of life, continuity, and order for her community.[21] Even though she is not a mother yet, Princess Peach is associated with domesticity and maternity. For all these reasons, *Super Mario* games strengthen the active-passive, subject-object, and nature-culture dichotomies on which the traditional distinctions between men and women rely.

Even though the damsel in distress trope has been an important target of feminist criticism for the past two decades, the portrait of the princess in the *Super Mario* series became more stereotypical over time.[22] In *Super Mario Bros. 3* (1988), Peach is depicted as less dependent and subordinate than in subsequent versions of the game. Indeed, she has the temerity to joke after Mario went through a long and perilous journey to save her: "Thank you. But our princess is in another castle! . . . Just kidding, ha, ha, ha!" Moreover, there is no clear indication that Mario and the princess will ultimately form a couple and no physical contact between them that suggests the necessity for a rescued woman to make her body available to her savior. During the 1990s, *Super Mario* games put more emphasis on Peach's distress, gratitude, or alignment with domesticity. In the final stage of *Super Mario World* (1990), for instance, the princess calls for help, falls from Bowser's vessel when he is defeated by Mario, and rewards her savior with a kiss on his cheek, before heart-shaped fireworks explode over their heads to symbolize their upcoming union. The end of the game therefore suggests that a woman must give herself to her rescuer as a rightful compensation and reinforces the archaic conception of women as spoils of war. At the beginning of the twenty-first century, Princess Peach, more than ever, was depicted as an object of exchange between male opponents. In *Super Mario Galaxy* (2007), Bowser Junior tells Mario, "Looking for Princess Peach? Too bad! Cause she's with me!" before Bowser adds, "I'll rule a great galactic empire with Peach by my side." In *Super Mario Galaxy 2* (2010), Bowser even holds Peach in his enormous hands—while she is begging Mario to help her—and declares, "Maybe I'll have Peach bake me something for once." During the final stage, Peach is imprisoned in a bubble, which literally appears like a ball that two men are trying to rip from each other's arms. These scenes highlight Peach's status as a rivalry-fueling object rather than a character with her own agency.

At the end of *Super Mario 64* (1996), Princess Peach kisses Mario to express her gratitude, announces that she will bake a cake for him, and enters the castle. Just like Snow White, who cleans the house and cooks meals for her seven male dwarf companions, Princess Peach appears as a natural-born happy homemaker. Because she is confined to a domestic space and associated with the activity of baking, the game implies that women's place is at home and reaffirms the conventional division of roles between the sexes. In her book *The Feminine Mystique*, published in 1963, Betty Friedan explains that media discourses consolidate the false conception that all women are naturally fulfilled as housewives and mothers, especially women's magazines in which topics are narrowed to cosmetics, furniture, and motherhood.[23] Half a century later, video games like *Super Mario Bros.* are playing a similar role.

The success of this princess-rescue formula established the standard for the game industry and the damsel in distress became one of the most extensively used stereotypes in video games.[24] According to Sarkeesian, the reiteration of this trope ad nauseam works to "normalize extremely toxic, patronizing, and paternalistic attitudes about women." In addition to reinforcing the false belief that women are biologically weaker than men, it gives credit to the idea that men necessarily have to be brave when faced with a tragedy and need to protect women in order to carry out their "natural" duty.[25]

Underrealized Critiques in *Super Mario* Animated Parodies

As a result of their stereotypical and anachronistic nature, Princess Peach and the damsel in distress trope make easy targets for parodies. Produced with the help of sprites and modeling software, the animated shorts "Princess Peach and Daisy vs. Michael Jackson" (2008, anonymous), "The Roast of Mario" (2010, College Humor), and "Mario and Princess Sex Tape" (2009, College Humor) comically revisit *Super Mario*'s story line and representations of women. Each of these parodies has its own way of breaking down the damsel in distress pattern, but not all of them are equally fighting gender disparity, empowering the princess figure, and introducing meaningful changes that move the damsel character beyond the stereotype.

The animation "Princess Peach and Daisy vs. Michael Jackson" re-creates the environment of early *Super Mario* games but twists the story line, adds new characters (Princess Daisy, Michael Jackson, Mario's and Luigi's babies), and integrates additional elements into the design (speech bubbles, firearms, etc.).[26] At the beginning of the video, Princesses Peach and Daisy are strolling with their babies when Michael Jackson suddenly distracts them with his fancy dance moves and kidnaps their children. The princesses decide to take matters into their own hands for a change and to save the day without the help of Mario. As they enter the first level of *Super Mario Bros. 3* and meet an angry Goomba, Daisy proudly crushes it by imitating Mario's move. Convinced that Mario's technique takes too long, Peach retrieves a pair of huge guns that will allow them to accomplish their quest faster. After she makes a noteworthy entrance in slow motion to the beat of hip-hop music and easily disposes of Mario's enemies with her weapons, she tells an astonished Daisy that she has learned to protect herself as a result of being kidnapped all the time. The princesses then find a clever shortcut to Michael Jackson's castle—navigating the game's map much more efficiently than Mario is able to—and Peach surprises the kidnapper by crashing through the window, pulling out a huge bazooka, opening fire on his minions, and flying toward him, à la *The Matrix* (figure 5.1). When Michael knocks Peach out with his flying hat, Daisy takes over and fights him in one-on-one combat.

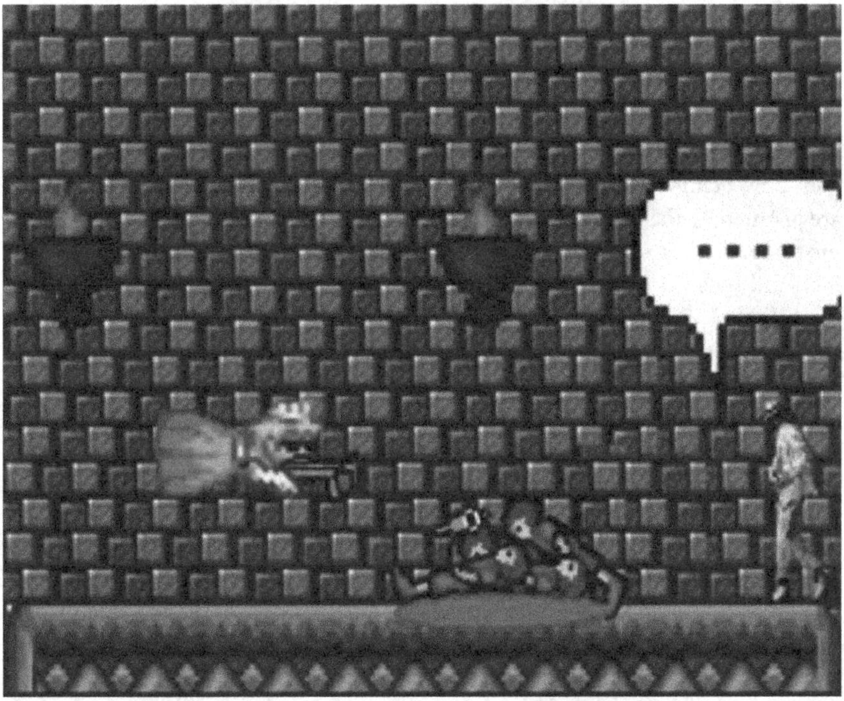

Figure 5.1. "Princess Peach and Daisy vs. Michael Jackson" (anonymous)

To this point, Princesses Peach and Daisy appear smarter and more efficient than *Super Mario*'s legendary Italian hero. The parody empowers the female characters by implicitly mocking Mario's methods of heroism and his obedient adherence to the game map's pathway. Because the damsels are the stars of the story instead of being the goals of a male protagonist, and because they are using their intelligence and strength to orchestrate the rescue of their loved ones, the parody subverts the traditional narrative expectations and offers a refreshing departure from the usual damsel in distress formula. This funny reversal of the princess rescue plot, coupled with the exaggeration of the damsels' combat skills and weaponry, deconstructs the idea that women are by nature weaker than men and puts into question their need to be sheltered. Instead of confining the princesses within the castle boundaries and reducing them to household functions, the parody relocates them outside of the domestic space, into the battle zone, and gives an absurdist overview of what they could accomplish if only they were given the opportunity to be playable characters. The parody therefore suggests that Princesses Peach and Daisy could be something other than inefficient damsels in distress whose existences are in suspension until Mario's arrival. By showing that Peach and Daisy can be the architects of their own destiny and that they can enjoy fighting villains, the parody overthrows the subject-object and the active-passive binary oppositions on which the conventional differentiation between men and women is based. The parody also introduces several moments of friendship and mutual assistance between women that are rarely displayed in the media.

However, this parody fails to fully dissociate the princess figure from her alleged nurturing instinct, because Peach and Daisy's quest revolves around the rescue of their children. Their courage and their willingness to fight villains violently are justified by their role as sacrificial mothers who are naturally devoted to their offspring. The parody's finale also reestablishes the traditional hierarchy between men and women, insofar as Mario barges in and saves the kids in a heartbeat. Nevertheless, Peach's frustrations regarding the fact that Mario ruined their moment of glory demonstrates that the traditional division of tasks does not rest on women's natural interests and competencies but is a socially constructed model imposed on women. In absence of clear guidelines for interpretation, the final intertitle—"Looks like Mario isn't getting lucky tonight ;)"—can either reinforce or challenge the idea of women's bodies as rightful compensations, depending on how it is interpreted by the viewer.

The short animation "The Roast of Mario" also muddies its criticism of the damsel in distress trope with its own instances of sexism. Reproducing the set of a television show roast, where the celebrated guest is mocked by friends and admirers in front of a live audience, this parody gives a voice to Princess Peach and allows her to complain about Mario instead of limiting her speech to begging for help or thanking him. While Mario is sitting on a throne, his opponents, allies, and competitors from other video games are invited one after the other to roast him. When Peach's turn comes, she confides to the crowd that Mario is far from being a perfect boyfriend: "The only way I can get his fat ass to save me is to say I baked him a cake. I don't even own a stove!" (figure 5.2).

Figure 5.2. "The Roast of Mario" (College Humor)

This comic allusion to Princess Peach's old-fashioned statements from *Super Mario 64* underlines the absurdity of depicting her as a homemaker in a game marketed to societies where women massively joined the labor force decades ago.[27] During her speech, Princess Peach also attacks Mario's sexual skills: "In bed, let's just say it's like someone's holding the B button the entire time. . . . Mostly, I'm jealous of world 3-1. At least, it's got something going into its pipes."[28] With these comments, the parody can subvert the players' assumption about the virility of video game heroes, but it also risks reinforcing the received idea that men's sexual stamina and size are all that matters for women. Finally, this parody does not push its criticism of gender stereotypes far enough, insofar as it is built around several sexist and homophobic jokes, like labeling Princess Daisy as "easy" and poking fun at Link from *The Legend of Zelda* (1986, Nintendo) by depicting him as a gay elf. Therefore, this parody cannot be considered subversive in a straightforward way: it overthrows some presuppositions about gender, while it fortifies other stereotypes.

A third animated video, "Mario and Princess Sex Tape," falls into the same sexist trap, as it depicts a sexual encounter between Mario and Peach that ends in disappointment. The opening scene recreates the final battle of *Super Mario World* (1990, Nintendo) with notable differences. When Princess Peach falls from Bowser's vessel, she grabs the diminutive Mario in her arms and eagerly smothers him with kisses without concealing her sexual drive. She also questions his heroism and proves that she is not the gullible type by asking him if he took a shortcut in order to reach her. Instead of being a passive object of desire that is exchanged among men, Princess Peach commands Mario to "do" her, leads him to the bedroom, initiates intercourse, and decides on the position. Unable to perform the sexual act, Mario has to eat a Super Mushroom that doubles his size and strength. After twenty seconds of action, Mario stops moving, and Peach asks him in a judging tone, "Is that it?"—to which he replies, "Sorry, babe, but Mario always goes first!" Nine months later, Princess Peach surprisingly gives birth to a mini Yoshi. The astonished Mario then turns his head toward his dinosaur-like sidekick before Yoshi swallows him in a single bite.

This parody depicts Princess Peach as a subject of desire who is concerned about her pleasure and who is sexually active with several partners on her own terms. However, it does not entirely move her sexuality away from functioning as a reward, insofar as infusing Princess Peach with more sexual drive confirms her role as a source of sexual enjoyment for the male protagonist and for heterosexual male players. Like in "The Roast of Mario," the princess character remains centered around a sexual fantasy—even if this fantasy is comically undercut by the parodies. We could therefore ask ourselves whether these two parodies actually react against boredom with Peach as a worn-out and not-very-sexualized female game character instead of seeking to address gender inequality and sexism. By mocking Mario's sexual skills and performances, the video "Mario and Princess Sex Tape" also supports harmful ideas about men's sexuality.

Each *Super Mario* parody challenges some aspect of the damsel in distress stereotype—whether it is her victimization, her passivity, or her confinement to the domestic space—without being entirely progressive. They unveil the anachronistic nature of the damsel in distress and shatter regressive ideas about women by producing "difference at the heart of similarity," but also reinforce other sexist beliefs.[29] In many ways, these parodies (especially the latter two) appear as surface-level efforts to modernize the damsel in distress figure.

Avatars and Beauty Norms in *World of Warcraft*

Unlike platform video games such as *Super Mario Bros.*, massively multiplayer online role-playing games (MMORPGs) such as *World of Warcraft* (*WoW*) give the possibility of choosing the sex, race, and class of the avatars, as well as some of their features (hairstyle, face, and skin). This type of game also breaks away from the damsel in distress pattern by favoring cooperation and mutual support between the male and female avatars.[30] However, MMORPGs never fully escape the influence of gender norms and beauty standards.

WoW offers a wide range of avatars that do not seem to conform to beauty norms, such as Orcs, Trolls, Taurens, and Dwarves, but a closer look at their bodies reveals that all of them comply with prevailing models of femininity or masculinity. Indeed, every female avatar is characterized by her firm breasts, well-rounded buttocks, tiny waist, and hourglass shape, while every male avatar can be distinguished by his large shoulders, oversized muscles, flat buttocks, and V-shaped torso. Moreover, all male characters are considerably more corpulent than their female counterparts, as if corpulence necessarily conflicts with femininity.[31] The Blood Elves remain the most problematic avatars in *WoW* because of their Barbie- or Ken-like appearance, their unrealistic body shapes, and their sexy clothing (especially those featured in *WoW*'s advertisements). The waist of a female Blood Elf is approximately the size of her head, while the shoulder-to-waist ratio of a male Blood Elf is abnormally disproportionate. Moreover, the dances executed by male and female Blood Elves are more virile or sensual, respectively, compared to those performed by "uglier" avatars such as Dwarfs and Taurens. *WoW* therefore sends the underlying message that only muscular men can be masculine and only slim women can be sexy. A study conducted by researchers from Palo Alto Research Center reveals that Blood Elves feature among the most popular avatars in *WoW*, especially when a female avatar is chosen.[32] *WoW* also facilitates the proliferation of hypersexualized female avatars by allowing them to walk around in their underwear and to buy skimpy clothes that connote sexual availability. In that sense, *WoW* does not break free from a tendency observed in earlier video games such as *Tomb Raider* (1996, Eidos) and *Everquest* (1999, Sony Online Entertainment).[33]

Far from providing real alternatives to conventional models of femininity and masculinity, *WoW* maintains stereotypical conceptions of the ideal woman's and man's bodies. Since the character creation interface allows players neither to choose from a wide range of body types nor to modify the morphology of their avatar, one of the few ways to protest against these limitations is to use the game's engine as a filmmaking tool in order to produce machinima parodies.

Fragile Critiques of Sexualized Avatars in *World of Warcraft* Machinima Parodies

Since the production of machinima does not require highly specialized skills and big budgets, it provides a valuable alternative to the creation of animation with complex modeling systems such as those used to produce the *Super Mario* parodies discussed previously.[34] Because machinima films are bound to their host game's assets, they make it easier for audiences to recognize what work is being parodied and for the parodist to create intertextual references and inside jokes.[35] However, machinima's intimate connection with parodied video games can make it more difficult for the parodist to incorporate incongruous elements and to generate irony, in order to achieve critical distance. The addition of dialogue, music, or special effects therefore becomes necessary to move away from the pixels on the screen and from the precoded animations.[36] These elements allow machinimators to find the compromises between "conservative repetition" and "revolutionary difference" on which parodies are usually based.[37] Machinimators, however, need to use these elements carefully to criticize stereotypes instead of reinforcing them.

The machinima series *Among the Blood Elves* (2010–2011, Britty), created within the environment of *WoW*, uses dialogue, mise-en-scène, music, and visual effects to criticize the Blood Elves' appearance and, implicitly, the players who choose them as their avatars. Each film of the series starts with a warning that makes obvious the intention of the parodist: "The following video is anti-Blood Elf. Some content may not be suitable for Blood Elf fans." The story revolves around Britty, a female Draenei who tries to overcome her hatred of Blood Elves by infiltrating one of their most popular guilds for one week, while her adventures are being secretly filmed for the reality show *Planet Azeroth*. As the days go by, it becomes more evident that Blood Elves are superficial beings who give more credit to appearances than to fighting skills and who do not fit into the medieval war zone of *WoW*.

At the beginning of her adventure, Britty covers her face with an oversized Blood Elf mask and meets the guild members for the first time (figure 5.3). A bossy blonde in a sexy outfit named Lisa fails to notice Britty's impressive battle gear and complains that she is too "fat" to be their new recruit. A couple of days later, Britty observes the female Blood Elves in the powder room spending hours primping and beautifying themselves. When she tries to fit into their social grooming group by walking around in her underwear, she is swiftly kicked out because her "big ass" is making Lisa "feel claustrophobic." Britty's imitation of the female Blood Elves' bodily practices has the potential to denaturalize gender conventions by showing that girly behaviors rely on performances. Britty's oversized mask highlights the fact that, in a figurative way, every Blood Elf wears a mask and takes part in a big masquerade. As Judith Butler points out,

Figure 5.3. *Among the Blood Elves* (Britty)

> The parodic repetition of gender exposes as well the illusion of gender identity as an intractable depth and inner substance. As the effects of subtle and politically enforced performativity, gender is an "act," as it were, that is open to splittings, self-parody, self-criticism, and those hyperbolic exhibitions of "the natural" that, in their very exaggeration, reveal its fundamentally phantasmatic status.[38]

The constant use of incongruous expressions such as "fatty," "big ass," and "fat cow" to describe the female Draenei—who is slightly curvier than the female Blood Elf—highlights the reality that the media industry's obsession with thinness has spread to digital environments.

Like many parodies, *Among the Blood Elves* contains reflexive devices such as a film-within-a-film structure and open display of the camera. After spending days among Blood Elves, Britty becomes impatient to meet the guild leader and to combat enemies, but the guild members keep bringing her to insignificant events such as "Justin Beaver's album release party" or the production of a "poorly lip-synced music video with a background that does not change." These multiple references to media productions and to their creation process draw attention to their fictional aspect and highlight the fact that media representations are not perfect copies of reality. They serve as a reminder that Blood Elves' gestures and stylized bodies are not the reflection of women's and men's inner natures, but the result of choices made during *WoW*'s own production process, by game designers and in compliance with dominant gender conventions and beauty criteria. The allusion to the young pop music icon Justin Bieber—who is idolized by teenagers for his beauty—underlines the superficiality of Blood Elves and, indirectly, the superficiality of the players who choose them.

At the end of the week, Britty is glad that the Blood Elves are finally raiding but shocked by the fact that everybody is wearing sexy clothing instead of battle gear. She gets the chance to meet the guild leader, who makes a marvelous entrance to the beat of the song "You Are So Sexy," but she is quickly disappointed in him when he commands the guilders to take down the dragon with their sexiness and when he starts to choreograph the guild by calling out "sexy" moves in an effeminate tone. After being kicked out of the group because she cannot dance properly, Britty removes her mask, reveals her true identity, and tells the guild leader that he is "the biggest douchebag [she] ever met." Deeply insulted, the guild leader flies away on the back of his pink magical unicorn, while Lisa and Britty insult each other and fight violently. The guild leader's detailed description of the Blood Elves' dance moves emphasizes the absurdity of these preprogrammed gestures and their arbitrary connection with sexiness. The effeminate behavior of the guild leader deconstructs the idea that muscles always go hand in hand with virility, but this stereotypical depiction of homosexuality, used for humor, does not help to fight generalizations about the LGBT community. The fact that Britty defeats Lisa with "PMS power" also reinforces the regressive idea that women are excessively sensitive because of their biology. Finally, the fact that both female protagonists keep calling each other "bitch," "slut," and "whore" in derogatory ways does not counter traditional representations of women's relationships with each other, which generally revolve around jealousy or vengeance instead of mutual aid.[39]

Nevertheless, Britty's participation in a reality show opens the door to more explicit criticisms of the Blood Elves' shallowness. When Britty makes her daily report on the guilders, she mentions that Lisa "likes to flaunt" and to judge people based on their appearance.[40] She depicts Lisa's minions as puppets who do not think for themselves and who fail to know which class they belong to. Finally, she portrays Lance as a narcissistic guy who is "full of himself," who looks at his reflection in the mirror, kisses his biceps, and congratulates himself for being so "hot" and "epic." During her final report, Britty confides that her adventure made her "hate Blood Elves even more," and therefore encourages viewers to revise their own opinion on these avatars. Britty's direct addresses to the camera and straightforward critiques minimize the risks of misunderstanding the parody as a glorification of superficial behaviors and beauty standards. Compared to *Super Mario* parodies, *Among the Blood Elves* appears as a more fully realized attempt to fight gender norms and stereotypes with complex narratives, reflexive devices, warnings, and direct criticisms—despite its own reinforcement of regressive ideas about gender at some points in the series.

One could believe that machinima parodies like *Among the Blood Elves* have little visibility on the web, but the series reached more than seven hundred thousand viewers on YouTube. Other popular machinima mock the sexiness or the virility of *WoW*'s avatars. In the short "I'm Too Sexy" (Bionic), for instance, the images of a male human avatar showing off his disproportionate muscles are resonating with Right Said Fred's lyrics "I'm too sexy for my love. . . . I'm too sexy for my shirt"—and especially with the superlative "too sexy," which underlines his excess of maleness. In the machinima "Cloudangel as Barbie in *World of Warcraft*" (2008, Cod), the images of a female human avatar with ideal proportions, who is dancing everywhere in a bikini, are put in perspective with Aqua's lyrics "I'm a Barbie girl in the Barbie world / Life in plastic, it's fantastic"—and more specifically with the word "plastic," which highlights her artificiality. The images of the female avatar performing oral sex on a male avatar, coupled with the lyrics "You're my doll. . . . Kiss me here, touch me there, hanky-panky," also remind audiences that female avatars are often hypersexualized and considered as pleasant-looking objects. Finally, the lyrics "You can brush my hair, undress me everywhere. . . . Dress me up, take your time, I'm your dollie. . . . Make me walk, make me talk, do whatever you please" serve as a reminder that players are partly responsible for their avatar's alignment with or divergence from gender and beauty norms. But because these machinima do not directly signal their parodic nature or highlight their criticism as strongly as *Among the Blood Elves* does, they may be interpreted literally in a way that bolsters rather than challenges stereotypes.

The avatar body is a site of regulatory norms that can also become a site of resistance, with the help of parodies. Even if *WoW*'s avatars embody traditional gender norms and beauty criteria, machinima parodies are a relatively accessible way for players to reflect on their gaming practices and to express their opinions on video game stereotypes. Machinimators should, however, be careful to avoid building their stories around derogatory dialogues and homophobic stereotypes, while including interpretative clues, direct criticisms, and reflexive devices to make clear their critical intention.

Conclusion

The analyses conducted in this chapter demonstrate that video game parodies hold both promise and peril for criticizing gender representations. At once encouraging and disappointing, audacious and conformist, useful and harmful, most video game parodies contain elements that jeopardize their subversive function. While animated parodies are less accessible to creators than machinima parodies, they offer more freedom to depart from the original narrative or from the initial design of a game in order to make powerful criticisms. However, their potential to fully challenge stereotypes remains generally underrealized. The animated parodies of the *Super Mario* series, found on YouTube, overturn the princess rescue plot and move the damsel figure away from the "weak and in danger" type but undermine their potential critiques because of their sexist and conventional elements. The close binding of machinima parodies with their targets makes it easier for parodists to reproduce video game environments and create a strong reference to their target but also constrains the possibilities of modification and restricts the insertion of revolutionary differences. Even though *Among the Blood Elves* does not fully elude the pitfalls of sexism and homophobia, it succeeds in highlighting

Figure 5.4. "FREE SPEACH: A Second Life Machinima Parody" (Gabrielle Trépanier-Jobin and MIT Game Lab)

the superficiality of Blood Elf avatars with the help of clever dialogue and reflexive devices. Compared to other machinima parodies that lack guidelines for interpretation, *Among the Blood Elves* reduces the risks of misinterpretations by using warnings, reflexivity, and straightforward criticisms.

To realize their potential as subversive tools, video game parodies need to avoid sexist humor, to prevent reactionary interpretations, as well as to unmask gender stereotypes instead of trivializing them. This is the challenge that I tried to meet by creating the machinina parody FREE SPEACH (figure 5.4) with the collaboration of the MIT Game Lab and a team of MIT undergraduate students.[41] Even if the preliminary reception study conducted with the video shows that this kind of work has the potential to open people's eyes to stereotypical depictions in video games and make them realize that video games' narratives could be different, it also indicates that it is difficult to remain entertaining while addressing gender stereotypes more directly and earnestly. Most viewers who participated in the reception studies, however, agreed that parodies can be good vehicles for the criticism of stereotypical representations. The question therefore becomes: To what extent is it necessary to sacrifice the entertaining value of a parody in order to send a clear message against gender stereotypes?

GABRIELLE TRÉPANIER-JOBIN is Assistant Professor in the School of Media at Université du Québec à Montréal, working on game studies, gender studies, and media sociology. In collaboration with the MIT Game Lab, she created a machinima parody titled *FREE SPEACH*.

Notes

1. Adrienne Shaw, *Gaming at the Edge: Sexuality and Gender at the Margins of Gamer Culture* (Minneapolis: University of Minnesota Press, 2014); Sheri Graner Ray, *Gender Inclusive Game Design* (Hingham, MA: Charles River Media, 2004); Helen W. Kennedy, "Lara Croft: Feminist Icon or Cyberbimbo? On the Limits of Textual Analysis," *International Journal of Computer Game Research* 2, no. 2 (2002), http://www.gamestudies.org/0202/kennedy.

2. Teresa de Lauretis, *Technologies of Gender: Essays on Theory, Film, and Fiction* (Bloomington: Indiana University Press, 1987).

3. Judith Butler, *Gender Trouble* (New York: Routledge, 1990).

4. Mike Mika, for instance, hacked the game *Donkey Kong* so that his daughter could play with the female character Pauline and rescue Mario instead of the other way around. Mike Mika, "Why I Hacked *Donkey Kong* for My Daughter," *Wired*, March 11, 2013, http://www.wired.com/2013/03/donkey-kong-pauline-hack.

5. Linda Hutcheon, *A Theory of Parody: The Teachings of Twentieth-Century Art Forms* (1985; repr., New York: Methuen, 2000), xii; Dan Harries, *Film Parody* (London: British Film Institute, 2000).

6. Matt Kelland, "From Game Mod to Low-Budget Film: The Evolution of Machinima," in *The Machinima Reader*, ed. Henry Lowood and Michael Nitsche (Cambridge, MA: MIT Press, 2011), 24.

7. Daniel Sangsue, *La Parodie* (Paris: Hachette, 1994).

8. Harries, *Film Parody*, 130.

9. Hutcheon, *Theory of Parody*, 60.

10. Anita Sarkeesian, "Damsel in Distress (Part 3): Tropes vs Women in Video Games," *Feminist Frequency*, August 1, 2013, https://feministfrequency.com/2013/08/01/damsel-in-distress-part-3-tropes-vs-women/.

11. Michele Hannosh, "The Reflexive Function of Parody," *Comparative Literature* 41, no. 2 (1989): 113–127.

12. Peach is a playable character in some video games of the *Super Mario* franchise but remains an NPC in most platform games of the core series. Even though her role expanded in games such as *Super Mario RPG* (1996) and *Super Princess Peach* (2005), her magical powers and her skills remained bounded to stereotypical feminine traits.

13. Nina B. Huntemann, "Pixel Pinups: Images of Women in Video Games," in *Race/Gender/Media: Considering Diversity across Audiences, Content, and Producers*, ed. Rebecca Ann Lind, 2nd ed. (Boston: Pearson, 2010), 250–257; Anita Sarkeesian, "Damsel in Distress (Part 1): Tropes vs Women in Video Games," *Feminist Frequency*, March 7, 2013, https://feministfrequency.com/2013/03/07/damsel-in-distress-part-1/.

14. Rebecca-Anne C. Do Rozario, "The Princess and the Magic Kingdom: Beyond Nostalgia, the Function of the Disney Princess," *Women's Studies in Communication* 27, no. 1 (2004): 36.

15. Jack Zipes, quoted in Ashlee Hynes, "Raising Princesses? Gender Socialisation in Early Childhood and the Disney Princess Franchise," *Critical Social Thinking: Policy and Practice* 2 (2010): 210.

16. Teresa de Lauretis, *Alice Doesn't: Feminism, Semiotics, Cinema* (Bloomington: Indiana University Press: 1984), 109.

17. Huntemann, "Pixel Pinups"; Sarkeesian, "Damsel in Distress (Part 1)."

18. Huntemann, "Pixel Pinups"; Anita Sarkeesian, "Damsel in Distress (Part 2): Tropes vs Women in Video Games," *Feminist Frequency*, May 28, 2013, https://feministfrequency.com/2013/05/28/damsel-in-distress-part-2-tropes-vs-women/.

19. Luce Irigaray, *Ce sexe qui n'en est pas un* (Paris: Éditions de Minuit, 1977), 167–185.

20. Huntemann, "Pixel Pinups," 253.

21. Do Rozario, "The Princess and the Magic Kingdom," 51.

22. Ray, *Gender Inclusive Game Design*.

23. Betty Friedan, *The Feminine Mystique* (New York: W. W. Norton, 2013).

24. Yi Mou and Wei Peng, "Gender and Racial Stereotypes in Popular Video Games," in *Handbook of Research on Effective Electronic Gaming in Education*, ed. Richard Ferdig (Hershey, PA: IGI Global, 2009), 922–937.

25. Sarkeesian, "Damsel in Distress (Part 1)."

26. The Michael Jackson character comes from the video game *Michael Jackson's Moonwalker* (1990, Emerald Software and Keypunch Software).

27. It would have been more subversive to hear her say, "I don't like cooking," questioning the so-called natural division of tasks more powerfully.

28. Holding the B button puts Mario in run mode.

29. Hutcheon, *Theory of Parody*, 8.

30. Sarkeesian, "Damsel in Distress (Part 2)."

31. Hilde G. Corneliussen, "*World of Warcraft* as a Playground for Feminism," in *Digital Culture, Play, and Identity: A "World of Warcraft" Reader*, ed. Hilde G. Corneliussen and Jill Walker Rettberg (Cambridge, MA: MIT Press, 2008), 63–86.

32. Nicolas Ducheneaut, Nick Yee, Eric Nickell, and Robert J. Moore, "Building an MMO with Mass Appeal: A Look at Gameplay in *World of Warcraft*," *Games and Culture* 1, no. 4 (2006): 281–317.

33. For more details, see Kennedy, "Lara Croft"; and T. L. Taylor, *Play between Worlds* (Cambridge, MA: MIT Press, 2006).

34. Kelland, "From Game Mod to Low-Budget Film," 24.

35. Jeffrey Bardzell, "Machinimatic Realism: Capturing and Presenting the 'Real World' of Video Games," in *The Machinima Reader*, ed. Henry Lowood and Micheal Nitsche (Cambridge, MA: MIT Press, 2011), 195.

36. Henry Lowood, "Video Capture: Machinima, Documentation, and the History of Virtual Worlds," in *The Machinima Reader*, ed. Henry Lowood and Michael Nitsche (Cambridge, MA: MIT Press, 2011), 16.

37. Hutcheon, *Theory of Parody*, 77.

38. Butler, *Gender Trouble*, 187.

39. Luce Irigaray, *Éthique de la différence sexuelle* (Paris: Éditions de Minuit, 1984), 106.

40. Her description of Lisa as an "Alpha female" reminds the audience that women can also dominate and therefore blurs the division of characteristics between the sexes.

41. Gabrielle Trépanier-Jobin and MIT Game Lab, "FREE SPEACH—a Second Life Machinima Parody," *YouTube*, July 27, 2015, https://www.youtube.com/watch?v=jKKcAJo6Fik.

Part II

RACE, IDENTITY, NATION

chapter six

DYSTOPIAN BLACKNESS AND THE LIMITS OF RACIAL EMPATHY IN *THE WALKING DEAD* AND *THE LAST OF US*

TREAANDREA M. RUSSWORM

WHILE THE MAINSTREAM VIDEO GAME INDUSTRY HAS BEEN WIDELY criticized for failing to prioritize diverse representations in narrative games, words like "race," "diversity," and "inclusiveness" have been appearing more often as topics of discussion at industry conventions like the Game Developers Conference (GDC). In 2015, for instance, Derek Mann and Dennis Matthews led a series of sessions on black characters in video games, and just one year before, at GDC 2014, Bioware Montreal game developer Manveer Heir issued an impassioned challenge to the same audience of game industry insiders. In his lecture "Misogyny, Racism, and Homophobia: Where Do Video Games Stand?," which *PC Gamer* called "the most important moment of GDC," Heir provocatively admitted during the talk that, "yes, we have a major representation problem."[1] Heir went on to argue that video game developers need to resist "the sales fallacy," the industry-held assumption that games with nuanced diverse representations will not sell. He told the crowd that solving "the representation problem," breaking away from white masculinity as a character norm, "starts with us, the developers, and it starts with us pushing back against our colleagues when they disagree with [the] race, gender, sexual orientation, and other non-typical characteristics of our characters." He further challenged, "I want us as an industry to stop being so scared."

Released in the years preceding Heir's talk, *The Walking Dead: Season One* (2012–2013, Telltale Games; *TWD*) and Naughty Dog's *The Last of Us* (2013; *TLoU*) seemed to anticipate and perhaps even facilitate some of the mounting public discourse around diverse representations of race in narrative games. Because both games appear to be progressive when it comes to the gaming industry's problems with representation and both games are depressively dystopian in terms of mood, setting, and plot, when examined together these games also invite questions about how dystopian tropes and storytelling conventions might uniquely inform wider conversations about gaming and inclusiveness. We might ask, for example, how central are "identity politics" to digital simulations of the end-times—and how does blackness function ideologically in such contexts?

Although there are many ways to approach the topic of racial representation in video games, the dystopian frame is a particularly compelling point of interest because of how common dystopian conventions are for the medium as a whole. Given the historical significance of blackness as an overdetermined signifier for abject suffering and dogged survival during bleak social and political times, this chapter examines the possibilities and limitations of representing black identity within a typical dystopian project. In the first part of the chapter, I contextualize the broader cultural interest in dystopian themes and explore what dystopian games like *TLoU* have in common with classic films like *Night of the Living Dead* (1968, Romero). Alongside this examination of how dystopian films and other media have represented black characters since the 1960s, I offer some guidelines for how writers and game designers might create what I theorize as a critical racial dystopia: a type of dystopian narrative that maintains a dialogic, progressive, and highly reflexive relationship to historical tropes of blackness. The second part of the chapter more closely examines how aspects of *TWD*'s game design, like the use of noninteractive cutscenes, work with and against historical representations of sacrificial and empathetic black characters in ways that create an ambivalent blend of utopian hope and dystopian dread.

Diverse Dystopias: Not All Bites Are Created Equal

But what makes a world dystopian in the first place, and what might it mean that the video game industry has become so heavily saturated with dystopian tales? The main stories in *TWD* and *TLoU* take place in environments that appear unequivocally worse than the present reality, feature zombie apocalypse scenarios, and generally represent the degradation of humanity. These elements place the games in proximity to a long narrative tradition of dystopian and anti-utopian writing, from George Orwell's *1984* to Alan Moore's *V for Vendetta*. In preceding art forms like literature, film, television, and comic books, dystopias have most typically appeared, as Tom Moylan defines in *Scraps of the Untainted Sky: Science Fiction, Utopia, Dystopia*, as

> [the narrative] ability to register the impact of an unseen and unexamined social system on the everyday lives of everyday people. Again and again, the dystopian text opens in the midst of a social "elsewhere" that appears to be far worse than any in the "real" world. As the mise-en-scène is established in an exponential

presentation of the society's structure and operation, the narrative zooms in on one of the subjects of the terrible place.[2]

If for Moylan and others the 1990s represented a decisive dystopian turn in Western narrative culture, video games like *TWD* and *TLoU* have replicated the success and popularity of dystopian storytelling so much so that we might easily argue that dystopias have functioned as a zeitgeist for the medium on the whole. The number of narrative games that invite players to explore fantastic terrible places as a part of their modus is compelling, and there are now video games that represent nearly every dystopian flavor and subgenre imaginable—from dystopias of catastrophic contingency and dystopias of authoritarian repression to nihilistic and critical dystopias.[3]

Entire video game franchises—many of them quite central to the medium's success—have perfected the virtual representation of disaster scenarios as a part of *Fallout* (1997–2010, Bethesda), *Half-Life* (1998–2004, Valve), *Deus Ex* (2000–2013, Ion Storm), *Mass Effect* (2007–2012, Bioware), *BioShock* (2007–2013, Irrational Games), *Crysis* (2007–2013, Crytek), and *Borderlands* (2009–2014, Gearbox Software). In addition to heavily influencing the production of mainstream video game franchises, dystopian world design has also become a defining feature of some notable nontraditional art games, independent games, and games featuring female protagonists, particularly *Papers, Please* (2013, Lucas Pope), *Nothing to Hide* (2014, NCase), the *Portal* series (2007–2011, Valve), and *Mirror's Edge* (2008, Digital Illusions CE). Any decline in, or cessation of, the current production cycle of digitally rendering dark times seems unlikely since the archive of such games developed for the current systems, next-gen consoles, and PCs only continues to grow with the steady production of a new wave of popular dystopian titles, including *Skyrim* (2011, Bethesda), *I Am Alive* (2012, Ubisoft), *Dishonored* (2012, Arkane Studios), *Day Z* (2013, Bohemia Interactive), *Watch Dogs* (2014, Ubisoft), *Resogun* (2014, Housemarque), *Middle-earth: Shadow of Mordor* (2014, Monolith Productions), and *Dying Light* (2015, Techland), to name a few.

With the exception of Marcus Schulzke's essay "The Critical Power of Virtual Dystopias," and a few blog posts and top ten lists, little has been written about the prevalence of dystopias in video game culture or about how games function similarly to and differently from other apocalyptically themed content.[4] In distinguishing his assessment of dystopian games from Raffaella Baccolini and Moylan's establishing, literary definitions of "critical dystopias" as narratives that ultimately maintain a hopeful, utopian impulse as a part of a larger deconstructive ambition, Schulzke argues that dystopian video games that nullify hope altogether offer an even more powerful mode of societal critique precisely because games make players complicit in the bleak "underlying logic of how these worlds are created and sustained."[5] As such, Schulzke discusses the *Fallout* series as successfully critiquing nuclear proliferation and cold war ideologies, *BioShock* as an active, cautionary illustration of a fall from utopia to dystopia, and *Spec Ops: The*

Line (2012, Yager Development) as a purposeful criticism of militarization and the use of unmitigated force in the chronic state of national emergencies.

With Schulzke's redefinition of the critical dystopia in mind, we can say that there has indeed been great diversity in terms of the range of types of dystopian video games produced in recent years. Specifically, when it comes to racial representation, we can also note that some of the most racially diverse video games are also dystopian tales, including *Beyond Good and Evil* (2003, Ubisoft), *Prey* (2006, Human Head Studios), *Afro Samurai* (2009, Namco Bandai Games), *Half-Life* and *Half-Life 2*, the *Mass Effect* trilogy, *Resident Evil 5* (2009, Capcom), *Deus Ex: Human Revolution* (2011, Eidos), *Remember Me* (2013, Dontnod Entertainment), the *BioShock* trilogy, and *Infamous: Second Son* (2014, Sucker Punch). These racially diverse dystopias grandly visualize and correlate representations of difference with dystopian tropes of survival and resistance.

To argue that video games have gotten very good at simulating diverse disasters is not to suggest, however, that such works will veer toward radical social critique when it comes to race. Case in point: Naughty Dog's *The Last of Us*, a game that is about who survives—both physically and emotionally—when the world has gone to hell. As a popular and critically acclaimed dystopian game released exclusively for the PlayStation 3 (and remastered for the PlayStation 4), *TLoU*'s plot is strikingly similar to *The Walking Dead*'s: a fungal virus threatens humanity and the emotional bonds established between a white adult male (Joel) and a young girl (Ellie) offers a human relational model for cherishing empathy and intersubjectivity (the psychological relationship between people) as the world around them falls. With its inclusion of four secondary, black NPCs, who are all presented without a diegetic awareness of their racial and cultural backgrounds, *TLoU* most evidently satisfies an uncritical multiculturalist imperative to merely include diverse characterizations in game worlds. For instance, all four of the black characters die in the game's story (they are either bitten, commit suicide, or are murdered by Joel), and throughout the game blackness labors to shore up white character agency—that is, Ellie needs her black friend, Riley, to teach her how to be more confident, exploratory, and politically subversive.

The empathetic relationship between these two characters is constructed as essential for Ellie and as one that has uneven consequences for Riley. For example, the story in the game's expansion pack, *Left Behind*, constructs a sweet and tender interracial love story between Ellie and Riley (they kiss)—until, that is, both girls are bitten by a swarm of infected humans. In one shot from the prequel, both characters sit side by side to imagine humanity's bleak future, share secrets, and vow to die slowly but assuredly together. Despite this meaningful exchange, their mutual death pact, and strong interpersonal connectedness, only Riley eventually succumbs to the dehumanizing effects of the fatal bites. Ellie, in turn, learns from Riley's sacrificial death that she alone is immune to the virus that is devastating the planet and turning other humans into the infected. Similarly, in the game's main story, witnessing the graphic deaths of two other black characters (brothers Henry and Sam) teaches Ellie and Joel that their lives and their bond are all the more worth fighting for. Such representations of sacrificial blackness evoke the kind of emotional responsiveness that Linda Williams critiques in *Playing the Race Card* as a pathos of black suffering and that Lauren Berlant problematizes in her work on race and sentimentalism.[6]

The most significant black character in the main story of the game is Marlene, the leader of the Fireflies, an underground group resisting the government's harsh military rule. Marlene functions in *TLoU* as an important sign of liberation and resistance not only because she fights the proponents of a corporatized and militarized police state but also because she works with a group of scientists who are trying to discover a cure for the fungal virus. At the same time, Marlene is positioned as the game's central antagonist because she and the group of scientists want to use Ellie's brain to create a vaccine. Even though Ellie is more than willing to die for a cure, in the game's final scenes Joel murders Marlene while she begs for her life, saves Ellie from the scientists, and thereby refuses to sacrifice Ellie for the greater good of humanity (figure 6.1). While Riley's death taught Ellie that not all bites are created equal, Joel's actions demonstrate that the interpersonal project of building attachment and empathy between white characters must be protected and prioritized at all costs, even at the expense of finding a cure. The fact that all the black characters die in order to teach Ellie and Joel to value their relational bond begs questions about the true costs of so-called empathy. In sum, although *TLoU* includes representations of black characters who are not overtly stereotypical, blackness nonetheless functions unimaginatively and unprogressively in this dystopian narrative frame that is so primed for social and political commentary.

Figure 6.1. Sacrificial blackness (*The Last of Us* game still)

Toward a Theory of Critical Racial Dystopias

If we are to believe that dystopian games have an emergent and distinct potential for criticism, then it also matters whether the game worlds are as self-consciously aware of the ideologies they reproduce as they are of the ones they ostensibly set out to critique. To my mind, irrespective of the cultivation of hope within the narrative, the most instructive and applicable part of Baccolini and Moylan's definition of a critical dystopia to the study of video games has to do with a given text's overall penchant for a "postmodern attitude of self-reflexivity."[7] Baccolini and Moylan clarify:

> With an exploration of agency that is based in difference and multiplicity yet cannily reunited in an alliance politics that speaks back in a larger though diverse collective voice, the new dystopias not only critique the present triumphal system but also explore ways to transform it that go beyond the compromised left-centrist solutions. These texts, therefore, refresh the links between imagination and utopia and utopia and awareness in decidedly pessimistic times.[8]

For a dystopian video game to function critically around matters of identity and race, then, we should expect to see a presentation of character agency that is not only rooted in "difference and multiplicity" but also skillfully and carefully connected to a broader project, an "alliance politics," that self-reflexively and implicitly critiques the present system of social and political organization through its construction of a dark future or alternate reality. Creatively constituted, a work can contain that utopian impulse within the text—through plot, character growth, mise-en-scène, and so on—or it might maintain a transformative import and agenda outside the text if its reflexivity and intentionality enliven a discourse community around its clear points of critique. Thus, even if a dystopian game—finally!—signals an investment in the politics of representation by visually representing racial difference and employing people of color for voice acting and motion capture, as my reading of the black characters in *TLoU* indicates, that attempt alone does not qualify it for doing rich, deconstructive work.

Through a set of four criteria, I propose one model for doing this deconstructive work and building critical racial dystopias. This model is most productively established by placing *TLoU* on a narrative continuum of works that have also combined race and disaster, a continuum that includes George Romero's 1968 classic *Night of the Living Dead*.

The first and most obvious criterion to consider when envisioning the possibility of a critical racial dystopia is Baccolini and Moylan's stipulation about textual reflexivity and self-conscious critical awareness. Romero's film, the first to feature a black protagonist in the lead role of a (notoriously graphic) zombie apocalypse narrative, is often read as a dense—if unintentional—political allegory. The black character, Ben (Duane Jones), becomes the leader of an enclave of survivors who are trapped in a house on the fateful night of the zombie outbreak. One by one, each of the other survivors (who are all white) succumb to the swarm of zombies descending on the house. After triumphing in a violent physical contest with Harry, a white male patriarch who challenges Ben's leadership, Ben survives the fantastical encounter with both human adversaries and the undead by barricading himself in the basement overnight. At daybreak, a mob of white men mistake Ben for a zombie, shoot him in the head, and perfunctorily burn his corpse. The film's diegesis never once references Ben's race nor does the story directly represent any aspect of 1960s racial tensions. Unlike a dystopian film like *The Brother from Another Planet* (1984, John Sayles), which is more overt in its engagement with race and the history of black oppression, *Night of the Living Dead*'s story concentrates on the more general harms inherent in the survivors' breakdown of communication and failure to relate intersubjectively and empathically.[9]

Second, while Romero's zombie classic does not include a diegetically reflexive relationship to its era's racial politics, we can see in the film's reception a complementary component of a critical racial dystopia: the creation of an active discourse community around the text. That is, the fact that the film's story is neither reflexive nor direct in its representation of racial difference and racial politics has not stopped viewers from receiving it as a complex racial allegory. As media scholar Robin Means Coleman explains, despite the fact that "the filmmakers have been unwavering in their assertion that the casting of a Black actor was happenstance" and despite the fact that the filmmakers never intended any social critique of American race relations, 1960s audiences and contemporary scholars have always read Ben as a symbol of black agency and resistance.[10] The same audiences have interpreted the film's ending as a condemnation of white vigilante justice. Thus, particularly if a text represents blackness sans racial reflexivity within the text—by subscribing to a color-blind multiculturalism, for instance—the extent to which that work creates a discourse community that nonetheless discusses the social and political implications of those representations remains essential for distinguishing a critical racial dystopia from other dystopias.

Here, of course, is where *TLoU*'s black representations struggle the most. The game's ending where Joel refuses to let Ellie be used for the cure does indeed create a critical discourse community. That is, players and reviewers have discussed to no end the moral implications of Joel's decision. The game's mechanics further encourage this deliberation about Joel's decision by employing character perspective shifting, which requires players to play the last moments of the game as Ellie rather than Joel. After Joel saves Ellie from Marlene and the scientists, you are literally distant from him as you play the final seconds of the game as a dazed Ellie who follows Joel toward their bright dystopian future together. Yet the fact that Marlene's identity as a black woman does not ever come up in the countless online debates about Joel's decision is also significant in a game that pits Ellie's humanity and right to live against Marlene's. Any racial anxieties that inform both this dynamic and Joel's cold-blooded murder of Marlene, which motivates the game's emotional climax, are completely divorced from the discussions of Joel's decision to forgo a cure.[11]

Third, although pessimism and bleak endings have traditionally been associated with dystopian projects, the critical dystopia as Baccolini and Moylan define it, importantly resists a resignation to utter hopelessness by maintaining some kind of transcendent, and I would add corrective, proximity to progressive ideals that "resist both hegemonic and oppositional orthodoxies" as they imagine "a space for a new form of political opposition."[12] Thus, a critical racial dystopia would engage and reference contemporary race relations, cultural identities, or historical oppressions in a way that also imagines some path for change. With the end of the film's graphic annihilation of Ben as a symbol of black resistance, *Night of the Living Dead* evidently fails to capture this third component of a critical racial dystopia. In fact, many scholars read the film's political orientation as relentlessly nihilistic, or as Matt Becker puts it, the film reflects "an overriding political ambivalence that was intimately related to a shift in the hippie counterculture's worldview from broad optimism to a foreboding sense of failure and doom."[13] Although *Night of the Living Dead* does not maintain the same type of utopian/dystopian political impulse of a critical dystopia, it is certainly possible to imagine that even a nihilistic dystopia could nonetheless foster a sense of hopeful disruptiveness within its discourse community. Whether or not conversations about social critique, hope, and change occur diegetically, or extra- or paradiegetically, the work's political ambition with regard to racial representation would include at least the spirit of what Henry Giroux describes as "a language of critique and possibility" and "hope" that also casts "democracy as a site of intense struggle over matters of representation, participation, and shared power."[14]

The fourth component of a critical racial dystopia includes a reflexive awareness that popular dystopian films and television shows since *Night of the Living Dead* have continued to almost obligatorily include black characters. As Sean Brayton summarizes in his assessment of sci-fi narrative conventions, "from *2012* and *24* to *Children of Men* and *Battlestar Galactica*, the relationship between disaster, dystopia, and diversity is increasingly apparent in SF film and television, where the end of the world is imagined in relation to multiculturalism."[15] In this regard, we can think of any number of films and television shows, including *Star Trek* (1966–1969, NBC), *The Brother from Another Planet*, *Terminator 2* (1991, James Cameron), *The Matrix* trilogy (1999–2003, the Wachowskis), *28 Days Later* (2002, Danny Boyle), *Children of Men* (2006, Alfonso Cuarón), *District 9* (2009, Neill Blomkamp), *I Am Legend* (2007, Francis Lawrence), and *The Book of Eli* (2010, Hughes Brothers), as establishing some additional precedent for how blackness has functioned both allegorically and reflexively in dystopian worlds. In many of these story lines, the black characters are signs of hope, as they are in *The Matrix*, *Children of Men*, and *I Am Legend*. As signs of hope amidst despair, black filmic characters like Laurence Fishburne's Morpheus, Clare-Hope Ashiety's Kee, and Will Smith's Robert Neville often work to save humanity by building empathetic and intersubjective relationships with others while the apocalypse threatens to shatter the relational potential of humanity. Other times, however, as with the black scientist Miles Dyson in *Terminator 2*, popular dystopian story lines reflect grave ambivalence about black characters' agency in reconstituting humanity and instead frame black identity as complicit in the destruction of humankind. In these instances, black characters routinely die sacrificial and symbolic deaths either in facile attempts to save humanity or as just desserts for their redemptive failures.[16]

Of course, the way blackness has labored overdeterminedly in fictional dystopian worlds is further informed by how black and brown bodies have historically functioned as signs of abjection and exclusion, on the one hand, and as catalysts for tolerance and radical change, on the other. Cultural theorist Jayna Brown persuasively argues that "there are meanings historically bound to Black diasporan subjects that explain this. Slavery and colonization were post-apocalyptic, and Black people's existence across the globe continues as a condition of alienation."[17] With few exceptions, then, the narrative patterns established by sci-fi television and film have consistently offered a mixed bag of dread and hope for the racial other as black dystopian characters like the citizens of Zion in *The Matrix* films have appeared as symbols who absorb a competing mix of historical tropes of blackness. Cultural critic Adilifu Nama concurs, concluding that despite the appearance of inclusion and change that dystopian texts may have tried to signal, sci-fi media has too often faltered ideologically and critically by only superficially challenging "racially biased representations of Blacks and other people of color" in order to avoid "criticism for promoting a particular racial politics."[18]

Black video game characters like Riley and Marlene in *TLoU*, Jacob and his father in *Mass Effect 2*, Afro and Ninja Ninja in *Afro Samurai*, and Lee and Clementine in *TWD* did not evolve in a cultural vacuum. This preexisting history of representing race and disaster provides some context for understanding why minority characters have become so easily associated with end-time scenarios in games.[19] The expectation that video game writers and developers have some familiarity with this history, that game design should be a dialogic process (which Bakhtin defines as the "constant interaction between meanings") and not just a procedural or algorithmic process, serves as this fourth and final guideline for crafting critical racial dystopias in digital culture.[20] This place where racial difference and the grand narrative tropes of disaster converge is also where African American studies and film and media studies have something unique to offer game studies. That is, the fact that both this representational history of dystopian media and the scholarship and criticism on these works exist means that game developers and writers do not have to start from scratch when trying to create meaningful and progressive black characters. Rather, there is every invitation here to build on these precedents, as the lessons learned from both the representational failures and successes in other media can serve as instructive models of departure for new media representation.

The Walking Dead and Lee's Reflexive Black Paternity

Much more so than *TLoU,* Telltale's *TWD* realizes at least some of the potential for video games to create dialogically centered critical racial dystopias. While the comic book and television show both feature white police officer Rick Grimes as the lead character around whom a multiethnic band of survivors of the apocalypse rally, the first season of Telltale's game inverts the franchise's racial power dynamic by weaving the story and game's principal action around black college professor and father figure Lee Everett. This power inversion comes with built-in limitations, however, as when the game starts, Lee is on his way to prison for committing a crime of passion—murdering his wife's lover. One way Telltale supported its decision to centralize Lee's race and background was to hire accomplished black voice actor Dave Fennoy, who has explained that he tried to use his recording sessions to make Lee's speech and enunciation resemble more of his own middle-class dialect and sensibilities.[21] In addition to what Fennoy contributes to *TWD* as the central voice actor, the story diegesis references Lee's race both directly and indirectly. For example, early in the game we learn that Lee's past and present were informed by his proximity to a southern black professional class; his mother and father were pharmacists in Macon, and he taught as a history professor at the University of Georgia. Other characters, particularly white men, are competitively and sometimes inexplicably hostile to Lee, whom the game situates as a de facto leader of the survivor groups he encounters. At times, the game's dialogue reflects an irrefutable awareness of some of the post-civil-rights American anxieties surrounding black masculinity and black exceptionalism. For instance, Larry, a large and volatile white male adversary, hates Lee from the moment he meets him. And even though the reason Larry gives for not wanting Lee to be around him or his adult daughter is that he knows about Lee's past as a convicted murderer, Larry's interactions with Lee also seem fueled by a history of racial bias and conflict. It is the narrative awareness of this history that gives Lee, in episode 3, the dialogue option to both call Larry a racist and express his own discontent with having to interact with the character and his equally reactionary daughter.

Throughout *TWD,* Lee's most significant interracial interactions are with Kenny, another white male southerner who—like Joel in *TLoU*—becomes an embodiment of white male depressive rage and social dysphoria. As Fennoy reads him, Kenny is, in fact, "this kind of racist guy. But [Lee and Kenny] have to learn to work together, and they develop a real bond. It's a troubling bond, but that's the guy he can depend on."[22] As Fennoy indicates, one of the reasons Lee's interpersonal connection to Kenny is troubling is because Kenny often expresses resentment toward Lee's achievements as a black professional. Some of these exchanges with Kenny will vary depending on the choices the player makes in the timed dialogue interactions, like when in episode 3, in a moment of heated verbal contest, Kenny blurts out a disapproving comment about Lee's "fancy job" and elite education. In my play-through, a grieving and despondent Kenny physically attacks Lee, pummeling him in the face. In other play-throughs of this moment, Kenny is more restrained if Lee works hard to empathically coax him along. Other times, the exchanges between Lee and Kenny that reflect the game's critical dramatizations of racial bias occur regardless of the choices the player makes. One narrative cutscene in episode 2, just after Kenny mockingly calls Lee "professor," satirically conveys some of the game's critical awareness of US race relations:

KENNY: Hey, Lee, you know how to pick a lock, right?

LEE: No, why would you say that?

KENNY: Well, you're . . . you know . . . urban?

LEE: Oh, you are not saying what I think you're saying!

KENNY: Jesus, man, I'm from Florida. Crazy shit just comes out of my mouth sometimes. Sorry.

Kenny's comments that link southern white masculinity with Florida and "crazy shit" have particular social and political resonance in the wake of the murders of Trayvon Martin and Jordan Davis, young black men murdered in Florida just before and during the game's development and episodic release. Importantly, as this scene is noninteractive, the player does not have a chance to push the issue further and challenge the way Kenny equates blackness and criminality—especially since Lee's backstory has already cemented that association. Even when Lee and Kenny do have conflict, then, the game's story eschews diegetic opportunities for more pointed critique in order to keep the project of building empathy and solidarity between the two characters open.

At the same time, some of the game's key story decisions exacerbate the flawed tradition of conflating black identity with the pathos of sacrifice and suffering. If one of the most classic conventions of the dystopian text is confirming humanity through acts of empathetic bonding among groups of survivors when all else seems to have gone to hell, the first season of the game hardwires this theme around black subjectivity. While it has become an accurate critical assumption that *TWD* game is about empathy and emotional identification, most reviewers and critics stop short of connecting this project to Lee's race.[23] Only journalist Ryan Smith, in "Empathy Games," infers some of the political and ideological implications inherent in building empathy around and through a black character. Smith writes,

> Part of what makes *The Walking Dead* so brave is that Lee is an African-American man convicted of murder, a marginalized minority in our society. There is no one-armed man to manipulate our sympathies, and the writers don't let Lee off the hook for his crimes. He is unequivocally guilty of killing his wife's lover, and he's headed to prison. In our society, Lee would typically be seen as a "bad guy," the type of character we'd likely be shooting down without mercy in another video game.[24]

In Smith's estimation, the apocalypse and the situational traumas that Lee experiences are culminating narrative events that successfully humanize blackness. The story events transform Lee from what appeared to be an ordinary dehumanized black criminal at the start of the game into "a complex vessel we pour ourselves into" by game's end.[25] Smith's reading suggests that Lee's race could potentially mean "a lot" in this context, and he notes that the grand upswing for violent video games like this one is that such games "could actually be creating empathy in us instead of destroying it."[26] Rather than unnerving the supposition that blackness must be made redeemable in order to become empathetic, Smith embraces the popularly held view that creating empathetic blackness is always beneficial. Such an analysis takes for granted that cultivating empathy is a good thing, a necessarily vaunted psychosocial and cultural norm. As we have seen, however, across sci-fi media and other dystopian tales about blackness, stories that uncritically and obligatorily signal and represent racial empathy also often produce disastrous and uneven consequences for the black characters at the center, or on the margins, of those works.

To return to *TWD*'s plot and mechanics of choice, notwithstanding Lee's interactions with white survivors like Kenny and Larry, it is Lee's relationship with Clementine that most evinces the celebrated project of exploring or maintaining empathy between central characters—and the fact that these two characters are black also matters.[27] Through both what D. Harrell Fox calls the "frontend" (visual representation) and "backend" (code, stats, gamic system), Lee is programmed and designed to be an empathetic black father figure.[28] This means that even if the player tries to play Lee with an edge and make him mostly reject the many opportunities to express empathy toward others, Lee simply cannot act this way with Clementine: their non-player controlled interactions are sweet and tender, and despite the elements of player choice and direction that the game's interactive design offers, Lee will above all be a compassionate father figure to her. This default paternal behavior coheres mostly in the noninteractive cutscenes, which set the overall tone for their relationship. For example, in one scene, the two characters ride in the back of an RV; Clementine nestles snuggly against Lee's chest, and he drapes his arm around her protectively. As they talk, Lee shares with her several hard truths about humanity and their circumstances—for example, some of the survivors they have been traveling with are not trustworthy or ethical. While the scene's quick time events (QTEs) give the player interactive opportunities to shape some of the details of this conversation, the visual assets of the shot's mise-en-scène firmly fix the interpersonal and emotional contours of their time together. Regardless of player input in this scene, Lee will always physically hold and comfort Clementine as they talk, and the way the cutscene is edited will always alternate close-ups of the child's facial expressions of contentment and trust with the wider shots of the two of them in filial embrace. As Clementine drifts off to sleep, Lee will always look down at her with his brow furrowed with fatherly concern (figure 6.2).

Figure 6.2. Fixed fatherly concern (*The Walking Dead* game still)

In scenes like this one, the emotional and physical staging of the two characters established within the noninteractive cutscenes (which by far outnumber the interactive QTE opportunities in the game) serves as a powerful critical retraction of the dominant negative imagery around black fathers as irresponsible, incompetent, and absentee, making this aspect of the game's design very much in line ideologically with what we might imagine as a critical racial dystopia.

Fans have been particularly attuned to this aspect of Lee's corrective image of black paternity. There is an extensive online archive of fan-created artwork for the game that mimics the relational dynamic set by the cutscenes in ways that further naturalize Lee and Clementine's bond as loving and playful. In one of the more popular examples of the critical discourse community around their relationship, one modder reimagined the characters using physics software (Garry's Mod) that allows players to alter gamic content and elements. In the resulting photo, *TWD*'s visual assets are manipulated to construct a Lee-Clem selfie that shows both characters goofing around, tongues out, as they pose together with one of Lee's arms resting on Clementine's shoulder and the other outstretched to capture their picture (figure 6.3). The photo foregrounds their warm humanity against the backdrop of the zombie apocalypse, the remnants of which can be seen incongruously lurking in the brightly rendered background.

In addition to critically resisting the dominant negative cultural associations to black paternity, the way both characters relate to each other in the noninteractive cutscenes services the game's general dystopian project of contrasting

Figure 6.3. Fan appropriations of *The Walking Dead* (by ChrisG; used with permission)

rampant moral degradation with empathetic acts and dialogue. The Lee-Clementine relationship also works, as Ryan Smith praises, to humanize and recuperate Lee from his criminal past. We come to know that Lee, who might otherwise be unrecognizably human as a black man and convicted murderer, is human because of his evident—algorithmic—ability to love and care for this adorable and vulnerable child. Even if we can say that the project of humanizing blackness succeeds and carries with it some measure of positive upswing here, that does not mean, however, that the decision to program Lee to have an intersubjective orientation toward Clementine remains unencumbered by other dominant anxieties about black subjectivity. That is, just as the cutscenes giveth, they also taketh away.

"You Are Dead": The Limits of Racial Empathy in *The Walking Dead*

The final episode of *TWD*'s first season, "Left Behind," depicts Lee's successful search for, and reacquisition of, Clementine after she has been kidnapped by the game's portrayal of yet another dysphoric and grieving white male. After their reunion, Clementine reciprocates by bravely and superhumanly saving Lee as he collapses in the middle of a zombie horde at the very moment when the two characters stumble on Clementine's zombified parents, who happen to be wandering hungrily and aimlessly in the streets of Savannah. At this point in the narrative, the player knows that Lee has been bitten (hence his blackout), but Clementine only now learns of Lee's deterministic proximity to her undead parents. One of the player's first tasks in this scene, then, is to break this news of Lee's impending death to Clementine and simultaneously protect her from Lee's dying rite of black paternity.

The player's options for controlling Lee during this part of the game's emotional climax veer heavily toward the expression of compassion and care. As he lays dying, Lee's primary role is a pedagogical one: to patiently coach Clementine toward her newfound independence and encourage the now nine-year-old child to demonstrate her budding acquisition of key survival tactics while she fights off a zombie and ultimately figures out how to free herself from the enclosed space—and from the soon-to-be-zombie Lee. Unlike *TLoU*'s use of character perspective shifting that allows the player to move between controlling Joel or Ellie at key moments of crisis, in *TWD* the player remains rooted in Lee's decomposing blackness even though Clementine has all the key points of action in the game's ending. From the moment Lee collapses to the ground (with about ten minutes remaining of gameplay) all of Lee's action QTEs create a symbiotic bridge and relay between the two characters that work to transfer his agency to the child. For instance, during these moments Lee provides minimal physical support to her, like in kicking a bat her way, but mostly the player controls and directs Clementine's actions from Lee's position on the floor by directing his gaze toward objects that she might use to save herself and by choosing dialogue options that assist her in problem solving. If at any time Clementine dies during this segment because you (as Lee) fail to blurt out the instructions to her soon enough, the kill screen reads YOU ARE DEAD, just as it does whenever Lee dies during other moments of failure in the game. Yet "you"—Lee—are not dead. Instead Lee looks on ashen and horrified, his face superimposed over the kill screen, as Clementine squeals and dies. In blurring the boundaries between one character who has been morally redeemed by his empathetic caretaking abilities but remains dying nonetheless and the other character who is presumably a youthful site of hope and progress, the game produces an instantiation wherein blackness deterministically lacks subjective distinctiveness.

Ultimately, the game's heavy use of tone-setting cutscenes pushes the characters' symbiotic bond to an ideologically problematic end. For example, in a noninteractive cutscene Lee instructs Clementine to handcuff him to a pole so that she will be protected from his undiscriminating violence when he inevitably dies and returns. Articulating her loyalty and attachment to her only remaining parental figure, Clementine protests, saying, "I don't want to do this," but Lee firmly and lovingly coaxes her to detain him nonetheless: "Just do it, sweetie," he sighs. In compliance, the child wrests a pair of handcuffs from a zombified law official who also inhabits the enclosed space. Despite all that their bond has signified up until this point, Lee's redemptive and punitive relationship to the prison industrial complex returns from the dead to fatally subordinate the intersubjective bond between the two characters, returning the black masculine subject back to his depressive and inevitable relationship to the state. Only this time, rather than function as signifier for a generalized threat to society (as he did riding in a police cruiser at the start of the game), Lee is refigured here as a specific threat to the only person with whom he has established reciprocal love. While the noninteractive cutscenes play the biggest role in cementing and cherishing the relational bond between these two characters throughout the other episodes, that bond is decidedly undermined with the same design tool at game's end.

The biggest and final test for Clementine, and the way she at last proves her readiness for the bleak realities of this new life, is initiated by Lee's symbolic death. In this game of limited choices, the player decides whether Lee will tell Clementine to shoot him (black humanity survives by dying) or whether Lee will spare her the emotional trauma of having to kill her caretaker (black humanity dies in rotting perpetuity). Herein lies a final test of the limits of racial empathy for the player, as well, since it is the player, and not a cutscene, who determines whether Clementine shoots Lee. Has the project of building empathy around and through black identity worked enough for players to make the right difficult, morally encoded decision? Have the players cultivated enough empathy for Lee to order a young child to shoot him point blank, squarely in the head? Telltale's endgame screenshot summary of player decisions shows that the majority of players do indeed instruct Clementine to shoot Lee—the decision that paradoxically stresses and preserves his humanity by refusing to let this rendition of Hortense Spillers's famously articulated culturally "banished" black father turn into a zombie.[29] After issuing the order for Clementine to kill him, Lee tries to paternalistically stress that she is making the difficult decision of saving his humanity. He tells her, "Close your eyes, and be thankful you'll never have to see me as one of them." In addition to humanizing and redeeming Lee, the grave reality of Lee's death or reanimation builds character for Clementine, hardens her, readies her for the brutal world outside the garage door. And so, with her face splattered with a mixture of dried blood and fresh tears, Clementine tightly closes her eyes, twists her head away, peeks several times to make sure that she has a straight aim—as Lee taught her to do—and then squeezes the trigger (figure 6.4).

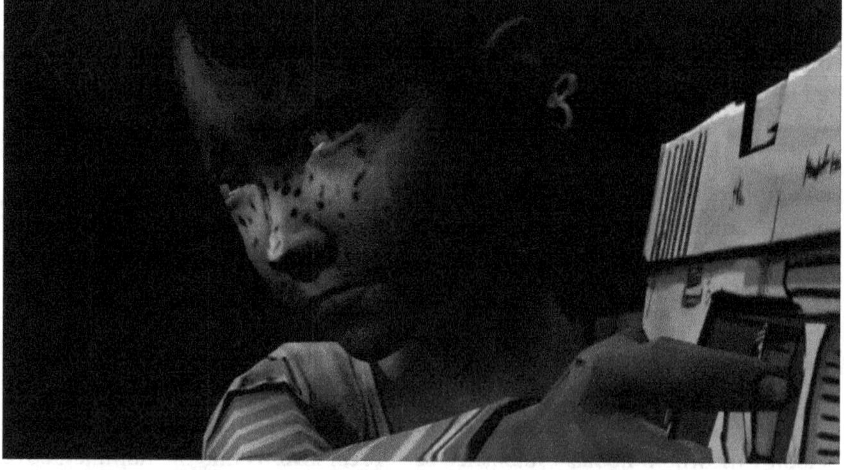

Figure 6.4. Murderous empathy (*The Walking Dead* game still)

This final action, along with the close-up of Clementine's aggrieved display of empathetic mercy, is certainly where the game earns its billing as an "emotional game." Everyone in the game's discourse community cries, it seems, when playing through Clementine's mercy killing. In fact, there are several YouTube compilations of player reactions to this moment.[30] Their teary-eyed and anguished facial expressions nearly mimic Clementine's as the players watch the cutscene of this empathetic climax. Yet there is nothing critical about *TWD*'s dystopian ending, least of all its racial politics, as black empathy has no real power here other than to evoke tears. The lesson in these final moments is that after empathy has been cultivated from several vantage points around Lee, and the narrative has gone to great lengths to demonstrate a black father-daughter love, Lee is reensnared with his original fate: he's back in handcuffs despite their powerful emotional ties. While the distraught player reactions and the high percentage of players who have opted to preserve Lee's humanity certainly confirm that some kind of empathetic identification with both characters has worked by this point in the story, there is also a costly sentimentalism here that draws on, spectacularizes, and then dissolves black intersubjectivity. Lee does not die here as Ben does in *Night of the Living Dead*, at the hands of an allegorically racist posse of white vigilantes. He seems to die harmlessly enough after being bitten by a zombie. Yet playing a black character who demands to be shot also plays out various racial anxieties through a diegetic gamic action that proves to be masochistic, melancholic, and critically unaware of either character's racial/social position. The payoff of Lee's death is its own reward: affected players cry over an emotional loss without discussing any of these consequences or allegorical meanings.

At game's end we are left with a prototypical image of sacrificial blackness—like we've seen so many times before in narrative history. In a game and franchise that self-consciously emphasizes humanity, empathy, and intersubjectivity as a contrast to the moral degradation of society, Lee's death reveals the limits of that overall project when it comes to the minority characters. An ending more attuned to the narrative history of dystopian blackness, perhaps one that radically and critically envisions an apocalyptic future where a black father and daughter survive together—by any means necessary—to fight another day would certainly represent something we have rarely, if ever, seen in visual culture.

Disaster by Any Means Necessary

Perhaps even more so than literature, film, television, or comic books, dystopian video games, because of their interactivity, have the potential to function as Jean Baudrillard's ultimate hyperreal simulations. Theorizing that the American cultural appetite for, and attraction to, scenes and images of destruction has only heightened since the attacks on the World Trade Center on September 11, 2001, Baudrillard argues that "every disaster made us wish for more, for something bigger, grander, more sweeping."[31] Yet Baudrillard's writings on disaster narratives and Baccolini and Moylan's theory of the critical dystopia represent opposing visions of how disaster and apocalyptic narratives may function in contemporary culture. On the one hand, there is Baudrillard's assertion that dystopian representations are primarily spectacles that evince our preference for simulations over and above any engagement with the real. Such works uncritically fuel an insatiable craving for nihilistic substitutions for lived experience as a way to cope with the inevitability of catastrophe. Critical dystopias, on the other hand, work in a mode of purposeful postmodern critique. These works use dystopian contexts to deconstruct from within as they attempt to unsettle present-day cultural norms, policies, and social hierarchies.

Dystopian video games, as ultimate simulations of disaster, have the potential for uniquely contributing in either vein. As video game narratives that both end with blackness represented as dead or dying in the future, *The Walking Dead* and *The Last of Us* contribute representations of gamic blackness that falter in their ability to function progressively. To simulate blackness using the oft-repeated tropes of muted or thwarted hope and resistance and obligatory sacrifice compounds the overall cultural pattern of creating spectacular and predictable urtexts, as the fate of black subjectivities remains as predictable as the narrative conventions of the next zombie apocalypse.[32] Gaming our way through the predictable mix of race and disaster parables does little more than assure us that although we may dread it, we can imagine with certainty the unchanging reality of the racial other's fate in the end-times.

As dystopian storytelling continues to remain attractive to both developers and gaming audiences, instead of continuing to demand "more" or "better" representations in games, with an interpretative framework like the critical racial dystopia I have aimed to make other narrative traditions and modes of critique valuable to this area of new media production. That video game developers are notoriously scrupulous when researching and constructing the lore and knowledge base for their game worlds means that there are tremendous opportunities for rich dialogic exchange between game design imperatives and interdisciplinary scholarship. So, too, can game studies as an emergent field better integrate the scholarship from African American studies, literary studies, and film and media studies. Part of what we can offer as interdisciplinary scholars are new ways to make critical discussions on topics like these—such as sacrificial blackness and the perils of empathetic racial friendships—accessible, relevant, and visible to the producers and fans of games.

TREAANDREA M. RUSSWORM is Associate Professor of English at the University of Massachusetts, Amherst, where she teaches classes on digital media, race, and popular culture. She is coeditor of *From Madea to Media Mogul: Theorizing Tyler Perry* and author of *Blackness Is Burning: Civil Rights, Popular Culture, and the Problem of Recognition.*

Notes

1. Manveer Heir, "Misogyny, Racism, and Homophobia: Where Do Video Games Stand?" *GDC Vault*, 2014, http://www.gdcvault.com/play/1020420/Misogyny-Racism-and-Homophobia-Where; Tom Senior, "Why Manveer Heir's Attack on Stereotypes in Games Was the Most Important Moment of GDC 2014," *PC Gamer*, March 23, 2014, http://www.pcgamer.com//why-manveer-heirs-attack-on-stereotypes-in-games-was-the-most-important-moment-of-gdc-2014/.

2. Tom Moylan, *Scraps of the Untainted Sky: Science Fiction, Utopia, Dystopia* (Boulder, CO: Westview, 2000), xiii.

3. For an excellent generic breakdown of dystopian and anti-utopian subgenres and classifications, see Antonis Balasopoulos, "Anti-Utopia and Dystopia: Rethinking the Generic Field," http://www.academia.edu/1008203/_Anti-Utopia_and_Dystopia_Rethinking_the_Generic_Field_ (accessed March 12, 2015).

4. See Marcus Schulzke, "The Critical Power of Virtual Dystopias," *Games and Culture* 9, no. 5 (2014): 315–334.

5. Ibid., 324. See also Raffaella Baccolini and Tom Moylan, eds., *Dark Horizons: Science Fiction and the Dystopian Imagination* (New York: Routledge, 2003), 7.

6. See Linda Williams, *Playing the Race Card: Melodramas of Black and White from Uncle Tom to O. J. Simpson* (Princeton, NJ: Princeton University Press, 2001); and Lauren Berlant, "Poor Eliza," *American Literature* 70, no. 3 (1998): 635–668.

7. Baccolini and Moylan, *Dark Horizons*, 2. For a discussion of "suspicions of the real," see Efraim Sicher and Natalia Skradol, "A World neither Brave nor New: Reading Dystopian Fiction after 9/11," *Partial Answers: Journal of Literature and the History of Ideas* 4, no. 1 (2006): 153.

8. Baccolini and Moylan, *Dark Horizons*, 8.

9. Several of Romero's sequels feature black characters in prominent roles and are more reflexive about their identities. See *Dawn of the Dead* (1978), *Day of the Dead* (1985), *Land of the Dead* (2005), *Diary of the Dead* (2007), and *Survival of the Dead* (2009).

10. Robin R. Means Coleman, *Horror Noire: Blacks in American Horror Films from the 1890s to Present* (New York: Routledge, 2011), 106. See also Kevin Heffernan, "Inner-City Exhibition and the Genre Film: Distributing 'Night of the Living Dead' (1968)," *Cinema Journal* 41, no. 3 (2002): 59–77.

11. Both fans online and scholars miss the opportunity to analyze the significance of Marlene's race in their discussions about the game and morality. See, for example, Amy M. Green, "The Reconstruction of Morality and the Evolution of Naturalism in *The Last of Us*," *Games and Culture* 11, no. 7–8 (2016): 745–763.

12. Baccolini and Moylan, *Dark Horizons*, 8.

13. Matt Becker, "A Point of Little Hope: Hippie Horror Films and the Politics of Ambivalence," *Velvet Light Trap* 57 (Spring 2006): 44.

14. Henry A Giroux, "The Terror of Neoliberalism: Rethinking the Significance of Cultural Politics," *College Literature* 32, no. 1 (2005): 15.

15. Sean Brayton, "The Racial Politics of Disaster and Dystopia in *I Am Legend*," *Velvet Light Trap* 67 (2011): 75.

16. Although I discuss visual culture in this chapter, it is important to note that black literary and print traditions (including the novels of Octavia Butler and Samuel Delany) have represented dystopian blackness with much more nuance than the visual culture's limited range of hope and sacrifice.

17. Jayna Brown, "The Human Project: Utopia, Dystopia, and the Black Heroine in *Children of Men* and *28 Days Later*," *Transition* 110, no. 1 (2013): 122.

18. Adilifu Nama, *Black Space: Imagining Race in Science Fiction Film* (Austin: University of Texas Press, 2008), 147.

19. I have argued that *Afro Samurai*'s feudal and futuristic dystopian world is productively postmodern. See TreaAndrea M. Russworm, "The Hype Man as Racial Stereotype, Parody, and Ghost in *Afro Samurai*," in *Game On, Hollywood! Essays on the Intersection of Video Games and Cinema*, ed. Gretchen Papazian and Joseph Michael Sommers (Jefferson, NC: McFarland, 2013), 169–182.

20. Mikhail Bakhtin, *The Dialogic Imagination: Four Essays*, ed. Michael Holquist, trans. Caryl Emerson, 2nd ed. (Austin: University of Texas Press, 1982), 426.

21. Kahlief Adams, "Dave Fennoy Drops the Knowledge," *Spawn On Me* (podcast), February 17, 2014, http://thespawnpointblog.com/spawn-episode-3-dave-fennoy-drops-knowledge/.

22. Ibid.

23. See Toby Smethurst and Stef Craps, "Playing with Trauma: Interreactivity, Empathy, and Complicity in *The Walking Dead* Video Game," *Games and Culture* 10, no. 3 (May 1, 2015): 269–290; and Jamie Madigan, "*The Walking Dead*, Mirror Neurons, and Empathy," *Psychology of Video Games*, November 7, 2012, http://www.psychologyofgames.com/2012/11/the-walking-dead-mirror-neurons-and-empathy.

24. Ryan Smith, "Empathy Games: Finding the Virtues amid the Violence of Telltale's *The Walking Dead*," *Gameological Society*, May 13, 2013, http://gameological.com/2013/05/empathy-in-the-walking-dead/; also quoted in Smethurst and Craps, "Playing with Trauma," 18.

25. Smith, "Empathy Games."

26. Ibid.

27. Clementine's race has been subject to countless public rumination. Although several developers have indicated that she is African American, fans continually change the character's wiki pages to state that she is Caucasian, Korean, or multiracial. The possibility for ambiguity here, along with the continual discussion, represents a highly reflexive decision in my mind, as it challenges the assumption that race and ethnicity can be determined on sight.

28. For "frontend" and "backend," see D. Fox Harrell, *Phantasmal Media: An Approach to Imagination, Computation, and Expression* (Cambridge, MA: MIT Press, 2013).

29. Hortense J. Spillers, "Mama's Baby, Papa's Maybe: An American Grammar Book," *Diacritics: A Review of Contemporary Criticism* 17, no. 2 (1987): 64–81. The number of players who opt to make Clementine shoot Lee has hovered around 67 percent and has been as high as 70 percent during my different play-throughs and viewings of walk-throughs on YouTube.

30. See "Youtubers Reaction to the Walking Dead Game Ending," *YouTube*, November 23, 2013, https://www.youtube.com/watch?v=xAOrGq7DQsI; and "Youtubers reaction to the Walking Dead Game Ending #2," *YouTube*, December 27, 2013, https://www.youtube.com/watch?v=lFSOdwiLVS4.

31. Jean Baudrillard, *The Spirit of Terrorism* (London: Verso, 2002), 11.

32. For more on the predictability of disaster narratives as urtexts, see Sicher and Skradol, "A World neither Brave nor New," 152.

chapter seven

JOURNEY INTO THE TECHNO-PRIMITIVE DESERT

IRENE CHIEN

> It takes centuries to invent the primitive.
>
> —Don DeLillo, *Americana*

IN THE SUMMER OF 1898, ART HISTORIAN JOHN C. VAN DYKE VENTURED ALONE into the American desert with barely more than a pistol. He was considered a fool—the desert was a no-man's-land that white men were forced to pass through to get to the abundant lands beyond. Yet Van Dyke emerged almost three years later from his solitary trek, utterly transfixed. Opposing the era's prevailing concept of the desert as blight and obstacle to modern civilization, Van Dyke's landmark 1901 book *The Desert* calls forth its profound beauty and power:

> Everyone rides here with the feeling that he is the first one that ever broke into this unknown land, that he is the original discoverer; and that this new world belongs to him by right of original exploration and conquest. Life becomes simplified by necessity. It begins all over again, starting at the primitive stage. There is a reversion to the savage. Civilization, the race, history, philosophy, art—how very far away and how very useless, even contemptible, they seem. What have they to do with the air and the sunlight and the vastness of the plateau![1]

For rapidly industrializing turn-of-the-century America seeking refuge from the ravages of modernity and the nonstop acceleration of urban life, Van Dyke's new vision of the desert was tantalizing. Van Dyke's desert is a barren but pristine natural space whose unfathomable desolation and immensity undoes human historical time. The desert offers a vision of the future and prehistory of civilization that is both the end and the beginning of the American colonial imperative: On the one hand, the desert seems to offer the last horizon of virgin territory, ripe for adventuring and conquest. On the other hand, its sheer vastness and radical indifference to human existence render all trappings of modern American culture insignificant. The desert reverts civilized man back to the innocent state of his primitive ancestors and offers an ecstatic reunion with his heretofore repressed inner "savage." This "savage," of course, is the Native American, whose systematic, and, in 1901, essentially complete subjugation through US military force produced a nostalgic longing for what the nation had destroyed. The desire for the desert apocalypse is therefore also a racialized, imperial desire to inhabit Native Americans' presumed primal connection with the natural desert environment, at the moment when Native Americans are no longer a threat.

Over a hundred years after Van Dyke's journey into the American desert, we arrive at another desert, in the form of a video game. In *Journey*, a 2012 game for the Sony PlayStation 3, you awaken alone in an endlessly sprawling desert. A mountain looms in the distance. Ruins half-buried in the sifting dunes are all that is left of human civilization. You have been reduced to the barest elements of a recognizably human form—eyes, robes, and the ability to walk and run (figure 7.1). But the beautifully rendered, wide-open space of the desert is yours to plunge into. Echoing Van Dyke's language of rapturous encounter, the game website entreats you to "travel and explore this ancient, mysterious world" and "discover the secrets of a forgotten civilization." Yet it also warns, "Your passage will not be an

Figure 7.1. *Journey*'s avatar (*Journey* game still)

easy one. The goal is to get to the mountaintop, but the experience is discovering who you are, what this place is, and what is your purpose."[2] Through a series of levels that include interactions with both benevolent and hostile remnants of the past, you slowly learn about and adapt to the environment surrounding you, and emerge at the journey's conclusion, like Van Dyke, spiritually transformed by your pilgrimage.

My juxtaposition of a contemporary video game with an early twentieth-century literary work serves to foreground some of the seemingly anachronistic consistencies between these two historical moments of seeking spiritual regeneration through a journey across the desert. Both texts construct the desert as an awe-inspiring site of cosmic reckoning rather than as an ugly and deadly wasteland. Both conceive of renewal and progress as requiring a regressive movement into a primordial past. And both suppress signs of technological modernity from their imaginary desert landscapes in favor of the natural, the primitive, the premodern, and the pretechnological, as emblematized in the figure of a "noble savage." By connecting Van Dyke's overtly racialized fantasy of the desert with the less overt one articulated in *Journey*, we can see how this new video game invests players in a very old desert trope. In the mode of Lauren Berlant's concept of "the double articulation of subjectivity and landscape," both *The Desert* and *Journey* attempt to construct an imaginary space of elemental purity and redemption.[3] In this space, the besieged white Western male subject may recover from the corruptions of modern technologized existence by way of radically othered geographies and identities. *Journey* works to counter the conventions of blockbuster military video games and their projections of demonized desert terrorists. Being dropped in the middle of nowhere and at the end of time provides a pleasurable escape from the destructive forward march of modern civilization. *Journey* has been widely and uncritically characterized as participating in a timeless, universal, and global human quest for meaning. But like Van Dyke's from a century ago, its efforts still require the excavation and display of racial difference across exotic bodies and distant landscapes.

Journey quickly became the fastest-selling game on the PlayStation Network upon its release.[4] The game has been almost universally acclaimed by critics, both in the gaming press and in mainstream media outlets, for its mesmerizing beauty and unprecedented emotional richness. Using terms rarely encountered in video game reviews, the *New York Times* praised it as "an almost transcendental experience" and *Entertainment Weekly* called it "a glorious, thoughtful, moving masterpiece."[5] *Journey* was selected as "Best Game of the Year" by gaming blogs *IGN*, *GameSpot*, and *Joystiq*. It won multiple awards at the Academy of Interactive Arts and Sciences (AIAS), the British Academy of Film and Television Arts (BAFTA), and the Game Developers Choice Awards. And the soundtrack was the first video game score ever nominated for a Grammy. *Journey* was created by thatgamecompany, an independent game studio founded by USC grad students Jenova Chen and Kellee Santiago. Thatgamecompany's self-stated mission is to create video games that explore emotions such as joy, wonder, tenderness, and melancholy, emotions that remain untapped by most commercial video games. Previous games developed by the studio, including *Flow* (2007) and *Flower* (2009), similarly eschew the standard competitive and aggressive action gameplay typical of contemporary gaming, in particular what Chen calls the "typical defeat/kill/win mentality" of war games, many set in blasted Middle Eastern or North African desert environments, which dominate the industry.[6]

Yet by evoking the Arab and Islamic world through the desert trope as a locus of enchantment and spiritual renewal that counters the exhaustions of Western modernity and its imperial projects, the game enacts a fantasy of the Orient and of Africa as primitive other to modern technology. This primitive desert dweller is governed by mystic religion rather than secular reason and is in intimate communion with, rather than alienated from, the natural world. *Journey* does foreground computational technology, but in a particular form that is soft, yielding, magical, and in tune with natural elements. This techno-primitive aesthetic, in which the traditional oppositions between primitive and high-tech, nature and human, magical and mathematical are conflated, allows the game to reciprocally articulate and manage the anxieties of technological difference through gender and racial difference. The desert as a sign of both ancient origins and apocalyptic futures allows the game to confound the logic of perpetual technological innovation and progress that drives video game development and technological development in general, a logic that also undergirds the dominance of normative white Western masculinity in mainstream video game discourse. *Journey* articulates an aporia of nostalgia—for the postapocalyptic future of a primitive, exotic, and more innocent pretechnological past. This nostalgia for the future seeks to imbue forward-looking computer game technology with genuine emotion through the affective authenticity guaranteed by backward-looking, atavistic, feminized, ethnic bodies.

I frame my examination of the game *Journey* not only within the contemporary historical moment of military shooter games and Middle Eastern warfare but within a much longer history of American imperial projects set in the desert, in order to move game studies away from its currently presentist orientation and toward more historically textured analysis. My examination of the historical precedents of the desert trope and primitivism are especially essential in examining *Journey*, whose neutralization of racial, sexual, and cultural difference and of historical specificity is central to the revelatory gameplay experience for which it is celebrated. For although *Journey* progressively undermines the authority of the white Western masculine aesthetic that dominates mainstream gaming culture, the universalizing discourse of the game's designers, players, and critics regressively works to deflect critical attention away from the historically constituted markers of race and gender that proliferate in the game despite their careful suppression. It also fails to examine how this deflection is animated by what Jennifer González identifies as "a recurring desire to see online digital spaces as sites of universal subjectivity that can escape the limitations of race."[7] Ultimately, I argue that *Journey*'s impressive destabilization of normative modes of online gaming is far more nuanced in its entanglements with difference than this universalizing discourse can account for.

Desert Warfare

Journey functions to provide an antidote to the violence and destruction of high-tech modern warfare, particularly US military operations in the greater Middle East, as figured in contemporary war gaming. The game stages its poignant encounters with music, other players, and the natural world in a desert world that resembles the Middle East and North Africa region as mediated through US news and entertainment, from the shimmering sand dunes down to the dark skin and hijab-like robes of the game characters. By reenchanting this distant and despised location through the tactile beauty of the desert environment and the fragility of its inhabitants against the majestic landscape, *Journey* opposes the prevailing contemporary vision of the region as a cultural wasteland and a site of chaos and jihadist terror. Recent news headlines and a documentary title sensationally equate desert topography with terrorist threat: "Pursuing Terrorists in the Great Desert," "The Danger in the Desert," "Africa Desert Helps Breed Radicals," and *Terror in the Desert*.[8] Military war games similarly cast the arid landscapes of the greater Middle East as hostile territory. The best-selling first-person shooters *Battlefield 3* (2011, EA DICE), *Call of Duty: Modern Warfare 3* (2011, Infinity Ward and Sledgehammer Games), and *Call of Duty: Black Ops II* (2012, Treyarch) feature battles in Iraq, Somalia, and Afghanistan, respectively, where the desert environment is a backdrop for warfare. In these games, the desert is a ruined landscape crowded with potential targets, the site of violent threats that can only be contained by the interventions of US military might.

The visual field in military first-person shooters is dominated by the weapon planted firmly in the foreground, and positions you, American soldier, as the agent of that weapon. The environment that you see beyond the barrel of your gun is overlaid by the heads-up display (HUD) that frames and filters your interaction with the space before you. The perceptual illegibility of the bleak, uniformly colored desert terrain and, by extension, its foreign inhabitants, is overcome by the surfeit of auxiliary information promised by the HUD. As Alexander Galloway observes, "The HUD exists as a supplement to the rendered world. It completes it, but only through a process of exteriority that is unable again to penetrate its core."[9] Data such as your remaining health and ammunition, the location of your mission objective, and the kill feed (real-time updates of who has been killed, by whom, and with what weapon) are designed to help you calculate the resources that you need from the environment and to assess your progress in the game so as to move through it with maximum speed and efficiency. The constant stream of metrics identifies exactly where you are and what you must do next to fulfill the game objectives at all times, fortifying you with its conflation of information, knowledge, and control. Both imbricated in and inherently external to the first-person experience of movement through space, HUD data emphasize the technological apparatus of informatic control—tracking, mapping, configuring, real-time data analysis and data flow—central to contemporary information warfare, of which Operation Desert Storm is considered the progenitor. The desert environment, like all game environments in military first-person shooters, is structured as inherently hostile foreign terrain, to be outmaneuvered and conquered through the force of the US military's superior command of technology in the form of both firepower and information control.

As Alenda Chang has argued, *Journey* replaces this military game concern with efficiency, speed, and legibility with a meditative experience of "distance, duration, and scale in ways that decenter typical player fantasies of mastery and control."[10] In the military first-person shooter, the field of sight is scaled to the player's eye and weapon range. Because you can see as far as you can shoot and shoot as far as you can see, all space is not only actionable but also destructible. The proportions of *Journey*, however, insistently reinforce the smallness of your game avatar, who is a fluttery wisp against the boundless expanse of the desert (figure 7.2). Without cutscenes and establishing shots to fill in your backstory and define your trajectory through the game, you do not initially know who you are, where you came from, or what you are supposed to do. There is no map or data feed to orient the space according to your objectives. Even after you discover that the mountain looming on the horizon is your goal, the drifting speed of your passage across the sand maintains the sense that you still have a long way to go. Your movements are fluid but very slow compared to the rattling staccato in a military shooter, and you spend a lot of time in the same place with the same resources rather than jumping between locations, vehicles, and weapons. And even as you

Figure 7.2. The desert as void (*Journey* game still)

fly over the sand, the camera remains positioned at a low angle that denies the visual mastery of the aerial view and instead emphasizes the monumentality of the surrounding environment. The details of the abandoned world you inhabit are never fully explained and remain a mystery, and there is throughout the game an elegiac tone of mourning for what has been lost.

Journey is designed to make players feel humble and insignificant in relationship to the immensity of the desert landscape. As Santiago describes, "In video games you're very powerful. You're usually immediately given a weapon of destruction. . . . We wanted to see what would happen when we took all that power away."[11] Yet in *Journey*, powerlessness and lack of knowledge is perceived as a source of wonder rather than as a threat or inadequacy. The game replaces the imperialist imperative to order and control what seems frighteningly unknown with what bell hooks calls an "imperialist nostalgia" that desires rather than denigrates the mysteries of the other. Hooks argues that in this mode of encounter, "the suffering imposed by structures of domination on those designated Other is deflected by an emphasis on seduction and longing where the desire is not to make the Other over in one's image but to become the Other."[12] The game consigns us to the desert, to the petite and delicate body of a feminized and ethnicized other, and absorbs us into a quiet and meditative experience designed to move us to tears. The valorization of frailty over omnipotence, innocence over knowledge, duration over speed, and nature over technology seems to challenge the prevailing power dynamic between the United States and its imagined Middle Eastern/Islamic other as articulated in contemporary military shooter games. Yet, as hooks points out, it leaves unexamined the asymmetries of power that produce and reproduce these binary categories and that privilege the white Western masculine subject with the ability to move between them.

In *Journey*, there is a reciprocal rather than instrumental relationship with the natural environment. Your movements emerge from and merge back into the sand in a tactile exchange that resists the figure-ground, subject-object divisions foundational to the environment design of military shooters. The sand is a living entity that moves with a fluidity analogous to your own. Like you, it billows and swirls when touched by the wind, and it responds with such sensitivity to your movements that you can draw patterns in it. Surfing down sand dunes, half directing the movement and half letting yourself go with the shared momentum, offers one of the most exhilarating experiences in the game. These disclose *Journey*'s primary mechanic—fluidity of movement—that is shared between you and the sand. Despite your lack of hands and feet, your small, robe-shrouded body seems to be perfectly adapted to the desert environment. Merging with rather than colonizing the Middle Eastern/Islamic topography allows for an intimate, ritualistic communion with the primitive other. As hooks argues, "The desire to make contact with those bodies deemed Other, with no apparent will to dominate, assuages the guilt of the past"—in this case, a continuing history of destabilizing US military interventions in the region centered on access to oil.[13] Indeed, the game hints, through the ancient murals that you uncover as you move through it, that this once-advanced civilization was wiped out by competition for natural resources and technologized war. *Journey* poetically unravels the logic of power, knowledge, competition, and warfare as epitomized in the military shooter game, but in doing so, it evokes a longing for the primitive and its more intuitive, elemental, and immediate connection to the environment. Like Van Dyke's desert trope, this closeness with the elemental forces of "the air and the sunlight and the vastness of the plateau" requires the essentializing valorization of a pretechnological savage who is more in tune with the land than civilized man.

Blank Spots on the Map

Many critics praise *Journey* for evoking the universal human experience of struggling for meaning. This universality, this openness to the rich emotional projections of the game player, is made possible by *Journey*'s radical refusal to provide any solid answers about the game's meaning or purpose, what game reviewers have called the "blank slate" that it provides for game players to mark up and fill in with their own personal desires and meanings. Ian Bogost also calls *Journey* a "tabula rasa." He explains, "It could be a coming of age, or a metaphor for life, or an allegory of love or friendship or work or overcoming sickness or sloughing off madness. It could mean anything at all. . . . Surely every sect and creed will be able to read their favorite meaning onto the game."[14] The game's music composer, Austin Wintory, describes his process of turning his soundtrack into a blank slate as well: "I gradually eliminated localizing concepts from the score to make it as universal and culture-less as possible."[15] This deliberate erasure of signs of difference is essential to achieving the global, universal appeal to which the game aspires.

Journey's ability to function as a blank slate is founded on the landscape of the desert, which has historically served as a metaphor for primordial void. The wide-open, horizonless, empty space of the desert evokes both desolation and limitless potential. This construction of the desert as barren expanse—a blank slate open to human invention—is what has allowed the American desert to be used as a nuclear weapons testing ground by the US military, and the greater Middle East to be a constant battle zone in successive US wars in Somalia, Afghanistan, Kuwait, Iraq (Operation *Desert* Storm), potentially Syria and Iran, and the more generalized War on Terror. As Trevor Paglen writes in his examination of covert military operations strategically situated in the deserts of the American West, "We enact what we imagine. When early explorers and settlers first came to the Basin and Range, they saw a wasteland. Then they laid waste to it." The assumed "non-existence" of these "blank spots on the map" invites destruction with impunity.[16] Moreover, the designation of deserts as uninhabitable wastelands at the same time that they are recognized as rich in energy sources like oil and uranium allows deserts from Nevada to Nigeria to be plundered through environmentally unsound extraction technologies. Even ostensibly environmentally sensitive green energy ventures like wind farms and solar power plants in the American West rely on a conception of these lands as otherwise blank and unused, ignoring the delicate ecosystems and the human inhabitants who depend on them that are devastated by these incursions.

The forces of high technology, big science, and military occupation take up what John Beck calls "a selective blindness" that eliminates the consideration of the desert's long-time native inhabitants in their eagerness to exploit the so-called desert void. Although *Journey* opposes the military shooter's construction of the implicitly Middle Eastern/North African desert as a territory to master and exploit, its reframing of this desert as a rapturous space of creative experimentation and profound personal discovery relies on and sustains the same fantasy of vacant lands. As Beck points out, "Speculators and aesthetes alike need the tropes of emptiness and uselessness in order to validate their construction of the landscape as available space."[17] This symbolic emptying out of the desert that is necessary for both those seeking to subjugate it as well as those seeking to redeem it helps to explain how the game evacuates the particular historical and cultural meanings attached to the game's desert iconography even as it puts raced and gendered icons of exotic otherness on display. The supposed blank slate of the game *Journey* is laden with direct and indirect cultural references that foreground difference only to subsequently disavow its significance in favor of the genderless and postracial universal.

Your avatar in *Journey* is a human-like creature with glowing eyes and no mouth, wearing a voluminous red robe and hood. As traceable in the concept art created during the development of the game, the final avatar evolved from discarded ideas for a more distinctly masculine presence, with outstretched hands and a warrior-like stance, as well as an overtly feminine version with long eyelashes and a veil.[18] The designers ultimately settled on a figure who producer Robin Hunicke declares "isn't a warrior" and "isn't a princess" but instead "transcends gender."[19] Players and reviewers consistently identify the game avatar's gender as indeterminate, but it has a light step, high-pitched chirp, and diminutive cuteness that suggest childness or femininity. The character's dark brown face points to an indefinite ethnic identity that is reinforced by its hijab-like head covering and the tribal patterns embroidered on its robe. The game designers cite many cultural inspirations in their design process—Native American rugs and symbols; Japanese kites; Egyptian hieroglyphs; Turkish, Greek, and Mayan architecture.[20] Matt Nava, the art director in charge of character design, writes, "I wanted the character to be iconic and universal, meaning that it would instantly resonate with people from many cultures."[21] In pursuit of a universal ideal, the specificity of each of these cultural sources, like the markers for male and female, were gradually erased from the character and the environmental design. Thus a character whose skin color and costume would signify gender and racial difference in any other game is consistently declared in *Journey* to be universal. The plethora of exotic references points to both a multiplicity of distant cultures and to nowhere in particular, reducing gender, race, and ethnicity to decorative styles that can be deployed at will by those with the power to appropriate the iconography of difference. However, this volitional identity implicitly posits a player who does not actually live in the desert and who does not actually look like the avatar on the screen.

Gameplay reinforces a traditional racial hierarchy. At the end of each game level, your small, red-robed avatar encounters a large, white-robed figure with a white face and blue eyes who towers over you with paternal benevolence. These are ostensibly ancestors from the once-great civilization that has been destroyed by its own technology, and their racialized contrast to the small, brown-faced avatar is striking. Moreover, to solidify the game's racial hierarchy between white, red, and brown, experienced players can collect enough glowing symbols throughout the game space to attain a white robe that replaces the red one and confers you a longer scarf and additional jumping power. The white robe also provides a distinct visual contrast to the warm earth tones of the game environment and signals to other players your superior level of experience. Once you have attained the white robe, you may change back to your red one at any time. This reaffirms the logic of what Lisa Nakamura calls online "identity tourism," in which racially unmarked white subjects can occupy black and brown identities at will. In her critique of internet ads from the late 1990s that display difference as a spectacle that can then be elided and erased by new network technology, Nakamura writes,

> This world without limits is represented by vivid and often sublime images of displayed ethnic and racial difference in order to bracket them off as exotic and irremediably "other." Images of this other as primitive, anachronistic, and picturesque decorate the landscape.[22]

The pleasurable consumption of gender, racial, and ethnic otherness—of a figure that is a fantastic amalgamation of Muslim child, African tribeswoman, and Bedouin Arab fixed in a faraway primeval desert—is foundational to *Journey*'s mythos of universal spiritual quest. The game's sense of journeying, of mobility and travel, is founded on the stable ground provided by both the open horizon of the desert and by the sympathetically powerless and vulnerable racial other who, "in contrast to the mobile and networked tourist/user, isn't going anywhere."[23]

Primitive High Technology

In his analysis of early twentieth-century spectacles like the 1893 Chicago World's Fair, close in date to Van Dyke's publication of *The Desert*, Mark Seltzer uses the term "techno-primitivism" to describe "a simulated primitivism mediated through and through by technologies of reproduction."[24] This techno-primitive aesthetic is manifested in "a formal division between technophilic interiors and anachronistic surfaces," in which the technologies that are necessary to recreate the primitive within the modern world are simultaneously fetishized and disavowed.[25] For Seltzer, techno-primitivism represents a "strange and violent coupling" between the primitive and the technological that is marked by a compulsive repetition of traumatic scenes of violence, such as US expansion into the western frontier as recapitulated in the fair's spectacular "Wild West" exhibit.[26] The techno-primitive seems to emerge from the nexus of technological and imperial advancement, suggesting that America's sense of progress is founded on a deeply embedded yet disavowed regression to mass violence, in which the state's imperial violence is displaced onto the debased atavism of racial others. *Journey*'s techno-primitive aesthetic emerges at another moment of disavowed mass violence—US military interventions in the greater Middle East and the War on Terror.

Rather than using high-tech implements like armor, guns, and vehicles that penetrate, map, and destroy the built environment as in standard war games, the player's avatar in *Journey* floats ethereally through the world devoid of technological aids, lacking even arms and hands to utilize tools. The PlayStation 3's processing power is marshaled in *Journey* to create an ancient, pretechnological world in which the rippling of sand, wind, and fabric are as lovingly rendered as bullet holes are in first-person shooters. *Journey*'s empty desert is one of the "forsaken geographies" that Nicole Fleetwood characterizes as "suffer[ing] from normative representational codes that frame them as timeless, faraway, and *forsaken* places where technology is useless, inaccessible, or at odds with the way of life."[27] Western digital divide discourses render the Middle East and Africa as technological deserts that, because of their assumed lack of access to computer technology, are "outside of futuristic narratives of progress and development."[28] By inviting the presumed Western male gamer to inhabit the diminutive body of the feminized ethnic other in an affective rather than combative relationship to the pretechnological desert environment, the game seems to position the primitive other as technologically handicapped by her innate affinity to nature.

What complicates this reductive association of the primitive with technological deficiency is the game's imbrication of nature into technology. The only technology implemented by the game avatar is your scarf, a ribbon of fabric covered with indecipherable symbols that flutters behind you. When lengthened and charged by encounters with glowing glyphs and floating strips of cloth, the scarf allows you to fly across the desert in breathtaking leaps and bounds. The longer your scarf, the longer you can stay aloft with each leap. And the more times you complete the game, the more ornate grows the embroidery pattern on your robes. Unlike the hard, impenetrable body armor in a military shooter, the scarf and robes of your *Journey* avatar ripple and flap in response to every puff of wind. Cloth envelops the avatar's body so thoroughly that it seems to be made of fabric (figure 7.3). The game's focus on cloth as the only technology wielded by the player and the only signifier of achievement offers a vision of a soft technology that runs counter to the hard technology paradigm of military games and traditional computing. As feminist scholar Sadie Plant has pointed out, the traditionally feminine craft of weaving plays a crucial but suppressed role in the history of computing. Charles Babbage, the inventor of the computer, modeled his famous Analytical Engine on early nineteenth-century textile looms. Plant mines the forgotten origins of computer programming in feminine weaving, in which there is continuity

Figure 7.3. Cloth as technology (*Journey* game still)

between the weaver, the weaving, and the woven, rather than in the strict subject-object relations of masculine technological control. Ethnomathematician Ron Eglash also charts an alternative lineage for modern computing by way of Africa rather than Western industrialization. He points to the fractal patterns that structure African textiles as expressions of mathematical concepts that are fundamental to computer programming. E-textiles and wearable computers extend these alternative paradigms of computation by integrating digital components directly into fabric and pushing toward a pervasive computing model of ubiquitous information systems that are intimately scaled and in tune with the vagaries of the human body.[29]

Journey takes up artist Joanna Berzowska's call for reinventing computing through textiles: "The tradition of electronics design and manufacturing is to produce hard components encased in square boxes. The tradition of textiles is to produce soft structures that encase the human body. By merging the two, we can create soft circuits and develop new methods for electronics design, sensing the body, and transmitting power and data."[30] The fabric in *Journey* is defined by its lightness and flexibility rather than the massiveness and hardness of the industrial forms of technology represented by the Guardians. Guardians are large, armored, mechanical beasts that hover overhead like airships, poised to attack and tear off your scarf if they catch you in their monocular spotlights. They are presumably leftovers from the more technologically advanced but now destroyed civilization, and a terrifying contrast to the playful, glimmering strips of cloth that energize your scarf and buoy you through the air like the Orientalist fantasy of flying carpets. Cloth in *Journey* is literally soft-ware—flexible, reconfigurable, ephemeral, taking on organic shapes, woven out of ancient runes reinvented as source code.

When the glowing glyphs that you collect swirl around you to lengthen your scarf, it is as if they are weaving fabric out of electricity and code. The game positions this primitive, magical, feminine technology of woven fabric against the hard, industrial, masculine technology of the warlike Guardians and their targeted, aerial vision. Cloth, despite its primitive origins, is actually the more nimble, regenerative, and modern technology in the game.

The Face of the Network

Alexander Galloway and Eugene Thacker point out that, following the September 11 attacks in 2001, international terror networks came into focus as a new enemy, but an enemy whose status as both effectively coordinated and amorphously distributed confounds attempts to pin it down and give it a name. As they argue, networks are never "integral whole objects" but rather characterized by multiplicity—"shapeless, amorphous, and faceless."[31] Thus "the topologies of netwar and the 'multitude' throw up a challenge to traditional notions of enmity: they have no face; they are instances of faceless enmity."[32] Although terror networks in the American cultural imaginary are loosely organized under the name al-Qaeda with a locus in the greater Middle East, they are threatening precisely because they cannot be conceived as a singular, individuated, territorially defined enemy in simple, binary form. Terrorists use the same dispersed, always-on global networks that we use to circulate communications, finances, and social relations, and they are imbricated in the same complex, technologically mediated circuits of transnational capital. As Patrick Jagoda suggests, in the age of networked warfare, there is little difference "between 'facing' an enemy and 'interfacing' with a hostile network collective."[33] It is within this new paradigm of terror networks, in which networks have come to evoke fear and interconnectivity is itself a threat, that *Journey*'s online multiplayer mode intervenes to reenchant the network as a source of simple human connection and to give it an individuated human face. This regenerative regression to the primal elements of human encounter both requires and disavows the authenticating presence of othered landscapes and bodies.

Journey's multiplayer mode produces encounters between networked online players that are nonverbal, noncompetitive, and in many ways, noncooperative. At different moments during gameplay, you might discover another figure, someone who looks almost exactly like you, appearing over the horizon. Whereas the sight of an unknown figure in a multiplayer military shooter signals danger and the reflex to shoot him down, in *Journey* it is a welcome relief from the radical isolation of your desert sojourn. It is not at first clear that this new figure is another player rather than a computer-controlled character, because, like you, the other player is without words, and that player's name and purpose in the game are not explained. You can play side by side, struggling toward the mountaintop together; you can ignore each other and go your separate ways; or any combination of the two. *Journey* does not allow you to harm each other, but it doesn't provide you with a mechanic to directly help each other either, as in conventional competitive and cooperative game modes. Rather, you mostly keep each other company, observing and following each other along the way. The game prioritizes proximity as the foundation of connection. The only player action that can directly affect another player is to move close to your companion, causing both players' scarves to recharge. Within this extremely circumscribed platform for interaction, players experience a powerful sense of intimate connection with their online companions. Fan sites are full of *Journey* players reaching out to express gratitude, affection, longing, curiosity, and regret to other players whom they have encountered in the game. "This stranger reminded me that there are beautiful people left in the world. That there is some hope for humanity," writes one player. "We continued walking forward, close together, singing our way to the end," writes another.[34] In *Journey*'s model of interconnection, our high-tech global networks return us to an elemental state of wordless, gestural, musical communication in which we simply exist together without acting on each other.

Journey suppresses the fluctuating multiplicity of other players in the online gaming network from its desert world. You only ever encounter one other figure in the game at a time, and as you move through the barren landscape in shared vulnerability, it feels as if you are the only two people in the universe. In the absence of interaction through language, you observe your companion closely, trying to read this other character's gestures and actions in terms of the distinct personality of another human being but well aware of the limits of your understanding. In this way, *Journey* attempts to reverse the dissolution of individual identity endemic to the faceless distributed network, while at the same time registering the inherent ambiguity of online presence. The matchmaking system's random swapping of other players in and out of the game is invisible to you during gameplay. It is not until after the game ends, when a list of the network IDs of those who shared the game session with you is displayed, that you can tell with whom you were playing. Sometimes after an intense experience of playing alongside a companion, it turns out that you have actually been playing with a series of players that you perceived as one. The network in *Journey* is experienced as simultaneously face and swarm, individual and multitude. The game maintains the uneasy sense of networks as "multi-modal, dynamic, distributed, and unpredictable" at the same time that it galvanizes players to experience deep connection with the network form as a partial and ambiguous but ultimately reassuring human presence.[35]

The developers of *Journey* work to counter the persistent hostility that characterizes anonymous online game interactions, often manifested in misogynistic and racist slurs, by systematically erasing player attributes in the game that highlight difference. As Chen describes the multiplayer mode, "It's about two strangers who meet online. They don't know who they are or how old they are. All they know is, that is another human being."[36] Players cannot see each other's names; customize their skin color and clothing; or accumulate points, objects, or resources to distinguish themselves. Rather than chatting via voice or text, which so often announces age, gender, and native language in online gaming, *Journey* players can only communicate through musical chirps and a limited range of gestures. The removal of the standard visual markers of communication technology—lobbies, text boxes, display names, call signs, and microphone headsets—strips down the multiplayer experience so that it feels like an existentially pure, face-to-face encounter. Left out of the discourse around *Journey*'s celebrated capacity for creating primordial human connection is how this leveling of identity between players takes place through the imputed blankness of the desert and innocence of the feminized, ethnically marked bodies that players occupy in the game. The oft-repeated praise that *Journey* allows players to cast away the cultural baggage of identity and face each other in the game with, as one reviewer states, "no race, no age, no gender, no body to be an advantage or disadvantage" reiterates the pervasive cultural fantasy of escaping the burdens of embodied difference in our globally networked online spaces.[37]

The elision of difference in favor of the universal claimed by both the makers and critics of the game detracts from the game's actual achievements. Chen, a US immigrant from China, frequently references his inability to fully inhabit either Chinese or American culture as the impetus for his desire to erase cultural specificity from the game world of *Journey* in favor of what he considers deeper, cross-cultural, universal experiences. "We're all the same," he states, and he cites Joseph Campbell's monomyth of the hero's journey as a key template for this homogenous universality.[38] Yet it is precisely because *Journey* imagines an alternately raced and gendered form of inhabiting game environments, and an alternate cultural lineage and future for global networks and technology, that its vision of online gameplay is so generative and compelling. The game's actual engagements with difference as negotiated, uneven terrain for ethical network interconnection should be acknowledged and examined for what they are, rather than suppressed under the vague banner of universality. As *Journey* enters the growing canon of video games that are taken seriously as works of art,[39] and as more independent games like *Journey* structure new emotional experiences through innovative design, we must also take these games seriously for their technologically and ludically mediated discourses of gender and race. For even as we critically examine a game like *Journey*'s groundbreaking reinvention of video game form, only by also attending to its retreading of very familiar cultural and historical ground can we fully account for its considerable affective power. *Journey* marshals the forces of contemporary computing and networking technology in the service of an anachronistic vision of interconnectivity based on shared vulnerability, physical proximity, communion with the natural environment, and interweaving fabric—forms of connection associated with women, children, and so-called primitive ethnic peoples. This nostalgia for the primitive within high technology finds a particularly evocative articulation in the desert landscape because of what William J. T. Mitchell calls the "double temporality" that governs the mythic image of the desert: "It is both the place of origin and the utopian prospect of the future, always fleeting beyond the present. This doubleness then defines a third space—the space between, of wandering, errancy, diaspora, and trial."[40] It is the nonhistorical, end-and-beginning time of the apocalyptic desert that allows *Journey* to embed the technological in the primitive and the mathematical in the natural, awakening the wasteland for a primordial encounter with networked computer technology.

IRENE CHIEN is Assistant Professor of Media and Communication at Muhlenberg College. She writes about the global politics of race and gender in video games, film, and other popular media forms, and has published on military gaming, embodiment in dance games, machinima, survival horror, and Nintendo aesthetics.

Notes

1. John C. Van Dyke, *The Desert: Further Studies in Natural Appearances* (Baltimore: John Hopkins University Press, 1999), 200.

2. thatgamecompany, "Journey," http://thatgamecompany.com/games/journey/ (accessed December 15, 2016).

3. Lauren Berlant, *The Anatomy of National Fantasy: Hawthorne, Utopia, and Everyday Life* (Chicago: University of Chicago Press, 1991), 35.

4. Jenova Chen, "Journey Is PSN's Fastest-Selling Game, Soundtrack Coming Soon," *PlayStation.Blog*, March 29, 2012, http://blog.us.playstation.com/2012/03/29/journey-is-psns-fastest-selling-game-soundtrack-coming-soon/.

5. Kirk Hamilton, "Game Theory: The Awkward Adolescence of Gaming," *New York Times*, December 27, 2012, http://artsbeat.blogs.nytimes.com/2012/12/27/game-theory-the-awkward-adolescence-of-gaming/; Darren Franich, "'Journey' Videogame Review: A Glorious, Thoughtful, Moving Masterpiece," *Entertainment Weekly*, March 14, 2012, http://www.ew.com/article/2012/03/14/journey-videogame-review.

6. Emily Gera, "Journey Hands-On Preview," *VideoGamer*, February 11, 2011, http://www.videogamer.com/ps3/journey/preview-2895.html.

7. Jennifer González, "The Face and the Public: Race, Secrecy, and Digital Art Practice," *Camera Obscura* 24, no. 1 (2009): 37.

8. Raffi Khatchadourian, "Pursuing Terrorists in the Great Desert," *Village Voice*, January 24, 2006, http://www.villagevoice.com/2006-01-24/news/pursuing-terrorists-in-the-great-desert/; "The Danger in the Desert," *The Economist*, January 26, 2013, http://www.economist.com/news/briefing/21570720-terrorism-algeria-and-war-mali-demonstrate-increasing-reach-islamist-extremism; Gillian Parker, "Africa Desert Helps Breed Radicals, from Al Shabab to Boko Haram to Mr. Marlboro," *Christian Science Monitor*, September 29, 2013, http://www.csmonitor.com/World/Africa/2013/0929/Africa-desert-helps-breed-radicals-from-Al-Shabab-to-Boko-Haram-to-Mr.-Marlboro; *Terror in the Desert*, BBC documentary aired on ABC television, October 7, 2013.

9. Alexander R. Galloway, *Gaming: Essays on Algorithmic Culture* (Minneapolis: University of Minnesota Press, 2006), 35.

10. Alenda Chang, "Games as Environmental Texts," *Qui Parle: Critical Humanities and Social Sciences* 19, no. 2 (2011): 79.

11. David Ciccoricco, "Narrative, Cognition, and the Flow of *Mirror's Edge*," *Games and Culture* 7, no. 4 (2012): 275.

12. bell hooks, *Black Looks: Race and Representation* (Boston: South End Press, 1992), 25.

13. Ibid.

14. Ian Bogost, "A Portrait of the Artist as a Game Studio," *The Atlantic*, March 15, 2012, http://www.theatlantic.com/technology/archive/2012/03/a-portrait-of-the-artist-as-a-game-studio/254494/. See also Scott Juster, "'Journey' and Seeing the Best in My Fellow Gamer," *PopMatters*, March 21, 2012, http://www.popmatters.com/post/156210-/.

15. Alex C., "Interview: Composer Austin Wintory on Journey," *TheSixthAxis*, March 15, 2012, http://www.thesixthaxis.com/2012/03/15/interview-journey-composer-austin-wintory/.

16. Trevor Paglen, *Blank Spots on the Map: The Dark Geography of the Pentagon's Secret World* (New York: Penguin, 2009), 56.

17. John Beck, "Without Form and Void: The American Desert as Trope and Terrain," *Nepantla: Views from South* 2, no. 1 (2001): 66.

18. Matthew Nava, *The Art of Journey* (Los Angeles: Blue Canvas, 2013), 14, 22–31.

19. Thomas Hobbs, "The Women Pushing Gender out of Gaming," *Vice*, December 4, 2015, https://broadly.vice.com/en_us/article/the-women-taking-gender-out-of-gaming.

20. Karen Moltenbrey, "Mysterious Journey," *Computer Graphics World*, June–July 2012, http://www.cgw.com/Publications/CGW/2012/Volume-35-Issue-4-June-July-2012/Mysterious-Journey.aspx.

21. Jason Cipriano, "'Journey' Art Director Discusses the 'Art of Journey' and Makes a Case for Games as Art," *MTV Multiplayer*, October 2, 2012, http://multiplayerblog.mtv.com/2012/10/02/journey-art-director-discusses-the-art-of-journey-and-makes-a-case-for-games-as-art/.

22. Lisa Nakamura, *Cybertypes: Race, Ethnicity, and Identity on the Internet* (New York: Taylor and Francis, 2002), 89.

23. Ibid.

24. Mark Seltzer, *Serial Killers: Death and Life in America's Wound Culture* (New York: Routledge, 1998), 81.

25. Ibid., 241.

26. Ibid., 213.

27. Nicole Fleetwood, *Troubling Vision: Performance, Visuality, and Blackness* (Chicago: University of Chicago Press, 2011), 200 (emphasis in original).

28. Ibid.

29. See Sadie Plant, *Zeros + Ones: Digital Women and the New Technoculture* (London: Fourth Estate, 1997); Ron Eglash, *African Fractals: Modern Computing and Indigenous Design* (New Brunswick, NJ: Rutgers University Press, 1999); and Diana Marculescu et al., "Electronic Textiles: A Platform for Pervasive Computing," *Proceedings of the IEEE* 91, no. 12 (2003): 1995–2018.

30. Joanna Berzowska, "Electronic Textiles: Wearable Computers, Reactive Fashion, and Soft Computation," *Textile: The Journal of Cloth and Culture* 3, no. 1 (2005): 11.

31. Alexander R. Galloway and Eugene Thacker, *The Exploit: A Theory of Networks* (Minneapolis: University of Minnesota Press, 2007), 12.

32. Ibid., 66.

33. Patrick Jagoda, "Terror Networks and the Aesthetics of Interconnection," *Social Text* 28, no. 4 (2010): 67.

34. "My Favorite Journey," *Journey Stories* (blog), January 29, 2014, http://journeystories.tumblr.com/post/74912097350/my-favorite-journey; "Companionable Silence," *Journey Stories* (blog), November 1, 2013, http://journeystories.tumblr.com/post/65634264279/companionable-silence. See also thatgamecompany's *Journey* forum, at http://www.thatgamecompany.com/forum/viewforum.php?f=11.

35. Jagoda, "Terror Networks and the Aesthetics of Interconnection," 66.

36. *Variety*, "Journey Game Creator Jenova Chen: 'Theories behind Journey'—Full Keynote Speech," *YouTube*, February 8, 2013, http://www.youtube.com/watch?v=S684RQHzmGA.

37. Linda Holmes, "Virtual Strangers: A 'Journey' with Anna," *NPR*, October 9, 2013, http://www.npr.org/sections/monkeysee/2013/10/09/230676658/virtual-strangers-a-journey-with-anna.

38. Albert Sabat, "How to Create Spirituality in a Video Game," *ABC News*, February 15, 2013, http://abcnews.go.com/ABC_Univision/Entertainment/jenova-chen-spirituality-video-game-journey/story?id=18501149.

39. For extended examinations of the aesthetics of *Journey*, see David Ciccoricco, *Refiguring Minds in Narrative Media* (Lincoln: University of Nebraska Press, 2015); Patrick Jagoda, *Network Aesthetics* (Chicago: University of Chicago Press, 2016); and Katherine Isbister, *How Games Move Us: Emotion by Design* (Cambridge, MA: MIT Press, 2016).

40. William J. T. Mitchell, "Holy Landscape: Israel, Palestine, and the American Wilderness," *Critical Inquiry* 26, no. 2 (2000): 213.

chapter eight

THE RUBBLE AND THE RUIN

Race, Gender, and Sites of Inglorious Conflict in Spec Ops: The Line

SORAYA MURRAY

SPEC OPS: THE LINE (2012), DESIGNED BY YAGER DEVELOPMENT AND published by 2K Games, is a third-person military shooter whose primary target is the military shooter itself. As Captain Martin Walker, you (the player) have been ordered to Dubai on a search and recon mission, after receiving a radio distress signal from deep within a city buried beneath shifting dunes for six months. Mega-sandstorms and domestic conflict have battered Dubai relentlessly, forcing its inhabitants to abandon the city. Privileged members of society and those accorded citizenship have been evacuated. Many were lost, but through on-screen messages, you gather that thousands of immigrant workers were left behind when the storms hit, and they are still fending for themselves as the tempests grow worse. Army Colonel John Konrad, a decorated war hero who once saved you in Kabul, is somewhere in the heart of Dubai with his men. As Walker, motivated by the loyalty of a life-debt and committed to leave no man behind, you are to find Konrad and any survivors and then radio for evacuation. Along with fellow Delta Force operators Adams and Lugo—whom you may minimally direct to neutralize a target, stun victims, or provide medical aid to each other—you explore the ruins in search of the source of a distress signal. The ensuing scenarios combine ecological apocalypse and humanitarian intervention with issues of race, gender, and moral culpability within a recognizable military narrative.

The Line—with its core game mechanic of shooting—is eminently playable, narratively rich, and visually gratifying. At first glance, one might mistakenly presume this game to be jingoistic, and perhaps not even the most exemplary of what the genre has to offer. However, it challenged the mainstream industry to deliver more thought-provoking content. With the aim of elucidating the game's genre iconoclasm, this chapter plumbs the significance of three notable aspects of *Spec Ops: The Line*: (1) the racialized world-making of an Arab megacity in ruins as a site of deep anxiety around non-Western modernity, (2) a mythic American construction of militarized masculinity as troubled and profoundly eroded under the duress of inglorious conflict, and (3) the mobilization of women and children as humanitarian symbols of victimhood to rationalize a military response. Through analysis of story, gameplay, and the establishment of a convincing sense of place, I discuss what the physical rubble and moral ruin visualized in the game mean within the context in which it was made. In its critical address of ideological tropes around the military action shooter, *The Line* allows us to consider its potentials, failures, and successes in mobilizing internal self-criticality within a dominant game genre. In a larger sense, this investigation provides one possible model of understanding playable representations, from a cultural studies and visual studies perspective, that form complex expressions of the "dream life" of a culture.[1] These playable representations are in conversation with and constitutive of the deepest fears, hopes, desires, and anxieties of their times.

Place as Race: Into a New *Heart of Darkness*

The affective impact of setting forms a key strategy of the game's intervention. *The Line* has been widely referred to as the *Apocalypse Now* of video games. Key developers of the content and imagery of the game have enumerated many filmic and televisual influences, such as *Jacob's Ladder* (1990, Adrian Lyne), *Spider* (2002, David Cronenberg), *Generation Kill* (2004, HBO), *Black Hawk Down* (2001, Ridley Scott), and *Apocalypse Now* (1979, Francis Ford Coppola). Certainly, many others, like *Platoon* (1986, Oliver Stone), the HBO series *Band of Brothers* (2001), and *Jarhead* (2005, Sam Mendes), bear mentioning. Walt Williams, lead developer and writer, created a story line that he describes as initially inspired by Joseph Conrad's 1899 anticolonialist novella *Heart of Darkness*, significant because it is the primary inspiration for *Apocalypse Now*.[2] *The Line* borrows affect from these earlier forms by distilling some of their most potent filmic moments and representing them in a new context.

In the cases of both the original novella, set in the colonial Belgian Congo, and Coppola's *Apocalypse Now*, set in Cambodia during the Vietnam War, a perilous and profoundly alien sense of place is established. Similarly, the game space is phantasmagoric, hostile, and uncanny. The first time a churning, howling sandstorm strikes during battle, you must cling tightly to a barrier so as not to be blown away, all the while firing on insurgents with your free hand. As you flail about in the wind like a rag doll, visibility is reduced by the red cloud of sand, and weapons aiming becomes unsteady and fallible. You (as Walker) might find yourself in a discotheque, the black-lit interior still glowing incongruously with garish decoration while you navigate the space, collecting ammunition and confirming enemy kills. Exterior scenes of resort-like locations, palm trees still decorated with twinkling lights, discarded Jet Skis, public sculpture, and billboard advertisements stand out against makeshift sandbag gun turrets and chunks of blackened human flesh that evidence recent carnage.

Williams, on the choice of Dubai as a backdrop, described a center of "luxury and overindulgence that has now become completely useless to the inhabitants of the city because it is cut off from the rest of the world."[3] The world of the game—a fictitious Dubai—is one of a megacity in ruins, "the world's most opulent ruin," in which the constructed value of worldly sumptuousness and grandeur stands revealed for its true worthlessness and absurdity.[4] The metropolis is now a place beyond domestication, taken over by nature, unlivable (figure 8.1). The once destination-city of Dubai is designated a no-man's-land for American troops, so one's very presence there is fraught from the beginning. The deviation of the narrative from a strictly wartime scenario typical of most realistic military shooters is key here. Dubai is not a site of aggressive military intervention but of a natural disaster, and the moving targets of this shooter are a combination of desperate refugees of varied and mostly unspecified origins, CIA operatives, and rogue US Army Thirty-Third Battalion soldiers, purportedly under Konrad's command. In this way, the game differs greatly from most military shooters and stealth games set in the present day, or that recreate historical conflicts. In most cases, there is a clearly defined foe, such as Nazi soldiers during World War II or terrorists in the post-9/11 War on Terror. *The Line*, however, immediately presents the moral ambiguity of an ill-defined enemy—one who is unexpected, or even a compatriot wearing the same uniform. As a player progresses through the increasingly hellish spaces of this third-person shooter, it becomes increasingly apparent that

Figure 8.1. A fictitious Dubai, destroyed (*Spec Ops: The Line* game still)

Walker (player), Adams, and Lugo cannot avoid wrenching choices between life and death for which there is no ethical high ground and that the humanitarian mission of rescue will quickly devolve into chaos and confusion. Over the course of fifteen chapters, a player moves deeper and deeper into a heart of darkness, and the game elicits intense visions of the worst of war, including civilian casualties, chemical and remote warfare, massacre, blight, torture, bare life, and extreme psychological breakdown.

What can this self-conscious choice of location mean, within the sociopolitical context in which *The Line* was made? *Heart of Darkness* has largely become an iconic representation of the brutality of conquest. The relationship between the original literary work, its liberal adaptation in film, and *The Line* is one in which the latter circles back to both earlier forms, while mining their cultural currency to maximum effect. This interlocking set of relations allows the game to engage with both the original colonial narrative and its cinematic reinterpretation, one that stands as an iconic cultural emblem of American moral feeling. Released four years after the war's end, Coppola's *Apocalypse Now* gathers up that moral feeling around the "bad" war, which resulted largely from the excessive visualization of war in mass media for the first time, made possible through news footage and photojournalistic reportage. *Apocalypse Now* adapts Joseph Conrad's narrative into a disorienting, nightmarish, acid-war vision of being caught in the turbine blades of the civilizing engine. The game draws on the capital and potency of these irruptions in culture but then recontextualizes them once again; it forms a palimpsest of imperialist ethical crisis, traumatic encounter with the other, with bad war, moral feeling, and now entanglement with conflicts in the Arab world.

Much has been written on the problems of imaging war in light of persistent questions of moral culpability—particularly in relation to the Vietnam War.[5] In her analysis of *Heart of Darkness* and *Apocalypse Now* as cultural refrains expressing imperialist moral foreboding and culpability, Neda Atanasoski writes, "The post-Vietnam ethical dilemma of how to portray the nation's encounter with its own heart of darkness, which played out largely in the realm of visual culture, can be read as an attempt to grapple with questions about how a nation maintains or loses its faith in its own ideals when it encounters their destructive and deadly force."[6] Similarly, *The Line*'s narrative reveals anxiety around the widening chasm between the idea of doing something good and the actual destruction that ensues in the mobilization of purported humanitarian effort.

Through Walker, the player is led to a place that is supposedly in a state of disorder and outside the light of civilization; but instead of bringing order, Walker reveals the darkness in himself. He commits atrocities that parallel the actions of both the literary and filmic characters of Kurtz; in doing so, he calls on their already-concentrated cultural potency. For example, in the beginning of the game, Walker and his Delta Force are drawn into conflict with nonspecific combatants who appear to be refugees, and even then the team attempts to communicate with the refugees before engaging in conflict. But by chapter 4, "The Refugees," the player is asked to openly fire on US soldiers in uniform—"our own guys," as Adams protests—with only the flimsy rationalization that they are "rogue" to validate these actions. Complicity with Walker's actions is established through play, as you must interact with the game for the narrative to move forward and for the game to progress.

The Line's variety of darkness is tied intimately to the sense of place created through natural elements, but notably, to human-made monuments as well. For example, the Burj Khalifa (Khalifa Tower), currently the tallest structure in the world, figures prominently in the landscape of actual Dubai, as well as in the iconography of the fictive, imagined city. In-game, it becomes a symbol of man's hubris, a twenty-first-century tower of Babel from which the rogue Konrad conveys his mad philosophy to Walker. An absurdity in such a place, the Burj Khalifa stands as a gleaming obelisk to failure. Particularly, one may draw out the Babel analogy further and think of the collapse of language and communication throughout: Walker and his team initially encounter men with whom they cannot converse; translation is botched with refugees of the storm who have splintered off into warlike tribal factions. This marks all future moments of communication, which are correspondingly misleading, broken, shot through with trickery, mistranslated, or unfulfilled. There are failed attempts to gather information from subjects who are dying (one, notably from sand in his lungs—a biological territory of language that is being taken back, as well). The so-called sand wall inhibits contact with the world beyond. There are communications that are traps, defunct news outlet spaces overrun by dunes and looting, and multiple instances of failure to communicate—or at times to even know precisely what one is seeing and hearing.

There is a cloying sense of the incomprehensibility of events, of rationalized motivations, of human nature as polymorphous and eminently destructive. With this hampered ability to gauge your own position as a player in a game that is too large to understand, the space of Dubai is a sublime nightmare. High capitalism in ruin is evidenced in the picked-through remains of luxury automobiles, jets, and yachts, partially consumed by the desert—a paradise of third-world riches lost. Oceans of sand dunes give way to the disorienting extreme verticality of skyscrapers virtually buried in sand, like an urban Grand Canyon.

Exteriors already give clear indication of the constructed value of worldly things, but it is with entry into interior spaces of abandoned hotels, clubs, aquatic centers, and other luxury sites that the uncanny nature of fictitious Dubai comes into view. For example, in chapter 3, titled "Underneath," Walker regains consciousness after crashing through a glass ceiling into a defunct hotel. The highly decorative interior features details proper to a grand hotel—rich blue and gold décor, with monumental peacock statues and ostentatious touches. Signs of excess such as bottles of champagne litter the site. The shifting sands have made it an underground cavern where it was once aboveground. The familiar made strange is heightened as Walker and his team engage in an extended firefight in an effort to escape their ultraconsumerist tomb alive. This spectacular setting is one of many instances in which the inside and the outside become confused, up and down reversed, and the spaces of civilization revert to sites of urban warfare and barbarity.

In short, the atmospheric, imagined Dubai of the game becomes a site of trauma for Walker, in a fictive heart of darkness of the Arab world. Upside-down ragged American flags—a sign of dire distress—and the evidential failure of humanitarian intervention dot the landscape. It is a hellish vision that owes much of its affect to films like *Apocalypse Now*. The obvious reading is of the rubble of Dubai as an externalization of Walker's crumbling mental interiority. Less charitable is a racialized vision of moral decay of the Arab world from within.

The Line certainly departs from its predecessors in its creative reimagining of a developed and wealthy city in the Arab world. *Heart of Darkness* was set in the Belgian Congo and underscored the degree to which the European colonizing presence defined itself in opposition to its African subjects and undomesticated land. *Apocalypse Now* was made during a time in which the United States defined itself in contradistinction to the hostile presence of communism in Asia, specifically Vietnam. Coppola's Captain Willard searches for Colonel Kurtz in a foreboding dark jungle that is constructed in the film as pure peril and savagery. The site of *The Line* departs from this by presenting a once-grand metropolis that has been reabsorbed by nature. This dystopia of the opulent space resonates readily with a more recent cultural moment in which the presence of rapid modernization and industrialization in Asia (particularly the Arab world and China) produces anxiety for the West, which has until now tenuously maintained its superpower status. Specifically, the Western fear of the rise of non-Western economic, industrial, and technological centers has manifested itself in framing the ideological construction of rapid modernization of these regions as rapacious in their exploitation of labor and destruction of the ecosystem.[7] This fear is ironic, considering the United States attained its dominant status by similar means.

The fictive Dubai becomes, in this context, a scene of both wish fulfillment and anxious disequilibrium. On the one hand, uncontrollable forces of nature, a seeming act of God, struck down an Arab megacity of indulgence. On the other hand, in its resultant disorder, one enters into the space to find a theater of war, with all its surreal atrocities. Location is key in that the megacity has become undomesticated, and trappings of civilization (social order, opulence, hypercapitalism) exist only as ruins. In fact, the modernization of non-Western centers is often denigrated as a pantomiming of Western and continental development, due to an ideological configuration of Europe and the West as the seat of scientific and technological advancement in the world. Modernization is coded as Eurocentric, and therefore its presence in Asia is correspondingly marked as inauthentic, or a parody. Non-Western modernity is fundamentally skewed as an imitation of what it means to be genuinely civilized. Under this reading, the storms do not destroy these Arab spaces; rather nature returns them to the savagery that lies beneath their gilded surface. The sandstorms tear away a veneer to reveal the essence of the space, which is conceived of as implicitly barbarous.

The shifting sands of this false Dubai's topography thus recall a destabilized space of constant reshaping and becoming. The land itself can become an asset too—piled heavily against windows, the sand can be released by shooting out the glass, causing a dune to shift and overwhelm enemies. Its shanty ruins of a global city, peopled by rogue insurgents and cast-off migrant laborers subsisting in the wreckage of Arab empire, bespeak a horror of order broken down, seepage between civilization and nature, self and other. What is the connection between that space and our space, between that context and our own? It is a hypothetical scenario of a "state of exception" in which extreme (martial) measures are necessary for survival and to stave off the chaos.[8] It has, in a sense, returned to an authentic state of disorder, certainly not Edenic, but nevertheless sublime. In this capacity, the game activates an anxiety around the global megacity and what it stands for but does not cogently critique that fear. This is interestingly discordant with the game's apparent critique of the ubiquitous military genre, which indicates that while the game questions the genre conventions of the military shooter, it does not critique its larger visual cultural politics of militarism. That is, it critiques neither the jingoistic militarism of the culture that gives rise to such representations nor the anti-Arab sentiments that (especially in the present political moment) tend to shore up those ideas.

Normative Soldiers, Good and Necessary Wars

Criticism of war games circulates around their pedagogical role in inuring players to militarized vision and violence, as well as their parallel uses as simulations for training and, more importantly, recruitment.[9] While there is much sociology-based discussion in the popular media of the direct connection between enacting violence in a game and doing the same in the lived world, what is understudied is the critical cultural approach that games may enlighten. Tanine Allison, for example, speaking primarily of World War II historical military shooters, analyzes an ideological sleight of hand through which such games point to a moment firmly constructed in history as good and necessary, and then nest contemporary conflicts within that sensibility. A player may then reenact the presented scenarios until they are surgically executed and perfected. This is achieved by presenting a system of missions that function within the formal structure of gameplay as goals and rewards, with no lived-world repercussions. Allison writes,

> Even if the current wars in Iraq and Afghanistan do not fit the model that is propounded by these games—a war of precision aiming and firing in which enemies are clearly located and there is no collateral damage—these games still reflect the fantasy of what modern war is: clean, precise, fast-paced, and with quantifiable success. Video games present war as something that can be controlled and mastered, without post-traumatic stress disorder or real death.[10]

This seems to resonate with a contemporary political affective moment that for some heralds the death of "traditional America"[11] or the erosion of the American way of life and its moral firmament, which was more stable in the historical configuration of World War II as a good war.

It is true that most military shooters presume the heroic and moral rectitude of their protagonists and that they may appeal to a player's desire to feel a certain way about the soldier-hero. However, *The Line* proves an exception to Allison's characterization by presenting compelling missions that beg for successful and efficient achievement on a game-mechanics level, while on a narrative level grating against the character's (and by extension the player's) presumed sense of righteousness and moral culpability. In this, *The Line* uniquely departs from its genre conventions.

In one scenario, for example, one must choose between shooting a man who stole water out of desperation—a grave offense—or the soldier who killed the thief's family in an attempt to apprehend him. Under threat of sniper fire, one must decide—shoot soldier or civilian, attempt to free them by shooting their ropes, attempt to shoot the snipers, or simply try to run (figure 8.2). While some nuances of narrative result from the varying options, none of them profoundly impact the trajectory of the story in terms of providing morally satisfying outcomes. The game has generally been praised for seeking to integrate ethical questions into the shooter genre and for its subversive narrative. As this particular example shows, possible ethical conversations issue not from providing a good option and a bad one but by making all the choices gut-wrenching ones.[12]

The cinematic referentiality of the game additionally recalls semantic and syntactic elements of contemporary war films and relies largely on preexisting visual culture to lend it authenticity. The game is replete with military clichés that are self-consciously, annoyingly saccharine to the critical viewer. Gregarious

Figure 8.2. Whom to shoot: soldier or civilian? (*Spec Ops: The Line* game still)

banter at the introduction of the core team of characters creates a sense of a preexisting bond; a strong physical manifestation of elite training is conveyed through practiced, efficient execution of commands; and stylized renderings of one-dimensional supersoldiers depict them banding together on a mission. However, as the narrative unfolds, these tropes turn in on themselves as the player begins to question Walker's thinning excuses for violence and his perpetual straying from the mission. Players begin to want to distance themselves from the very character with which they should most identify.

Load screens didactically signal critique with phrases like:

> "Do you feel like a hero yet?"
> "You are still a good person."
> "You cannot understand, nor do you want to."
> "This is all your fault."
> "What happens in Dubai stays in Dubai."

These messages are charged with a kind of reverse polarity to the action of the game, which is itself dubious. They undermine the presumption that one plays from a central position of good, or as the hero of the narrative. Particularly, the lattermost phrase makes reference to a popular advertising slogan, "What happens in Vegas, stays in Vegas," which suggests letting go of one's inhibitions in the sequestered party zone of Sin City. In the case of the game's fictive Dubai, it is not pleasure but an orgy of violence that is to remain behind—which configures the central figure as villain. In an interview, Williams insists that anything there purely for shock value was removed. He wanted all moral dilemmas to be realistic. The game, he asserts, asks the player to "hold a mirror up to [himself] and say, 'Why am I playing this game the way that I am playing it?'"[13] This notion of self-reflection appears as a refrain in *The Line*, through the use of mirrors and reflective images as a trope, to which I return later.

Players and game critics alike conveyed a marked affective response to the murky moral scenarios. A flurry of reviews reflected on how the game made reviewers feel. This likely attested to the potency of the narrative and aesthetic elements that encouraged rumination on the cost of military violence and framed Captain Walker's treacherous journey as stingingly tragic. While moral quandaries are presented, gameplay consistently denies the player the chance to perform as good or evil Walker. Brendan Keogh explores this in his critical analysis of *The Line*. He writes, "I may not have always had a choice in my actions in *The Line*, but I was still responsible for being present in those choice-less situations. Or, put another way, what I chose to do doesn't matter so much as what I did."[14] The game, he asserts, invokes criticality by forcing you as a player to consider your intentions while you play, and your own rationalizations of in-game brutality as having been enacted without choice or, in other words, as inevitable.

Williams seized his opportunity at the 2013 Game Developers Conference in San Francisco to do a wrap-up of the game and his team's intentions. He spoke precisely about the tools they used to intervene in the typical genre conventions of military action shooters, which operate on ludic and narrative levels. He identified the importance of "ludonarrative dissonance" or, in other words, the oppositional friction between the stated narrative contract of the game and its mechanical contract.[15] This term was initially constructed by Clint Hocking as a way of characterizing a flaw in a game, whereby the message contained within the narrative is somehow contradicted by actions undertaken in gameplay—or perhaps in the point-scoring system. For example, Hocking critiqued the purported narrative of self-sacrifice in *BioShock* (2007, 2K Boston and 2K Australia) because the gameplay itself, through its opportunism and violence, ultimately sends a message of self-interest. In his presentation "We Are Not Heroes: Contextualizing Violence through Narrative," Williams summarized his stance on the subject of violence in his own game, and games in general:

> I don't believe that violent games make violent people, and I don't believe that violent games desensitize us to violence. I do, however, believe that violent games desensitize us to violence in games, and I think that has to do with how we treat our games and how we treat our genres, which is that our genres are defined by action, and that action is how you are going to be interacting with the world. It's going to be how you overcome obstacles, how you effect change, how you progress in your goals. If it is a platformer, you are going to do that by jumping. If it is a shooter, you are going to do this by killing someone with a gun.[16]

Fundamentally, the core game mechanic of *The Line*, he explained, shapes the limitations of what the player can do. A shooter requires shooting, plain and simple, so it is not as if Walker is going to do much else. But this dissonance between the ideals of a humanitarian mission and the use of excessive violence in the process can be maximized, the apparent hypocrisy mined as constitutive of the main character, as opposed to being a flaw of the game design. As one critic opined, "as the game goes forward, it becomes weirder and weirder that he's killing so many people."[17]

Gender and the Theater of War

Evan Watts has discussed ruins as a prevalent aesthetic of many game spaces and what this might mean symbolically in terms of social structures and the toppling of a phallic order. In this interpretation, architectural structures become "monuments of a masculine-dominated society" and a ruin then functions as "a space that offers freedom from the same gender-oppressive institutions that once permeated them, and thus sites of empowerment."[18] In the case of the ruin aesthetic of *The Line*, the site does engender a kind of freedom, but of the nihilistic variety. In this mythic structure, men can be men, but their violent mark-making is aberrant. Watts analyzes this through several games, most notably the underwater ruins of *BioShock*, arguing that in a larger sense, even though the new social order arising is "horrific," it at least reveals the heteronormative order to be socially constructed and therefore malleable.[19] While in the case of *The Line*, where gender reversals may not be at play in the same way that Watts lays out, it is important to consider the imaging of white (normative) masculinity in crisis and its relation to an imagined site of social chaos.[20]

Watts is correct insofar that, as sophisticated expressions, games do model gender standards, power relations, racial biases, class differentials, and sexual norms. Women in *The Line* exist only as victims of torture and friendly fire; as the subject of casual joking between men; as burned, dead, casualties—precious, perhaps, but fundamentally secondary. Though the patriarchal order is disrupted in the false Dubai, the result is chaos, as opposed to an alternative or gender-reversed solution. Jennifer Terry, a scholar working at the intersection of war, technological innovation, and humanitarian intervention, traces the ways in which history has shown gender and the promise of women's liberation to be a tool of empire. Through a reading of Amy Kaplan's work, she elucidates the ideological role of gender in garnering support for expansion:

> Humanitarian claims have been at the forefront of all modern American military excursions, claims that have been mobilized to rationalize the seizing of territory and resources from Native Americans; from Native Hawaiians; from peoples living in Cuba, Puerto Rico, the Philippines, Korea, Vietnam, and now Iraq. Humanitarian salvation, Kaplan notes, has been a powerful ideological mechanism for justifying U.S. empire to the masses in the United States. A rationale of liberating others—of bringing democracy to allegedly backward cultures—and particularly claims of liberating women: these are fundamental ideological mystifications burying wounds and deaths that continue to haunt the United States.[21]

Terry ultimately contends that militarism, humanitarianism, and imperialism are of the same order, that their destructive powers are mobilized through ideologies of saving the other, and that the wounds this destruction leaves are legible traces of geopolitical and biopolitical ideology. Similarly, the scorched or otherwise traumatized bodies of women imaged in *The Line* become both a moral motivation for the ensuing conflict, as well as a necessary collateral cost of the conflict (figure 8.3). That they are neither playable characters nor secondary interactants points to their configuration as pawns as opposed to agents—at least in the world of the game.

Still, the heteronormative, white male shooter trope is also undermined in the narrative. Watts writes of this, particularly the frustrated "'masculine' satisfaction accompanying gameplay mechanics of dominating one's environment using violence and aggression,"[22] Sara Humphreys discusses games as cultural expressions that "influence the development of cultural, racial, political, social, and national identities."[23] Games, she argues, re-present myth models: "powerful paradigmatic myths that serve as models for the construction of similar myths."[24] She cites the Western action genre of games, specifically *Red Dead Redemption* (2010, Rockstar San Diego), as proselytizing American exceptionalism, neoliberalism, and white

Figure 8.3. Female refugee from a cutscene (*Spec Ops: The Line* game still)

supremacy. In *The Line*, Captain Walker performs his role of supersoldier, seeking to dominate every scenario with military aggression. However, as the game progresses, he and his team physically transform from a well-oiled and surgically accurate unit to burned, bloodied, traumatized aggressors. Their psychological breakdown mirrors this, but particularly Walker's verbalizations to his men shift from jocular confidence to stern aggression and then finally to psychotic rage. His metamorphosis under the duress of battle from the beginning to the end, and his mounting rationalizations that become tantamount to dementia, agitate a preexisting longing for the stability of that normative male role. But it is eroded throughout the game until what remains is psychopathy and a figure of hero as menace who uses pure, excessive violence as a destructive form of expression. He is effective in the execution of his elite training, but his motivations are flawed and his ultimate endeavor to save lives is utterly impotent.

This transformation from supersoldier to mass murderer occurs across the arc of fifteen chapters of gameplay. In the early portions of the game, the narrative models hackneyed homosocial relations in terms of the mythmaking of soldiering as an unconditional, loving bond between men. This depoliticizes the image into a band-of-brothers myth, which functions through its focus on the individual and interpersonal relations, rather than larger political forces at play in the circumstances of soldiers in battle.[25] This is consistent with the military shooter genre. But as key characters of *The Line* become more exhausted, injured, filthy, surly, hopeless, and morally bankrupt, verbal cues by the primary character move from clichéd war film dialogue to unhinged bloodlust. Walker transforms into a menacing figure, a terrorist who imposes his ideology and will on others in pursuit of unsanctioned objectives no one else shares. Through this shifting representation, which is slowly revealed by play, the image of the ideal soldier as the embodiment of righteous justice is tarnished, and the critique takes shape.

The literal and metaphorical use of mirroring as an analog of self-criticality, or in other words, looking at one's self in the mirror, becomes a leitmotif within the game. Culpability and ethical clarity are closely connected to key peaks in the game's narrative arc, as well as moments of revelation that interrupt the character's coherent sense of self. The most potent example is in the pivotal white phosphorous assault in chapter 8, "The Gate," during which Walker uses incendiary warfare on American Thirty-Third Battalion soldiers that far outnumber his team. If the player wishes to continue, there is no viable alternative but to play through Walker's choice. This comes at roughly the middle of the game, after a geographic descent that generates an aesthetic vision of this place as ever more hellish, treacherous, and unconscionable. This incident is imaged in a very sophisticated use of visual signifiers to conjure the act of playing the game in relation to the excessive cruelty that will take place—and which mirrors recent lived-world events. The controls for the white phosphorous mortars are not unlike those used for gameplay—a case with toggles, buttons, and a screen. First, despite the outspoken protest of Lugo, your team launches a camera device that will provide a bird's-eye view, to be observed on the monitor within the player screen. Most poignantly, Walker's face is imaged in the reflective surface of the camera monitor, so that you (the player) simultaneously see an on-screen self and the remote bomb-vision of white phosphorous charges deployed at your command. It is self-reflection, literalized. The resultant casualties—chemically burned soldiers writhing on the ground in pain and frozen in grisly death poses—are agonizing to survey later. Worse yet is the collateral damage of noncombatant refugees, many of them women and children, who have suffered the same fate. A close-up of a charred woman and child, huddled together, her hand held over the child's eyes, drives home the not-so-subtle message (figure 8.4). Again, here women and children are configured not as having agency but as passive victims; more importantly, they are civilian victims of excessive use of force by a supposed hero. Internal fighting flares again when Lugo reacts to the horror, claiming they have gone too far this time. The question of who exactly has gone too far may point to Walker, Adams, and Lugo on one level; to the game designers, who painfully conjure the recent use of this weapon in Iraq by both Saddam Hussein and the United States; and the US military itself, which has defended its use of white phosphorous as not being in violation of chemical warfare prohibitions on account of its official classification as "incendiary."[26]

In blurring the ethical boundary between soldier and mass murderer, *The Line* indicts the supposed civilizing mission or "white man's burden" of protecting the globe from degenerating into disorder, darkness, and barbarism. In this, the line that is crossed may also refer to the dissolution of stable white masculinity as it is put into crisis through a racial encounter with the other in the Arab world.

Figure 8.4. Victims of white phosphorous (*Spec Ops: The Line* game still)

The protagonist of most first- and third-person military shooters assuredly fights on the side of right. In this game, fantasies of full-spectrum dominance remain technically fulfilled, but morally frustrated. As a player, this frustration results largely from feeling dragged into Walker's insanity and self-righteous military display, without having any real power to choose otherwise. In fact, after using the aforementioned cinematic elements and military shooter signifiers to present a conventional vision, *The Line* deftly exploits morally condemnable tactics as a strategy for confounding players' expectations that they represent the good.

Conclusion

In "War Bytes: The Critique of Militainment in *Spec Ops: The Line*," Matthew Payne suggests that "indeed, *Spec Ops* might be the game industry's first major, anti-war military shooter."[27] Arguing that the game breaks with the tradition of military entertainment games by injecting the whole scenario of its play with "discordant feeling," Payne concludes that a genre critique is at work.[28] By interrupting the basic pleasures of the military shooter (which he describes as a pleasure of escapism within the context of an affective bond to the lived world), *Spec Ops* creates a productive discomfort for the player that gives rise to internal self-reflection on the "banal pleasures of militainment."[29] What, ultimately, are the possibilities for self-critical address of ideological constructions that typically populate the military game genre? This is, after all, a fraught time for creative contribution. The ongoing actions in the Arab world—namely, the Gulf Wars and the Global War on Terrorism—have been incessantly and immediately represented in visual culture (with the repetition of animated graphics of war, smart-bomb vision, and planes striking towers). The global effort demands a political unity that charges any critique with being antiwar and anti-nation. The question for a creative producer then becomes how to respond through visual culture when the only two viable options seem to be support or silence. Critique virtually guarantees censure, while complicity engenders propaganda. The work of the imagination demands more than this, so what becomes of the expression? What generation of meaning is possible?

Yes, *The Line* does contain a critique of the cost of war (particularly the psychological toll) at the story level. It does borrow from the visual culture of the antiwar film (*Apocalypse Now, Full Metal Jacket*, etc.), and it does break with the military shooter genre's jingoism by turning its core action against itself. From a gender equity perspective, women are configured as victims without agency or as absent, in both the diegesis of the game and as a tool of the larger critique it seems to make—a retrograde maneuver in an otherwise sophisticated intervention. As Keogh has remarked, "In a game that subverts and works against so many conventions, an entirely conventional lack of any real representation of women—without any real commentary on this lack—is incredibly disappointing."[30] More interestingly, the racialized sense of place points to fears around what the modernization of non-Western centers mean for the United States, with its imperiled superpower status. But the pleasure in the game comes from tapping into a deeper American cultural imaginary of the Arab world as regressing into calamity and mired in extreme poverty, reinforced through continual media representation. "Being a spectator of calamities taking place in another country," Susan Sontag once wrote, "is a quintessential modern experience, the cumulative offering by more than a century and half's worth of those professional, specialized tourists known as journalists. Wars are now also living room sights and sounds."[31] With this game, the horror of the everyday imaging of ruin and agony in remote places is brought into our living rooms in a new way. *The Line* presents a playable opportunity for those of a particular socialization—who see themselves mirrored in and functioning through Walker—to play their part in the destruction of a region that occupies a deep-seated racialized fear, that of a dark world rising up as a technological, wealthy, and research-rich competitor on the global stage. Returning Dubai, a gleaming symbol of that Arab world modernity, to a state of savagery, no doubt constitutes a cathartic vision for a certain type of nationalist, whose American identity is bound up in global dominance and the other as a manifestation of lack. And all this is achieved while Walker deludes himself that he (and by extension you) are on a humanitarian mission. The melancholic irony of *Spec Ops: The Line* issues, finally, from a friction between its call for technical mastery of gameplay and a moral bankruptcy that lies beneath it.

What are the rubble and ruin of this game? The rubble is of fallen empire. This is wishful thinking as it represents a rising Arab empire with all the fears and fantasies this possibility engenders. It also represents the conceit of a moralistic claim of judgment over the burgeoning modernization, opulence, and global economic dominance of that other space. Is the affective force of the atrocity witnessed—and enacted within gameplay—not only one of violence but one of the dissolution between the self and the other? The ruin is of an ideal, in this case the psychological and ethical ruin of a Western soldier ideal, whose time has passed and whose prescribed role as a protector/gatekeeper against the encroaching chaos of an Arab heart of darkness is defunct.

SORAYA MURRAY is Assistant Professor in the Film and Digital Media Department at the University of California, Santa Cruz. She teaches contemporary visual culture, with a particular interest in art, digital media, and games. She is author of *On Video Games: The Visual Politics of Race, Gender and Space.*

Notes

Acknowledgments: I thank Derek Conrad Murray, Neda Atanasoski, Felicity Amaya Schaeffer, the anonymous readers, and the editors for their generous feedback during the development of this chapter. Earlier versions of this chapter were delivered at the Center for Cultural Studies at the University of California, Santa Cruz, in May 2013, the Leonardo Art Science Evening Rendezvous (LASER) lecture series at Stanford University in June 2014, and California College of the Arts in February 2015.

1. This notion of a culture's "dream life" comes from Stuart Hall, *The Origins of Cultural Studies: A Lecture*, produced and edited by Sut Jhally (Northampton, MA: Media Education Foundation, 2006), DVD.

2. The connection to *Heart of Darkness* was frequently mentioned in interviews with Walt Williams. See, for example, Hollander Cooper, "Spec Ops: The Line—Learn about the Story with Lead Writer Walt Williams," *GamesRadar+*, March 30, 2012, http://www.gamesradar.com/spec-ops-line-learn-about-story-lead-writer-walt-williams/.

3. Gillen McAllister, "Spec Ops: The Line GRTV Interview," *Gamereactor*, June 21, 2012, http://www.gamereactor.eu/news/33921/Spec+Ops%3AThe+Line+GRTV+Interview/.

4. From the game documentation included with PlayStation 3 version packaging.

5. For a thorough deconstruction of the relationship between *Heart of Darkness, Apocalypse Now*, and shifting attitudes around the Vietnam War and humanitarian intervention, see Neda Atanasoski, "The Vietnam War and the Ethics of Failure: *Heart of Darkness* and the Emergence of Humanitarian Feeling at the Limits of Imperial Critique," in *Humanitarian Violence: The U.S. Deployment of Diversity* (Minneapolis: University of Minnesota Press, 2013), 73–101.

6. Ibid., 76.

7. Among the many recent examples, see the nine-part Showtime documentary television series focusing on climate change, *Years of Living Dangerously* (Season 1, directed by Joel Bach and David Gelber), which premiered April 2014. See also the documentary of photographer Edward Burtynsky, *Manufactured Landscapes*, directed by Jennifer Baichwal (Foundry Films, 2007), whose photographs of ecological destruction and labor abuse in China starkly point to Western anxieties around the ascension of China to superpower status through rapid industrialization, urbanization projects, and energy revolution.

8. Giorgio Agamben, *State of Exception*, trans. Kevin Attell (Chicago: University of Chicago Press, 2005).

9. There are many examples, but see especially Nick Dyer-Witheford and Greig de Peuter, *Games of Empire: Global Capitalism and Video Games* (Minneapolis: University of Minnesota Press,

2009); and Nina B. Huntemann and Matt Payne, eds., *Joystick Soldiers: The Politics of Play in Military Video Games* (London: Routledge, 2009).

10. Tanine Allison, "The World War II Video Game, Adaptation, and Postmodern History," *Literature/Film Quarterly* 38, no. 3 (2010): 192.

11. Bill O'Reilly, American television host of *The O'Reilly Factor* on Fox News Channel, uses this common terminology, with which conservatives speak about what they believe to be a break from "traditional" America. Bill O'Reilly, "Talking Points Memo: Is Traditional America Gone for Good?" *Fox News*, November 12, 2012, http://www.foxnews.com/transcript/2012/11/13/bill-oreilly-traditional-america-gone-good.

12. For an excellent analysis of the ethical gameplay design in *The Line*, see Miguel Sicart, "Into Play," in *Beyond Choices: The Design of Ethical Gameplay* (Cambridge, MA: MIT Press, 2013), 111–116.

13. McAllister, "Spec Ops."

14. Brendan Keogh, *Killing Is Harmless: A Critical Reading of Spec Ops: The Line* (Marden, Australia: Stolen Projects, 2013), Kindle edition, loc. 2394.

15. Williams's discussion is part of a 2007 debate that resulted from Clint Hocking's coining of the phrase "ludonarrative dissonance" on his blog. See Clint Hocking, "Ludonarrative Dissonance in *Bioshock*: The Problem of What the Game Is About," *Click Nothing*, October 7, 2007, http://clicknothing.typepad.com/click_nothing/2007/10/ludonarrative-d.html.

16. Walt Williams, "We Are Not Heroes: Contextualizing Violence through Narrative," presentation at Game Developers Conference, March 27, 2013, http://www.gamasutra.com/view/news/188964/Video_Spec_Ops_The_Line_contextualizes_violence_through_story.php.

17. Kirk Hamilton, "*Spec Ops* Writer on Violent Games: 'We're Better Than That,'" *Kotaku*, March 27, 2013, http://kotaku.com/spec-ops-writer-on-violent-games-were-better-than-th-460992384.

18. Evan Watts, "Ruin, Gender, and Digital Games," *WSQ: Women's Studies Quarterly* 39, no. 3 and 4 (2011): 248.

19. Ibid., 255.

20. Here I want to be clear that although there are three soldiers, including Walker, Lugo, and Adams (Euro-American, Italian American, and African American, respectively), it is Walker who is losing his mind.

21. Jennifer Terry, "Significant Injury: War, Medicine, and Empire in Claudia's Case," *WSQ: Women's Studies Quarterly* 37, no. 1–2 (2009): 200–225.

22. Watts, "Ruin, Gender, and Digital Games," 255–256.

23. Sara Humphreys, "Rejuvenating 'Eternal Inequality' on the Digital Frontiers of *Red Dead Redemption*," *Western American Literature* 47, no. 2 (2012): 202.

24. Ibid.

25. Dyer-Witheford and de Peuter discuss this in "Banal War: *Full Spectrum Warrior*," in *Games of Empire*, 97–122.

26. "US Used White Phosphorus in Iraq," *BBC News*, November 16, 2005, http://news.bbc.co.uk/2/hi/middle_east/4440664.stm.

27. Matthew Thomas Payne, "War Bytes: The Critique of Militainment in *Spec Ops: The Line*," *Critical Studies in Media Communication* 31, no. 4 (2014): 265–282. See also Matthew Thomas Payne, *Playing War: Military Video Games after 9/11* (New York: New York University Press, 2016).

28. Payne, "War Bytes," 266.

29. Ibid., 268.

30. Keogh, *Killing Is Harmless*, loc. 1239–1241.

31. Susan Sontag, *Regarding the Pain of Others* (New York: Picador, 2003), 18.

chapter nine

REPRESENTING RACE AND DISABILITY

Grand Theft Auto: San Andreas *as a Whole Text*

RACHAEL HUTCHINSON

RESEARCH ON RACE IN GAME STUDIES HAS FOCUSED MORE ON THE disenfranchisement of certain populations in the world of game texts rather than on the reasons that developers may construct particular images of race for particular reasons. Analysis of racial representation in games is often based on stereotypical imagery found in short segments of game text, isolated from narrative context and divorced from cultural meaning. I argue that to understand the representation of race in video games, it must be placed in the context of the narrative whole. Diegetic elements such as character motivation and gameplay dynamics like player-character identification must be taken into account. It is also useful to examine racial imagery in terms of broader aims of the game text, such as social critique, and to analyze its construction along different axes of identity. Race is not represented in a vacuum, but as a marker of identity and difference used in conjunction with other markers such as social class, sexuality, disability, age, and so forth. Rockstar North's *Grand Theft Auto: San Andreas* (2004) is a useful case study, as a game that has attracted much scholarly and media criticism for its depictions of racialized violence. At the same time, it was the first game from a major studio to feature a black man as the main playable character. I argue that when taken as a whole, the game provides a thoughtful examination of race relations in mid-1990s California.

As a whole text, the representational complexity of *GTA: San Andreas* resists attempts to simplify and isolate images of racial violence and stereotype. Racial stereotypes serve a purpose in the central story, and player-character identification is strengthened as interracial cooperation in the plot gives the player access to different sections of the game world. However, the dual identity construction of blind Triad boss Wu Zi Mu, on the axes of race and disability, points to the limitations of Rockstar's social commentary. Despite the emphasis on race in the text, disability is treated in a less thoughtful manner. To access these elements by examining the narrative whole does not preclude the study of gameplay or limit analysis to a pure cultural studies approach. Instead, I aim to show how narrative, representation, and gameplay dynamics are intertwined and interdependent.

Critical Reception and the Fantasy Other

GTA: San Andreas was developed by Rockstar North and released for the PlayStation 2 in October 2004. The main character is Carl Johnson (CJ), a young black gang member who negotiates his way through intergang warfare and police corruption to save his brother and restore peace to his community, Grove Street, in the city of Los Santos. The in-game world is a vast, open environment, explorable on foot or by a wide variety of vehicles. Los Santos approximates real-world Los Angeles, featuring territorial warfare between black and Latino gangs. San Francisco and Las Vegas are represented by the in-game cities of San Fierro and Las Venturas, dominated by the Chinese Triads and Italian mafia, respectively. The map opens up to the player in stages, as missions are passed and the plot develops. Set in the 1990s, the game features music, fashion, and slang from the period as well as a riot scene reminiscent of the Los Angeles riots of 1992. Like other games in the franchise, *GTA: San Andreas* was seen as controversial for its violent and sexual content. Negative criticism against violent video games is not new, but *San Andreas* brought a racial dimension to violence that many found offensive.

While the game raised ire among parents and politicians, it was a critical and commercial success in industry terms, praised for its realism and open-ended environment, engaging story line, action-adventure gameplay, high production values, and new role-playing elements.[1] *IGN* rated it 9.9 out of 10, the highest rating it awarded any PlayStation 2 game, and it won Game of the Year Awards from *GameSpot*, *IGN*, and Spike TV. Adding to its profile, *San Andreas* featured recognized voice actors like Samuel L. Jackson, James Woods, Chris Penn, and Peter Fonda. It remained the highest-grossing game for the PlayStation 2 in the United States through the end of the console's commercial influence, with sales of over 17.3 million units.

Scholarly articles on the game have tended to focus negatively on the image of black and Latino gangs in Los Santos. David Leonard criticizes the characters as "an array of Black and Latino men, all with braids, bandanas, and guns," even though many black and Latino characters in the game are merely bystanders, shopkeepers, or city officials.[2] Charles Dickerman and his collaborators describe the narrative as that of "a young African American man trying to get rich and succeed through violent and criminal gang activity."[3] This assessment overlooks the character's motivation; while CJ does amass a certain amount of wealth, his main aim is to seek his mother's killer and eliminate the drug-dealing empire of corrupt police officials in Los Santos. Paul Barrett characterizes CJ's neighborhood as "a pseudo-shantytown literally under a bridge," even though the Grove Street cul-de-sac features a mix of one- and two-story houses on individual plots of land, with garages, driveways, and basketball hoops.[4] CJ's house is well-appointed with a full kitchen, living room with a TV and video game console, upstairs bedrooms, walk-in closet, and art on the walls. Leonard argues that the academic emphasis on racialized violence is symptomatic of hierarchical discourses of race in America, but the narrow focus on black gangsta imagery means that other elements of identity construction and narrative context have been overlooked.[5]

Critics have also focused on the whiteness of the Rockstar developers, and their skewed representation of minorities that enables white supremacy discourse.[6] It is true that Rockstar North is mostly run by white men, and that Los Angeles is constructed as a fantasy place in the game, much as Miami is in *GTA: Vice City* (2002). However, the main difference between the two games is that the player-controlled main character in *San Andreas* is black, whereas the main character in *Vice City* is white. There is a corresponding difference in the accusations of racism leveled against the two games. In *Vice City*, the main character has to eliminate the Haitian rivals of a Cuban drug lord. The instruction to "kill the Haitians" has been interpreted by some as a racist order for a white character to exterminate an ethnic group.[7] Accusations against *San Andreas*, however, focus on possible actions that players could take with the main character. Because the player embodies a black character, scholars see the gameplay as "digital blackface" or minstrelsy, where the player enjoys the fantasy of playing as the other.[8]

Lisa Nakamura and Peter Chow-White argue that the element of player performance or embodiment distinguishes the study of representation in video games from its study in many other media.[9] It is therefore important to analyze the representation of race through player-character interaction, embodiment, and identification. However, studies on embodiment in *San Andreas* have limited race to a strict black-white binary and overestimated the statistical dominance of white male players.[10] Assuming the whiteness of players of *San Andreas* makes "embodiment" transracial in nature, which is not always the case. Current studies also tend to assume that all black players will have similar reactions to the stereotyped representation, although as André Brock's discourse analysis of *Resident Evil 5* (2009, Capcom) demonstrates, individual players have vastly differing reactions to racial representation.[11] Further, critics have not considered that black and other minority players of the game are also enjoying playing as the other when playing *San Andreas*. If the fantasy cities of Los Santos and Vice City function as spaces where the other can be constructed in a particular way, the other in question does not have to be racially defined. The dangerous world of criminal activity is already an other space for most gamers, who enjoy the transgressive environment as an exciting alternative to their own socially acceptable lives.

In short, criticism of *San Andreas* has not taken into account the interplay between embodied, individual players and the game's narrative. The study of racial representation has been based on the surface visuals of characters, rather than how they act in the narrative or interact with other characters of different races, and on misguided assumptions about who is playing the game and how players embody CJ as a character. *San Andreas* is a rich narrative text that does not offer static representations of black and Latino men in isolation, but explores how these men negotiate racial prejudice and overcome biased attitudes. Player choices about how to play the game, and the development of player-character identification over the course of the narrative, both provide strong evidence that *San Andreas*—contrary to its popular and scholarly reputation—is a text deeply concerned with issues of race, prejudice, and how people see each other in society.

Choosing Violence: Player Agency and the Narrative Whole

Criticism of racialized violence in *San Andreas* has focused on the radical possibilities of action available to the player, as well as the violent missions of the central story, often conflating the two. Many critics do not distinguish between the sandbox play of exploring the open-ended game environment ("paidea") and the mission-centered objectives of the central narrative ("ludus").[12] However, for open-ended environments like *San Andreas*, the distinction between gameplay modes is crucial. Zach Whalen describes the game as "a reflexive space that contains modalities of play and the freedom to select between them as its overarching structure."[13] The narrative whole is thus made up of different gameplay modes negotiated by the player—as Nate Garrelts observes, "the act of playing the game has become an act of choosing which content will surface."[14] The narrative of sandbox play is largely determined by player choice, resulting in a spectrum of activity from the socially acceptable to deranged mayhem. The player chooses whether CJ should help or harm strangers, compliment or insult passersby, indulge in random drive-by shootings or take on ambulance missions, ferrying needy passengers to the hospital.[15] Bill Loguidice and Matt Barton argue that the element of choice in sandbox play makes the game text a mirror of the player's moral compass as well as social values: "Rockstar can always fall back on the position that they merely create possibilities—it's up to the player to enact them. If living the life of a criminal is more fun than being a law-abiding citizen, what does that say about our society?"[16]

In this reading, the game system acts as a critique of our own attitudes toward violence. As Gonzalo Frasca observes, paidea structures carry their ideological agendas in the "manipulation rules" of what the player is able to do in the game, not just the "goal rules" of what is needed to win.[17] In *San Andreas* the two systems work together: negative actions on the street bring consequences (raised wanted levels, police attention, attacks from pedestrians) while positive actions bring better statistics, many of which help the player in achieving central mission objectives. Rewards for civic-minded behavior are built into the level-up system:

completing optional ambulance missions raises health to 150 percent, while completing fire engine missions makes CJ impervious to flames. Scholars have noted the conservative outlook of a game where passersby scream at violent acts and CJ is rewarded for his hard work ethic, whether pumping iron at the gym or earning respect on the streets.[18] But in the open world environment, CJ can potentially emerge as a civic-minded citizen rather than the violent thug of media perception.

In contrast to sandbox play, the central missions follow a linear script involving a great deal of violence. Player agency is limited to deciding whether to attempt the missions, although Ian Bogost observes that the game constantly "reorients the player back toward the missions."[19] The player is also restricted to a small area of the map until a certain number of missions are passed. While some missions involve positive actions (such as rescuing someone from a fire), the player must commit robbery and murder to complete the story. However, this must be taken in the context of criminal activity elsewhere in the game world, as well as the overall objective of the central missions. As in previous *GTA* games, the criminal activity of the main character in the central missions pales in comparison to the organized crime of other gangs, politicians, and city leaders.[20] In *San Andreas* this includes human trafficking by Vietnamese gangs, drug dealing and distribution by corrupt police, money laundering by the Italian mafia, and international armament smuggling by the CIA. It is the job of the main character to shut these operations down, making CJ the good guy by comparison. It is also significant that the larger crimes are not monopolized by black characters. While black officer Frank Tenpenny (voiced by Samuel L. Jackson) is the mastermind behind police corruption in Los Santos, the other major criminals are either Asian or white. Critics who focus on negative racial representation of African Americans are therefore focusing on the gang warfare of Los Santos rather than the organized crime that provides its context.

The gang violence itself serves a specific purpose in the game, as CJ's story is tied to a broader narrative of Los Santos as a city plagued by drug addiction. The first part of the game is dedicated to driving out the rival gangs and drug pushers, reclaiming Grove Street territory, and cleaning up the neighborhood. In the second half of the game, CJ becomes distracted by the allure of a hip-hop lifestyle, befriending the rap star Madd Dogg and helping him set up a recording studio at a mansion in the hills. It is CJ's brother Sweet who reminds CJ he has forgotten his roots, prompting an all-out mission to rid Grove Street of drugs for good. A critical point near the end of the game sees Sweet tempted by crack himself, bending over to inhale from a pipe just as CJ bursts through the door. The brothers join forces to drive out the corrupt police behind the drug racket and reinstate decent standards of life in the neighborhood.

The essentialist depiction of particular ethnic communities also serves a purpose, observed in scenes and missions that show CJ and Sweet overcoming the racial prejudice of others and themselves. For example, in the early mission

"Cesar Vialpando," CJ discovers that his sister, Kendl, is dating a Chicano gangster from the south side. Sweet tries to prevent Kendl from seeing the "cholo," joking that their offspring would be named "Leroy Hernandez" or "Leroy Lopez." In response, Kendl calls her brother a "no-good, narrow-minded, hypocrite gangbanger" and a "racist." It is significant that this charge of racism is quoted in the BradyGames official strategy guide, as direct quotes from the script are rarely included.[21] The quote frames the mission as one concerned with breaking down cultural barriers to achieve progress in the game. When CJ meets Cesar in person, he seems trustworthy and a good match for Kendl. Befriending Cesar allows CJ (and therefore the player) to undertake further missions like car racing and, more importantly, advances the central narrative: it is Cesar who tracks down the car used to kill CJ's mother, and Cesar who enters CJ in a car race against Wu Zi Mu in the badlands. When CJ wins the race, Wu Zi invites CJ to call him if he is ever in San Fierro, opening that area of the map. Narrative progress and player-character identification are thus deeply enmeshed, as CJ and the player can only gain access to certain sections of the game world through overcoming racial barriers and expanding their range of contact with other ethnic communities.

Racial stereotypes are similarly challenged and reassessed through the game, as racist attitudes are exposed through dialogue, and CJ cooperates with the Latino and Chinese gangs to achieve his goals. At the end of the game, a team comprising all different races (including a nerdy white computer whiz voiced by David Cross) pulls off a major casino heist, while CJ enlists the help of Chinese Triad members to recapture the Mulholland mansion and recording studio. Although most academic criticism focuses on a black-white binary when discussing race in the game, the narrative is more concerned with establishing cooperation between the black and Latino gangs in the first instance, and then with the Chinese gangs in San Fierro. Racial representation in *San Andreas* is thus multiracial in nature, while communication across ethnic lines is crucial to success. In terms of gameplay, ludus—following the central mission objectives—is what forces the player to commit crimes, but ludus is also what gives the player access to CJ's redemptive rationale for action as well as the experience of transcending prejudice through the narrative.

Complicating Race: Wu Zi Mu, Orientalism, and Disability

While the representation of black and Latino masculinity in *San Andreas* has attracted much attention, the significant role of Chinese identity in the game has been overlooked.[22] The identity of Wu Zi Mu, the blind Triad boss of San Fierro, is constructed along two lines of otherness—race and disability—raising questions about Orientalism in the process of character construction as well as the dynamics of player-character identification. The self-reflexive narrative mode brings a level of nuance to the identity construction, but this aspect of the text may be lost on many players, raising additional questions about the nature of a whole text and how the developer's vision is experienced through actual gameplay.

Wu Zi Mu is constructed primarily as a gang leader, but the toughness of his gangster persona is inseparable from his Chinese identity since the gang is a Triad group. Wu Zi is tall, handsome, and elegantly dressed. He has neatly cut black hair and is clean-shaven, always wearing dark sunglasses, and is usually surrounded by admiring female assistants or Triad members, emphasizing his role as leader. In terms of character, he is honest, values the family, and emphasizes the idea of duty. He is supremely self-confident in all tasks, well-spoken, and a loyal friend.

Looking at the wider context of the character, we see the construction of Chinatown as other—a common trope of literature, film, and other media that fits the overall gangster narrative of the game and makes the Triad boss a good ally for CJ. Rockstar's representation of Chinatown follows convention, with a preponderance of the color red, dragon gates, Asian passersby, Chinese characters on shopfronts and street signs, and Triad members hanging around the territory with guns. Wu Zi's office is decorated in traditional Chinese style, with moon-shaped doors, red lattice cornices, fans and swords on the walls, and so on. Later in the game, the player finds Wu Zi's casino, The Four Dragons, similarly decked out in flamboyant Oriental style, featuring a four-tiered pagoda and moon gate on the building's exterior as well as lion-dogs, giant Buddhas, and "Asian-themed" game rooms inside.[23] This is a comfortable, normative representation of China as other with which players all over the world are familiar from other media. While it is clearly an Orientalist construction, it is notable that there are two sets of visual symbols operating here—the flamboyant and the minimalist. Although Wu Zi's office is decorated in splendid exotic fashion, he and his colleagues dress in minimalist black, pointing simultaneously to China's imagined past and present.[24]

The figure of Wu Zi Mu is thus established as a conventional Chinese other from his context and surroundings. But Rockstar makes efforts to de-racialize the character. First, his name is Anglicized to "Woozie," increasing relatability for the average North American player. In the mission titled "Wu Zi Mu," he introduces himself saying, "My friends call me Woozie," immediately establishing CJ as one of his friends and promoting feelings of goodwill for the player. Onscreen instructions refer to the character as "Woozie," while his health bar is also labeled "Woozie," reinforcing the friendly nickname. Second, although he often lapses into Cantonese when speaking with his associates, Wu Zi has no Asian accent when speaking English. The lack of an accent produces a binary contrast in opposition to other Asian characters in the game. In the "Woozie" mission strand, he and the other Chinese Triads (the Mountain Cloud Boys and the Red Gecko Tong) are directly contrasted against the Vietnamese Da Nang Boys, making an interesting example of "good" versus "bad" Asian in the game.

The negative construction of the Vietnamese gang members begins with their thick accents in English, barely understandable to the player. They are also referred to as Snakeheads, implying they are involved in human trafficking.[25] This implication is borne out when CJ attacks their container ship and finds one container full of people. In the strategy guide and in-game instructions, these people are referred to as refugees, but to anyone who has heard the term "Snakehead" before, they are clearly victims of human trafficking. The Snakehead leader is a caricature of an aged martial artist—an old, ponytailed man practicing sword dancing on the ship's bridge. He tosses CJ a similar sword and they fight to the death. CJ loses all other weapons here and is forced to perform in a stereotypical Asian fight scene. The Vietnamese characters are thus caricatured to a far greater extent than any other racial group in the game. Strong characters, both good and evil, may be found in white, black, Latino, and Chinese groups. However, the Vietnamese representation is so exaggerated as to provide cautionary evidence against claims to Rockstar's racial sensitivity. One could argue that the parody itself points to a critical metacommentary on racist stereotyping, but this nuance would undoubtedly be lost on most players.[26]

The de-racialization of Wu Zi Mu may thus be seen as a process by which he becomes less threatening and more relatable to the average player. As the Vietnamese are made more strange and exoticized as the other, so Wu Zi Mu becomes more familiar and closer to the self. This process itself could be criticized as perpetuating Orientalist discourses of racism and power.[27] However, the relationship between self and other here has implications for the process of player-character identification, which is undercut and emphasized in various ways throughout the game. This results in a high degree of self-reflexivity, where the Rockstar developers are constantly drawing attention to the constructed nature of the game world.

CJ's ignorance of Chinese culture and name pronunciations provides a good example, producing a clear disjunction between CJ's knowledge and the player's. The player has a better idea of Chinese characters' names because they are often written on the screen in text, as part of the mission title. A good example is the mission titled "Ran Fa Li." Here we meet the head of the Red Gecko Tong, Shuk Foo Ran Fa Li, threatened with assassination. CJ lures the Vietnamese assassins away from San Fierro, using Ran Fa Li's car as a decoy. CJ calls the Tong leader "Mr. Farlie," running the syllables together and linking them with a strong *r* sound. Even players unfamiliar with Chinese names can laugh at CJ's mispronunciation here, because the text of the mission title has given them knowledge unavailable to CJ himself. This sequence emphasizes CJ's status as a complete outsider to Chinese culture but also draws a clear line between character and player.

Players are constantly taken out of the diegetic world of the game to recognize their own actions as those of a person playing a game. *GTA: San Andreas* is a step forward from *GTA: Vice City* in this respect. *Vice City* has many visual puns and references to 1980s culture from a modern standpoint, constructed primarily in terms of nostalgia. *San Andreas* has a similar kind of nostalgia in terms of music and fashion, but also evokes the memory of consequential events in US racial history. The player is inevitably reminded of the 1992 Los Angeles riots, Rodney King, and the racial tension of California depicted in such films as *Boyz n the Hood* (1991). The mission "Riot" toward the end of the game sees fires in the streets, people looting, cars exploding, and random gunfire from all sides, connecting the diegetic gameplay and narrative to a nondiegetic historical moment. The construction of racial identity in the game—whether Chinese, black, Latino, or white—must be taken in the context of this wider retrospective on California race relations in the 1990s.

In this context it is tempting to argue that Wu Zi's blindness, as a marker of difference, minimizes racial difference as a distinguishing feature. Although China is exoticized in the game, this also holds true for other groups: the Italian mafia, black American gang culture, the Spanish-speaking Latino community, and so on. All have their instantly recognizable cultural symbols, like the street mural of Madonna and child indicating the Catholic faith of the Latino community. If all cultural groups are equally exoticized in the game space, the exoticization of China does not stand out. Similarly, the good guys in the narrative represent a range of racial identities: CJ is African American, Cesar is Latino, Zero is white, Wu Zi is Chinese. However, in this mix of racial difference, Wu Zi alone is marked out as more different by his disability. Wu Zi's blindness thus acts to further exoticize the Chinese other.

Wu Zi Mu's blindness is masked by the fact that he wears dark glasses throughout the game. CJ does not realize his new friend is blind until he visits Wu Zi's betting shop in San Fierro and is told about "the boss's curse." At the same time, CJ is told that the boss has "incredible good fortune," as if to compensate for his disability. Wu Zi himself acts as if he is not blind—he runs fast, shoots guns, races cars, and so on. His self-confidence in games like golf and cards is enabled by his cronies, who move the putting hole and deliberately fold their hands at cards so the boss will always win. This ploy is highlighted when CJ appears in their midst and plays cards to win, prompting some confusion from Wu Zi, who mutters that he is having an off day. It is only at the end of the game, when CJ and Wu Zi are planning a bank heist, that Wu Zi admits he may not be the best person to pilot the getaway helicopter.

This kind of humor points to the self-conscious nature of player-character identification in the game. The player encounters Wu Zi solely through his meetings with CJ, discovering Wu Zi's blindness when CJ does, feeling CJ's confusion at Wu Zi's ability to race cars, and (perhaps) laughing along at the visual gags occasioned by Wu Zi's inability to see. In the "Mountain Cloud Boys" mission, CJ tests Wu Zi's blindness by waving a hand in front of his face, and Wu Zi runs straight into a wall when leading CJ to their destination in Chinatown. The humor operates on one level to defuse potential negative associations with disability. David Annandale describes the humor as "affirmative" and optimistic, the laughter between friends that signals the breaking down of barriers caused by difference.[28] But it also places the player in the uncomfortable position of laughing at the blind. Player reactions of laughter or disbelief can reinforce initial expectations that a blind character will be limited or otherwise defined by disability. That we think about Wu Zi's abilities in terms of real-world possibilities highlights the fact we are playing a game, underscoring the self-reflexivity of the game text. However, while some players may question their complicity in laughing at the disabled other, others will be content to read the game on a surface level. The game's self-reflexive mode is not strong enough here to overcome the element of caricature. As a result, the identity construction of Wu Zi Mu on the axis of disability is problematic, following conventional rhetoric that remains at the level of spectacle and exoticism.[29]

It has often been noted that many Rockstar games have strong satire and parody elements to make a critical point.[30] The humor in Wu Zi's representation could be acting as satire, pointing to a society that makes others of people with disabilities, just as the open possibilities of paidea and sandbox play point to our own failings in the areas of morals and ethics when playing video games. But many players will not read the text in this way. There is thus a disjunction between the possible intentions of the Rockstar developers, who built a metanarrative of social commentary—relying on savvy and intelligent consumers to see past surface visuals to get the critique—and the vast spectrum of players who can read the text in different ways.[31] When we talk about the whole text, then, do we look at Rockstar's presumed intentions or player responses? These questions bring us back to the hoary chestnuts of literary studies, authorial intent and reader response, but deserve to be explored anew with regard to video games as a medium.

In this case, the theoretical framework of Orientalism can help illuminate the disjunction between construction and reading. Rockstar may have given the Asian character a disability in order to draw attention to Orientalist discourses operating not only on culture and race but also on the disabled body. However, the disability chosen is blindness, which resonates in a particular and racialized way. Blindness in Asian and European culture has long been associated with the sacred, bestowing otherworldly powers of divination or other abilities to compensate for the lack of sight. Particularly in martial arts films of China and Japan, blindness sharpens the senses and allows the hero superhuman abilities to defeat unseen enemies.[32] Blindness of an Asian character thus comes with its own set of rhetorical expectations.

Following convention, blindness empowers Wu Zi with mysterious skills, as he completes drive-by shootings and wins car races on his own. At the beginning of the mission "Amphibious Assault," CJ and Wu Zi are shown playing video games together (using PlayStation controllers, of course). CJ loses the game and stands up, cursing as the Triad boss easily wins. "Shit, how'd you do that?!" asks CJ, and Wu Zi just laughs. This seemingly mystical power adds to the otherness of the Chinese figure. But pointing to disability as the source of that mystery produces a positive exoticization of disability in itself. Tobin Siebers argues that this kind of mythologizing contributes to the marginalization of people with disabilities: "The challenge is not to adapt their disability into an extraordinary power. . . . The challenge is to function."[33] Disability in *San Andreas* is made into an other beyond the reach of CJ's comprehension. The conjunction between Wu Zi's race and disability is determined by Orientalist rhetoric, highlighting China as other and blindness as special. While *San Andreas* gives a serious treatment of race relations overall, it remains subject to problematic rhetorical patterns, showing the deep reach of Orientalist structures into the way we think about identity. Although reading the game as a whole text redeems the racialized violence in the game narrative, the depiction of disability remains static.

Conclusion

This chapter argues that *GTA: San Andreas* should be taken as a narrative whole in order to understand the meaning of particular representations of identity. Criticism of the game has focused on racial representation, but when we examine narrative context, gameplay choices, and player-character identification, the game emerges as a critical reflection on racial conflict in America. Rockstar's generally thoughtful treatment of race in contrast to disability raises its own questions about Orientalizing processes in game development. The construction of race does not take place in a vacuum, either in the real world (game development) or the game world (narrative context). Focusing just on race in games, therefore, means missing out on the complexity of the overall text and how other elements of identity construction are also subject to processes of exoticization. The figure of Wu Zi Mu in *San Andreas* may be approached as an object of study at the nexus of cultural studies, disability studies, and game studies—disparate yet connected fields that can work productively together to discover more meaning in game texts as the products of specific development teams in specific times and places.

Examining identity representations in a game text also means accounting for different gameplay modes—including ludus and paidea—as well as video game genres. In this case, the complex intersections between race and disability in *San Andreas* cannot be grasped by the player unless the entire central mission strand is completed successfully. The riot scene and bank heist come at the end of the central narrative, but the sheer length of the mission strand coupled with the vastness of the open-ended interactive environment makes the whole text of *San Andreas* inaccessible for many. Some players simply prefer sandbox play while others will speed-run the missions, doing only what is needed to beat the game and get to the end of the story. As David Parry points out, the statistic "100% completion" means little in a game with an endless number of statistics to provide new challenges for players, limited only by their imaginations.[34] Vast game environments like those in the *Grand Theft Auto* series thus need a different analytical approach than, for example, highly linear Japanese role-playing games (JRPGs) with little opportunity for player agency.[35] Further research is needed on what constitutes completing a game and what this means for narrative studies in relation to games.

The people most likely to be powerfully affected by a cultural text are the people who consume the whole text—those who read the whole book, see the whole film, play the whole game. If I have invested one hundred hours of my time playing *GTA: San Andreas*, I have spent one hundred hours submerged in its worldview, with time to absorb the cultural attitudes of the game designers regarding race, gender, sexuality, and class. Players more immersed in the game will spend more time on side missions or replayable scenes, manipulating various cinematic effects and creating an admirable photo gallery, to fully experience everything that the game has to offer. These players are the people for whom the narrative meaning would make the most impact, who are most likely to realize that interracial cooperation is valued highly and that CJ's ultimate goal is to clean up Grove Street for good. Gamers most immersed in the fashions, hairstyles, radio music, and street slang of Los Santos are most directly experiencing the mid-1990s cultural milieu of California, including the shock and terror induced by the sudden riot scenes toward the end of the game. The sense of chaos and limitless possibility is invigorating at the same time as threatening imminent danger to CJ. The player experiences excitement, fear, and complicity—understanding the will to riot, the desire to loot, and the compulsion to destroy for destruction's own sake. These players will take away an embodied experience that may redefine and complicate their own understanding of race relations in America today.[36]

As Kiri Miller has observed, the virtual space of Los Santos carries its own ideology, making Grove Street a safe haven for the player returning to CJ's house after a mission. Miller describes a "wash of relief" at familiar sights of black faces, chain-link fences, and the highway overpass that signals the entrance to Grove Street and home. The experience "reshaped my sense of public space and public safety. . . . [I]t added a visceral dimension to my intellectual understanding of racial profiling."[37] This kind of embodied experience, coupled with the self-reflexive nature of *San Andreas* as a text, can make players reflect on race, politics, and historical events in new ways. The sociopolitical dynamics that inform racial representation are encountered in both paidea structures of sandbox play and ludus structures of the central missions. The whole text thus encompasses not only what was created by the developers but also the multiple possibilities of narrative created by players in their own gameplay experience.

For our part, as scholars, we should also play the whole game to analyze it successfully. One would not write a study of *Pride and Prejudice* or *Heart of Darkness* based on the first thirty pages of the text. However, as Mia Consalvo points out, it is often the case that game analyses focus on introductory levels or the first thirty minutes of gameplay.[38] While this most often applies to broad quantitative studies addressing a large number of games at once, rather than qualitative studies examining a single title, the fact that these large studies deal with representations of gender, race, and other forms of identity makes the issue more pressing.[39] If journalists, parents, politicians, and even players find the whole text of a game inaccessible, then it is surely the scholar's duty to reach the end of the narrative and experience different modes of gameplay in order to provide an accurate and useful commentary on representation in the game text. If that means spending one hundred plus hours in a place like San Andreas, then so be it.

RACHAEL HUTCHINSON is Associate Professor of Japanese Studies and Game Studies at the University of Delaware. She has written about representation and identity, Orientalism, and Occidentalism in a range of Japanese narrative texts, in publications including *Games and Culture*, *NMEDIAC: The Journal of New Media and Culture*, *Monumenta Nipponica*, and *Japan Forum*.

Notes

1. Although play is limited to one main character, CJ is customizable in terms of dress, hairstyle, tattoos, and body type. For more on the limitations of the single-character subject position, see Kiri Miller, "Grove Street Grimm: *Grand Theft Auto* and Digital Folklore," *Journal of American Folklore* 121, no. 481 (2008): 257–258.

2. David Leonard, "Young, Black (and Brown) and Don't Give a Fuck: Virtual Gangstas in the Era of State Violence," *Cultural Studies ↔ Critical Methodologies* 9, no. 2 (2009): 265.

3. Charles Dickerman, Jeff Christensen, and Stella Beatriz Kerl-McClain, "Big Breasts and Bad Guys: Depictions of Gender and Race in Video Games," *Journal of Creativity in Mental Health* 3, no. 1 (2008): 24–25.

4. Paul Barrett, "White Thumbs, Black Bodies: Race, Violence, and Neoliberal Fantasies in *Grand Theft Auto: San Andreas*," *Review of Education, Pedagogy, and Cultural Studies* 28, no. 1 (2006): 101.

5. Leonard, "Young, Black (and Brown)."

6. Ibid. Anna Everett criticizes hegemonic racial structures in video games, emphasizing the whiteness of game discourse and peripheral industries, in "Serious Play: Playing with Race in Contemporary Gaming Culture," in *The Handbook of Computer Game Studies*, ed. Joost Raessens and Jeffrey Goldstein (Cambridge, MA: MIT Press, 2005), 311–325; see also Anna Everett, *Digital Diaspora: A Race for Cyberspace* (Albany: State University of New York Press, 2009).

7. For more on the Haitian controversy, see David Kushner, *Jacked: The Outlaw Story of "Grand Theft Auto"* (Hoboken, NJ: Wiley, 2012), 162–165.

8. Joshua Green, "Digital Blackface: The Repackaging of the Black Masculine Image" (master's thesis, Miami University, Ohio, 2006).

9. Lisa Nakamura and Peter Chow-White, eds., *Race after the Internet* (New York: Routledge, 2012), 8.

10. A Kaiser Family Foundation study, for example, shows that black and Hispanic teens spend more hours per day playing video games than white teens. Victoria J. Rideout, Ulla G. Foehr, and Donald F. Roberts, "Generation M^2: Media in the Lives of 8- to 18-Year-Olds," January 2010, pp. 5, 11, 25, http://kaiserfamilyfoundation.files.wordpress.com/2013/04/8010.pdf.

11. Brock analyzed the *Kotaku* forum "Black Looks on RE5 Racism," finding varied responses to both the game itself and a blog about race in the game: André Brock, "'When Keeping It Real Goes Wrong': *Resident Evil 5*, Racial Representation, and Gamers," *Games and Culture* 6, no. 5 (2011): 429–452.

12. James Newman expands on these terms, suggested by Roger Caillos's study of games. See James Newman, *Videogames* (New York: Routledge, 2013), 17–21.

13. Zach Whalen, "Cruising in San Andreas: Ludic Space and Urban Aesthetics in *Grand Theft Auto*," in *The Meaning and Culture of "Grand Theft Auto,"* ed. Nate Garrelts (Jefferson, NC: McFarland, 2006), 147.

14. Nate Garrelts, "An Introduction to *Grand Theft Auto* Studies," in *The Meaning and Culture of "Grand Theft Auto,"* ed. Nate Garrelts (Jefferson, NC: McFarland, 2006), 13. David Parry's chapter in the same book argues for "negotiation" of play modes as the best analytical framework for game texts; see David Parry, "Playing with Style: Negotiating Digital Game Studies," 226–243.

15. CJ can speak to NPCs by using the directional buttons—left for positive comments and right for negative. CJ's repertoire includes over 4,200 comments, separate from the 3,500 scripted cutscene comments. Bill Loguidice and Matt Barton, *Vintage Games: An Insider Look at the History of "Grand Theft Auto," "Super Mario," and the Most Influential Games of All Time* (Burlington, MA: Focal Press, 2009), 116 n19.

16. Ibid., 121.

17. Gonzalo Frasca, "Simulation versus Narrative: Introduction to Ludology," in *The Video Game Theory Reader*, ed. Mark Wolf and Bernard Perron (New York: Routledge, 2003), 230–232.

18. Miller, "Grove Street Grimm," 262; Ian Bogost, "Videogames and Ideological Frames," *Popular Communication* 4, no. 3 (2006): 165–183.

19. Bogost, "Videogames and Ideological Frames," 180.

20. Loguidice and Barton observe this about *GTA II*. See Loguidice and Barton, *Vintage Games*, 110.

21. Tim Bogenn and Rick Barba, *Grand Theft Auto: San Andreas Official Strategy Guide* (Indianapolis: BradyGames, 2005), 31.

22. See Norma Mendoza-Denton, "The Semiotic Hitchhiker's Guide to Creaky Voice: Circulation and Gendered Hardcore in a Chicana/o Gang Persona," *Journal of Linguistic Anthropology* 21, no. 2 (2011): 261–280.

23. Rockstar Games, *San Andreas: Local Business Advertiser's Guide* (New York: Take-Two Interactive, 2004), game manual, 14.

24. This minimalist modern China resembles the rhetorical constructions of "Techno-Orientalist" Japan. David Morley and Kevin Robins, *Spaces of Identity: Global Media, Electronic Landscapes, and Cultural Boundaries* (London: Routledge, 1995).

25. The term "Snakehead" (*shé tóu*) refers to Chinese gangs, mostly from Fujian province, active in human trafficking since the 1990s.

26. Hugo Dobson makes a similar case for racist stereotyping in *The Simpsons* to be read as "carnivalesque" and "hyper-ironic," but this did not prevent viewers in Brazil, Japan, and Australia being offended. See Hugo Dobson, "Mister Sparkle Meets the Yakuza: Depictions of Japan in *The Simpsons*," *Journal of Popular Culture* 39, no. 1 (2006): 44–68.

27. For more on Orientalist discursive structures in the game industry, see Everett, *Digital Diaspora*, 118–120; and Anthony Sze-Fai Shiu, "What Yellowface Hides: Video Games, Whiteness, and the American Racial Order," *Journal of Popular Culture* 39, no. 1 (2006): 113–116.

28. David Annandale, "The Subversive Carnival of *Grand Theft Auto: San Andreas*," in *The Meaning and Culture of "Grand Theft Auto,"* ed. Nate Garrelts (Jefferson, NC: McFarland, 2006), 93–94.

29. For more on such conventions, see Rosemarie Garland-Thomson, "Seeing the Disabled: Visual Rhetorics of Disability in Popular Photography," in *The New Disability History: American Perspectives*, ed. Paul Longmore and Lauri Umansky (New York: New York University Press, 2001), 335–374.

30. Annandale, "Subversive Carnival," 95–98; Tanner Higgin, "Play-Fighting: Understanding Violence in *Grand Theft Auto III*," in *The Meaning and Culture of "Grand Theft Auto,"* ed. Nate Garrelts (Jefferson, NC: McFarland, 2006), 77–79; Dennis Redmond, "Grand Theft Video: Running and Gunning for the US Empire," in *The Meaning and Culture of "Grand Theft Auto,"* ed. Nate Garrelts (Jefferson, NC: McFarland, 2006), 104–114.

31. Matt Sienkiewicz and Nick Marx raise this caveat regarding anti-Semitic humor in *South Park*, as viewers may miss the critique and take jokes at face value. See Matt Sienkiewicz and Nick Marx, "Beyond a Cutout World: Ethnic Humor and Discursive Integration in *South Park*," *Journal of Film and Video* 61, no. 2 (2009): 518.

32. Takeshi Kitano's film *Zatōichi* (2003) deconstructs this cinematic staple. Rutger Hauer in *Blind Fury* (1989) provides a humorous parody.

33. Tobin Siebers, "Disability in Theory: From Social Constructionism to the New Realism of the Body," in *The Disability Studies Reader*, ed. Lennard Davis, 2nd ed. (New York: Routledge, 2006),

180. For a discussion of "supercrip" representation, see Russell Meeuf, "John Wayne as 'Supercrip': Disabled Bodies and the Construction of 'Hard' Masculinity in *The Wings of Eagles*," *Cinema Journal* 48, no. 2 (2009): 88–113.

34. Parry, "Playing with Style," 231–237.

35. For more on player agency in the JRPG, see, for example, Rachael Hutchinson, "Embodied Experience and Social Critique: Anti-nuclear Discourse in *Final Fantasy*," in *Introducing Japanese Popular Culture*, ed. Alisa Freedman and Toby Slade (New York: Routledge, forthcoming).

36. James Paul Gee argues that the embodied experience in video games has a powerful effect on learning, fundamentally different from written or filmic texts, due to the situated meaning gained from gameplay. See James Paul Gee, *What Video Games Have to Teach Us about Learning and Literacy* (New York: Palgrave Macmillan, 2003), 83–90.

37. Miller, "Grove Street Grimm," 265.

38. Mia Consalvo, "Videogame Content: Game, Text, or Something Else?" in *The International Encyclopedia of Media Studies*, ed. Angharad N. Valdivia and Erica Scharrer, vol. 5, *Media Effects/Media Psychology* (Chichester, UK: Wiley Blackwell, 2013), 411.

39. For an overview of quantitative content analyses, see ibid., 408–410.

chapter ten

ENTERING THE PICTURE

Digital Portraiture and the Aesthetics of Video Game Representation

LISA PATTI

"IF ANYTHING, MY AVATAR HAS TO CONCENTRATE ON BEING ME," EXPLAINS Harisu, an actress and singer from Seoul, South Korea, who describes herself as the "first Korean transgender celebrity."[1] Her comments about her experiences inhabiting male and female avatars in virtual worlds in comparison to her reception in the "real" world appear in the book *Alter Ego,* a collection of British artist Robbie Cooper's photographic portraits of over fifty people. Harisu's portrait, like the others in the book, appears opposite a portrait of one of her avatars. Featuring almost identical compositions—outdoor settings, medium close-ups of her torso(s) turning slightly away from the camera while her face(s) address the camera directly—the portraits invite a visual comparison of the subject and her avatar. They are at once both uncannily similar—the slender yet strong frame, the long neck, the full lips—and adamantly different, with Harisu's long brown hair, hoop earrings, and low-cut pink T-shirt replaced by her avatar's long blonde braids, large elfin ears, and elaborate armored corset. The avatar both is and is not Harisu, or as she explains, "It's more like your partner. I definitely don't get confused between my real and my virtual self."[2]

Harisu works in Korea, China, and throughout East Asia and maintains virtual lives as several male and female avatars in the online game *Lineage II.* In *Alter Ego,* Harisu reflects on the affinities and disjunctions between her real and virtual selves, implicitly challenging the assumption that off-line experiences are more real than online ones. She describes a confrontation with transphobia in *Lineage II*:

> I came upon a group of avatars who were chatting about transsexuals. They were making jokes and saying how much they disliked them. I asked "Why do you hate transgendered people?" and they answered with more negative comments. So I just told them who I was. They were embarrassed and tried to take back what they'd said. The virtual world is very much like the real one.[3]

Harisu's comments point to the affordances and the limits of exploring identities and identification through digital avatars. *Lineage II* offers Harisu the flexibility to design and inhabit multiple avatars of different genders and races. Participants in online worlds, however, are subject to the same forms of intolerance and aggression that people with minoritized and marginalized identities in the off-line world confront. Harisu's analysis of her digital lives addresses both of these dimensions of online identification and interactivity. Her off-line and online portraits form a network of representation that acknowledges yet resists the boundaries of representation and identification. In effect, the combination on facing pages of the two portraits and the first-person narrative that accompanies them as an extended caption reminds the viewer of the aesthetic and social agency of avatar designers.

Contemporary digital portraiture projects like *Alter Ego* provide an important conceptual grid for mapping the representational possibilities of digital games and other virtual worlds. An investigation of portraits of both digital avatars and players bridges the academic field of game studies with the fields of film studies and art history. The methodological emphases in these fields on the formal analysis of still and moving images and the theoretical analysis of the experience of the spectator provide new ways to reflect on avatar design and player interactivity in digital games. Portraits of avatars and gamers like those featured in *Alter Ego* extend the visual representation of gaming to the institutional spaces of museums and galleries and assert diverse rosters of participation.

The formal analysis of the digital portraits presented in this chapter seeks to unsettle popular and critical assumptions about gender and race in gaming cultures, linking screen aesthetics to virtual agency. The analysis of digital portraits of players and avatars complements previous work in the field of game studies that analyzes representation both within game worlds and within game cultures by engaging directly with players. For example, Adrienne Shaw's *Gaming at the Edge: Sexuality and Gender at the Margins of Gamer Culture* provides an ethnographic exploration of the ways that players understand the imbrication of identification and representation within their gaming experiences. Her interviews with players reveal that identification was not a central concern for them, but this lack of investment in identification among the players enables a more nuanced discussion of identification and representation to unfold:

> At times we want to see ourselves in the place of characters who are as we wish to be. At other times we use media texts as fodder for imagining what else might be possible in our everyday lives. In either case, while identification *as* a member of

a group does not define how audiences identify *with* media characters, representations of different types of bodies remains crucially important to shaping what types of worlds we can imagine.[4]

The portraits curated in the projects I analyze activate our critical engagement with the movement between "identification *as*" and "identification *with*," not only in relation to players and avatars but also to the spectators who view these portraits. While the image of a single player or avatar may be framed by the camera, the presentation of those images places the viewer in a contextual network that includes the textual world of the game, the player's social environment while engaged in gameplay, and the viewer's position in relation to the portrait, a strategic vantage point from which we can reflect on the aesthetic expressions of representation in gaming.

In this chapter, I turn to Andy Warhol's *Thirteen Most Beautiful* (1964–1966), a rotating archive of silent black-and-white 16mm screen tests of celebrities and unknowns who passed through Warhol's Factory, as a framework for rethinking the aesthetics and politics of video game representation. I link Warhol's screen tests to video games and other interactive virtual worlds by analyzing three contemporary art projects that directly or indirectly cite *Thirteen Most Beautiful*: Eva and Franco Mattes's installation *13 Most Beautiful Avatars* (2006), Cooper's ongoing video series *Immersion* (2008–), and his book of portraits, *Alter Ego* (2009). *13 Most Beautiful Avatars* presents a set of digital portraits of avatars from the virtual world *Second Life* that both confirm and destabilize conventional definitions of human beauty, *Immersion* records the reactions of players from the point of view of the screen (through the use of a specially designed camera and projector installation) as they play popular console video games, and *Alter Ego* juxtaposes the portraits of digital avatars in virtual worlds—including Harisu's—with portraits of the people who designed them. The transformation of players into portraits in these projects prompts a reexamination of the ways that they identify with or as screen images when engaging video games and other virtual worlds.

These projects also assert, through their selection of featured avatars and subjects, a more diverse constituency on- and off-screen than many video games (and discussions of games) allow. Scholarly studies of in-game character demographics have chronicled persuasively the consistent underrepresentation of women and racial minorities in digital games.[5] Industrial analyses of game players reveal a much more diverse profile of digital gaming. For example, the 2016 Entertainment Software Association (ESA) survey determined that in the United States 41 percent of players are female and that "women age 18 or older represent a significantly greater portion of the game-playing population (31%) than boys age 17 or younger (17%)."[6] *13 Most Beautiful Avatars* and *Immersion* provide visual rosters that complement those statistics, curating portraits of male and female avatars and players with different racial identities. These art projects thus establish a new census of representation in both virtual worlds (in *13 Most Beautiful Avatars*) and console games (in *Immersion*). This diversity is one of the most significant alterations of Warhol's experiments with cinematic portraiture generated through its extension into digital forms. Warhol's screen tests were not racially diverse; almost all of his subjects were white. Warhol, however, explored the representation of gender and sexuality throughout his films in relation to popular expressions of beauty and the apparatus of the camera. His project thus serves as a formal model for contemporary digital portraiture and a provocation to analyze representation in relation to aesthetic forms.

Interactive Stillness: Andy Warhol's Screen Tests

Warhol's 472 screen tests, originally called "stillies," followed rigid formal protocols. Shot with a 16mm Bolex camera fixed to a tripod, each film was approximately three minutes long, the length of one roll or one hundred feet of film. Warhol cited mug shots, photo booth photos, and passport photos as inspirations for these films. His screen tests attempted to capture and intensify the awkwardness of these semipublic portraits by expanding the duration of the image's production, from the brief instant of a snapshot to the several minutes that elapsed during a single roll of 16mm film. Warhol insisted on a stationary camera, so his interventions (and those of his assistants and fellow artists at the Factory, where the films were shot) were focused on the design of the set and the direction of the subjects. The sitters were placed against a plain background (with light or dark backdrops selected to contrast their appearance) and lit with a bright key light. Typically centered in a close-up or medium close-up shot, the subjects were instructed by Warhol or one of his surrogates to remain still and, if possible, not to blink. These screen tests were not aesthetic auditions for roles in Warhol's other films as the name of the series might suggest; the films complement Warhol's other portraiture projects, exploring the possibility of recording a portrait in time.

The formal austerity and consistency of the conditions that Warhol imposed on these portraits generate a revealing range of responses, from Ann Buchanan's inscrutable stare as tears stream down her cheeks from her unblinking eyes (figure 10.1) to Lou Reed's antic interactions with a Coke bottle while stubbornly refusing to remove his sunglasses. Callie Angell, the curator who organized the large and unwieldy collection of Warhol's films into a cataloged archive for the Whitney Museum of American Art, observes that the portraits are performances or "allegorical documentaries about what it is like to sit for your portrait, with each poser trapped in the existential dilemma of performing as—while simultaneously being reduced to—his or her image."[7] The viewer experiences this discomfort in an exaggerated form because the films are projected at a slower frame rate, increasing the duration of each film by over one minute and creating an almost visible expansion of the subject's anxiety. The viewer witnesses the subject's performance in slow motion.

Angell argues that the films "should be recognized as true collaborations, films in which the subjects have at least as much control as the artist in determining the

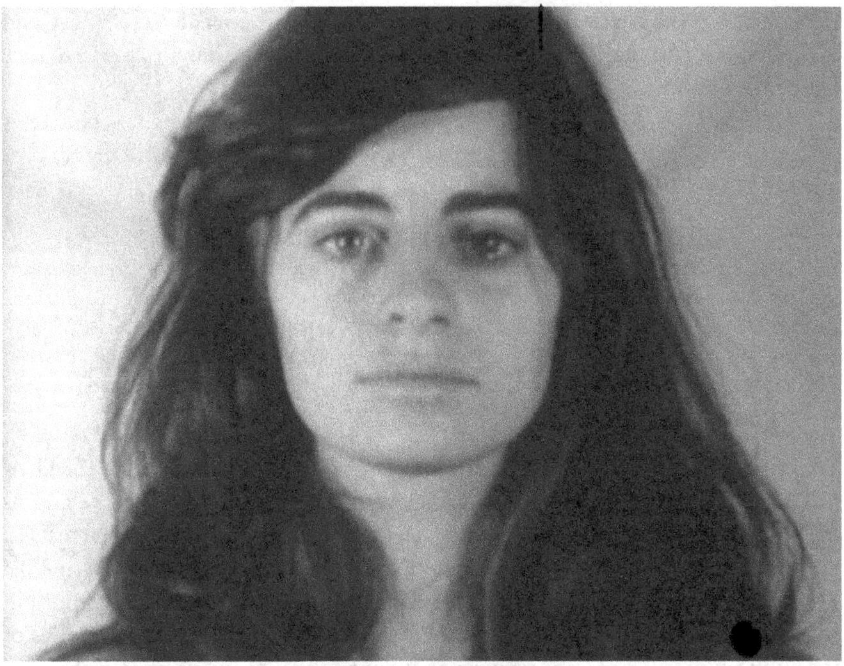

Figure 10.1. Ann Buchanan's screen test (*Thirteen Most Beautiful* film still)

outcome of the finished work."[8] This collaboration must also include the viewer, implicitly dared by many of the screen test subjects to return their gaze. Warhol's screen tests were originally featured in a limited series of screenings in New York with the titles *Thirteen Most Beautiful Boys* or *Thirteen Most Beautiful Women* (with different films substituted into the program to satisfy either the whims of Warhol or the egos of subjects in attendance at the screenings).[9] While many of the films remain accessible only through the Whitney archive, some have been included in the DVD compilation *13 Most Beautiful . . . Songs for Andy Warhol's Screen Tests*, featuring a soundtrack for the silent films composed by the band Dean and Britta. The release of this DVD, promoted by a limited tour of live shows during which the band performed the songs as the screen tests were projected on large screens behind it, has led to the circulation of some of the screen tests online.[10]

Several versions of Buchanan's screen test appear on YouTube. Officially labeled "Girl Who Cries a Tear" by Warhol (or one of his collaborators), the film was included in Warhol's exhibition *The Thirteen Most Beautiful Women*; and an image of Buchanan was featured in a *New York Herald Tribune* article discussing the exhibit, bringing Buchanan and her screen test a measure of fame.[11] On YouTube, Buchanan's screen test has provoked several comments that acknowledge the inclusion of the viewer in the film's circuit of endurance: "Did anyone see her blink? I don't think I saw her blink." "I tried staring her down without blinking—and she won." "She has the power to hold our attention through this whole 'screen test' and make you cry with her. She should have been a star."[12] Buchanan's performance enlists the viewer as a collaborator, a competitor, and a critic.

Hal Foster's assessment of the ways that viewers can confront the screen tests anticipates one of the connections I draw between Warhol's films and digital portraits of virtual avatars:

> In Warholian cinema at large, to film a person often meant to provoke and/or to expose him or her, and to be filmed meant to parry this probing or to be laid bare by it. As a result the viewer cannot idealize the filmed person, as is usually the case with Hollywood cinema. One can only empathize, intermittently, with his or her travails before the relentless camera, that is, again, to empathize with the vicissitudes of the subject becoming an image—with wanting this condition too much, resisting it too much, or otherwise failing at it.[13]

The viewer's empathy with the image in a digital portrait responds not to the identity of the subject as an image but to the desire of the subject to become an image. Warhol exposed and exploited this desire by collecting sets of screen tests in his *Thirteen Most Beautiful* series. *Thirteen Most Beautiful Boys* and *Thirteen Most Beautiful Women* extended the reach of the "relentless camera" to the exhibition venues, subjecting the performers in the screen tests to the renewed anxieties of the public exhibition of their performances or to the disappointment of their exclusion from the unstable canon of thirteen featured films.

Virtual Beauty: Eva and Franco Mattes's *13 Most Beautiful Avatars*

The conceptual artists Eva and Franco Mattes directly appropriate Warhol's investigation of performance, beauty, and exhibition in *13 Most Beautiful Avatars*. The thirteen digital portraits of avatars from *Second Life* appear in a museum installation in a series of 36 by 48 inch digital prints on canvas, arranged in a straight line on white walls in a large room. The transition from the moving images in *Thirteen Most Beautiful* to the still images in *13 Most Beautiful Avatars* entails several aesthetic and critical alterations. The avatar portraits present a series of faces in poses of maximal and inert beauty. The still image eliminates the endurance required by both the subjects featured in Warhol's screen tests and the viewers who watched them. *13 Most Beautiful Avatars* thus transforms the featured avatars into icons, obscuring the agency of the avatars in *Second Life* as performing subjects who articulate their identities through movement, speech, and other physical expressions. The interactive architecture of *Second Life* could enable the production of moving images by adapting Warhol's formal conditions to a virtual world, but the decision by Eva and Franco Mattes to curate screen shots rather than screen tests focuses their project on the avatars that players designed rather than on their designers. The avatar exhibition posits virtual beauty as a design achievement and invites the viewer to contemplate whether digital beauty is worthy of exhibition and recognition.

In her brief reading of the avatar gallery, Emily Apter answers this question by arguing that *Second Life* users "adapt the principles and procedures of cosmetic surgery—augmentation, enhancement, nose jobs, liposuction, botox—to virtual body-construction," and yet she also acknowledges that they "move beyond the commercialized beauty ideal towards an aesthetics of virtual surface and augmented bodies: skin, jewels, and tattoos, extreme morphology, intersectional race and gender, cross-speciation."[14] The thirteen close-up portraits in the *13 Most Beautiful Avatars* series do participate in the virtual translation and perfection of a culturally pervasive set of beauty standards. While Warhol's shifting set of "most beautiful" subjects included both subjects who embodied dominant beauty ideals and others who challenged them, the faces of the "most beautiful avatars" resemble those found on the covers of glossy fashion magazines and in the couture advertisements they contain.

The portraits do not subvert these conventional assertions of beauty, but they do present a racially diverse profile of virtual expressions of beauty through portraits of avatars of different races and portraits of racially ambiguous avatars. The images of Nubiian Craven and Modesty Galbraith offer two examples of this racial diversity and uncertainty.[15] In both portraits, the avatar's face fills the frame, concealing the avatar's body (and its costuming) and the environment in which the avatar appears. Both avatars look slightly away from the viewer: Nubiian Craven directs her gaze above the viewer, and Modesty Galbraith casts her stare slightly downward. Whether these looks imply a coquettish invitation to examine the avatar, a defiant refusal to look at the viewer, or a distracted or purposeful engagement with another avatar, object, or event in *Second Life,* they permit the viewer to analyze the close-up images without confronting the avatar's gaze. Craven and Galbraith do not look alike, but they share specific facial features with each other and with the other "most beautiful avatars": large eyes adorned with eyeliner, glamorously long eyelashes, full and pouty lips covered in lipstick, and flawless skin combine in each portrait in perfect symmetry.

It would be impossible to produce a demographic analysis of the installation. Three of the thirteen avatars have very dark skin, including Nubiian Craven, and several of the avatars may identify or be identified as white. Any attempt to assign a racial identity to each avatar beyond these observations of visual surfaces rests on the viewer's speculation. Does the extreme close-up of Modesty Galbraith's face provide visual evidence that she is Asian? How can that question be answered when her avatar, like the others in *13 Most Beautiful Avatars,* has been detached from the other markers of identity that the people who designed the avatars may have activated? Would answering that question change the installation's investigation of digital beauty and voyeurism in any way? Do names like Nubiian Craven make different claims about racial identity than names like Modesty Galbraith, either confirming or obscuring the race of each avatar? Every avatar has a different skin tone, and this visual diversity undermines the standard grid that frames most statistical analyses of racial composition. Racial identity remains indeterminate for most of the featured avatars, and racial indeterminacy emerges in the collection as a salient feature of virtual beauty.

The presentation of these portraits in a gallery of "most beautiful avatars" does not insulate the avatars from virtual interactions that deploy the same racist and misogynistic discourses and actions used in off-line social encounters, as noted by Harisu in her description of transphobia in *Lineage II*. B. Coleman probes the ways in which "virtual identity markers work analogous to how they work in the real world."[16] Including images from the *13 Most Beautiful Avatars* portrait gallery to accompany her theoretical reflections, Coleman notes that "avatar images, as well as gestures and voice, translate cultural information that we believe in: if we see a black avatar, we comprehend this as a black person and treat that avatar accordingly."[17] Coleman's ethnographic research in virtual worlds addresses the importance of acknowledging the social consequences of avatar design: "For better and for worse, putting a face on things also attaches the societal associations that such a face bears."[18]

The collection of digital portraits in *13 Most Beautiful Avatars* obscures the impact of these associations, but the procession of images of idealized and augmented beauty formalizes several registers of representational diversity in virtual worlds. First, the creation of an avatar is a performance of the self as a screen image, similar to the performances improvised and sustained in front of Warhol's Bolex camera. Whether or not the viewer is aware of the "avatar effect" that Coleman describes, "in which we find persuasive signs of virtual identity that are aggregated with the identity of the media participant," the avatar's presence bears witness to the subject's desire to become the image.[19] Second, the thirteen avatars do not fit neatly into demographic categories of race. A viewer may speculate that specific avatars match common racial designations, but the variety of skin colors available to avatar designers in *Second Life* complicates these divisions. Digital code generates more permutations of racial difference than demographic analysis. The *13 Most Beautiful Avatars* installation thus not only catalogs the virtual construction of beauty but also exhibits the ways that aesthetic explorations of identity in virtual worlds may simultaneously resist and reassert social realities. These digital portraits enact a reversal of Warhol's slow surveillance of the subject. Warhol's screen tests define beauty through or in relation to the subject's performance. The avatar installation dwells instead on the visible contours of virtual beauty by freezing the avatars as still images.

Moving Portraits: Robbie Cooper's *Immersion*

Cooper's *Immersion* series does not explicitly cite Warhol's screen tests as an influence, but the projects share several formal features and a fascination with what Foster describes as "the vicissitudes of the subject becoming an image."[20] Cooper began the *Immersion* project in 2008, and—as of this writing—the geographic, medial, and formal scope of the project continues to expand. While this chapter discusses the edited video of children playing popular video games that Cooper circulated under the title "Immersion," the larger *Immersion* project documents subjects of all ages as they watch various screen media, including television shows, live sporting events, pornography, and music videos. Inspired by documentary filmmaker Errol Morris's "Interrotron" apparatus, Cooper designed a recording environment that projects the screen image (of the video game being played) onto a glass surface with a camera positioned behind the glass. While the subject watches the "screen," the camera records the subject from the point of view of the screen. By fusing the position of the camera and the screen, the apparatus allows the filmed subject to look directly at the viewer of the completed film. The glass operates as a surface of projection and a scrim over the camera rather than a screen. While the subjects in "Immersion" are aware that they are being filmed, both the location of the camera and the immersive (and social) experience of gameplay prompt them to engage directly with the games and to perform their roles as players without the attendant anxieties of performance visible in the screen tests.

Like the screen tests, "Immersion" features a stark mise-en-scène—a well-lit gray background with no objects in the frame other than the subject or subjects (some children play alone and others in pairs or small groups). Shot in color, with most of the children framed in close-ups or medium close-ups, the video's framings resemble school portraits. Unlike Warhol's silent films, however, "Immersion" includes a complicated soundscape sourced from the games and their players—explosions, gunfire, hip-hop music, in-game dialogue, and exclamations from the players ("Come back here, and let me stab you." "Haha, you'll get knifed!"). These sounds provide the viewer's only access to the games that the children are playing, beyond their reactions to the games. Cooper never reveals any images from the games, choosing instead to transform the player into an image. The viewer watches the player, while the player watches and plays the game. This arrangement of looks creates the illusion that the player on the screen is looking not at but through the viewer of "Immersion." Cooper's elaborate recording apparatus enables the viewer to occupy an otherwise impossible viewing position. While the player becomes an image on-screen, the viewer becomes the game, or to be more precise, looks at the player from the vantage point of the game.

This position disrupts the economies of spectatorship that dominate film studies because the viewer's position within the virtual space of the game does not involve identification but rather a radical distanciation. The descriptions of the cinematic spectator that dominate psychoanalytic film theory and apparatus theory—for example, in its most generic form, the description of the spectator identifying with the image projected on a large screen in a darkened room—break down in "Immersion"; and the aesthetic, social, and political effects of the cinematic apparatus unravel in turn.[21] Cooper's video aligns the spectator with the game itself—not with a character or an avatar within the game but with the surface of the game as it unfolds on the screen. By occupying this abstract and dispersed point of view, the spectator wields the ability to examine the player directly yet covertly. Experiences of identification or resistance are not structurally embedded in the textual apparatus, thus permitting a wide range of affective and critical responses to the video within the ambit of Cooper's provocation to dwell on the consequences of immersion.

Cooper's editorial interventions depart from Warhol's more passive procedures; he organizes the individual shots in "Immersion" into a compilation that documents the diversity of digital gaming. He uncovers diversity not in the individual games the children play (which include *Grand Theft Auto IV* [2008, Rockstar North] and *Call of Duty IV* [2007, Infinity Ward]) but in the identities of the children and in the forms of interactivity they exhibit. "Immersion" begins, for example, with footage of a female player: Jessica Hardy, a thirteen-year-old white girl from Grimsby, England, plays *Tekken: Dark Resurrection* (2006, Namco). Jessica's silent and rapt investment in the game emerges as she stares open-mouthed, twisting her head as she operates the controller (which is hidden beneath the frame of the image). Her performance telegraphs concentration, determination, and expertise. Of the dozen children featured prominently, only three are female, but the opening performance of Jessica Hardy anchors the video, introducing the viewer to its formal protocols and immediately challenging any assumptions the viewer may have about who plays video games and how they play.

If a star emerges from among the excerpts included in the video, it is the seven-year-old African American boy Drew Hugh (figure 10.2). In Drew's segment, the most direct connection between Warhol's screen tests and Cooper's videos takes shape. In the video, Drew plays the game *Hulk* (2003, Radical Entertainment), and a single tear falls down his face as he stares at the screen. The shot lasts for exactly ten seconds at the midpoint of the short film, and it dramatically shifts the tone of the video. The previous subjects appear immersed in their gameplay, but their immersion seems at times competitive ("Come back here, so I can stab you."), and at times irreverent ("Haha, you'll get knifed!"). These exclamations, analyzed in tandem with the open-mouthed intensity of the players, may alarm viewers of the video, especially those who associate violent video games with acts of violence in the off-line world.[22] Drew's tear, however, realigns the viewer's engagement with the video, inciting empathy for the subject as he endures the "relentless camera" that Foster describes in relation to watching Warhol's films. Is Drew distressed by an event in the game world? Is he overwhelmed by self-consciousness in response to Cooper's video surveillance of his gameplay? Is his tear provoked by an event or circumstance unrelated to the game and the video recording? The viewer enters the speculative mode similarly prompted by Buchanan's tears. Viewers who discover "Immersion" through a slideshow of still images from the video featured on the *New York Times* website, however, learn that Drew's tear was a physiological response rather than an emotional one. According to the introduction to the slideshow, Drew "stares so intently at the screen that he doesn't blink, and his eyes quickly fill with tears, according to his mother."[23]

Figure 10.2. Drew Hugh, New York, 2008 ("Immersion" video still)

The revelation that Drew's tears are evidence of the physical rigor of his immersion in gameplay rather than an emotional response to the game itself or the circumstances of Cooper's filming fails to neutralize the falling tear's disruption of the video. While Drew's mother's explanation is logical and persuasive, the tear remains as an unsettling inscription on the surface of the video. Drew does not twitch or sigh or groan or stick out his tongue or hold his breath or perform any of the other (conscious or unconscious) physical and vocal gestures that the other players express during their segments; he remains still. All the digital portraits included in "Immersion" share the same formal elements, but Drew's ten-second-long portrait almost arrests the passing of time in the video. For viewers watching the video on a computer screen (as most viewers will who do not have access to the museum installations of *Immersion*), it may seem as if the video has frozen for a moment. Only the sound of the game itself and the slow movement of the tear assure the viewer that the video is still playing, and that Drew is still playing. In both Buchanan's screen test and Drew's gameplay portrait, the image vibrates with the tension between stillness and movement and asks viewers to contemplate their complicity in the production of the image. The affective speculation set in motion by Drew's tear shifts the parameters of the discussion of race and video games. The image complicates Anna Everett and S. Craig Watkins's observation that "in the context of video games, players are not only watching race; they are also performing and, as a result, (re)producing socially prescribed and technologically mediated notions of race."[24] *Immersion* presents Drew as a player and as a representation, challenging audiences to locate him within the existing discourses of racial representation. Whether the tear indicates emotion or immersion, its appearance positions Drew as a new representation; expanding the industrial and cultural frameworks that define the black male in video games as an absence or as an agent or victim of violence.

Alter Egos: Digital Portraiture and Diversity

Cooper's projects resist the articulation of a clear argument. In his introduction to *Alter Ego,* Julian Dibbell notes: "Look for any single theme to which the varied images and attitudes on display here might be reduced, and you will look in vain. These photos, and the words that frame them, tell us quite a bit about the emerging relationships between real people and virtual realities, but very little of what they have to say is final."[25] Indeed, a review of the portraits in *Alter Ego* confirms the meticulous diversity of the subjects, and this may be the connecting theme or argument that Dibbell finds so elusive. Cooper's subjects in *Alter Ego* include equal numbers of men and women of various ages and races. Cooper photographs participants living in the United States, the United Kingdom, France, Greece, Denmark, Austria, Germany, South Korea, China, and Belgium. While this geographic range is not truly global, it attests to Cooper's ambition to track engagement with virtual worlds across geographic borders.

More striking than the geographic sprawl of his portraits is the range of approaches the subjects take to designing their avatars and theorizing their designs and their experiences in virtual worlds within their written accounts. In some portraits, the avatar approaches the uncanny valley of resemblance, sharing all of the subject's facial and bodily features and even wearing the same clothes and accessories that the subject wears in the portrait. The juxtaposition of these portraits suggests that the subject has successfully transgressed the border between worlds and entered the virtual world as an almost exact graphical replica. In other portraits, no visible connection between the subject and his or her avatar appears. Subjects choose avatars of different races and genders and with different body shapes and styles of adornment. Fantasy worlds also enable subjects to design avatars of different species, with wings, tails, and magical powers. Close readings of these portraits and their accompanying mini-autobiographies do not point to any patterns. Avatar design remains unpredictable, and the accumulation of portraits resists reconciliation into a unifying theory of virtual experience. The relationship between the two portraits in each set—the desires, experiences, resemblances, and differences that define each pair of subject and avatar—reflects individual matrices of identification and interactivity that a single model of avatar design could not describe. *Alter Ego* establishes its argument through the quantity of portraits it includes rather than the presentation of a single quality that all of the portraits share.

Immersion operates through a similar quantitative logic. The formal continuity among the portraits promotes a simultaneous reading of the experience of immersion that each subject shares and the unique ways in which they inhabit that immersion. "Immersion" serves as a critical intervention in the representational politics of video games by asserting that not all children who play games are white males. One of the portraits features two children playing *Star Wars: Battlefront*

(2004, Pandemic Studios) together—the white male Niamh Byers and the black female Tilly Geddes, both ten years old, filmed in Acton, England. Niamh and Tilly telegraph a subtle awareness of the camera that the other children do not, with Niamh smiling and giggling as he almost hides from the camera's stare. Tilly seems to be suppressing a smile as she remains still and otherwise expressionless. Because the camera obstructs the view of their hands, it is difficult to determine at first whether Tilly is playing or merely watching Niamh play. A slight movement in her body later suggests that she is in fact playing. Her performance in the portrait is otherwise unremarkable. She does not laugh or cry. She does not threaten a character or cheer her victory or talk to Niamh. She just plays. While the introduction of Jessica's assertive absorption in the opening frame of the video or the pivotal take of Drew's enigmatic tear may invite more formal attention, Tilly's presence in the video as a black girl playing a video game may be equally powerful as a representational intervention.

13 Most Beautiful Avatars canonizes the presence of racially diverse and racially ambiguous avatars. By curating a collection of portraits of the "most beautiful" avatars in *Second Life* and hanging them on a gallery wall, Eva and Franco Mattes formalize a canon of virtual beauty and link that beauty to racial diversity. *13 Most Beautiful Avatars* defines beauty through commercially dominant regimes, selecting avatars that resemble contemporary fashion models; but the installation also presents racial diversity and racial ambiguity as aesthetic ideals. The transformation of active avatars into still portraits invites the spectator's contemplation of the ways that virtual beauty both supports and subverts dominant aesthetic ideals in the off-line world.

Alter Ego, *Immersion*, and *13 Most Beautiful Avatars* share an investment in using digital portraiture as a means to expose the diverse aesthetic and social experiences that define online identification and interactivity. The virtual world is neither a utopian space where the expression of different gendered and racial identities can proceed free from scrutiny or harassment nor an industrially codified sphere that neatly replicates off-line structures of power. The portraits collected in these projects draw our attention to the diversity of gaming cultures and other virtual worlds both by enshrining the presence of people who play games (and who may or may not look like the people you imagine playing games and whose avatars may or may not resemble their off-line selves) and by establishing formal conventions that provoke the investigation of these players as images in the off-line world and as actors in virtual worlds. Harisu's reflection that her avatar "has to concentrate on being [her]" directs our attention back to Harisu and the many other people who comprise the diverse and irreducible roster of players and their avatars.

LISA PATTI is Assistant Professor in the Media and Society Program at Hobart and William Smith Colleges. She is coauthor of *Film Studies: A Global Introduction* and coeditor of *The Multilingual Screen: New Reflections on Cinema and Linguistic Difference.*

Notes

1. Quoted in Robbie Cooper and Tracy Spaight, *Alter Ego: Avatars and Their Creators* (London: Chris Boot, 2007), n.p.

2. Quoted in ibid., n.p.

3. Quoted in ibid., n.p.

4. Adrienne Shaw, *Gaming at the Edge: Sexuality and Gender at the Margins of Gamer Culture* (Minneapolis: University of Minnesota Press, 2014), 93 (emphasis in original).

5. See, for example, Dmitri Williams, Nicole Martins, Mia Consalvo, and James D. Ivory, "The Virtual Census: Representations of Gender, Race, and Age in Video Games," *New Media and Society* 11, no. 5 (2009): 815–834.

6. Entertainment Software Association, "2016 Sales, Demographic and Usage Data: Essentials Facts about the Computer and Video Game Industry," April 2016, p. 3, http://essentialfacts.theesa.com/Essential-Facts-2016.pdf.

7. Callie Angell, *Andy Warhol Screen Tests: The Films of Andy Warhol Catalogue Raisonné*, vol. 1 (New York: Harry N. Abrams and the Whitney Museum of Art, 2006), 14.

8. Ibid.

9. For recent discussions of the screen tests in relation to the extensive filmography of experimental cinema produced by Warhol, see J. J. Murphy, *The Black Hole of the Camera* (Berkeley: University of California Press, 2012); and Douglas Crimp, *"Our Kind of Movie": The Films of Andy Warhol* (Cambridge, MA: MIT Press, 2012).

10. The thirteen screen tests included in the Dean and Britta project are Paul America, Susan Bottomly, Ann Buchanan, Freddy Herko, Jane Holzer, Dennis Hopper, Billy Name, Nico, Richard Rheem, Lou Reed, Edie Sedgwick, Ingrid Superstar, and Mary Woronov.

11. Angell, *Andy Warhol Screen Tests*, 45.

12. For a complete list of comments, see starlett lopez, "Andy Warhol's Screen Test: Ann: The Girl Who Cries a Tear," *YouTube*, June 30, 2010, http://www.youtube.com/watch?v=rQEiOoMyvos.

13. Hal Foster, "Test Subjects," *October* 132 (2010): 41–42.

14. Emily Apter, "Technics of the Subject: The Avatar Drive," *Postmodern Culture* 18, no. 2 (2008), http://www.english.illinois.edu/-people-/faculty/schaffner/w4w/readings/apter.pdf.

15. For a complete portfolio of the portraits included in *13 Most Beautiful Avatars*, see http://www.postmastersart.com/archive/01org_07/01org_07_window1.html.

16. B. Coleman, *Hello Avatar: Rise of the Networked Generation* (Cambridge, MA: MIT Press, 2011), 72.

17. Ibid.

18. Ibid., 74.

19. Ibid.

20. Foster, "Test Subjects," 42.

21. The long bibliography chronicling these strands of film theory includes Jean-Louis Baudry, "Ideological Effects of the Basic Cinematographic Apparatus," *Film Quarterly* 28, no. 2 (1974–1975): 35–47; and Laura Mulvey, "Visual Pleasure and Narrative Cinema," *Screen* 16, no. 3 (1975): 6–18.

22. For a brief overview of leading counterarguments responding to the popular representation of media effects research, see Henry Jenkins, "Reality Bytes: Eight Myths about Video Games Debunked," *PBS*, http://www.pbs.org/kcts/videogamerevolution/impact/myths.html (accessed December 19, 2016).

23. A series of seven screen shots from *Immersion* is included in the online slideshow "My Game Face," *New York Times Magazine*, November 18, 2008, http://www.nytimes.com/slideshow/2008/11/18/magazine/20081123-games_index.html.

24. Anna Everett and S. Craig Watkins, "The Power of Play: The Portrayal and Performance of Race in Video Games," in *The Ecology of Games*, ed. Katie Salen (Cambridge, MA: MIT Press, 2007), 149.

25. Julian Dibbell, "Introduction," in Cooper and Spaight, *Alter Ego*, n.p.

Part III

QUEERNESS, PLAY, SUBVERSION

chapter eleven

PLAYING TO LOSE

The Queer Art of Failing at Video Games

BONNIE RUBERG

WHEN WE PLAY VIDEO GAMES, WE PLAY TO WIN, DON'T WE? SOMETIMES WE fail—very often we fail—but failure itself amounts to little more than an unpleasant, if necessary, obstacle on the road to success. It's normal to hate to fail; taking pleasure in failure itself, playing a game intentionally to lose, would be very queer indeed. At least, these are the assumptions that underlie recent writing on failure in video games. These same assumptions are being challenged by contemporary queer theory, which explores the functions of failure but doesn't address video games. This chapter brings these two contemporary discourses into dialogue, in order to question and ultimately refute a set of accepted notions about games: that players find pleasure only in success, that players find only pain in failure, that the power of losing lies in the power of winning, and that it would be bafflingly abnormal and dismissively unlikely to revel in defying a game's expectations for success—to lie down willingly under the blows of our opponents, to crash our cars in a blaze of self-destruction.

My ultimate goal is to bring together queer theory and game studies to argue for failure as an inherently queer mode of play. To do this, I interweave two recent theoretical works of such strikingly similar titles that they beg us to read them together. In 2011 queer theorist Jack Halberstam published his book on failing and cultural resistance, *The Queer Art of Failure*. In 2013, games scholar Jesper Juul published his own treatise, an extended essay on "pain in video games," *The Art of Failure*. The two texts share almost no common material and do not reference each other.[1] Halberstam doesn't talk about video games; Juul doesn't talk about queerness. However, considered as two pieces of one puzzle, these works, at once surprisingly similar and surprisingly different, form a conceptual basis for exploring queerness in video games beyond representation. That is, the abstract nature of their connections allows us to look for the queer, in its many guises, in games that have no explicitly LGBT content. After presenting some of the ways that one might fail for failure's sake, I use the racing game *Burnout Revenge* (2005, Criterion Games) both to illustrate and nuance my basic claim: that, contrary to common assumptions, failure in video games can be pleasurable and powerful—a spectacular, masochistic mode of resistance that disassembles normative expectations in and out of the game world. To conclude, I propose a new understanding of play through queer failure, a new understanding of queer failure through play, and a framework for future crossovers between queer studies and game studies, two currently disparate disciplines with much to gain from opening their doors to one another.

Beyond LGBT Representation: On Queering "Straight" Games

Putting queerness and games in dialogue is a nascent practice, for academics and game makers alike. Traditionally, mainstream video games have shied away from including LGBT characters or story lines—and what elements they have included often promote reductive or harmful stereotyping.[2] In this sense, approaching games through the lens of queerness seems at first counterintuitive. Lately, though, a number of independent game developers whose work directly addresses queerness have received national attention.[3] Meanwhile, recent years have seen the inauguration of multiple conventions and conferences exploring everything from LGBT discrimination in the games industry to different approaches to designing LGBT content to the LGBT "geek" lifestyle to the academic intersection of queer studies and game studies.[4] Scholarship around these issues has only recently begun to circulate. Previously, queer games writing frequently focused on questions like, "What are the experiences of LGBT gamers?" or "How do existing games depict LGBT characters, and how could they improve?"[5] This important work has played a crucial role in orienting our thinking around queerness and games. However, my focus lies elsewhere. I do not discuss literal representations of queer characters or the alienation of queer gamers denied representation. I do not lay out the history of queerness in games or the games industry or prescribe for queer content a brighter tomorrow. Instead, in the tradition of ludologists like Juul, algorithmic thinkers like Alexander Galloway, and classic theorists of play like Johan Huizinga, Roger Caillois, and Sigmund Freud, I focus on ludics, and I do so queerly. I don't mean to imply that we shouldn't dedicate attention to explicitly queer games elsewhere, that queerness is somehow inept by association with failure, or that player masochism equates to player sickness. Indeed, failure, masochism, and the queer are all used here as powerful, positive, and fluid concepts that allow us to see queerness where it often goes overlooked.

Before diving into Juul's and Halberstam's queer arts, I unpack the stakes of this proposition, that we might look for queerness beyond LGBT representation. What happens when we call a work—a video game, movie, and so on—"queer" even if it doesn't seem to contain any explicitly queer content? If players can't play at gay marriage or choose transgendered avatars, if they can only race cars or throw punches, doesn't that make a game by default "straight"—or at least not gay? It's likely that the queer-free game in question includes no overt references to sexuality at all. To the player who sees queer as synonymous with gay, this game appears sexless, benign. Games like these make up a huge majority of commercially released titles. Yet it's specifically because this presumed straightness so dominates the medium that we need to challenge the mold and look at all types of games through the lens of queerness, not just those rare few where schoolboys kiss schoolboys (*Bully*, 2006, Rockstar Games) or women seduce women in the far reaches of outer space (*Mass Effect* series, 2007–2012, BioWare).

Queering the seemingly un-queer is a particularly touchy, and therefore particularly powerful, practice when it comes to video games, an artistic form with close ties to its historically homophobic player base.[6] The traditional wisdom from gaming's outspoken online community objects that when we explore queerness in "straight" games, we "read too much" into them, polluting the hetero safe space of queer-free play with our "gay" interpretations. The pervasiveness of this homophobia has been well documented.[7] Allow me to illustrate. Shortly after the release of the widely popular *Portal* (2007, Valve), I wrote a blog post for the *Village Voice* about lesbian overtones in the relationship between the game's female protagonist and GLaDOS, her taunting, female-coded robot tormentor.[8] In the post's comment thread, a reader left this response, one of many like it: "There is nothing gay about this game, you just made that up. No one ever says lesbian. You're just a dyke bitch who doesn't know what you're saying. If you want to think like that in your own home go ahead but don't force it down our throats."[9] This comment neatly encapsulates what I would identify as the main tenets of gamer homophobia. First, any game not clearly marked as gay must be straight. Second, any interpretation of a game not spelled out explicitly by the game itself must be personal, invented, and therefore invalid (e.g., "you just made that up"). Third, anyone who talks about queerness must be gay. Fourth, reading games queerly, like queerness itself, belongs in the closet (e.g., do it "in your own home"). Fifth, making queerness visible constitutes an act of violence against the hetero status quo. Sixth, this imagined violence is itself charged with unacknowledged homoerotics (e.g., "don't force it down our throats"). Seventh, there is a "we," and there is a "you"; women and queers fall in the "you" and stand outside an imagined, invisible community of "we"—real, normal, straight, male players. Needless to say, the beloved game itself, in this case *Portal*, is claimed without question for the "we"—up until the imagined moment when the word "lesbian," had it been included in the game, would have satisfactorily solidified the doubtful "queer" into the comprehensible, categorical "gay."

Game designers and scholars, arguing for the legitimacy of video games as an art form, often draw parallels between the tumultuous history of film and the current state of interactive media—young and wobbly but blossoming in the face of criticism, as cinema did in its earliest decades. A similar parallel exists between queer film studies and queer game studies. The homophobic, anti-analytical community response exemplified by the *Portal* comment mirrors with surprising familiarity the dismissive, heterocentric backlash that film scholars faced in the mid-1990s when they began to queer classic straight movies. In *Flaming Classics: Queering the Film Cannon* (2000), Alexander Doty describes the reactions of his peers to his queer readings of supposedly safe, sexless favorites like the movie *The Wizard of Oz* (1939). "It often seems as if people think that since you have chosen to read something queerly," Doty laments, "you need to be pressured or patronized into feeling that you have made the wrong or the 'less common and therefore easy to undermine or put in its place' choice."[10] Under the truism that mass media is produced for and by the average straight, white, middle-class male consumer—and is therefore itself straight—attitudes like those Doty encountered insistently categorize queer readings of mainstream films (or games) as "pathetic and delusional attempts to see something that isn't there."[11] At best, this hegemonic thinking posits that queer readings focus excessively on small tidbits of homoeroticism that are insubstantial, subtextual, subcultural, and always second-rate alternatives to the allegedly obvious, reasonable, literal, ostensibly hetero interpretation of bodies on-screen.

How do we argue for queerness in the face of such insistently narrow perspectives? First, we must understand the word "queer," in its contemporary usage, to mean much more than gay, or even LGBT. Individuals who identify as queer might see themselves as defying heterosexual norms in any number of ways: through sexuality, gender queerness, non-mainstream relationship styles, and so on. And queerness isn't just confined to the flesh. More abstractly, queerness means both desiring differently and simply being differently (or, in this case, playing differently): a longing to live life otherwise, a resistance to social structures, and an embrace of the strange.[12] So when we explore queerness in supposedly straight games, we're not declaring them gay. We're also not calling their players or makers gay. We're not saying that developers intentionally built queerness into their games or that every player experiences queerness similarly. We're not even necessarily labeling this queerness as sexual. These caveats may seem obvious, but for the video game community "queer" still represents untried and uneasy territory. The multiplicity of ways to interpret queerness also reminds us that there are many, equally valid ways to interpret games. Queer readings don't necessarily seek to override straight ones. Instead, they offer queer ways of seeing games. These modes of seeing value experience above content, a particularly important approach for video games, where player input shapes the interactive world. Any game becomes queer, in a sense, when we experience it queerly.

Of course, to explore the queerness in all games, we must move past the homophobia and anti-intellectualism exemplified by my reader's remark. If we want games to flourish as a rich, artful medium for entertainment and study, we'll have to set aside our knee-jerk, heterocentric defenses. Games may be fun, but that doesn't mean they're just fun. As Juul writes, video games speak to "something deeper, something truly human, something otherwise invisible" about their players and the world around them.[13] Games are fictional, fantasy, but they are also always at least half-real.[14] Understanding fantasy helps us understand desire, pleasure, pain, and ourselves. Besides, what does it mean to read a game too closely? "Too close" implies intimacy, inappropriate contact, poking and prodding and pressing—an almost sexual and certainly ludic encounter with the video game itself. It means caring too deeply. Gamers, of all people, know what it's like to be told by those who do not share their passion for games that they care too much. These intimacies are queer intimacies, alternate visions of the control-freedom dynamic—the intimacy between player and game, between flesh and the controller in our hands.

The Arts of Failure: Halberstam and Juul

Juul opens *The Art of Failure* with a personal account of how much he hates to lose, admitting and proclaiming:

> I am a sore loser. Something in me demands that I win, beat, or complete every game I try, and that part of me is outraged and tormented whenever I fail to do so. Still, I play video games though I know I will fail. . . . On a higher level, I think I enjoy playing video games, but why does this enjoyment contain at its core something that I most certainly do not enjoy?[15]

To illustrate this contradiction, this "pleasure spiked with pain," Juul describes failing at a level of the Japanese rhythm game *Patapon* (2008, Pyramid). Again and again, angry and dejected, he fails, puts the game away, then picks it up again, and then puts it away once more, returning as if compulsively to the site of his tantalizing torment—recalling Freud's fort-da game, in which a child repeatedly throws away and retrieves a toy that reminds him painfully of his absent father.[16] Everyone who plays video games participates in the same illogical dance, Juul asserts: "It is safe to say that humans have a fundamental desire to succeed and feel competent, but game players have chosen to engage in an activity in which they are almost certain to fail and feel incompetent, at least some of the time."[17]

These opening paragraphs make clear that Juul hates failing, and that he assumes everyone else hates failing too. Failure makes Juul viscerally upset. Therefore he tells us, unequivocally, to put any thoughts of masochism out of our minds. He "most certainly" does not enjoy his repeated demise, as we might be tempted to suggest. Indeed, Juul founds *The Art of Failure* on the presumption that displeasure is the logical and normal response to losing. Players who lose feel rotten, and loss jolts them out of the game with such a nauseating punch to their self-esteem that they contemplate giving up entirely. Yet players' drive to win pushes them forward past failure, inspiring them to walk over the emotional broken glass of lost levels in a rush of determination, pride, and testosterone. What Juul names the "paradox of failure" sits at the crux of his argument—the confusing fact that we return time and again to play through what we hate (temporary defeat) in order to experience what we love (success). Though often overlooked, Juul reasons, failure is a crucial part of the play experience—so crucial, in fact, that Juul suggests we might call video games as an art form "the art of failure." The presumption operating here, for Juul, is that meaning in failure comes not from the pleasure or pain of failure itself, but instead from the frustrations and rewards of struggling to overcome it. That failure might be its own success, its own pleasure, its own art—performed not by the game but by the player—does not enter into Juul's equation.

Juul suggests and dismisses a number of possible explanations for this paradox. Perhaps video games offer a safe space for failure, a magic circle where falling on our faces is "neither painful nor the least unpleasant." No, in some sense video game failure really does hurt, he insists. Perhaps failing in video games allows us to purge our reserves of pity and fear in response to fictional tragedy. No, writes Juul, "when we experience a humiliating defeat, we really are filled with emotions of humiliation and inadequacy. Games do not purge these emotions—they produce the emotions in the first place."[18] Maybe failure motivates us to continue playing. Maybe failure keeps us agreeably honest. Maybe failure doesn't matter.[19] Juul come closest to a decision about the paradox of failure when he posits that games make us feel flawed and deficient but also promise us the opportunity to overcome our flaws.[20] In each of these proposed answers, though, the appeal of failure remains inextricably linked to eventual success—to failure's roundabout ability to cleanse bad feelings or encourage us to win. The solution, tautologically, replicates the assumptions of the paradox itself—success is good, failure hurts, and no one likes to hurt.

Though Juul's *The Art of Failure* and Halberstam's *The Queer Art of Failure* have nearly identical titles, Halberstam offers a very different take on losing. Halberstam's book doesn't discuss video games, but questions of success and self-destruction sit at its heart—making it a logical, if unexpected bedfellow for Juul's distinctly queerness-free text. What's more, because it so prominently uses language like "losing" and "winning," we can easily reenvision it as a treatise about play. The basic imperative behind Halberstam's argument is to stop thinking about failure as an onerous frustration to be overcome. Instead, think of all the heteronormative expectations we undermine when we refuse to succeed, to play along, to win. Think of the havoc we wreak on the status quo when we, under the charge of queer nonconformity, play to lose:

> Heteronormative common sense leads to the equation of success with advancement, capital accumulation, family, ethical conduct, and hope. Other subordinate, queer, or counter-hegemonic modes of common sense lead to the association of failure with nonconformity, anticapitalist practices, nonreproductive lifestyles, negativity, and critique. . . . [They] recategorize what looks like inaction, passivity, and lack of resistance in terms of the practice of stalling the business of the dominant. . . . Rather than searching for ways around death and disappointment,

> the queer art of failure involves the acceptance of the finite, the embrace of the absurd.... Rather than resisting endings and limits, let us instead revel in and cling to all of our inevitable fantastic failures.[21]

In this vision, queer failure does not just mean falling facedown in the mud; it means taking pleasure in that fall. It means getting up, not because determination drives you to "die tryin'," as Derek Burrill describes in his book on video games and performances of masculinity, but because you want to fall all over again.[22] Meanwhile, clean, happy, "normal" people pass by and shake their heads—their idea of happiness for a moment unsettled. The one who revels in "fantastic failures" is the one who loses, embraces losing, and likes it. If we adjust Halberstam's language for games, we can read normative "advancement" as advancement through levels (or a refusal to advance), and "capital accumulation" as in-game points accumulated (or ignored, wasted). "Nonreproductive lifestyles" becomes the squandering of extra lives, the abandonment of hard-fought unsaved games. The queer takes on the guise of the bad subject, the bad player who rejects the regulating logic of the game and "[stalls] the business of the dominant," the cheater who exercises her unsanctioned agency not so much to win as, in Mia Consalvo's terms, "to challenge the notion that there is one 'correct' way to play."[23]

Juul and Halberstam disagree on what exactly constitutes the art of failure. For Juul, it refers to games themselves as an art form, interactive experiences carefully designed to bring us to our knees and convince us to stay there. For Halberstam, by contrast, the art of failure isn't an object that punishes us; it's an art we enact, an art of being differently, of embracing self-destructive agency. When we fail fantastically, we are the queer artists. Halberstam's use of "queer" in the phrase "the queer art" highlights the word's double meaning—both sexually nonnormative and simply bizarre. Traditionally, artistry equates to being good at something; failure equates to being bad at it. Any art of failure would be queer indeed. After all, who throws themselves in the mud for fun? Someone masochistic. Someone exploring fun's absurdities and abjections, playing with the meanings of pleasure, playing queerly. Thus, to play queerly means to play the wrong way around, to jump our unsuspecting, pixelated avatars into pits instead of over them, to choreograph the most unfortunate disasters. If Juul's art of failure is games, in this sense Halberstam's is also a game, one of our own making. It is a playful art, a ludic art, which makes a game of dying.

Fail Fantastically: *Burnout Revenge* and the Pleasure of Self-Destruction

To question the notion that players simply hate failing, we need look no further than the multitude of "fail" videos accruing views on YouTube. In these videos, players record their own epic in-game fails and then post them proudly. Whereas live-action fail videos feature real bodies putting themselves in real peril, the failure in game videos is the failure to play well—or it's the success of playing so badly it becomes absurd. A YouTube compilation uploaded in May 2013 composed of clips from games like *Call of Duty: Modern Warfare 3* (2011, Infinite Ward) and *Halo 4* (2012, 343 Industries) promises scenes from "ULTIMATE Gaming Fails."[24] In this montage, avatar after avatar finds a way to self-destruct in violent ecstasy. Players accidentally launch grenades at their own feet or blithely fire handguns into nearby caches of explosives. Game fail videos are most often filmed and uploaded by the very players who fail in them. These players find pleasure, not shame, in the infinite replay of their failure, which comes to function as an inverted performance of non-skill and bravado. The pleasure viewers take in watching these videos similarly speaks to the complex feelings surrounding failure. Spectators are bound to enjoy a fail video more if they have played the game in question. Through this identification, they imagine themselves failing by proxy. If, as Juul tells us, all players hate failing, who would watch these videos? Who would make them?

As we think through the potential pleasures of game failure, a taxonomy begins to emerge. Juul discusses many types of games at which we might fail: games that are difficult to master, games that can never really be completed, games that insult us, games that make us feel like failures to coax us into learning, fair games, unfair games, games of skill, sadistic games, cathartic games, suicide games.[25] This seemingly endless enumeration makes sense; after all, failure plays a role in almost every game. We can imagine failing in even more ways than Juul lists: failing with our bodies versus failing with our minds (e.g., messing up in a dancing game versus miscalculating in a tactical one), failure through inaction versus failure through action (e.g., forgetting to avoid an incoming missile versus stepping in front of it), failure by accident or failure on purpose (e.g., tripping over versus stepping on a ticking bomb). I want to stress one distinction I find particularly important for queer failure—the distinction between failing toward or against a game system. By this I mean the difference between failing in the way that a game wants us to (e.g., flinging one's avatar to a gruesome demise in *Stair Dismount* or walking toward the inevitability of death in *Passage*) versus failing in the way that a game does not want. Determining what any given game "wants" is itself tricky, but I am thinking here about what outcomes the game instructs us to strive for, what outcomes it rewards, what outcomes it punishes, what outcomes it renders impossible.

To explore the pleasure of failing against a game, we might forfeit, allow ourselves to be beaten, or even commit virtual suicide. Failing on purpose takes on a particularly queer appeal in fighting games, where the express and monolithic goal is victory. Like many other long-standing fighting games series—*Mortal Kombat* (1992–2015, Midway Games), *Street Fighter* (1987–2014, Capcom), *Dead or Alive* (1996–2015, Tecmo)—*SoulCalibur IV*'s (2008, Namco) basic unit of gameplay is the two-person, attack-and-defend match. If you win, the game sings your praises and subjects the loser to a playback of his defeat. In my experience, the game unintentionally offers two ways to play that are more enjoyable than winning. Option one: let yourself be slowly and beautifully beaten by your opponent. While I am losing, I get the chance to appreciate our rippling on-screen flesh, which I would normally miss while slashing away, and to revel in the physicality of my in-game proxy. With each hit, I am temporarily disabled; my avatar flies up into the air; my controller rumbles. This long, teasing self-torture makes me feel tantalizingly present. Option two: commit suicide after you've already won. The fighting stages in the *SoulCalibur* games frequently end in treacherous ledges. After winning a match, when the loser's body lays motionless on the ground, the winner is allowed a few seconds to gloat. I prefer to take that moment, when success looks certain, to jump off the edge of the level into oblivion. Out I go into the gorgeous, green-blue, soft-focus scenery. I am both victor and failure.

Alternatively, we might choose to fail against a game through nonaction. Racing games are another genre unambiguously oriented toward winning, making them a poignant site for experimenting with non-goal-oriented play. *Need for Speed: Most Wanted* (2012, Criterion Games) presents players with an open world where they can roam a wide network of urban streets dotted with racing challenges. Yet this same open world unintentionally affords players the opportunity to opt out of racing altogether. The *Need for Speed* series promises entertainment in the form of fast cars, illegal maneuvers, and high-speed chases. I therefore take great pleasure in driving slowly and respectfully. I stop my shiny coupe at red lights; I follow other cars at a safe distance. The game itches and aches, sending a frantic stream of pop-ups to remind me that I should be off actually playing. This tactic takes a slightly different form in the independent game *Nidhogg* (2014, Messhof), which combines fighting mechanics with classic platformer levels. Two players face off, attacking each other with pixelated epees. Here, I spend inordinate amounts of time dancing. Since *Nidhogg*'s characters have fast, agile movements, leaping about produces something like an extemporaneous dance. But, because any contact between swordsmen results in a temporary death, the trick is to dance circles around an opponent without making contact. In an appropriately queer paradox, failing (i.e., playing in a way that the game refuses to recognize) requires something like success (i.e., staying alive).

While it's possible to fail in almost any type of game, I am particularly interested in games that blur the line between failing toward and against the system. These games illustrate, enrich, and yet ultimately complicate our thinking about queer play. The *Burnout* games, a long-standing racing series, have no explicitly queer content. They do, however, set themselves apart from other popular racing intellectual properties (like *Need for Speed*) with their emphasis on fantastic destruction rather than simulated realism. They boast failure in their very title. *Burnout Revenge* (2005, Criterion Games), released for the Xbox 360 and PlayStation 2 as the fourth *Burnout* console title, continues the series' obsession with daredevil demises. Whereas most commercially successful racing games focus on impressive cars and driving physics, *Burnout* embraces the pleasures of the crash. In *Burnout Revenge*'s primary racing mode, players earn rewards for swiping or taking down other racers in a show of sparks and metal. Traffic Attack mode ups the ante, making destruction, not speed, the goal of each round. Players, unleashed on city streets buzzing with oblivious civilian vehicles, ram into as many cars as possible without getting caught in head-on collisions. However, it's in the Crash challenges that *Burnout*'s fervor for failure becomes clearest. Though the game doesn't present Crash as its primary mode, Crash succinctly distills important elements from across the game, and some form of Crash exists in almost all *Burnout* titles. Succeeding at Crash mode means one thing—failing as spectacularly as possible. Players have their choice of location and vehicles. While the lightweight cars, designed for racing, have sleek curves and shiny finishes, the heavyweight crash cars (all the better to rear-end you with) wear their failure on their automotive skins. The paint chips off the sides of an old sedan. A pickup truck, covered in dents, looks like a fighter sporting yesterday's bruises. After players select a trusty, crappy steed, the game shoots them speeding down a street dotted with obstacles. Stay unharmed just long enough to spot the perfect crash site, where a traffic accident will do the most damage. A well-calculated leap off the side overpass rail might, for example, land you smack in the side of a semitruck. This truck, now stopped on a busy highway, swipes other cars, causing a pileup of screeches and explosions. Seventy-two cars in a row, seemingly unperturbed by the danger, happily plow into you without breaking or swerving—compelled by the logic of a world designed and destined for destruction, where the only choice is the choice to crash.

Success in *Burnout Revenge*'s Crash mode—that is, self-destruction—feels undeniably good. Points, dollar signs, and other achievements accumulate onscreen throughout the pileup. Then there's the cinematic pleasure. Before beginning a level, the game presents a long tracking shot through the peaceful cityscape you are about to ravage. This establishing shot, to borrow a cinema term, serves equally as tactical shot, a chance to plot the exact path of your wreckage. Once you crash, tapping the B button rapidly at the right moment causes your car to explode, sending out an impressive mushroom-cloud boom that breaks apart nearby vehicles. A replay video shows each crash from multiple, dramatic angles, including swooping crane shots that seem to transform your humble handiwork into the culminating scene from *True Lies* (1994, James Cameron). Meanwhile, the raucous, punk-inspired soundtrack adds aural adrenaline. After the moment of crash, however, the music cuts to silence, broken only by the surprisingly distant sound of crashing cars and the cheers of an invisible crowd of male voices applauding your accomplishment. These cheering voices are as much confusing as congratulatory. There are no people in *Burnout Revenge*. No drivers, no pedestrians. The cars' tinted windows, when they crumble off the side of wrecked vehicles, reveal empty cabs. No blood. No victims. No victor. Instead, the bodies on-screen are the bodies of cars—their bumpers askew, their windows shattered. The blood is the blood in the veins of the player, who at once pushes to lose and to win.

Is it possible to fail at a game that you win by failing, to fail against the system in a game that encourages you to fail toward it? Yes, but this type of failure looks different than we might expect. In *Burnout Revenge*'s Crash mode, success means going out in a violent blaze; failing, however, means getting stuck on the shoulder of a highway while your engine lazily puffs out smoke. On your way to impale a tractor trailer, you accidentally swipe your car against a bollard. Here your turn comes to an end. The game again offers an array of epic shots of the (in this case decidedly nonepic and unsatisfying) destruction you have caused. A few other cars spin out around you, but for the most part traffic passes by unharmed. The action-movie pleasure of success becomes fail-video shame, inverted as a display of dullness, not bravado. As for the game's primary Race mode, it technically never wants you to crash your own vehicle, no matter how fantastically. Make contact with another car at the wrong angle and, instead of triumphantly sending them off course, the game forces you into a three-second, third-person, noninteractive slow-motion scene of your own car smashing itself to bits (only to appear, reconstituted and ready to race, once the scene is done). The game wants us to feel inconvenienced by the crashes in Race mode, and we do; for those three seconds we squirm as our competitors zoom by. At the same time, Race mode does want us to enjoy the spectacle of our own destruction, even as it incentivizes standard racing goals, like clocking in a record-breaking lap or simply finishing first. The cutscenes of our undesirable demise are as aesthetically appealing—shiny metal, flashing sparks—as those in which we receive cash and applause for our failure. The game also uses the same load screens for Race as for Crash—images of two cars smashing together at great speed. The images foreshadow the crashes sure to follow, taunting us with our imminent loss, and reminding us of the game's real goal, thinly veiled in talk of points and winners: destruction.

Juul addresses the *Burnout* series directly, but quickly dismisses it as an unremarkable example in the pantheon of video game failure. During a discussion about suicide games, Juul notes that a similar suicidal instinct does occasionally appear in commercial games, though in less direct forms. About failure in the *Burnout* series and its pleasures (or lack thereof), Juul writes:

> This experience of self-destruction has an unpleasant aspect to it, but the game presents no human characters, and furthermore restarts immediately after a crash with no cost to the player, hence deemphasizing any human suffering caused. *Burnout Paradise* is part of a small trend that does not involve the long-time suffering of the protagonist, but rather fascinates through the immediate joyful discomfort of witnessing (bodily) destruction.[26]

Again, Juul emphasizes the unpleasantness of losing, but with a few new caveats. He proclaims *Burnout*'s brand of self-destruction to be unpleasant but not unpleasant enough. Without any mangled bodies to mourn, without a suffering protagonist to identify with, surely players will never rise from petty fascination to true self-flagellation. Instead, they'll continue their victimless massacres without consequence, which by extension renders the massacres themselves inconsequential. To my eye, contrary to Juul's reading, accidents definitely do come at a cost in Race mode. And in Crash mode, they're not the cost; they're the point. Also, how can we blithely group *Burnout*, in which there are no human bodies, with games that center around "witnessing (bodily) destruction"—all while shrugging off the game's impact for its lack of bodies? Most importantly, Juul is wrong about self-destruction in the game: it isn't unpleasant. It's highly pleasurable. In fact, it's fantastic.

Of course, since Halberstam's book doesn't reference video games, he doesn't discuss *Burnout*. However, his approach to understanding self-destruction helps fill in the missing pieces of Juul's interpretation. By joining Halberstam in insisting on the queer in the game's art of failure, we can reinstate *Burnout Revenge*'s masochistic pleasure. We can also begin to uncover the full queer potential of playing to lose. Halberstam, in his chapter on masochism and feminism, insists that we see self-destruction not as a pathological behavior from which the queer artist needs rescuing, but as a form of resistance against mainstream power structures. He writes, "I propose a radical form of masochistic passivity that . . . offers up a critique of the organizing logic of agency and subjectivity itself. . . . The masochist tethers her notion of self to a spiral of pain and hurt. She refuses to cohere, refuses to fortify herself against the knowledge of death and dying."[27] Halberstam's masochist, like the loss-driven player, defines herself not through tenacity and recognition, but through her choice to embrace pain and death (one "dies" regularly in games). Juul argues that the suffering *Burnout* offers (that "immediate joyful discomfort") feels so good we hardly know whether it's suffering at all. Yet, if we look at *Burnout Revenge* through a masochistic lens, we see that the power of such games lies specifically in their combination of pain and pleasure, which scrambles our prescriptions for success and loss: the pain of seeing our automotive avatar splattered on the highway, the pain of not seeing our automotive avatar splattered on the highway, the pleasure of the fantastic crash when we go up in flames, the pleasure of living to die another day.

Playing to Lose: The Queer Art of Failing at Video Games

What, then, can we call the queer art of failing at video games? Between queer theory and game studies, we have triangulated a new perspective. Failure is integral to games, and failure is queer. That leads to a handful of coherent, if controversial propositions: that failure (whether toward or against a game) must be a queer way to play, that failure brings queerness to games with no explicitly queer content, that a game based on failure must be a queer game, and that queerness (in the guise of failure) is itself integral to all games. Far from being a merely inconvenient and inconsequential obstacle on the road to success, video game failure matters and can be leveraged as a form of resistance. Together, these claims allow us to see a supposedly straight game like *Burnout Revenge*—with its fast cars, presumed heterosexual male player base, and war-gasm explosions—as something other than normative or sexless. The game becomes, in this view, one that plays differently, that we play differently, a queer game that queers us as we play. If failing at video games is an art of playing the wrong way, every game has its own wrong way. In *Burnout Revenge*, it might take the form of lingering too long over destruction, or playing Crash mode on fort-da repeat as the game tries to inch us toward new levels. In these moments, the beautiful, painful, pleasurable vision of self-destruction, which players enact through their queer artistry, itself takes on the caliber of an undeniably alluring art.

However, before unambiguously claiming failed play in the name of queer game resistance, I want to complicate this calculation, as the *Burnout* games themselves demand. Keep in mind the distinction between failure toward and against a system. Here is the particular paradox of failure at work in *Burnout*: how can we claim to play queerly by failing in a game where failing is the way to win? In *Burnout Revenge*'s Crash mode, we win when we fail well. In the game's Racing mode, crashing makes it more likely that we'll lose, yet the game clearly wants us to take pleasure in crashes. Any way we fail, we seem to be failing toward the game. At the same time, cultural expectations outside of the game dictate that driving successfully doesn't mean catapulting into a semitruck, and that succeeding doesn't mean watching yourself go up in flames. When we crash in a brilliant blaze, then, we both conform to and ostentatiously reject systems of dominant logic—one belonging to the game, the other belonging to the social context in which we play it. What would it mean to fail against the game in *Burnout*? It might look quite similar to my dull, lawful meandering in *Need for Speed*. In *Need for Speed*, though, refusing to engage with the goal of the game (racing to win) is relatively easy: don't enter into a race. However, in *Burnout Revenge*, opting out takes skill, and even this form of failure is bound to inevitably fail. Opting out would mean driving but not crashing at all, and everything in the game is designed for impact. Like the *Nidhogg* dance, which requires avatar proximity but breaks with avatar contact, playing crashless in *Burnout Revenge* navigates a precarious line. It seems whatever system players choose to fail against, they fail into the arms of another. Admittedly, that basic contradiction does some queering of its own. Try gingerly navigating the streets of *Burnout Revenge* in a stubborn attempt to play at being the good subject in a world gone wrong. It makes driving in the real world, with all its reasonable precautions and normative regulations, seem equally absurd. When we embrace failure, we also queer success.

Ultimately, the true usefulness of *Burnout* isn't just in how it exemplifies the pleasures of self-destruction but also in how it lays bare the infinite and uniquely queer dialectical tangle between system and player, failure and success, pain and pleasure. It shows us that winning can be equal parts subversive and conformist, and that a player's hurt and joy are not contradictory, but interwoven blurs that shape and color experience. When it comes to queer failure in video games, this ambiguity is apt. Games allow us to play at queer failure, to examine it from different angles, to try and fail at failing. Juul posits many reasons why we return to game failure time and again, though we (supposedly) hate it. We could similarly posit many reasons for why we play at queer failure. The drive toward queer failure itself reveals a contradiction within the queer art of failing at video games. When we throw ourselves in the mud for the hundredth time, we do it better than we did the first time. When we replay failure, we replay toward perfection, failing more and more fantastically. New games to fail at mean more elaborate deaths, deaths rendered more and more impressive by better graphics, an endless proliferation of ways to self-destruct. Perfecting the art of failure, an art defined by imperfection, abjection, and artlessness, puts us back in the realm of paradox. What we've learned, therefore, is to embrace the paradox, to explore alternate longings and nonnormative desires as they speak to us from within our play.

I close by reasserting an incendiary conjecture: that if we accept failure as fundamental to games and we accept failure as coded as queer, all games become queer, in a nonrepresentational sense. This doesn't just apply to games in which players willingly blow themselves to pieces. To the extent that no game can exist without failure, no game can exist without queerness. In response, then, to the homophobic voices who would silence queer thinking as marginal, this conjecture lays claim to all games as fair territory for exploring queerly. It also offers a platform on which future queer studies and game studies might intermingle and models how we can uncover and unleash the queer, subversive tensions inherent to any game.

BONNIE RUBERG is Provost's Postdoctoral Scholar in the Interactive Media and Games Division at the University of Southern California. She is coeditor of *Queer Game Studies: Gender, Sexuality, and a Queer Approach to Game Studies* and is lead organizer of the annual Queerness and Games Conference.

Notes

1. Though their books do not reference one another, Halberstam and Juul did present a conversation, "Queer Arts of Failure," at the 2013 Queerness and Games Conference in Berkeley, California.

2. For an overview of the history of LGBT representation in games and its discontents, see Edmond Chang, "Queer(ing) Video Games and Video Game Studies," presentation at the 129th Modern Language Association Annual Convention, Chicago, January 9, available at http://www.edmondchang.com/2014/01/08/mla14.

3. Brendan Keogh, "Just Making Things and Being Alive about It: The Queer Games Scene," *Polygon*, May 24, 2013, http://www.polygon.com/features/2013/5/24/4341042/the-queer-games-scene.

4. Electronic Arts hosted Full Spectrum, a one-day event addressing discrimination in the video games industry, in March 2013; New York University hosted Different Games, a collaborative conference on diversity and inclusivity in games, in April 2013; Gaymer Connect hosted GaymerX in August 2013 in San Francisco, a fan expo that drew thousands of attendees; and the University of California at Berkeley hosted the Queerness and Games Conference in October 2013, bringing together scholars and game developers.

5. Adrienne Shaw's work epitomizes this field. See *Gaming at the Edge: Sexuality and Gender at the Margins of Gamer Culture* (Minneapolis: University of Minnesota Press, 2014).

6. Many articles, both inside and outside the gaming community, have addressed this issue. For a representative piece, see Erik Kain, "Homophobia at BlizzCon: Is Gamer Culture Anti-Gay?" *Forbes*, October 27, 2011, http://www.forbes.com/sites/erikkain/2011/10/27/homophobia-at-blizzcon-is-gamer-culture-anti-gay/.

7. See *Gaming in Color*, directed by Philip Jones (MidBoss, 2015).

8. Bonnie Ruberg, "'Portal' Is for Lesbians," *Heroine Sheik*, October 17, 2007, http://www.heroine-sheik.com/2007/10/17/portal-is-for-lesbians/.

9. This comment, along with other overtly hateful remarks, were shortly thereafter removed from the post at the request of the *Village Voice*.

10. Alexander Doty, *Flaming Classics: Queering the Film Canon* (New York: Routledge, 2000), 4.

11. Ibid.

12. Jack Halberstam, *The Queer Art of Failure* (Durham, NC: Duke University Press, 2011), 2; Lee Edelman, *No Future: Queer Theory and the Death Drive* (Durham, NC: Duke University Press, 2004), 4; Kathryn Bond Stockton, *The Queer Child, or Growing Sideways in the Twentieth Century* (Durham, NC: Duke University Press, 2009), 1.

13. Jesper Juul, *The Art of Failure: An Essay on the Pain of Playing Video Games* (Cambridge, MA: MIT Press, 2013), 22.

14. Jesper Juul, *Half-Real: Video Games between Real Rules and Fictional Worlds* (Cambridge, MA: MIT Press, 2005).

15. Juul, *Art of Failure*, xi.

16. Sigmund Freud, *Beyond the Pleasure Principle* (New York: Bantam, 1967).

17. Juul, *Art of Failure*, 2.

18. Ibid., 4–5.

19. Ibid., 9, 15, 5.

20. Ibid., 7.

21. Halberstam, *Queer Art of Failure*, 89, 88, 187.

22. Derek Burrill, *Die Tryin': Video Games, Masculinity, and Culture* (New York: Peter Lang, 2008).

23. Mia Consalvo, *Cheating: Gaining Advantage in Videogames* (Cambridge, MA: MIT Press, 2009), 2.

24. LOL Cod Comedy, "ULTIMATE Gaming Fail Compilation 2013!" *YouTube*, May 4, 2013, https://www.youtube.com/watch?v=dpROt6ipiwE.

25. Juul, *Art of Failure*, 31, 48, 52.

26. Ibid., 100.

27. Halberstam, *Queer Art of Failure*, 131, 144–145.

chapter twelve

ROMANCING AN EMPIRE, BECOMING ISAAC

The Queer Possibilities of Jade Empire *and* The Binding of Isaac

JORDAN WOOD

> You are meant to learn, but not too much. To see, but not too clearly. To succeed, but not completely.
>
> —The Water Dragon, *Jade Empire*

> To play the game means to play the code of the game. To win means to know the system. And thus to interpret a game means to interpret its algorithm (to discover its parallel allegorithm).
>
> —Alexander R. Galloway, *Gaming: Essays on Algorithmic Culture*

ALEXANDER GALLOWAY'S OFT-CITED PORTMANTEAU, THE ALLEGORITHM, distills the video game's relationship with the real to one of systemic analogy and critical comparison.[1] The allegorithm is the point of contact between the internal logic of the game and the social constructs that produce it. McKenzie Wark extends the concept of the allegorithm into a spatial metaphor: "The real has become mere detritus without which gamespace cannot exist but which is losing, bit by bit, any form or substance or spirit or history that is not sucked into and transformed by gamespace. Beyond gamespace appear only the spent fragments of nameless form."[2] Wark sees the relationships that have been generated amid the electronic productions of the early twenty-first century as a gradual topological refashioning of Western social space. This re-creative posture toward the spatial (and thus toward the temporal) provides fertile ground for fresh approaches in how we theorize the gendered body. If indeed the game space contains the potential to rework the real as both Galloway and Wark would have it, then it seems high time to begin the work of queering the game space itself.

Of course, the potential for queering the game space is only as useful as the texts that capitalize on it. Therein lies one rather obvious reason for queer theory's apparent oversight of video games as an aesthetic place of reconfiguration: the sexual politics of video games—here construed as industry, praxis, and product—have been deeply problematic. To say that video games and their contingent industries and cultures have struggled to adequately represent or include perspectives from LGBT communities is an understatement. The host of criticisms that have been levied on the gaming industry in this regard are numerous to the point of redundancy and have already created new opportunities for sexual minorities to engage in productive discourse about gaming and sexuality. For instance, the *Border House* blog has been for several years a productive site of discussion. The blog's "About Us" blurb reads, "The *Border House* is a blog for gamers. It's a blog for those who are feminist, queer, disabled, people of color, transgender, poor, gay, lesbian, and others who belong to marginalized groups as well as allies."[3] This inclusiveness echoes in response to the general absence of queer bodies from any representation at all in video game texts. As Adrienne Shaw asks, "Why then, when video games have been a popular medium since the 1970s, are questions about the representation of diverse sexualities and gendered identities only now being discussed?"[4] I suggest one possible answer to this question: we have not adequately explored the form itself to understand how principles of queer theory might be organically inscribed within the video game. The intuitive solution to the haze of monolithic heteronormativity would be to increase the number of queer characters in games—to, in keeping with other modes of queer advocacy in popular culture, generate more visibility. However, even when the representational content of games deviates from heteronormativity, it often does so only within the broader context of what we might call heteronormative spatiotemporal logics. Some games, however, are able to break out of, or at least unsettle, these logics that underwrite heteronormativity both in the game text itself and the game space that produced it. These games both predict and present the question: What would it mean for queer temporalities and queer spaces to find representation or inscription in a game?

In this chapter, I offer an analysis of two very different games as a way to begin answering this question. After all, if Galloway is right about the relationship games have to the cultures that produce them, then it will be in the games themselves that potential modes for the inscription of queer bodies and queer times emerge. Though their production contexts, generic investments, and fictional worlds are incredibly different, BioWare's *Jade Empire* (2005) and Florian Himsl and Edmund McMillen's *The Binding of Isaac* (2011, Valve) offer a dramatic point of contrast in the kinds of queer representation that digital gaming has made possible. This queer potential unfolds primarily at the representational level for *Jade Empire*, whereas *The Binding of Isaac* works to incorporate on a basic structural level the dynamic, embodied kind of queering in which Halberstam himself finds value. I deploy Halberstam's concept of the queer archive in order to uncover how *The Binding of Isaac* enacts its own ludoaesthetic strategies to create a virtual space of queer performativity. These strategies of structured, compositionally rooted, queer spatiotemporality take place within the context of a kind of virtual becoming. Within the formal aesthetic boundaries of the video game, heteronormative formations of space and time become newly fluid and in that fluidity become open to myriad reworkings of the queer body.

Queer Representation in *Jade Empire*

Jade Empire was not the first game in which players could pursue sexual relationships as either a man or woman with either men or women, but it was nevertheless groundbreaking in its inclusive posture toward the player's sexual relationships with other characters.[5] Exploring a fictional historical setting based loosely on dynastic China, *Jade Empire* players take on the role of a heroic martial arts prodigy with a mysterious past who must gather a group of followers to rescue his or her master from a power-obsessed emperor and his sadistic lieutenant. Players guide their hero and his or her companions through a series of magically exotic settings, obstacles, and enemies, growing more powerful with each step. The player's ultimate goal is to restore spiritual balance to a kingdom whose souls, both alive and dead, have been thrown into upheaval by an emperor's arrogant crime against the gods. Though the game was praised for its story as well as its strategic yet frenetic action, the central feature of *Jade Empire* was its rich characters and potential for romantic liaisons with what seemed like virtually every consenting adult in the player's party.

BioWare's approach to romantic liaisons in its narrative role-playing games is by now well established and can be traced back through game releases from well before *Jade Empire* saw the light of day in 2005. While other games like Black Isle Studio's *Fallout 2* (1998) and Lionhead Studio's *Fable* (2004) featured some rudimentary romance options for players, these games rarely gave the non-player character (NPC) partners any sense of their own agency in the matter, making it hard to imagine any kind of sexuality or gender actually at work beyond arbitrary, computerized assignment. In contrast, BioWare games offer players the opportunity to articulate their character's sexuality in relation to companion NPCs with backstories that give a degree of social and political context, as well as the suggestion that their potential partners have some level of agency in the way the romance eventually unfolds. For instance, BioWare's *Baldur's Gate* franchise features full-fledged narrative subplots involving the flirtation, pursuit, and eventual partnership between player-characters and their NPC counterparts. The success or nonsuccess of these courtships depends on a mixture of player morality (often framed as a question of how the player uses his or her hero's growing power) and conversational choices. This latter quality proved essential to the

BioWare romance model moving forward, as the conversations between BioWare protagonists and their faithful companions are the stages on which these often melodramatic pairings play out. While *Jade Empire* did little to innovate with this framework, it nevertheless introduced the most robust support for straight, gay, and even bisexual pairings yet seen in this style of mainstream video gaming.

What seems to have been particularly unique about *Jade Empire*'s representation of queer relationships at the time was the way in which it normalized bisexuality and homosexuality alongside heterosexual romantic pairings. The game's narrative is wholly agnostic to the player-character's sexual orientation. All of *Jade Empire*'s romantic options are entirely elective, meaning players can choose to woo any of three possible romantic partners (Dawn Star, Silk Fox, or Sky), or even to completely ignore them without affecting the outcome of the game narrative proper. In other words, the world's salvation cares little for the sexual preference of any of its denizens, even those who carry the weight of fate more heavily than others. It isn't clear, in fact, whether sexual orientation matters, in the political sense, to anyone at all in the world of *Jade Empire*. Moreover, two of the three characters (Silk Fox and Sky) with whom players can have a fling are evidently bisexual and will respond to the player-character's advances irrespective of his or her gender, thereby suggesting a fluidity in sexual identity in not only the player-character but the sexual preferences of the NPCs as well. This, too, seems to be unremarkable to the denizens of *Jade Empire*.

This normativizing effect is compounded by a small, but significant formal departure that *Jade Empire* made from the typical BioWare party-based narrative format. In other games by the studio—like *Baldur's Gate 2* (2000) or *Star Wars: Knights of the Old Republic* (2003)—the player's relation to potential romantic partners exceeded that of the player-created protagonist. These games feature exploration and combat systems in which at any moment players can switch from controlling their bespoke protagonist to controlling any of his or her companions, and in the case of *Baldur's Gate*, even to all companions at once. In other words, the player's relation to NPCs actually shifts to a relationship with a player-character after all. These games, therefore, posit two avenues of player-character relation: a narratively contextualized relationship mediated through the protagonist's conversations with her compatriots, and a mechanically mediated relationship in which the player ruptures NPC autonomy by bringing them under the aegis of player agency. In contrast, *Jade Empire* removes the traditional capacity for players to directly control the protagonist's companions, meaning that their relationship to these followers is always only filtered through the protagonist's diegetic experience of them. By grounding these relationships exclusively in the perspective of the protagonist rather than in that of the player at the helm, the romantic partners of *Jade Empire* reserve a degree of their own bodily autonomy away from the player, which in turn reinforces the game world's overall tacit endorsement of queer sexual possibilities.

Thus *Jade Empire* appears to queer its game space by offering players the freedom to represent themselves in the game's diegesis on four axes: gender identification, sexual orientation, sexual desire (or forwardness), and sexual desirability. What's more, each axis has been rendered equally valid via both its inconsequential relationship to the game's win condition and the game's refusal to make any meaningful distinction in visual representation between heteronormative couplings and queer ones. Even in the most salacious of sexual endings, wherein the hero apparently convinces both Dawn Star and Silk Fox to join him in his tent, the camera refuses to leer, thereby avoiding the tendency of later BioWare games, and mainstream visual culture at large, to render lesbian sex as pure visual spectacle even as they closet visual representations of gay male sexual encounters.[6]

Yet for all of its apparently progressive gestures toward queer representation, *Jade Empire* only queers the game space so far as narrative and visual representation can take it. If digital games afford us the possibility of generating a particular kind of temporal and spatial experience, as Wark and Halberstam suggest, then it seems likely that the kind of queer representation found in a game like *Jade Empire* makes only shallow use of the formal tools at its disposal. Moreover, a medium that works by generating a sense of alternate embodiment and temporality via simulation necessitates a queer theory that accounts for these aesthetic emphases, interrogating time and space sites of representation distinct from narration and characterization.

The Archive and the Queer Logic of Becoming

Halberstam's provocative work *In a Queer Time and Place* offers just such a framework for reorienting our approach to aesthetic conceptions of space and time. For Halberstam, queer theory and praxis have their basis in "an outcome of strange temporalities, imaginative life schedules, and eccentric economic practices."[7] Halberstam construes these "strange temporalities" as the various ways in which the queer body is out of step with heteronormative conceptions of progress, reproduction, and evolution. In other words, queerness lies at the disjuncture between heteronormative time and bodies that, in their vexed relation to mainstream culture, point to alternative temporalities. Imagining a queer temporality to counter heteronormativity carries no small amount of risk. To imagine a way of life that runs counter to reproduction and heteronormative teleologies of progress is to acknowledge the precarity of queer life in the face of hegemonic oppression and then to use that precarity as a position from which to articulate a social and political identity. But it is the very riskiness of this venture that allows for a broad rejection of heteronormative demands on the body. Halberstam clarifies this subversive dynamic in the context of queer subcultures, which he says, "produce temporalities by allowing their participants to believe that their futures can be imagined according to logics that lie outside of those paradigmatic markers of life experience—namely, birth, marriage, reproduction, and death."[8] In these new logics, the queer subject seeks out the temporal norms that authorize the heteronormative life and either refuses them outright or subverts them. In particular, Halberstam isolates "reproductive time" as a powerful temporal concept that defines the parameters of domesticity for all couples, even those who never choose to raise children.[9] Queer time unsettles the domestic reproductive space, it undermines the productive logics of capital, and it refuses linearity. It is, in other words, essentially ludic.

The ludic quality of queer temporality is evocative for our consideration of a queer gameplay. That both queer aesthetics and the video game contain some sense of playfulness suggests an intriguing formal affinity. We might even imagine the "trifler" from Bernard Suits's *The Grasshopper* who plays chess according to the rules, but in a spirit that runs counter to the game's demand for a winner. The trifler plays the game, yes, but she also rejects the notion that winning is the best way to play. The archive is the formal aesthetic strategy of just such queer trifling. Contrary to heteronormative temporality, which denies the validity of the risky life and forces every history to tell a single, carefully managed story, the archive is "simultaneously a resource, a productive narrative, a set of representations, a history, a memorial, and a time capsule."[10] The archive is, at bottom, a logic to be deployed, a communal practice, rather than a history book to consult, although it is that too. In the archive, queer temporalities come to bear on the unfolding and enfolding of history, creating a bundle of potential meanings wherein equal value is given to every contribution. The archive makes the myth of progress and the dominance of domestic reproductive time untenable. The logic of the queer archive therefore commits to combining and sustaining multiple disparate realities—whether historical or physical—in tension with one another. It refuses to resolve the multifarious practices, identity markers, or sensations that the queer body may contain. This irresolution, this playfulness, forms the bedrock of Halberstam's vision for a queer temporality that can counter heteronormative control. The ludic always challenges the productive, and just as postmodern art and architecture work against the monolith of rational capitalism, so might video games operating according to the logic of the queer archive disrupt heteronormative disciplining of the body.

The body that functions according to queer archival logic is, therefore, a liminal body that resists external definition by virtue of its own continual unfolding. Queerness is not a state of being but rather one of becoming. If a queer body maintains the playfulness of archive, then it is always shifting through a whole range of spatial and temporal states. When a queer life is living "on the margins of social intelligibility [it] alters one's pace; one's tempo becomes at best, contrapuntal, syncopated, and at worst, erratic, arrested."[11] Queer becoming escapes the control of heteronormative narration. The dominant culture of straight gender and sexuality cannot make sense of the queer subject because it is not playing to win. Instead, it trifles.

This ethic of archival becoming necessitates a pivot away from the identity politics that have come to define much of the liberal LGBTQ advocacy that filters into the mainstream. As Clare Colebrook argues, a queer advocacy based in becoming "requires a radical and distinct break from identity politics."[12] Identity politics are rooted in an Enlightenment conception of what it is to be human, and as such rely on the heteronormative temporalities that enforce regimes of capital and reproduction. The queer body, on the other hand, is an affirmative nonbody, for which amalgamation and combination becomes the key to political advocacy, not stable identity categories. Thus, to aesthetically and narratively represent queer logics of time and embodiment, we must push for forms that can work out the archival on its own terms, rather than insist on the Enlightenment path of normalization. The video game is uniquely situated to represent queer becoming, a capacity that *The Binding of Isaac* begins to take advantage of while *Jade Empire* remains rooted in the personalization of identity politics.

The Queer Practice of Gaming

And here we can turn to the video game as a potential aesthetic and historical site for the working out of queer temporality and queer bodies. Much of the discourse on LGBT and queer representation in video games has focused on the hostile environment of the game industry and the need for LGBT characters that exist beyond the level of stereotype and tokenism. Though the game industry surely needs more queer characters, Halberstam shows us that we must stop thinking of queer representation only in terms of narrative presence and begin to look at the video game form for its queer aesthetic potential. While *Jade Empire* is certainly more inclusive than most of its contemporaries in terms of sexual identity, it nevertheless neglects the specifically ludic potential of a game that *The Binding of Isaac* brings to the fore. It seems, then, that the first question to ask is: What are the specific ways in which the video game has the capacity to represent the queer archival? I submit that video games are uniquely situated to represent these ludic queer temporalities by deploying archival logic in the myriad bodily configurations of gameplay. Though the inherent safety of simulated experimentation might restrict the riskiness with which a queer community forges its position amid heteronormative time and space, as an aesthetic object, the video game points toward new possibilities for the representation of queerness.

Graeme Kirkpatrick helps make this link by associating the video game with particular social rhythms, establishing a necessary connection between the form and conceptions of temporality: "Video games are integral to the contemporary structure of feeling; they are an important example of how social relations are becoming increasingly dance-like and animated by a distinctive set of rhythms."[13] In Kirkpatrick's model, the game derives from the rhythms of a technologically oriented society, and the aesthetic products of that society reciprocally structure that society's emotional economy. Vivian Sobchack corroborates this perspective in her analysis of an electronically mediated civilization:

> In sum, just as the photograph did in the last century, so in this one, cinematic and electronic screens differently demand and shape our "presence" to the world

and our representation in it. Each differently and objectively alters our subjectivity while each invites our complicity in formulating space, time, and bodily investment as significant personal and social experience.[14]

Video games are therefore not merely passive representations of social temporality: they invite and shape our participation in the temporal rhythms that already structure our lives. Herein video games have their first mode of queer potential: they offer the possibility of inscribing temporalities that disrupt heteronormative rhythms of life. A video game can, theoretically, reject linearity, contain multiple unresolved narratives, and offer a space-time that rejects reproductive norms in much the same way Halberstam's archive demands. What's more, the time of the video game is already necessarily ludic, and therefore contains the potential to rupture productive hetero temporalities in its capacity to divert the economic energies of the gamer into nonproductive, simulated modes of nonproduction.

The video game also supplies its gamers with the potential to experiment with bodily reconfigurations. Most video games already operate on a principle of bodily extension, amplification, or limitation. Players are always already participating in a complex negotiation of identity between themselves and their avatars on-screen. That is, in the translation of subjectivity from the player to the avatar, the player constantly negotiates an ongoing process of mutual embodiment between herself and the on-screen representations of her actions.[15] *Madden NFL 13* (2012, EA Sports), for example, extends player subjectivity into the bodies of an eleven-person football team. Many action games, like *DmC: Devil May Cry* (2013, Capcom) or *Bayonetta* (2010, Platinum Games), operate according to principles of amplification, engaging in a sort of power fantasy wherein players are given incredible supernatural powers to flashy, often violent effect. Still other games work to limit and constrain players, like *Journey* (2012, thatgamecompany), whose incredibly narrow scope of interaction focuses what little player interaction exists into potent little bursts of affect. Each of these cases relies on a dynamic translation of real-world activity by the player into game space activity by the avatar, and within that translation identities can begin to entangle in interesting ways. One critic suggests that there is "an enfolding of the physical body in game space in ways that expand or extend the body and its capacities through onscreen representations."[16] Players take on a simultaneous digital embodiment alongside their physical one, submitting to the demands of the game space and performing according to their avatars' abilities. The on-screen bodily representation of the gamer is from the outset a technological reconfiguration of the body in much the same way that Halberstam's archives reconfigure history and narrative. The reciprocal mediation of on- and off-screen bodies bears the markings of a semiliving mesh, one animation animating the other, and vice versa.

This simultaneous, reciprocal embodiment of the gamer and her avatar lies at the bottom of the video game's unique capacity for queer bodily recombinations. Jenny Sundén, reflecting on her sexual experiences in *World of Warcraft*

(2004–2014, Blizzard), notes the connections between the gendered expression of her troll avatar and her own sexual orientation:

> Lesbian is not being, but becoming, it enters into an assemblage of other (machine) parts, into a sequence of flows and disruptions, of varying speeds and intensities. Lesbian is not an identity, it is not a position, but a mode of moving and changing, of always being in the process of becoming otherwise, always unstable, fleeting, provisional.[17]

Sundén finds *World of Warcraft* receptive to this constant state of sexual unfolding, in part because of the fluid potential of the digital body. Her troll warrior is capable of articulating a shifting embodiment that might otherwise be inaccessible to her own existence, in part because *World of Warcraft* has the capacity for nonreproductive temporal organization. Because there are no externally enforced constraints on her body (or rather, because such constraints are made explicit and mechanically transparent through processes of character creation), Sundén is free to reconfigure her troll's gender, attraction, and bodily expression via the game's menus and in-world shops. She is responsive to the ludic temporalities of the game itself, and her relation to those temporalities through the mediation of her troll avatar.

There is, of course, the sense in which the video game temporality must necessarily coincide with, yet be other than, the temporality of "real life." Juul articulates this notion quite well in his discussion of the formal construction of games. For Juul, it is the specifically rule-based nature of the game (any game, not only the computerized game) that sets game time apart from real time. He argues, "'Rules' describes games as formal systems. That a game is outside 'ordinary life' describes the relationship between the game and the rest of the world."[18] This sense of being "outside ordinary life" is especially interesting when we take it in the context of queer praxis also being outside the modes of life that have been authorized as ordinary, sufficient, or productive by heteronormative space and time. The game already operates along geographies external to capital productivity (industry demands aside) and thus, much like art, provides a ludic space for queer experimentation. Queer theory is in a position to adapt the magic circle of the video game and inscribe its own subversive temporalities and bodies therein. In the video game, the queer community has the opportunity to establish a new allegorithm that moves according to its own queer logics, exposing the constructed, social nature of heteronormative space-time.

Straightening the Empire

Given the way the formal properties of video games respond to bodily and temporal reconfigurations, we can reexamine the status of queer representation in video games in a new light. Perhaps this reconceptualization of the queer game may even point a way forward in queer aesthetic praxis. In any case, if we conceive of queer theory's expression at the ludic level of the video game in the way that I have laid out, the canon of video games suddenly opens up to criticism in ways it hasn't before. In that spirit, I turn to examine both *Jade Empire* and *The Binding of Isaac* according to logics of queer space and time rather than the simple presence or absence of diegetic queer representation. Under this critical rubric, these games offer concrete examples of both the pitfalls and the potential of queer representation in digital games.

Two pitfalls emerge in particular from the application of queer space and time to *Jade Empire* that would otherwise have remained hidden behind a veneer of LGBTQ inclusiveness. The first extends out of the exoticized setting of *Jade Empire*. Explicitly drawing inspiration from martial arts films, Orientalist travelogues, and Western conceptions of East Asian spectacle, *Jade Empire* works out its decidedly Western notions of sexuality against a backdrop of Oriental exoticism. This setting limits somewhat the allegorithmic potential of any subversive queer politics in *Jade Empire* as it masks the fluid sexualities of its characters with the distance of a fantastical, magical Chinese empire. Beneath this Orientalist mask, any subversive queerness seems at best attributable to the foreign erotics of an ancient Asian civilization and, at worst, completely invisible amid the muck of a racialized fantasy. There is no winking satire to the Imperial City of *Jade Empire*; there is only the sober narrative of a hero arisen, a hero betrayed, and a hero triumphant, and this sobriety works to foreclose the possibility of ludic, queer disruption.

It is that linear narrative of a restored civilization that most significantly undermines the queer potential of *Jade Empire*. As a narrative-driven role-playing game where quests provide the narrative motivation for player progress, *Jade Empire* always foregrounds the fact that players are interacting with a broken world that desperately needs a hero for its restoration. An early sequence in the game features the wanton destruction of the avatar's bucolic home, which showcases the central domestic scene of the game—the master and student. There is constant talk of destiny, and the hero is fated to grow in power and alliances until he can restore that domestic scene that the emperor has ruptured. In fact, the game's direst sin is easily figured as an act of violence against heteronormative temporality. The emperor imprisoned the water dragon, the god of water and life, in order to end a drought that had long parched the empire. Construed as the ultimate act of arrogance, the emperor's actions prevented the water dragon from performing its primary function, ushering the souls of the dead through the karmic underworld. Without the water dragon to guide them, the empire has begun to fill up with violent ghosts who seek vengeance on any living soul unlucky enough to be in their way. Thus, the actions of the player are explicitly figured as a heroic quest to restore the proper, sanctioned temporal equilibrium of *Jade Empire*'s spiritual and social economy.

The implications for queer representation in *Jade Empire* are clear. Though characters with some degree of gender and sexual fluidity abound in terms of genital sexual attraction, the collective weight of *Jade Empire*'s queer population is marshaled in service of a basically heteronormative temporality. The bodies and pleasures of *Jade Empire* converge in unconventional ways, but in the end, they are an unimportant sideshow. They exist only on the terms that the player commit to a necessarily heteronormative temporal teleology of proper life and proper death. The romance plots will not advance without the primary narrative's progress. The queer body never emerges because it is always articulated within the context of heteronormative narrative progress. Against the backdrop of reproductive restoration, the potential queer politics of *Jade Empire* stage a limited resistance indeed.

The Queer Allegorithm of Isaac

A work of artisanal craft rather than big-budget production, *The Binding of Isaac* is a strange little downloadable title that follows in the venerable footsteps of *Rogue* (1980), triggering a fresh wave of rogue-like games in its wake. The labor of only two game developers rather than an entire studio, *The Binding of Isaac* is a rigorously independent production (though distribution deals have now put it on most major console platforms), and as such offers more transgressive potential for queer representation than many AAA games that present only diegetic or characterological representations of queerness. Lo-fidelity (lo-fi), independent games often lack the budget and resources to craft a fully realized fictional world populated with well-written and painstakingly animated characters for players to interact with. Moreover, they also lack the industry pressures that come along with AAA game development. Both of these factors make formal and generic experimentation more viable within independent game development, which in turn opens up avenues for queer representation that remain quite difficult within the aesthetic and industrial pressures of AAA games. As a result, therefore, of its thoroughly independent industrial origins, *The Binding of Isaac* is able to deploy generic conventions and formal mechanics that are often unavailable to bigger budget releases that have to recuperate their enormous costs.

In *The Binding of Isaac,* players guide Isaac, a tiny, naked boy, through six randomly generated levels of psychosexual, scatological horror as he flees his mother. The game's opening cinematic sets the tone for what follows. It runs a scant four minutes, but in this brief span players are introduced to the game's cartoonish art style, pitch-dark subject matter, and quiet sense of humor. Characters are crudely and cartoonishly drawn, and the quality of the animation is equally rudimentary. Narratively, the opening animation explains that Isaac's mother, a religious fanatic who watches too much Christian television, believes that God has commanded her to kill her son in order to prove her faith. In terror, Isaac escapes down a trapdoor in his bedroom, but instead of safety, he finds level after level of monsters and traps. A narrator relates the events in deep, sinister tones. In keeping with these opening moments, the game that ensues is rife with biblical allusions, graphic and disturbing cartoon violence, and a thoroughly biological horror aesthetic.

At first, *The Binding of Isaac* seems an unlikely candidate for queer representation. Outside of the opening cutscene, there is hardly any characterization. The production quality is decidedly lo-fi, offering none of the narrative richness of many contemporary AAA games within which queer representation could unfold amid a relational network. The main character is a disturbed child, and the only narrative premise to speak of in *The Binding of Isaac* is that of an abusive relationship between the child and his mother, a decidedly negative context within which to work out a positive political advocacy.[19]

However, *The Binding of Isaac* actually inscribes at the formal level the very queer temporality and embodiment that Halberstam identifies in *In a Queer Time and Place*. It accomplishes this inscription in three ways: First, by rejecting the video game convention of saving your progress and embracing the permadeath of the rogue-like genre; second, by relying on a procedurally generated randomization for the content and form of its levels; and third, by figuring all of the various magical abilities and power-ups that are available to players as physical modifications and transformations that are thrust on Isaac himself.

Unlike many mainstream video game titles in which the avatar's death is rare and inconsequential (a quick trip back to the last checkpoint and you're good to go), in *The Binding of Isaac*, death is permanent. Permadeath in *The Binding of Isaac* entails a complete reset of your progress through your levels, sending the player and Isaac himself back to the first basement level without any of the power-ups he may have accrued. At no point through the entire game is there anything resembling saved progress. There is only a single run through the six levels, and in the event of death, a total loss of all assets. This rejection of continuity from play session to play session is a fascinating refusal of narrative teleology. Though *The Binding of Isaac* certainly has narrative aspects that frame the action, the majority of the player's time is spent in cyclical play. Here we should hear echoes of the riskiness of a queer life in the face of heteronormative time and space. The centerpiece of *The Binding of Isaac* is not the quest, the object that must be achieved, but rather it is the experience of Isaac's body. The game is quite difficult, meaning that for most gamers, the experience is one of incremental progress followed by death and reset, over and over. Though technically the game has an endpoint in its final maternal boss battle, players spend the majority of their time recycling through the levels, reexperiencing the actual play itself, rather than a steady, linear progression toward the end. The goal here is not to transcend Isaac's situation and set everything right again but rather to spend cycles of constant iteration in the explorative mode.

That process of iteration and reiteration highlights the diminished degree to which narrative resolution figures into the pleasure of *The Binding of Isaac*. Given the rather dire premise of a child making an escape attempt away from his murderous mother, one might expect the game to push toward that final triumph with some degree of melodramatic pathos. Instead, the bulk of the game circulates around that affect of peril, never really getting out from under the threat of the mother's heel, and knowing that even if he does escape, the little boy would be irrevocably altered for the experience. In contrast to *Jade Empire*, which must at all costs resolve the fallout of the emperor's destructive actions into either a "good" or "bad" ending, *The Binding of Isaac* simply presents its players with a set of oppressive circumstances and, rather than cajoling them into saving the day, invites them to play around with the myriad possibilities that even this awful environment affords. What could be more evocative of Suits's trifler who plays not to win but for something far more elusive?

Within this cyclical structure of reiteration, *The Binding of Isaac* generates all of its levels, monsters, power-ups, and obstacles procedurally. The random nature of *The Binding of Isaac*'s gameplay ensures that, in addition to keeping the gameplay fresh, there is never a time in which the gamer can say that she has truly figured the game out, so to speak. Secret rooms move. Monsters appear in different combinations. Bombs are never hidden in the same place as before. Though there are parameters within which each level operates (the game increases in difficulty the farther down you go, for instance), they provide only a rough framework of any given experience. This means that the game always obscures any attempt to carry over knowledge from a previous play-through to the current one. Some knowledge persists from play-through to play-through, but that knowledge is always necessarily incomplete. A certain rejection of narrativized history lurks in this random generation. The always unfolding logic of the queer archival represents a narrative approach that is generative rather than authoritative. *The Binding of Isaac* enacts the direct allegorithm to Halberstam's queer logics. Unlike *Jade Empire,* whose branching plot lines must all, inevitably, result in some kind of seizure of power and the restoration of the reproductive regime, *The Binding of Isaac* offers a space (limited though it may be) for endless temporal and spatial configurations. Heteronormativity's record of progression dissipates into an archive of jumbled histories.

Amid these rather queer temporalities stands the game's centerpiece: Isaac's body. Naked from the outset and armed only with his tears, Isaac—and by proxy, the player—only gains in power through highly visible, grotesque alterations to his corporeality. When Isaac picks up a wooden spoon, he gains movement speed but his body also becomes covered in marks from being swatted. When he finds a rock, his tears do more damage but the rock also lodges bloodily in his head. What's more, the physical alterations stack onto each other, so the farther down Isaac delves and the more powerful he becomes, the more marked his body becomes. The implication here for the queer archival is clear. Isaac himself has become a kind of semiliving object, whose very physical comportment resists heteronormative logics of wholeness and stable embodiment.[20] Like a living, biological archive, Isaac's body gradually becomes an amalgamation of organic and inorganic materials. Margrit Shildrick's work on the connections between the disabled body, the prosthetic, and queer embodiment are particularly illuminating to Isaac's queer situation. Outlining what it means for a queer body to become, Shildrick argues, "is not that there is no distinction to be made between one corporeal element and the next, or indeed between the human and animal, or human and machine, but rather that becoming entails an inherent transgression of boundaries that turns the pleasures—sexual or otherwise—of the embodied person away from dominant notions of human subjectivity."[21] As flesh and machine mesh, the categories of embodiment are constantly being reinvented, reconceived, and rearticulated. In that Isaac's entire arsenal of powers—everything from laser eyes to dog food—has visually represented effects on the comportment of his body, Isaac is an essentially queer body. That the majority of these power-ups are visually represented in terms of bodily harm only serves to confirm the radical rejection of heteronormative safety.

Perhaps even more subversively, it is his very queerness, his constant bodily becoming, which grants Isaac the abilities that set him apart from the monsters throughout the game and enable him to navigate the nightmarish world in which he finds himself. On the one hand, the monsters, grotesque as they may be, are wholly restricted by their particular biological traits: the giant fly with a red abdomen will always fire a missile of blood in the same way, the decapitated children will always shamble aimlessly toward Isaac in predictable patterns, and so on. Isaac's beleaguered body, on the other hand, constantly changes, marked at all times by his own vulnerability. It is not that Isaac is the only creature in the basement with special powers that makes him unique. Rather, it is his status as a precarious queer body, one that is constantly at risk of harm and therefore always in the flux of becoming, that empowers him to press on past his adversaries.

For a game to possess the allegorithmic potential to extend queer counterpublics out from the game space onto the real, it must do so on the level of formal function. By holding the archival body up against heteronormative constructions of time and embodiment, *The Binding of Isaac* provides an alternative queer politic over and against the linear, reproductive, capitalist subject. The potential of the allegorithm extends beyond what it can offer as an interpretive framework. If the video game is indeed central to structuring contemporary social relations, then we may look to *The Binding of Isaac* as an example of how the allegorithm puts the game space into the service of queering the real.

JORDAN WOOD is a PhD candidate in the English department at Syracuse University, where he studies video games, queer theory, embodiment, and the affects of pleasure. He develops and manages a laboratory for the study and teaching of games on the Syracuse University campus where he helps students and faculty alike encounter video games in a rigorous academic atmosphere.

Notes

1. Alexander Galloway, *Gaming: Essays on Algorithmic Culture* (Minneapolis: University of Minnesota Press, 2006), 90–91.
2. McKenzie Wark, *Gamer Theory* (Cambridge, MA: Harvard University Press, 2007), sec. 019.

3. Border House, "About Us," http://web.archive.org/web/20150812054306/http://borderhouseblog.com/?page_id=2 (accessed February 22, 2017).

4. Adrienne Shaw, "Putting the Gay in Games: Cultural Production and GLBT Content in Video Games," *Games and Culture* 4, no. 3 (2009): 229.

5. Numerous games up to this point had featured gay or transgender characters, such as Birdo in *Super Mario Bros. 2* (Nintendo, 1988) or Vamp in *Metal Gear Solid* (Konami, 2001). These games, however, did not render the player-character's sexuality fluid in the way that *Jade Empire* does, and therefore feature a different mode of representing queer sexuality.

6. In *Mass Effect* (2007, BioWare) and *Mass Effect 2* (2010, BioWare), for instance, players can have relatively graphic sexual encounters of the heterosexual and lesbian varieties, but not between phenotypically male bodies.

7. Judith Halberstam, *In a Queer Time and Place: Transgender Bodies, Subcultural Lives* (New York: New York University Press, 2005), 1.

8. Ibid., 2.

9. Ibid., 5.

10. Ibid., 23.

11. E. L McCallum and Mikko Tuhkanen, "Becoming Unbecoming: Untimely Mediations," in *Queer Times, Queer Becomings*, ed. E. L. McCallum and Mikko Tuhkanen (Albany: State University of New York Press, 2011), 1.

12. Clare Colebrook, "On the Very Possibility of Queer Theory," in *Deleuze and Queer Theory*, ed. Chrysanthi Nigianni and Merl Storr (Edinburgh, UK: Edinburgh University Press, 2009), 21.

13. Graeme Kirkpatrick, *Aesthetic Theory and the Video Game* (Manchester, UK: Manchester University Press, 2011), 195.

14. Vivian Sobchack, "The Scene of the Screen: Envisioning Cinematic and Electronic Presence," in *Electronic Media and Technoculture*, ed. John Thornton Caldwell (New Brunswick, NJ: Rutgers University Press, 2000), 138.

15. Veli-Matti Karhulahti, "A Kinesthetic Theory of Videogames: Time-Critical Challenge and Aporetic Rhematic," *Game Studies* 13, no. 1 (2013), http://gamestudies.org/1301/articles/karhulahti_kinesthetic_theory_of_the_videogame.

16. Jenny Sundén, "Desires at Play: On Closeness and Epistemological Uncertainty," *Games and Culture* 7, no. 2 (2012): 165. "Game space" here literally refers to the space of the game itself, rather than the very specific theoretical notion of "gamespace" from Wark's *Gamer Theory*.

17. Ibid., 178.

18. Jesper Juul, *Half-Real: Video Games between Real Rules and Fictional Worlds* (Cambridge, MA: MIT Press, 2005), 29.

19. Although, as one responder at a panel for an earlier version of this chapter shrewdly remarked, painful parental rejection has long been a touchstone of narrativizing the queer experience.

20. Halberstam, *In a Queer Time and Place*, 113.

21. Margrit Shildrick, "Prosthetic Performativity: Deleuzian Connections and Queer Corporealities," in *Deleuze and Queer Theory*, ed. Chrysanthi Nigianni and Merl Storr (Edinburgh, UK: Edinburgh University Press, 2009), 124.

chapter thirteen

A GAME CHOOSES, A PLAYER OBEYS

BioShock, *Posthumanism, and the Limits of Queerness*

EDMOND Y. CHANG

ACCORDING TO THE GAME'S WEBSITE, *BIOSHOCK* (2007, IRRATIONAL GAMES) is a "'genetically enhanced' first person shooter that lets you do things never before possible in the genre: turn everything into a weapon, biologically mod your body with plasmids, hack devices and systems, upgrade your weapons and craft new ammo variants, and experiment with different battle techniques in an incredible and unique underwater city."[1] *BioShock* is set in the mysterious city of Rapture, "an underwater Utopia torn apart by civil war."[2] The game features various political, economic, and ideological factions as well as biotechnologies that offer "instant genetic modifications that empower you with different abilities."[3] Like other first-person shooters, the game allows players to see, fight, and interact with the world from the perspective of the player-protagonist—in this case Jack, whose plane crashes in the middle of the Atlantic Ocean and who discovers the secret entrance to Rapture. As Jack, the player plays through seven areas of the city from medical and industrial facilities to fishing ports and botanical gardens to red-light and residential districts, encountering an array of mutated enemies, mechanical traps, and gruesome scenarios, all culminating in the discovery of the truth behind and eventual destruction of Rapture. The game offers the player many of the conventions of first-person shooters, blending them with other genres like horror survival and role-playing games, but *BioShock* also allows for ludic opportunities to analyze and critique said conventions, mechanics, and narratives. According to Ken Levine, the creative director of Irrational Games, "If people take anything intellectual away from this game, I hope it's just 'here [are] some new ideas, think about them.'"[4] With this invitation in mind, one new way to think about *BioShock* is to queer it, to explore and challenge the norms and expectations of games and gaming.

To queer *BioShock*, then, is to explore "the open mesh of possibilities, gaps, overlaps, dissonances and resonances, lapses and excesses of meaning" across player, platform, story, and avatar.[5] To queer *BioShock* is to invite "experimental linguistic, epistemological, representational, political adventures" that reveal the ways that game narrative and mechanics open and foreclose on alternative identities and embodiments.[6] Although Irrational Games did not set out to make a queer game, to queer *BioShock* is to attempt to answer the question: Is it even possible to create a queer video game? In *BioShock*, queerness is encoded, embedded not only in characters and plot but more importantly in the very relationship between game and player, algorithm and adventure. Rather than turn to ostensibly queer(er) games, *BioShock* provides a critical potential in addressing and analyzing a popular, mainstream title as well as reveals the ways most digital games strategically deploy and ultimately recuperate queer possibilities.

Most intentionally queer games—from BioWare's *Dragon Age* (2009–2014) or *Mass Effect* (2007–2012) titles to Lion Head Studios' *Fable* (2004) to Maxis's *The Sims* (2000–2015)—focus on content, on same-gender sex, and queer couple or marriage plots in ways that are, by and large, still window dressing, as the games provide menu-driven identities and represent sexuality as a series of yes-or-no choices. This arrangement replicates the rather limited binary of hetero or homo, gay or straight, and, perhaps problematically, the conservative belief that sexuality is merely a choice. Anna Anthropy, an openly transgender, independent game maker, argues, "In this world, 'gay' is a checkbox on a character sheet, a boolean, a binary bit, not an experience that greatly changes one's life, identity, and struggle. Token characters are not the product of queer experiences. Actual queer experiences offer perspectives on identity, on struggle, and on romance that could be entirely different."[7] On the surface, a game like *The Sims 3* (2009, Electronic Arts) seems to privilege a kind of gamic bisexuality where characters are happily open to same- or opposite-gender encounters and relationships, providing a more heteroflexible gameplay. However, the choice is still limited to one or the other and the experience of this binary might too easily fall into a cartoonish stereotype of promiscuity.

Anthropy's indictment of the "straight, white, able-bodied cis-gender" privilege in games and in the game industry provides a scatter plot of terms and tensions that frame the problem of queer games: tokenized content versus inclusive experience, Boolean check boxes versus the multiplicity of identity, and the inescapable binary structure of digital computers. Video games execute and play for us what I call the technonormative matrix, the technologically enhanced and informatically infected version of Judith Butler's heteronormative matrix, "the matrix of power and discursive relations that effectively produce and regulate the intelligibility of [sex, gender, or sexuality]."[8] Video games are not only normative and reductive in their content, narratives, and imagined worlds but normative and conservative in terms of the technology itself, the very medium of digital games. The tyranny of the binary, of the Boolean, of the matrix is what Alexander Galloway defines as protocol. This "proscription for structure," this regulation of game space, is fundamental to digital computers and to games.[9] After all, what is a game but "a system in which players engage in an artificial conflict, defined by rules, that results in a quantifiable outcome."[10] The technonormativity extends to game companies, industry circles, and gamer communities as well. As dramatized in recent attempts to trouble the privileged magic circles of games and gaming cultures and in the subsequent virulent, often violent, misogynist, and phobic backlashes, technonormativity is the default mode from code to console, from programmer to player, from development teams to gamer communities.[11] To queer *BioShock*, then, is to unpack the intersections of heteronormativity and digital technology, game mechanics, and content and to close read and close play three intersecting frames: the queer promises of posthumanism, the queer promises of video games, and the queer promises of Rapture, the city and setting of *BioShock* itself.

Posthumanism, the Interactive Fallacy, and *BioShock*

The first frame concerns a broad engagement with the perils and possibilities of life- and body-changing technologies shorthanded here as the posthuman. Cary Wolfe defines posthumanism as the "historical moment in which the decentering of the human by its imbrication in technical, medical, informatic, and economic networks is increasingly impossible to ignore."[12] Imaginings of posthuman futurity are decidedly polar: on the one hand, dystopian fears over machine intelligence, cloning, and the loss of life, liberty, and humanity; on the other hand, dreams of transcendence, immortality, global harmony, and enlightenment. What I want to highlight here is the latter, addressing particularly the idea that technology will ultimately make people (and society) better, stronger, faster. This is a brand of posthumanism—or, more precisely, transhumanism—that Wolfe critiques as merely the intensification of traditional liberal humanism. In fact, Humanity Plus (formerly the World Transhumanist Association) espouses "the possibility of broadening human potential by overcoming aging, cognitive shortcomings, involuntary suffering, and our confinement to planet Earth."[13] These ideals have been extended to queer bodies and lives. For example, Dale Carrico, an academic and author of "Technology's Making Queers of Us All" on BetterHu mans.com, wants to take conventional gay and lesbian politics to "far more subversive places. Queerer places."[14] Carrico argues, "Queer politics . . . is predicated on the assumption that what is not 'normal' should nevertheless often be valued and celebrated. Queer sensibilities tend to be supremely suspicious of the gay vision of equality and normality, and are drawn instead to vision of diversity and proliferation."[15] He believes that transhumanist technologies and politics can provide queers this opportunity of "diversity and proliferation," which, he continues, "unite technological development with human self-creation in the hope of unleashing varieties of desire queers themselves have rarely (but sometimes) dreamt of."[16] The fantasy of transhuman queerness, of queer transhumanism, is then repurposed and skinned by games—including *BioShock*—about the fantasy of individual freedom and self-creation.

The second frame, the queer promise of video games, confronts the mainstream belief that video games empower players with choice, control, exploration, even escape. Mainstream games—from gameplay to packaging to advertising—highlight an incredible array of rhetoric about both game content and game design that exhort openness, flexibility, freedom of action, movement, and choice. These are overlaid by calls to be the hero, the star, the rich, the famous, the best of the best. The very beginning of *BioShock*, for example, opens with a short monologue by the main character, Jack, who says, "They told me . . . son, you're special. You were born to do great things. You know what? They were right." It is Jack's specialness that players want to play, to access, to embody. But is all this hype and hoopla just fantasy? Do players really exert control and have power? Might all this playing and pretending reveal the ways that control and power work in the real world? As Galloway writes, "Video games render social realities into playable form."[17] After all, video games are about actions and interactions, activity and interactivity. Julian Stallabrass highlights these elements, writing, "The distinctiveness of computer games lies in interaction. . . . [It is] an environment in which the player's actions have a direct, immediate consequence on the world depicted."[18] This all certainly sounds like control; this all certainly sounds like power. With the push of a button or a tilt of a joystick, something happens, things change, the world responds. Video games enact and invite interaction with the logics of cyberspace, convincing players to suspend disbelief to believe that they are in full control of the action even as they consent to the rules and limits of the game. Video games require players to give in to what Katie Salen and Eric Zimmerman call the "immersive fallacy"—the notion that "the pleasure of a media experience lies in its ability to sensually transport the participant into an illusory, simulated reality."[19] In other words, players must learn, navigate, and even exploit the rules and constraints of a game and simultaneously deny them—mystify them via the fantasy of choice, power, immersion, and interactivity—a curious kind of digital double-consciousness.

The desire for control, for freedom, and for choice is further dramatized in the 2008 film *Second Skin*, a nerd-core documentary that follows the lives of three groups of video gamers that play massively multiplayer online role-playing games (MMORPGs). In the documentary, a *World of Warcraft* (2004–2014, Blizzard) player says, "An MMO is a world within a world. It's a completely different set of rules; you're a completely different person while you're there. Just to have that kind of freedom, to be able to get away with it and not have anybody question you, makes it a world unto itself."[20] It is this notion that video games offer gamers control, power, and worth that once again recapitulates the standard narratives of cyberspace. For many gamers, playing games like *World of Warcraft* is part escape, part adventure, and part self-actualization where players and their avatars feel empowered and important and resourceful. Nick Yee, online game researcher and founder of the Daedalus Project, says in the documentary, "A lot of players have what they perceive as dead-end jobs . . . and they log on to these worlds, and suddenly they're someone with power."[21] Video games, then, advertise and facilitate the thrill of being someone different, someone important, someone powerful—deploying commonsense definitions of control and power as the ability to affect, change, and better yourself and the world around you. Like the transhumanist fantasy of technological transcendence, video games offer a similar promise of the right to life, liberty, and the pursuit of happiness, and the liberal humanist virtues of choice, free will, and success.

Given these rhetorics of interactivity and immersion, of sandbox synthetic worlds, of democratization through gamification, *BioShock* serves as an excellent example of video games as a vernacular posthuman technology. *BioShock* is, then, a critique of posthuman possibility and the transhumanist fantasies of technological self-fashioning, possessive individualism, and liberation from the limitations of embodiment through the cyborg medium of video games. As Galloway further warns, "The more emancipating games seem to be as a medium . . . the more they are in fact hiding the fundamental social transformation into informatics."[22] In other words, even as a video game evinces a player's power and agency, it naturalizes and obscures its own algorithmic and protocological control. Players playing Jack often feel powerful given the conventions and tropes of the first-person shooter genre—players see what Jack sees; they run, jump, and fight as Jack; and they win or lose seemingly based solely on their own skill, effort, and choices. Salen and Zimmerman add, "The immersive fallacy is symptomatic of contradictory ideas about technology. On the one hand, there is a technological fetishism that sees the evolutionary development of new technology as the saving grace of experience design. On the other hand, there is a desire to erase the technology, to make it invisible so that all frames around the experience fall away and disappear."[23] Salen and Zimmerman's immersive fallacy becomes interactive fallacy as *BioShock* simultaneously dramatizes the posthuman fantasy of self-fashioning and body modification, and on a metalevel, critiques the player's belief that he is in control, making substantive choices, and driving the narrative.

The third and final frame is *BioShock* itself and its rich game world. To reiterate, *BioShock* is set in 1960, just after the New Year, and takes place in the retrofuturistic Rapture, an underwater Art Deco city-state utopia tacitly modeled on Ayn Randian objectivist philosophy. The game world riffs on Rand, particularly *Atlas Shrugged*, Rand's fourth and final novel, which describes a dystopian, economically and socially ruined world that can only be saved by reason, individualism, free-market capitalism, and noninterference from any government. According to the novel and Randian philosophy, "If man is to live on earth, it is *right* for him to use his mind, it is *right* to act on his own free judgment, it is *right* to work for his values and to keep the product of his work. If life on earth is his purpose, he has a *right* to live as a rational being: nature forbids him the irrational."[24] The sometimes science-fictional world of *Atlas Shrugged* is repurposed and reconfigured as Rapture. The player-protagonist, named only Jack, mysteriously arrives in Rapture after the plane he is on experiences some sort of calamity and crashes in the middle of the ocean. Jack is the only survivor. He conveniently discovers a strange tower nearby, jutting up out of the ocean, which leads him to Rapture. The player arrives in media res, finding the city in turmoil and near collapse after the introduction of body-hacking technology called "splicing," which results in civil war between the humans and the posthuman splicers. The opening cinematic introduces the mastermind behind Rapture, an entrepreneur and visionary named Andrew Ryan (clearly anagrammatically rhyming Ayn Rand), who proclaims the city's manifesto and the central dilemmas of the game: "A man has choices; I chose the impossible. I built a city where the artists would not fear the censor, where the great would not be constrained by the small, where the scientist would not be bound by petty morality. I chose to build Rapture. But my city was betrayed by the weak. So I ask you, my friend, if you live with pride, would you kill the innocent? Would you sacrifice your humanity? We all make choices, but in the end, our choices make us." Ryan's words clearly resonate with the passage from *Atlas Shrugged* and frame the game's plot and programmatic imperatives: *BioShock* is about choice, about choosing between weakness and strength, between losing and winning, between staying human and becoming posthuman. Rand's rationality, the right to act on one's own judgment, is coded into the game, but Ryan's final line—"We make choices, but in the end, our choices make us"—foreshadows the game's attempt to critique this fantasy and to reveal how games always make choices for players.

By employing these three frames, my goal here is to avoid just a "straight" queer reading of the game, to do more than just go bird-watching for queer characters. Rather, because *BioShock* dramatizes the transhumanist dream of self-fashioning via splicing and because it relies on the interactive fallacy of video game freedom and control—in a sense, allowing one to play an alternative past and posthuman future—the game invites queer possibilities that might be leveraged to critique normative gender, sexuality, even race. In the end, though, *BioShock* forecloses on these possibilities, recuperating them back into hetero- and technonormativity.

Queer (Im)Possibilities in Rapture

The player-protagonist is thrust into Rapture, is introduced to splicing technology, and must navigate not only the crumbling city but also the political factions at war. To escape Rapture, Jack is led to believe he must help a resistance fighter named Atlas (another Randian reference) and overthrow Ryan. Aside from the usual first-person shooter arsenal of guns, ammo, and the ever-popular pipe wrench, the player-protagonist is enhanced by splicing technology (called plasmids) derived from a deep sea slug. Adam and Eve, drug-like derivatives of the sea slug, allow the player-protagonist to enhance health, strength, and skills, and they grant an array of superhuman powers like throwing bolts of electricity, summoning an insect swarm, and telekinesis. Mapped onto these technologies are the libertarian and individualist mores of Rapture's society, which promises freedom for all to be beautiful, talented, rich, and powerful. Littered throughout the game world are Gatherer's Garden vending machines where players can purchase genetic modifications and upgrades, which improve the character's health, stamina, and offer special abilities. The vending machine spews in a little girl's voice, "My daddy's *smarter* than Einstein, *stronger* than Hercules, and lights a fire with a snap of his fingers. Are you as good as my daddy, Mister? Not if you don't visit the Gatherer's Garden, you aren't! Smart daddies get spliced at the Gardens!"

Ironically, at the very start of the game, in the first level of Rapture, Jack discovers a Gatherer's Garden and before the player has any say or choice injects himself with the florescent-red hypodermic. The player-protagonist walks up to the machine, takes the enticingly glowing plasmid sitting in the vending slot, and then the game takes over, seamlessly switching to a short in-game cutscene. The player can only watch as Jack looks at the plasmid injector in his right hand, weighing it as if considering what to do, lifts his left hand into view, and then jams the needle into his left wrist (figure 13.1). Immediately, there are sounds of pain and discomfort, everything glows with a rosy haze, and Jack's flesh begins to twist and crackle with bright blue-white electricity. Atlas, ever helpful, crackles over the radio in his Irish brogue, "Steady now! Your genetic code is being rewritten—just hold on and everything will be fine!" Curiously, this momentary lapse of player choice and volition is quickly passed over, rationalized as necessary exposition and the introduction of the plasmid mechanic. After all, the "electro bolt" power is necessary in order to pass through a locked door on the first level and one of many powers

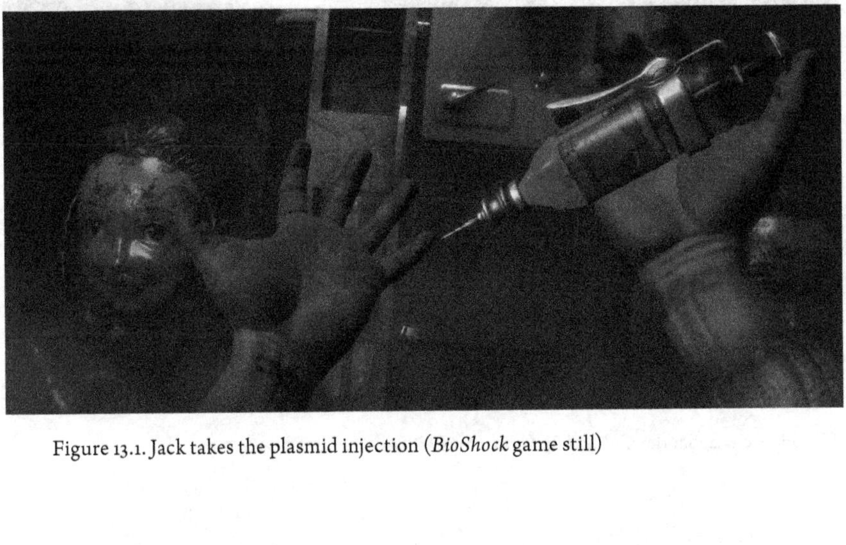

Figure 13.1. Jack takes the plasmid injection (*BioShock* game still)

needed for success. Atlas says, "You all right, boyo? First time plasmid's a real kick from a mule. But there's nothing like a fistful of lightning, now is there?" To become posthuman is no longer a choice, rather necessity or utilitarian destiny. Even though the game constrains the player and character, symbolized by the tattoos of chains on Jack's wrists, the interactive fallacy confirms for us that in this case, Jack is different. He is special, individual, and will not become a monster like the splicers that are ruining Rapture but the hero that will have the competitive power to save it.

It is in this setting, this set of tensions, that we find Sander Cohen (figure 13.2). He is described as a poet, composer, sculptor, and playwright. He wears a tailored tuxedo, a red flower boutonniere, and black-and-white saddle shoes; he is in theatrical white face with exaggerated eyelashes, penciled eyebrows and mustache, and red lips. Though the game does not out Cohen, there is enough textual evidence to support reading him as the stereotypical Hollywood or Broadway fey fatale: he is the boss of the seventh level and pleasure zone Fort Frolic, which is full of bars, theaters, strip clubs, and boutiques; he is a suffering artist, musician, and director given to lavish melodramatics. He is coded as flamboyant, effeminate, and raucously queer. He is a token character and meant to be a foil to the hardscrabble toughness of characters like Atlas or the generic masculinity of Jack himself. Leigh Alexander of *GameSetWatch* waxes anecdotally,

> I spent two years [at New York City acting conservatory] with some of the most archetypal "theatre people" imaginable—black-cloaked, emotional Method actors, flamingly homosexual dancers, proudly egomaniacal Shakespearians, and hysterical, demanding pianists prone to throwing fits. Sander Cohen's pitch-perfect

Figure 13.2. Sander Cohen (*BioShock* game still)

rant—"my muse is a fickle bitch with a very short attention span!"—might have been snatched from one of their mouths.[25]

It is this coding, from algorithm on up, that marks Cohen as different, crazy, and bent on half-seducing, half-sadistically playing with the player-protagonist. Again, though the game does not dare speak the name of the love that Cohen represents, he fulfills a long-standing, easily recognizable trope—from Hollywood to television to digital stereotype, or cybertype, borrowing Lisa Nakamura's term.[26] The figure of Cohen illustrates the normative logic of how video games include and encode queer characters.

During gameplay, Atlas describes him: "Cohen's an artist, says some. He's a Section Eight, says I. I've seen all kinds of cutthroats, freaks, and hard cases in my life, but Cohen, he's a real lunatic, a dyed-in-the-wool psychopath." Here the language of mental illness, pathology, and being unfit for military service recalls for the player the beliefs and narratives about homosexuality in the mid-twentieth century. To be queer meant to be different, subversive, even dangerous to the normative fabric of society, security, and country:

> Considering the time period, and the eras of nostalgia *BioShock* evokes, it is useful to keep in mind the Hays Code that was at one time enforced in the United States. Homosexuality was forbidden to be discussed outwardly in films, though this did not prevent the inclusion of topics broaching such. Instead, "coding" became a way of recognizing when people were discussing a man or woman who may not be of the heterosexual sort.[27]

From 1930 to 1968, films released in the United States were constrained by the Motion Picture Production Code, or Hays Code (named for Hollywood's chief censor, Will H. Hays), which prohibited a range of "don'ts" and "be carefuls" from profanity to drug use to miscegenation to sex perversion.[28] To get around the code, filmmakers relied on an arsenal of euphemism, double entendre, and other filmic cheats and codes to signal or disguise that which could not be shown. Queer characters then became legible, recognizable in their dress, in their speech, and in their subordination to normal or straight characters. The Hays Code was abandoned and replaced by the now standard and recognizable MPAA rating system, which has in part been adopted as a model for rating video game content by the ESRB. Like film producers, game designers and marketers often walk the ratings tightrope trying to balance violence, mature themes, vulgarity, nudity, and especially, sexuality. And like in films, queerness in digital games often is relegated to shadow and stereotypical shorthand. According to journalist Jagger Gravning,

> While there is no modern Hays Code equivalent in contemporary American video games (the ESRB rates but does not censor) the manner that LGBT characters are being introduced to a broader audience in major games is through this same blowback-wary method of diligent self-policing. The writers allow space for an audience member to overlook or deny the homosexuality of a particular character if that's the way they would prefer to see things.[29]

Cohen's in-game sexuality, then, is in part obscured by his mania, like the bunny mask or actor's makeup that hides his face, and in part self-explanatory given that insanity has been stereotypically used as an outward manifestation of an interior perversion. In one of Cohen's audio diaries, titled "The Wild Bunny," he says:

> I want to take the ears off, but I can't.
> I hop, and when I hop, I never get off the ground.
> It's my curse, my eternal curse!
> I want to take the ears off but I can't!
> It's my curse! It's my fucking curse!
> I want to take the ears off!
> Please!
> Take them off!
> Please!

The subtext of the closet here is undeniable. Cohen laments his need to remain hidden, to know himself as different, to pass as not queer. However, Cohen's actions speak much louder than his words. What is most compelling in reading Cohen as queer is that he vindictively requires the player-protagonist Jack to kill the remaining three of his four young, male protégés. All these men point a bent finger at Cohen. Among them, Martin Finnegan calls Cohen an "old fruit" and an "old grape." Hector Rodriguez laments, "The things that man had me do." Kyle Fitzpatrick, whom Cohen kills by chaining him to an exploding piano, cries, "Oh Cohen, you sick fuck, let me out of this!" Finally, in the confrontation with Silas Cobb, one of Cohen's favorites, Cobb says to Cohen, "I used to love you, I used to think you were a musical genius. You know why? Because you paid my rent, you ancient hack!" He later spits at Jack, "It's all a game, errand boy! Cohen, Ryan! Two old birds pullin' on each other's milk sticks!"

According to Denis Farr, a contributor to GayGamer.net, who extends the queer reading to include a possible connection between Cohen and Ryan himself, the developers wanted to make Cohen a full-fledged character. The developers wanted to "create human beings, which meant that everyone was treated equally. Everyone also had the same capacity to fall and become depraved killers."[30] In other words, the creators of *BioShock* could imagine queerness within the game, but that imagined queerness is given short shrift. Of course, all this talk of equality obscures the problematic logics at work in Cohen's characterization and reveals a failure to recast the intersections of queerness, technology, and agency.

What is important is that Cohen allows for a game space and body open to queerness where "artists would not fear the censor," yet simultaneously perpetuates a stereotypical representation of the homo-homicidal aesthete complete with dance numbers and bitchy repartee. The figure of Cohen is Eve Kosofsky Sedgwick's "open mesh of possibilities, gaps, overlaps, dissonances and resonances, lapses and excesses of meaning."[31] Even Cohen's powers enact this queer possibility. He is a unique form of the Houdini Splicer allowing him to teleport from place to place, appearing and disappearing like a rabbit pulled out of his own hat. If the player-protagonist chooses to engage Cohen in combat, he shouts as he fights, "I'm Sander-Fucking-Cohen!" and "Look at me, boy!" Both are commands that invoke both desire and recognition. In a sense, Cohen demands the player-protagonist's attention, to see and acknowledge his difference, his queerness.

Whether Cohen is homosexual or not is beside the point; rather what is more important is not who he sleeps with but what his queerness, his difference, portends and produces in this close playing. To decide that he is gay or straight would mean succumbing to the binary logic of digital computers and games. In fact, games often resort to the Boolean choice, as Anthropy argues, rather than reveling in ambiguity or ambivalence. The game and its discursive and cultural codes result in fixing Cohen's status and sexuality. Unfortunately, as with most video games, the queer spaces opened by Cohen are quickly closed and both his story and gameplay come to an end. In order to proceed in the game, the player must defeat Cohen (though not necessarily kill him). This inevitability—required by the game's programming and narrative and by the larger, cultural policing of queerness—reveals the ambivalent positioning of the player and protagonist in gaming's posthuman fantasies. It is possible, on the one hand, to see the killing of Cohen as a phobic response, as the final fix to Cohen's queerness. On the other hand, the sparing of Cohen might be read as a magnanimous act, an act of acceptance of queerness. But either way, as the player moves forward toward escape and success, Cohen's irredeemable descent into madness (and eventual death by the player's hand or by the destruction of Rapture) ultimately censors him, recuperates him. If the player kills Cohen, he is complicit in this recuperation. If the player spares Cohen, he is still playing the part of the straight savior. The problem of Cohen as a queer character and a set of design choices eventually succumbs to the algorithmic and narrative need for straight and clear-cut resolutions.

A Game Chooses, a Player Obeys

Overall, in a game world and a cyborg medium that argue for a kind of technopossessive individualism ("it is *right* for him to use his mind") and liberation from the limits of the mind, body, and culture ("it is *right* to act on his own free judgment"), *BioShock* attempts to enact a critique of Randian objectivism and posthuman choice via its own interactive medium and a story about power, control, and self-determination. Central to the game is the showdown between Jack and Ryan. Until this aptly titled level, "All Is Revealed," Jack believes himself to have discovered Rapture and become trapped in its civil war by chance and accident. What is revealed in the confrontation with the father of Rapture, however, is that Jack was in fact born in Rapture, fathered by Ryan himself, and bioengineered to be the inheritor and defender of the utopia. Most importantly, the player learns that

Jack's body modifications included mind-control implants, which are triggered by the polite request, "Would you kindly?" The player and protagonist simultaneously realize that they have been duped by the game and the game world. The player's desire to follow the plot, to pass each successive level, and to eventually win is concomitant and conflated with each "Would you kindly?" command. The illusion of self-will and fantasy of individual choice are broken within and without the diegesis.

As argued earlier, video games seduce their players with fantasies of power and control, the chance to play as superhuman heroes battling wrongdoing, injustice, and oppression. Yet the one power that gaming can never fully offer its player is choice. Some—even most—of the choices within a game have already been decided, mapped onto decision trees, and embedded in scripted encounters, cutscenes, and command structures. The player is always caught between limited gamic action and algorithmic control. Even moments where players and characters seem to go off script, they are never off the map and eventually must return to the main action in order to proceed. In the "All Is Revealed" scene, *BioShock* violates the player's trust that the game will reveal how to approach, inhabit, and navigate the game world. However, in that positioning, it is directing the player: "Would you kindly move forward?" "Would you kindly kill that boss?" "Would you kindly win the game by playing the game *this* way?" Even as Ryan screams, "A man chooses; a slave obeys," and commands the player-protagonist to kill him with the golf club, the game dramatizes what Thomas Foster calls the "key antimony" of posthumanism, the irony that these technologies can serve both liberation and domination.[32]

All three frames—transhumanist fantasies of technological power, the immersive and interactive fallacies of digital games, and the queer promise of Rapture undermined by *BioShock*'s mind-control conceit—coincide in the confrontation with Ryan. Despite an arsenal of plasmids and weapons; of overcoming puzzles, predicaments, and foes; and despite doing everything right, the player and Jack—like Cohen—are recuperated by the game. Alas, as with Cohen, *BioShock* does not end the game at the defeat of Ryan. Instead, the game extends the narrative by forcing the player-protagonist to seek out and defeat the true end boss, Frank Fontaine, who is Ryan's rival and who has ultimately been manipulating Jack too. Luckily, Jack is given the ability to overcome the "Would You Kindly" mind control, and with the defeat of Fontaine—an end gambit with no more nuance than a tank-and-spank—Jack escapes Rapture and restores his status as hero in full possession of his individuality and free will. The player then is also recuperated and fed back into the interactive fallacy. The status quo of video game freedom is restored and the fantasy of posthuman agency is reassured. The technonormative must be reestablished even as Jack has his posthuman cake and eats it too, keeping his augmentations without succumbing to the same degeneration suffered by all the splicers now destroyed. For *BioShock* to end with Jack duped and defeated by Ryan would indeed be too threatening—too queering—to the ideals and ideologies that ensure the gaming industry and the larger gaming culture's popularity, profitability, and status quo.

Even the three possible endings of *BioShock* further reveal the winnowed and narrow possibilities for narrative and play. One of the selling points of *BioShock* was its promise of different endings, which would be revealed depending on the strategies and choices made by the player-protagonist, even as she or he was led by the nose through fifteen levels and hours and hours of gameplay. For example, the back of the game's box reads,

> *BioShock* is a shooter unlike any you've ever played, loaded with weapons and tactics never seen. You'll have a complete arsenal at your disposal . . . but you'll also be forced to genetically modify your DNA to create an even more deadly weapon: you. . . . No encounter ever plays out the same, and no two gamers will play the game the same way.[33]

From the start, the game promises newness, choice, and multiplicity, but ultimately, the choices funnel down to a very limited set of possibilities. The central decision of the game is whether to help or harvest the Little Sisters, genetically modified little girls who have been altered and conditioned to gather Adam from the dead corpses around Rapture. Saving the Little Sisters means the player-protagonist gains in strength, power, and ability more slowly (ostensibly being rewarded with a feeling of heroic righteousness). Harvesting the Little Sisters, which kills them, means the player-protagonist gains power earlier and more quickly (though the consequences of this moral and ethical choice bear little impact on the game itself).

After finishing the game, if Jack harvests all, some, or even just one of the Little Sisters, the player-protagonist is given the bad ending. The geneticist, Dr. Brigid Tenenbaum, who discovered the plasmid biotechnology and created the Little Sisters, says in a voice-over,

> They offered you everything, yes? And in return, you gave them what I've come to expect of you: brutality. You took what you wanted. All the Adam. All the power! And Rapture trembled. But in the end, even Rapture was not enough for you. Your father was terrified that the world would try to steal the secrets of his city. But not you. For now you have stolen the terrible secrets of the world!

Within this bad ending, harvesting some of the Little Sisters earns the sad voice-over. Dr. Tenenbaum speaks slowly, plaintively, disappointedly. Harvesting and killing all the Little Sisters earns the same ending but with an angry, harsher voice-over. Both versions of the bad ending are word for word the same save for a difference in the voice acting. The bad ending chastises and treats the player-protagonist as no different than Fontaine, Ryan, Cohen, or the other mad-with-power characters.

If the player-protagonist resists the temptation of quick and easy power and Jack saves all the Little Sisters, she or he is rewarded with the good ending. The

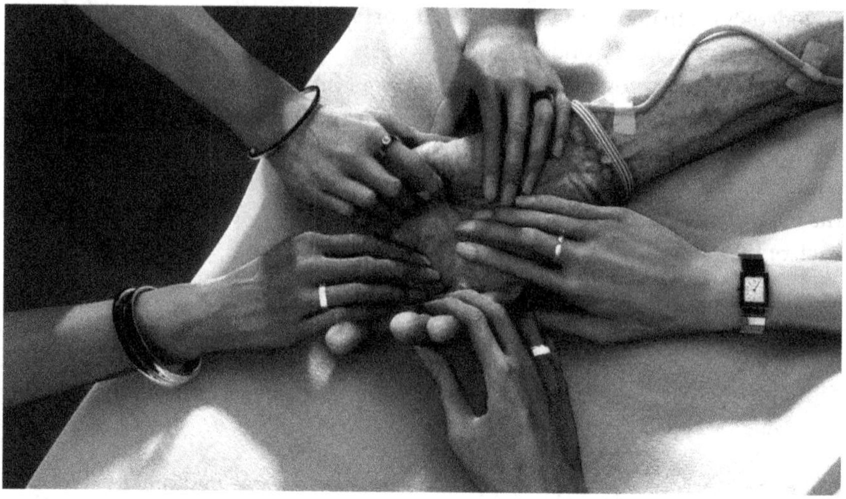

Figure 13.3. "Family" (*BioShock* game still)

cinematic at the end says proudly, "They offered you the city and you refused it. And what did you do instead? What I've come to expect of you. You saved them. You gave them the one thing that was stolen from them: a chance. A chance to learn, to find love, to live. And in the end, what was your reward? You never said it, but I think I know: a family." Presumably on his deathbed, the final image is a close-up of Jack's hand, palm up; his skin pale, aged, and wrinkled, liver-spotted, the chain tattoo faded, and some sort intravenous tube or monitor taped to his arm. In a circle, five different hands, younger and feminine, reach out to hold Jack's in a farewell gesture. Each of the women's hands and wrists, ostensibly belonging to Little Sisters now grown up, are adorned with jewelry—a bracelet here, a watch, and more importantly, rings (figure 13.3). Where the bad ending renders the player-protagonist as villain, the good ending is equally as flattening and limiting in its heroification. Individuality, agency, self-making, and righteous courage are rewarded with the most important prizes: life, liberty, and the pursuit of marriage, children, and family. Both good and bad endings recuperate the player and the protagonist, but the good ending literally and figuratively binds the player-protagonist with symbolic wedding bands, with the narrative and teleology of fatherhood, with heteronormativity. Like the fixed battle with Ryan and the fixed heroism of the defeat of Fontaine, the ending of *BioShock* offers little nuance and reveals its fixed reward tables and decision trees.

Queergaming

Ironically, it is the bad ending that leaves the game the most open ended, with the most unanswered questions. Perhaps the lesson here is to queer the endings as neither good nor bad, to recover them from the closed designs of game worlds and the real world. Given the previous examples from *BioShock*, how might we imagine and develop a different understanding of the posthuman possibilities offered by technology? How might we resist the move to recuperation and open queer opportunities? How might we read against the game's desire to recuperate Cohen, to tie up loose and errant ends, and to restore Jack's normative masculinity, family, and humanity—perhaps even superhumanity—to reposition him as already challenging these categories precisely because of his mediation and penetration by technology? How might we extend these critiques to find ways to resist the technonormative matrix? The inability to imagine alternative or radical identities, narratives, and possibilities, particularly those allegedly transformed by posthuman technologies, may result in "the same narrow concept of personhood used to legitimate racism, sexism, and homophobia."[34] Therefore, is it possible to see the "point of potential intersection between posthumanism and new social movements like feminism, gay and lesbian liberation, civil rights," to imagine worlds that challenge the limited binary of good and bad endings?[35] Is it possible to make different choices, play against the grain, develop queer algorithms in a medium that in the deepest sense maintains a strict binary: zero or one, no or yes? If the popular promise and mythology of posthumanism is that of liberation—whether it is liberation from human frailty, singular identities, oppression, or even mortality—then games and players must not give in to the seductions of these narratives and technologies, in the way *BioShock* and its players have. They must be mindful that, in the words of Nakamura, "only too often does one person's 'liberation' constitute another's recontainment."[36]

For instance, extending the close playing of Cohen, what if the sparing of Cohen by the player-protagonist yielded more than a few modest resources? What if the game took seriously the choice to not kill the Fort Frolic boss by substantively affecting the outcome of the game, perhaps providing a stratagem or advantage that helped not only Jack to survive but Cohen as well. What would it mean to stop play after "All Is Revealed" and decide the game ends in critique rather than recuperation? Or, if the player-protagonist forges ahead, how might the Little Sisters narrative and mechanic be reconfigured so that every Little Sister saved, not harvested, meant an additional ally in the final battle with Fontaine. Instead of the first-person shooter convention of Jack against Frank, mano a mano, the ultimate fight could be a collective, collaborative effort rather than a lone hero-savior's triumph. And, finally, might the endings reflect a deeper critique of the player-protagonist's choices and, more importantly, lack of choices? In the end, what might the game reimagine to embrace queer possibilities rather than reject or repudiate them, including queerer relationships, kinships, coalitions, and world making.

Players, developers, scholars, and game designers must resist the interactive fallacy and the transhumanist fantasy of power and control. The acts of designing, playing, and queering video games, then, must grapple with the fact that interface, mechanics, programming, platform, and electromagnetic states simultaneously, ambivalently allow for some flexibility and heterogeneity yet are also determined and controlling, often in unseen and naturalized ways. A queer and critical approach to video games provides further critique of the pleasures and pitfalls of this cyborg medium and imagines different kinds of games—

> games that encourage players to constantly shift the frame of the game, questioning what is inside or outside the game; games that play with the lamination between player and character, pushing and pulling against the connection through inventive forms of narrative play; games that emphasize metagaming, or that connect the magic circle so closely with external contexts that the game appears synchronous with everyday life.[37]

A queer and critical approach must think about ways to play games and make games that take advantage of the affordances of digital computers as well as the happy accidents, workarounds, and transformations that provide alternative practices, opportunities, and endgames. A queer and critical approach must think about what Galloway calls "countergaming," which does not simply identify "alternate formal strategies" of gaming but actively employs and gleefully explores those strategies.[38] By extension, a queer and critical approach might imagine what might be called queergaming, ways of playing against the grain, against normative design, and ways of designing gamic experiences that foreground not only alternative narrative opportunities but ludic ones as well. Or, in the words of Adrienne Shaw, "more than just studying the presence of queerness in games, I think the time is ripe to push forward with work that uses queer theory to confront the norms within game studies and push queer theory to engage more directly in challenging the homophobic norms of game culture."[39] Cohen's strutting and fretting on *BioShock*'s stage might look and feel different, Jack's role and goal might break with convention, and the player's integration into the circuit of game narrative, mechanic, and play might be disrupted, even oppositional. To reiterate and bring the three frames back around, queergaming—ultimately unrealized in the illusory promise of *BioShock*—embraces the meshes and messes, the possibilities and improbabilities, the gaps and glitches, the overlaps and undertexts, and the dissonances and resonances of play, player, and program. It delights in creativity and uncertainty. Queergaming is, to reprise Tenenbaum's phrase, "a chance to learn, to find love, to live" beyond the technonormative matrix, to imagine play, exploration, even failure that resists the check box, the Boolean, that rewrites protocol and refuses the posthuman fantasies of choice and control.

EDMOND Y. CHANG is Visiting Assistant Professor in the Department of Women's and Gender Studies at the University of Oregon. He writes about technoculture, gender and sexuality, digital games, popular culture, and contemporary American literature. A recent publication, "Love Is in the Air: Queer (Im)Possibility and Straightwashing in *FrontierVille* and *World of Warcraft*," appeared in *QED: A Journal of GLBTQ Worldmaking*.

Notes

1. *BioShock*, "Information," http://www.bioshockgame.com/site/us/ (accessed February 22, 2017).
2. Ibid.
3. *BioShock*, "Gene Bank," http://www.bioshockgame.com/site/us/ (accessed February 22, 2017).
4. Julian Murdoch, "BioShock," *Gamers with Jobs*, June 5, 2007, https://www.gamerswithjobs.com/node/1008276.
5. Eve Kosofsky Sedgwick, *Tendencies* (Durham, NC: Duke University Press, 1993), 8.
6. Ibid.
7. Anna Anthropy, "Now We Have Voices: Queer Games Are Important," *Auntie Pixelante*, January 12, 2013, http://www.auntiepixelante.com/?p=1888.
8. Judith Butler, *Bodies That Matter: On the Discursive Limits of "Sex"* (New York: Routledge, 1993), 42.
9. Alexander Galloway, *Protocol: How Control Exists after Decentralization* (Cambridge, MA: MIT Press, 2004), 30.
10. Katie Salen and Eric Zimmerman, *Rules of Play: Game Design Fundamentals* (Cambridge, MA: MIT Press, 2004), 80.
11. For more on these challenges to dominant game culture and their backlashes, see chapters 2, 3, and 4.
12. Cary Wolfe, *What Is Posthumanism?* (Minneapolis: University of Minnesota Press, 2010), xv.
13. Humanity Plus, "Transhumanist Declaration," 2009, http://humanityplus.org/philosophy/transhumanist-declaration/.
14. Dale Carrico, "Technology Is Making Queers of Us All," *Armor Mundi*, March 5, 2006, http://amormundi.blogspot.com/2006/03/technology-is-making-queers-of-us-all.html.
15. Ibid.
16. Ibid.
17. Alexander R. Galloway, *Gaming: Essays on Algorithmic Culture* (Minneapolis: University of Minnesota Press, 2006), 17.
18. Julian Stallabrass, "Just Gaming: Allegory and Economy in Computer Games," *New Left Review*, March–April 1993, http://newleftreview.org/?page=article&view=1706.
19. Salen and Zimmerman, *Rules of Play*, 450–451.
20. Quoted in *Second Skin*, directed by Juan Carlos Pineiro Escoriaza (Pure West Films, 2009), DVD.
21. Ibid.
22. Galloway, *Gaming*, 106.
23. Salen and Zimmerman, *Rules of Play*, 451.
24. Ayn Rand, "Man's Rights," 1963, https://ari.aynrand.org/issues/government-and-business/individual-rights.
25. Leigh Alexander, "'The Aberrant Gamer': An Evening with Sander Cohen," *GameSetWatch*, September 6, 2007, http://www.gamesetwatch.com/2007/09/column_the_aberrant_gamer_an_e.php.
26. Lisa Nakamura, *Cybertypes: Race, Ethnicity, and Identity on the Internet* (New York: Routledge, 2002), 3.
27. Denis Farr, "Queer Characters: BioShock," *Vorpal Bunny Ranch*, September 9, 2016, https://vorpalbunnyranch.wordpress.com/2016/09/09/queer-characters-bioshock.
28. Though the code itself remained in effect until 1968, the provision against any mention of homosexuality was scaled back in 1961 (with the impending release of William Wyler's *The Children's Hour*, whose producers threatened to release the film without code approval if the provision stood).

29. Jagger Gravning, "How Video Games Are Slowly, Quietly Introducing LGBT Heroes," *The Atlantic*, February 25, 2014, http://www.theatlantic.com/entertainment/archive/2014/02/how-video-games-are-slowly-quietly-introducing-lgbt-heroes/284017/.

30. Farr, "Queer Characters."

31. Sedgwick, *Tendencies*, 8.

32. Thomas Foster, *The Souls of Cyberfolk: Posthumanism as Vernacular Theory* (Minneapolis: University of Minnesota Press, 2005), xxvii.

33. *BioShock* (Irrational Games, 2007), Xbox 360.

34. Foster, *The Souls of Cyberfolk*, xxvi.

35. Ibid.

36. Nakamura, *Cybertypes*, xv.

37. Salen and Zimmerman, *Rules of Play*, 455.

38. Galloway, *Gaming*, 111.

39. Adrienne Shaw, "Circles, Charmed and Magic: Queering Game Studies," *QED: A Journal in GLBTQ Worldmaking* 2, no. 2 (2015): 87. See also chapters 11 and 12.

AFTERWORD

Racism, Sexism, and Gaming's Cruel Optimism

LISA NAKAMURA

> The future of the culture wars is here, and it's Gamergate.
>
> —Kyle Wagner, "The Future of the Culture Wars Is Here, and It's Gamergate"

I HAVE BEEN LUCKY ENOUGH TO TEACH UNIVERSITY-LEVEL COURSES ON VIDEO game studies for several years. While my other digital media courses have a good mix of female and male students, my game courses have attracted very few women. In their earliest iterations, a full class of thirty students might enroll only one or two women, making me dreadfully afraid that they might drop the class; the numbers have improved but are still unbalanced. My game classes have, however, been quite racially diverse. These classes have been a laboratory for learning about what students really think of racism and sexism in video games and gaming culture. My students readily admit that racism and sexism are pervasive, that these issues are serious obstacles to equal participation, and that gamers and the game industry can be brutal to women, people of color, sexual minorities, and anyone who signals difference online. These students care about gaming, enough to devote serious thought and attention to this problem both during class discussion and in their written work.

Over the years my students have been extremely consistent in advocating two strategies to address gaming's racism and sexism. The first is to rehabilitate games by diversifying game makers; they believe that hiring more women and programmers of color is the only way to teach the industry how to make diverse games. This strategy imagines that the games themselves and their industries produce racist and sexist games and cultures, and that different games can solve this problem. This argument has a long tradition in media studies: the notion that the presence of more female and racialized bodies will immunize the media products that they help to produce from inequality can be found in debates about diversity in film and television as well.

The second and more chilling strategy is to posit that it is "bad" female and nonwhite gamers themselves who are the problem. My students certainly don't mean this in a moralistic sense; what they mean, rather, is that if marginalized gamers become elite players they can rehabilitate other gamers' race and gender problems. They agree that the best strategy for creating social justice—the freedom not to be harassed while playing games—is for stigmatized players to create habitable spaces for themselves by displays of superior skill, by proving their worth by dominating other players, in other words by using procedural meritocracy. They believe that rights accrue to those who can leverage the mechanics of the game to create a win-condition for themselves and by implication for their gender, race, and sexuality.

This strategy invariably comes along with a story, and the story is always a variation of the one that follows. If from a man: "A buddy of mine was playing *Halo* once, and a bunch of other players were hassling a female player really bad, calling her a cunt, telling her to make them a sandwich. And she was a really good player, and she pwned all of them, and that totally changed the way that I view women in gaming now. It also shut them up." If from a woman: "I was playing as a female, and other players could hear my voice over the chat, and I was getting catcalled, but when they found out that I was a girl but that I knew how to play, it stopped because I earned their respect and showed I was a real gamer."

As Carol Stabile found in her study of gender-swapping as a form of "making gender" in *World of Warcraft* (2004–2014, Blizzard), some of the female players she interviewed saw their skillful play as a form of gender uplift within the game. One player explained that "she thought it was important to play the game and play it well as a female toon because it communicated a positive message about female identity; that women could be powerful, strong, and excellent players."[1] Helen Kennedy's writing about female *Quake* (1996, id Software) players notes the same: her informants reveled in beating male players as women. Though they disavowed the term "feminist" to describe themselves, Kennedy defined them as such since their labor within the game helped to make the space more diverse.[2] The satisfaction that comes from talking softly and carrying a big stick is real. However, it perpetuates meritocratic ways of thinking about freedom from racism and sexism within games that make these things seem not rights at all but rather privileges to be earned.

Believing in meritocratic play as the path to acceptance and respectability for minorities and women in sexist and racist gaming cultures is the cruelest kind of optimism.[3] In an interview about her book *Cruel Optimism*, Lauren Berlant writes,

> Why is it so hard to leave those forms of life that don't work? Why is it that, when precariousness is spread throughout the world, people fear giving up on the institutions that have worn out their confidence in living? . . . In all of these scenes of "the good life," the object that you thought would bring happiness becomes an object that deteriorates the conditions for happiness. But its presence represents *the possibility of happiness as such*. And so losing the bad object might be deemed worse than being destroyed by it. That's a relation of cruel optimism.[4]

What are games but the "possibility of happiness as such"? Women, minorities, and queers who play in this way are doing "social justice" the right way. They are embodying liberal virtues: self-reliance, unfettered competition in unregulated space, in short, a neoliberal fantasy of the entrepreneurial self's power in precarious times. They are not breaking the game by seeking to changes its rules, customs, or its liberal contract. Gaming's cruel optimism exploits minority gamers' fierce attachment to the medium and sutures it to a notion of social justice that can only be earned, not given.

Instead of advocating for procedural meritocracy—earning the right to question or change the rules by excelling at the game, I agree with science-fiction writer John Scalzi, author of the viral blog post "Straight White Male: The Lowest Difficulty Setting There Is."[5] As he writes, the "game" is stacked against many of us, and life is already on the highest difficulty setting for queers, for women, for people of color. Becoming the gamic model minority by outperforming others within the game is not going to change that. Leveling up in-game isn't a path to social justice; instead, as Berlant reminds us, believing that it is exemplifies a uniquely technocratic form of cruel optimism.

As Berlant writes, the period between the 1990s and the present in the United States is characterized by the development of a new "historical sensorium" that reflects the "frayed fantasies" of "postwar optimism for democratic access to the good life."[6] As opportunities for this life recede, the very idea of fairness seems to recede as well. Berlant explains that the desire for this idea, for a "meritocracy, the sense that liberal-capitalist society will reliably provide opportunities for individuals to carve out relations of reciprocity that seem fair and that foster life as a process of adding up to something and constructing cushions for enjoyment," drives unproductive, even painful attachments to objects that can't satisfy it.[7]

Thus it is that games are particularly cherished during our economically precarious times; not only do they let users feel what a particular vision of "the good life" is like—acquiring and owning the trappings of hyperconsumptive luxury such as rare and exotic cars, extravagant houses, and virtual women that look like models or porn stars—they produce these things as a consequence of ones' own behavior or play. Players can have that elusive and satisfying feeling of having earned privilege, of engaging in a meritocracy that works the way that it should.

As game scholar Ian Bogost writes, video games are procedural media; they fundamentally index user activity to the computer's programmed responses to that input.[8] They are algorithmic. And while the algorithms or set of rules that many Americans believe have governed access to the good life—defined as job security, a comfortable retirement, the right to be safe and secure and free from violence—have proven themselves broken, games appeal all the more because they embody this very promise.

Thus, gamers' intense attachment to games reflects the opposite of guilty pleasure, much less time wasting. In a viciously neoliberal economy, gaming feels like a virtuous pleasure, for games reward player labor, while, in contrast, labor in the real world is often undervalued, treated as surplus or even as worthless.

Though Berlant does not write about video games at all in her work, the period of US culture she examines in *Cruel Optimism* overlaps with the rise of video games as a mass medium, and her description of cruel optimism describes gaming's dynamic in interesting new ways. As she writes, "optimism is cruel when the object/scene that ignites a sense of possibility actually makes it impossible to attain the *expansive transformation* for which a person or a people risks striving."[9] Games make vividly visible what transformation might look like. The strict procedurality of games both satisfies and ignites desires for fairness in the context of a US culture that is patently unfair, particularly for racial minorities and women. The attachment to games can be a cruel one for all players, but especially for those who are subject to even more unfair proceduralities and forms of systematic discrimination in real life.

What can we learn from queer theory and critical ethnic studies as practiced by scholars such as Berlant, who do not study games but are centrally concerned with questions of nation, desire, attachment, feeling, and identity? There is much at stake in bringing this kind of work to bear on the state of video games and race, especially as moments of racial and gendered violence coalesce around the cultural debates surrounding gaming's famously uncivil cultures.

Gaming is a bellwether medium. And in 2014, it became more apparent how the two are related. The summer of 2014 saw two major cultural crises in the United States involving violence against women and minorities. These crises brought together racial violence, gendered violence, and gaming within the same chronological framework, and looking at them together reveals how rule-based systems such as the law and algorithmic ones such as gaming share a similar dynamic. The first of these centered around protests against shootings of young black men by white police officers, and the second, dubbed Gamergate, showed the world the extent of gaming's misogyny and internal conflicts over death threats made against female gamers, critics, and game developers by a cadre of male gamers.

A black teenager, Michael Brown, was shot by Darren Wilson, a white police officer, on August 9, 2014, in Ferguson, Missouri. This incident dominated both the traditional media outlets and social media as intense protests, vigils, and public anger proved that black and white people held strongly differing opinions about the majority white police department's lack of respect for black lives. A viral media campaign would ensue and travel along social media such as Twitter. The ferment continued into November, when a grand jury decided not to indict Wilson for the murder of Brown. The #BlackLivesMatter movement, which started in 2012 to protest the killing of another young black man, Trayvon Martin, by a police officer, trended during this period. It served as a channel for users' frustrations that widespread institutional racism made it such that the good life, indeed the possession of life at all, might be unattainable for young black men in the United States.

Another incident that proved the precariousness of the good life for those who are not white males surfaced almost exactly at the same time. In early August 2014, game developer Zoë Quinn received a number of death threats from members of the gaming community who had read claims from a former boyfriend that she had slept with a writer for *Kotaku*, a popular gaming blog, in order to receive positive reviews for her game *Depression Quest*. Quinn was subjected to a campaign of harassment so virulent that she was forced to flee her house. A few months later games critic Anita Sarkeesian received (a new round of) death threats as well for her video series *Tropes vs Women in Video Games* that critiqued misogyny in video games and was also forced to flee her home.

Both Gamergate and the Michael Brown case made it abundantly clear that the United States does not offer a level playing field to women and people of color. Players of color must negotiate intense and sometimes painful attachments to a dream of equality and respect earned through good play both within and without games. It is precisely because games are such important sites of attachment for players that they merit the nuanced critique and careful research from scholars such as those whose essays appear in this book. Much of the writing produced on games appears in ephemeral media such as blogs, written by gamers with varying amounts of interest in questions of identity who do not have the time or mandate to produce carefully researched game scholarship. This is precisely the moment for games scholarship originating from ethnic studies, women's studies, queer studies, film studies, and cultural studies to intervene in this ongoing conversation, and to strategize about the future of race, gender, sexuality, and digital media.

For strategy is central to many forms of race critique. For example, the foundational woman-of-color feminist anthology, *This Bridge Called My Back*, is about tactics and strategy, two notions at the heart of gamic structure.[10] This book's shared vision shows the reader how to make another world when the one you're in excludes you. It has a radical vision for letting go of the things that may have given you joy—the faith in meritocracy, for example, that if we work twice as hard we can get almost as much—because they are not only false but very harmful to the self. Games are far too valuable, and pleasurable, to let go. The chapters in this book bring together an appreciation of these pleasures and an analysis of their politics that we badly need.

LISA NAKAMURA is Gwendolyn Calvert Baker Collegiate Professor of American Cultures and Digital Studies at the University of Michigan, Ann Arbor, and

Coordinator of the Digital Studies Program. She is the author of four books on race, gender, and digital media.

Notes

1. Carol Stabile, "'I Will Own You': Accountability in Massively Multiplayer Online Games," *Television and New Media* 15, no. 1 (2014): 43–57.

2. Helen Kennedy, "Female Quake Players and the Politics of Identity," in *Videogame, Player, Text*, ed. Barry Atkins and Tanya Krzywinska (Manchester, UK: Manchester University Press, 2007), 120–138.

3. Kyle Wagner, "The Future of the Culture Wars Is Here, and It's Gamergate," *Deadspin*, October 14, 2014, http://deadspin.com/the-future-of-the-culture-wars-is-here-and-its-gamerga-1646145844.

4. Lauren Berlant, "Lauren Berlant on Her Book *Cruel Optimism*," *Rorotoko*, June 5, 2012, http://rorotoko.com/interview/20120605_berlant_lauren_on_cruel_optimism/ (emphasis in original).

5. John Scalzi, "Straight White Male: The Lowest Difficulty Setting There Is," *Whatever*, May 15, 2012, http://whatever.scalzi.com/2012/05/15/straight-white-male-the-lowest-difficulty-setting-there-is/.

6. Lauren Berlant, *Cruel Optimism* (Durham, NC: Duke University Press, 2011), 3.

7. Ibid.

8. Ian Bogost, *Persuasive Games: The Expressive Power of Videogames* (Cambridge, MA: MIT Press, 2007).

9. Berlant, *Cruel Optimism*, 2 (emphasis added).

10. Cherríe Moraga, Gloria Anzaldua, and Toni Cade Bambara, *This Bridge Called My Back: Writings of Radical Women of Color* (New York: Kitchen Table, 1983).

INDEX

Page numbers in italics indicate material in figures or tables.

Aarseth, Espen, 48
Ackerman, Forrest "Forry," 74, 77
Adam (in *BioShock*), 239
Adams (in *Spec Ops: The Line*), 147, 150–151, 159, 163n20
Adorno, Theodor, 68
affirmative humor, 172
Africa, tropes of, 133, 136–137, 139–140. *See also Journey* (thatgamecompany)
"Afrogeek," 5
Afro Samurai (Namco Bandai Games), 112, 117, 128n19
agency, player, 167–169, 174; illusion of, 238; in *Jade Empire*, 214–215; parody and, 90; and queering of "straight" games, 198–203, 208–210, 235–237; race and, 5, 11, 112, 114–117, 159; in *Second Life*, 184; and women and children, 21, 31, 64, 93, 123, 159, 161
age of gamers, xi
Alexander, Leigh, 61, 234–235
allegorithm, 212, 221
Allison, Tanine, 153–154
Alomar, Sheva, xii
Alter Ego (Cooper), 179, 181, 190–191
American tropes, 62, 133, 136–139, 157–158
Among the Blood Elves (Britty), 99–102, *100*
Anable, Aubrey, 45
Andromeda, 92
Angell, Callie, 182
Annandale, David, 172
Anthropy, Anna, 7, 228
anxiety, real-world versus play, 47
Apocalypse Now (Coppola), 12, 148, 150, 152, 162n5
Apter, Emily, 185
The Art of Failure (Juul), 197, 201–203
Ashiety, Clare-Hope, 116
Assassin's Creed 3: Liberation (Ubisoft), xii
Atanasoski, Neda, 150
The Athena Factor (Hewlett et al.), 66, 69
Atlas Shrugged (Rand), 231–232
"attention whore" label, 82–84
authorial intent, 173
avatar(s): beauty norms in *World of Warcraft*, 98–99; exploring identities through, 180; as "partner," 179; race/ethnicity of, 185–186; sexualization of, 63; universal figure in *Journey*, 137–138

Babbage, Charles, 139
Baccolini, Raffaella, 111, 114, 116, 125–126
Bakhtin, Makhail, 91, 117
Baldur's Gate (BioWare), 214–215
Band of Brothers (TV series), 148
Banks, Miranda, 79
Barbie parody, 102
Barrett, Paul, 166
Barthes, Roland, 91
Barton, Matt, 167
Battlefield 3 (EA DICE), 133
Baudelaire, Charles, 38–39, 43, 52–53
Baudrillard, Jean, 125–126
Bayonetta (Platinum Games), 23, 37n20, 219
"Beat Up Anita Sarkeesian" (Ben Spurr), 58
Beck, John, 137
Ben (in *Night of the Living Dead*), 114–116, 125
Berlant, Lauren, 131, 246–248
Berzowska, Joanna, 140
"Best Friends Forever" skill tree, 41
BetterHumans.com, 229
Beyond Good and Evil (Ubisoft), 112
Bieber, Justin, 100
The Binding of Isaac (Valve), 213–214, 218, 221, 222–225

BioShock (Irrational Games), 85–86, 111, 112, 156, 227–240
BioWare, 214–216
Birdo (in *Super Mario Bros. 2*), 226n5
"bitch-goddess" in *The Last Seduction*, 34
Bittanti, Matteo, 43
Bittman, Michael, 46
"black cyberflaneur," 5
Black Girls Code, 64
Black Hawk Down (film), 148
#BlackLivesMatter movement, 3, 249
blacks in cosplay, 82–83
Blacks in Gaming, xiv. *See also* race/ethnicity
"blank spots on the map," 136–137
blindness as distinguishing feature, 169, 172–174
BlizzCon, 78
Blomkamp, Neill, 116
"Blood, Gore, Sex and Now: Race" (Marriott), xiv
Blood Elf avatars, 91, 98
bodies in cosplay, 76, 81, 83
Bodies That Matter (Butler), 76
bodily reconfigurations, 219
Body Heat (film), 34
body shaming, 83, 99–101
Bogg, Jan, 67
Bogost, Ian, 136, 168, 247
Bolton, Michele, 45, 47, 51
The Book of Eli (film), 116
booth babes, 62, 68, 84–86
Border House (blog), 213
Borderlands (Gearbox Software), 41, 111
Bound (film), 34
Boyle, Danny, 116
Boyz n the Hood (film), 171
Brayton, Sean, 116
Britty (*World of Warcraft* parody character), 99–101, *100*
Brock, André, 166
The Brother from Another Planet (film), 115–116
Brown, Jayna, 117
Brown, Michael, 248–249
Bryce, Jo, 6
Bryson, Valerie, 46
Buchanan, Ann, 182–184, *183*, 188
Bully (Rockstar Games), 199
Burj Khalifa (Khalifa Tower), 151
Burnout Revenge (Criterion Games), 198, 205–209
Burrill, Derek, 203
Burt, Martha, 66
Burtynsky, Edward, 162n7
Butler, Judith, xiv, 76, 99–100, 228
Butler, Octavia, 127n16
Byers, Niamh, 191
Byrne, Ciara, 66

Caillois, Roger, 198
Cake Mania (Sandlot), 43
California in mid-1990s, 164, 172
Call of Duty, 62, 133, 204
Cameron, James, 116, 206
Campbell, Joseph, 143
Capcom, 66
Carrico, Dale, 229
Cerberus Productions, 78
CGA (Casual Games Association), 40
Chang, Alenda, 134
Chen, Jenova, 131–132, 142–143
Chess, Shira, 46, 56n34
Chicago World's Fair (1893), 138–139
Children of Men (film), 116
The Children's Hour (film), 243n28
Chow-White, Peter, 166
CJ (Carl Johnson; in *GTA: San Andreas*), 165–172, 176n1, 177n15
Clementine (in *The Walking Dead*), 117, 120–125, 128n27, 128n29
"Close Enough" skill, 41
cloth as technology, 139–140, *140*
"Cloudangel as Barbie in *World of Warcraft*" (Cod), 102
Cobb, Silas, 236
codes of representation, 3–4
Cohen, Sander (in *BioShock*), *234*, 234–235, 238
Colebrook, Clare, 218
Coleman, B., 186
Coleman, Robin Means, 115
Collier, Mary, 53
Comic-Con, 77, 80, 84
comments on gaming sites, 60–62
Conrad, Joseph, 148, 150
Consalvo, Mia, 6, 59, 175, 203
CONsent, 86–88
constructivism and gender, 90
conventions, 62, 74, 77–78, 86–88, 109. *See also* cosplay
conversations within games, 214–215
Cook, Nathalie, 85
Cooper, Robbie, 179, 181–182, 186–190
Coppola, Francis Ford, 148
cosplay, 74–75; as becoming mainstream, 87–88; body manipulation and crossplay in, 82; and criticism of revealing costumes, 82; DIY culture of, 79; gender of panelists on, 78; harassment during, 76–77, 82–87; industrial

incorporation of, 85–86; and Morojo Douglas, 77–78; negative and positive coverage of, 74–75; networking of, 79–90; as pathway to producer role, 76; presence of women in, 78–80; professionalizing of, 84–85; as providing legitimacy for women, 80; and public body shaming, 83; scholarship on, 75–77; skin color in, 82–83; transformative potential of, 76
Cosplay Tutorial, 80
countergaming, 242
Crane, Luke, 57
Crash Override Network, 68
Craven, Nubiian, 185
critical dystopias, 110–112
"The Critical Power of Virtual Dystopias" (Schulzke), 111–112
Croft, Lara, xii, 23, 36n7, 37n20, 48, 85
Cronenberg, David, 148
Cross, David, 169
crossplay, 82
Cruel Optimism (Berlant), 246–248
Crysis (Crytek), 111
Csikszentmihalyi, Mihaly, 46
Cuarón, Alfonso, 116
cultural policing, 39, 59
"The Culture Industry" (Adorno and Horkheimer), 68
Cumberbatch, Chaka, 82

Daedalus Project, 231
damsel in distress trope, 92–96
Da Nang Boys (in *GTA: San Andreas*), 170
Davis, Jordan, 119
Dawn Star (in *Jade Empire*), 215–216
Day Z (Bohemia Interactive), 111
Dead Reckon (blog), 66
Dean and Britta, 183
"deep flow," 46
Delany, Samuel, 127n16
Delicious (Zylom), 43
DeLillo, Don, 129
demographics of gamers, x–xi
DePass, Tanya, 68
Depression Quest (Zoë Quinn), xii, xiii, 60, 249
de-racialization, 171
desert, double temporality of, 143–144
The Desert (Van Dyke), 129, 131, 138
Deus Ex (Ion Storm), 111
Deus Ex: Human Revolution (Eidos), 112
DeviantArt and cosplay, 79–80
Diaper Dash (Zemnott), 43
Dibbell, Julian, 190
Dickerman, Charles, 165
Dickwolves incident, 63–64
Dietrichson, Phyllis (in *Double Indemnity*), 22, 27
Dietz, Tracy, 62
digital blackface/minstrelsy, 166
digital portraiture in gaming, 180, 190–191
Dill, Karen, 62
Diner Dash (Gamelab), 40, 43–52, *44*, *49*
disability as distinguishing feature, 169, 172–174, 177–178n33
Dishonored (Arkane Studios), 111
Disney princesses, 92
District 9 (film), 116
DIY (do-it-yourself) cosplay culture, 79
DmC: Devil May Cry (Capcom), 219
Doane, Mary Ann, 21
Dobson, Hugo, 177n26
Donkey Kong hack, 104n4
Doty, Alexander, 200
Double Indemnity (film), 22, 24, 27
Douglas, Myrtle "Morojo," 74, 77–78
Dragon Age (BioWare), 66–67, 228
"dream life" of a culture, 148
dress code for promotional models, 84
Dying Light (Techland), 111
Dyson, Miles (in *Terminator 2*), 117
dystopias and racial representation, 110–113, *113*

Eglash, Ron, 140
Electronic Arts, 64
Electronic Entertainment Expo (E3) events, xiii
Elizabeth (in *BioShock Infinite*), 85–86
Ellie (in *The Last of Us: Left Behind*), 112–113, 115, 123
embodiment and race, 166
"Empathy Games" (Smith), 119–120
empathy of the viewer, 184
Entertainment Software Association (ESA) 2016 survey, 181
Entertainment Weekly, 131
epistemological trouble, femme fatale as, 21
e-textiles and wearable computers, *140*, 140–141
Eurogamer Expo, 62
Everett, Lee (in *The Walking Dead*), 117, 118–125, 128n29
Everquest (Sony Online Entertainment), 98
exoticization of disability, 173–174

Fable (Lionhead Studio), 214, 228
Facebook, 14, 43, 81, 83, 86–87
FAIL Blog, 83
failing at video games: by accident versus on purpose, 202, 204; paradox of, 201–202;

failing at video games (*continued*)
pleasure from, 203; queering of "straight" games, 198–203, 208–210; toward and against the system, 205–207, 209; varieties of, 204. *See also* queering of "straight" games
fake geek/gamer girls, 34, 71n30, 80–82
Fallout (Bethesda), 111
Fallout 2 (Black Isle Studio), 214
fan identity, 76
"fantastic failures," 203
Farr, Denis, 236
fascism, production of, 68
Fashion Boutique (Total Eclipse), 43
Fat, Ugly or Slutty (website), 62
fat shaming, 83
"fed" comments, 83
fem-ing characters, 82
The Feminine Mystique (Friedan), 93–94
feminism as perceived threat, 22, 34
Feminist Frequency, xii, xiv, 36n7
feminization of mass gaming, 40–43, 52
femmes fatales: in film, 19–24, 27–28, 34, 35n1, 36n12; in gaming, 22–34, *26*, *28*; as threat to male dominance, 34
Fennoy, Dave, 118
field of sight, 134
Filamena on #1reasonwhy, 62
"final girl" of slasher horror, 37n27
Finnegan, Martin, 236
Firefall (Red 5 Studios), 85
Fishburne, Laurence, 116
Fitzpatrick, Kyle, 236
Flaming Classics (Doty), 200
Fleetwood, Nicole, 139
flexibility in gameplay, 29, 45, 52–53, 140, 180, 230
Flo (in *Diner Dash*), 43–52
flow, 45–46
Flow (thatgamecompany), 132
Flower (thatgamecompany), 132
Fonda, Peter, 165
Fontaine, Frank, 238
fort-da game, 201, 209
Foster, Hal, 184, 188
Foster, Thomas, 238
Fox, D. Harrell, 120
Fox, Jesse, 63
Framed (Loveshack), 35
Frasca, Gonzalo, 167
freedom of speech defense of abuse, 63
"FREE SPEACH: A Second Life Machinima Parody" (Gabrielle Trépanier-Jobin and MIT Game Lab), 103, *103*
Freud, Sigmund, 198, 201
Friedan, Betty, 93–94
Fron, Janine, 59

Gaider, David, 66–67
Gaige (in *Borderlands 2*), 41
Galbraith, Modesty, 185
"The Gallant Marksman" (Baudelaire), 38–39, 43, 52–53
Galloway, Alexander R., 133, 141, 198, 212–213, 229–231
Gamasutra, 64
Game Developer Magazine salary survey, 65, *65*, 67
Game Developers Conference (GDC), 109
gamer demographics, xii, 6, 40, 57–61, 64, 67, 179–181
Gamergate, xii–xiii, 34, 42, 60, 66–68, 72n56
Games and Culture, 1
game space, 64, 212–213, 219
GameSpot (blog), 131
Game Studies, 1
Gaming (Galloway), 212
Gaming at the Edge (Shaw), 6–7, 180
gaming journalism, xiv
Garrelts, Nate, 167
GayGamer.net, 236
Geddes, Tilly, 191
Gee, James Paul, 178n36
Geek Out (blog), 81
gender and war, 156–160, *158*, *160*
Gender Trouble (Butler), xiv, 76
Generation Kill (TV series), 148
GIC (gaming industrial complex), ix–xii
"girlfriend mode," 41
Girls Who Code, 64
"Girl Who Cries a Tear" (Warhol), 183
Giroux, Henry, 116
"goal rules" versus "manipulation rules," 167–168
González, Jennifer, 132
Good Morning America, xi
Grandpré, Aveline de, xii
Grand Theft Auto (Rockstar Games), xi–xii, 6
Grand Theft Auto V (Rockstar Games), 61
Grand Theft Auto: San Andreas (Rockstar North), 164–175
Grand Theft Auto: Vice City (Rockstar North), 166, 171
The Grasshopper (Suits), 217
Gravning, Jagger, 235
Graziano, Crystal, 85
Grimes, Rick (in *The Walking Dead*), 118

Grubb, Amy, 63
Guardians (in *Journey*), 140–141
Gun Crazy (film), 26

Halberstam, Jack, 197, 202–203, 208, 214, 216–217, 219, 223
Half-Life (Valve), 111, 112
Hall, Stuart, 3
Haniver, Jenny, 61–62, 68, 73n64
Hannosh, Michele, 91
harassment and intolerance: combating, 42; documenting, 57–58, 62, 64–66, 86; Gamergate, xii–xiii, 34, 42, 60, 66–68, 72n56; of trans people, 179–180
Haraway, Donna, 56n38
hard-core versus casual gaming: and adolescent male sensibility, 59; as code for male versus female gaming, 40–41, 54n7; and hard-core pornography connotations, 58; and interruptibility and leisure, 45–46, 53. *See also* *Diner Dash* (Gamelab)
Hardy, Jessica, 188, 191
Harisu, 179–181, 186, 191
Harrell, D. Fox, 6–7
Harries, Dan, 91
Harris, Tony, 81, 82, 87
Harry (in *Night of the Living Dead*), 115
Hays Code (Motion Picture Production Code), 36n4, 235, 243n28
heads-up display (HUD) in military games, 133–134
Heart of Darkness (Conrad), 148–150, 152
Heavy game magazine, 83
Heavy Rain (Quantic Dream), 20, 28–34, *31*, *32*
Heir, Manveer, 109
Hemingway, John, 41
Hernandez, Patricia, 61
Heroes of Cosplay (TV series), 75
heteronormativy in gaming, 213, 221–223
Hills, Whitney, 66
Himsl, Florian, 213
Hjorth, Larissa, 75–76, 79
Hochschild, Arlie, 53
Hocking, Clint, 156, 163n15
homosexuality. *See* LGBTQ gaming
hooks, bell, 135
Horkheimer, Max, 68
"How to Gank a Girl Gamer" (ShrineNI), 67
Hugh, Drew, 188–191, *189*
Huizinga, Johan, 198
Hulk (Radical Entertainment), 188
humanitarian missions, 157
Humanity Plus, 229
Humphreys, Sara, 157
Hunicke, Robin, 137
Hutcheon, Linda, 91

I Am Alive (Ubisoft), 111
I Am Legend (film), 116
identification *as* versus identification *with*, 181
identity construction in cosplay, 76
identity politics, 110, 217–218
"identity tourism," 138
"I" design methodology, 66
IGN (blog), 131
Immersion (Cooper), 181–182, 186–191, *189*
"imperialist nostalgia," 135
"I'm Too Sexy" (Bionic), 101–102
In a Queer Time and Place (Halberstam), 216, 223
I Need Diverse Games, 3, 68
Infamous: Second Son (Sucker Punch), 112
Inman, Matthew, 64
"Interrotron" apparatus, 187
interruptibility, 45–46
interventionist criticism, x, xiv
"Intimidation Game" (*Law and Order: SVU* episode), xiii–xiv
Irigaray, Luce, 92
Irrational Games, 85–86
Islamic State terrorism, xiii
iterability, 76
Ito, Mizuko, 43

Jack (in *BioShock*), 227, 230–233
Jackson, Samuel L., 165, 168
Jacob (in *Mass Effect*), 117
Jacob's Ladder (film), 148
Jade Empire (BioWare), 212, 213–216, 218, 221–224
Jagoda, Patrick, 141
Japan, cosplay in, 74, 88n2
Jarhead (film), 148
Jenkins, Henry, 75–76, 79
Jezebel, 86
Joel (in *The Last of Us: Left Behind*), 112–113, 115, 123
Jones, Duane, 114
Journey (thatgamecompany), *130*, 130–138, *134*, 141–143
Joyrich, Lynne, 42–43
Joystiq (blog), 131
Juul, Jesper, 45, 52, 197, 201–203, 207–209, 220

Kaiser, Rowan, 41
Kaplan, Amy, 157

Kee (in *Children of Men*), 116
Kendl (in *GTA: San Andreas*), 168
Kennedy, Helen, 246
Kenny (in *The Walking Dead*), 118–120
Keogh, Brendan, 155, 161
Kerr, Aphra, 59
Kickstarter crowdfunding, xii
Killer, Sushi, 86–87
kill feed, 133
killing time as gaming genre, 43
King, Rodney, 171
Kirkpatrick, Graeme, 218
Konrad, John (in *Spec Ops: The Line*), 147, 149, 151
Kotaku, 60, 61, 68, 87, 249
Krahulik, Mike, 63
Kurtz (in *Apocalypse Now*), 148–152

Lamerichs, Nicolle, 76
Larry (in *The Walking Dead*), 118
The Last of Us (Naughty Dog), 109–115, 117–118, 123, 126
The Last Seduction (film), 34
Lauretis, Teresa de, 92
Law and Order: SVU, xiii–xiv
Lawrence, Francis, 116
League of Legends (Riot Games), 83
The Legend of Zelda (Nintendo), 97
leisure gap, 39, 40, 43, 46, 53, 55n29
Leonard, David J., 5–6, 165–166
Levine, Ken, 227–228
Lewis, Joseph H., 26
LGBTQ gaming: and *Border House* (blog), 213; homophobia in game interpretation, 199–201; homosexuality in parody, 101; lesbianism as becoming, 220; queering of normative space-time, 218–219, 223; queering of "straight" games, 198–203, 208–210; queer logic of becoming, 216–218, 221–225; queer representation in *Jade Empire*, 214–216; Sander Cohen as fey fatale, *234*, 234–235; scholarship on, 198; self-policing against overt content, 235–236
Lineage II, 179–180, 186
Lisa (*World of Warcraft* parody character), 99, 101, 105n40
Little Sisters (in *BioShock*), 239–241
lo-fi independent games, 222
logic of the game, challenging the, 203
Loguidice, Bill, 167
Lollipop Chainsaw (Grasshopper Manufacture), 84
"The Loneliness of the Female Coder" (Byrne), 66
"ludonarrative dissonance," 156, 163n15
ludus versus paidea, 167, 174
Lugo (in *Spec Ops: The Line*), 147, 150, 159, 163n20
Lyne, Adrian, 148

machineries of representation, 3–4
machinima parodies, 91, 99–102, *100*
Madd Dogg (in *GTA: San Andreas*), 168
Madden NFL 13 (EA Sports), 219
male gaze, 86–87
"manipulation rules" versus "goal rules," 167–168
Mann, Derek, 109
Manufactured Landscapes (film), 162n7
"Mario and Princess Sex Tape" (College Humor), 94, 97
marketing of sexism, 42
Marlene (in *The Last of Us*), 113, *113*, 115, 117
Marriott, Michael, xiv
Mars, Ethan (in *Heavy Rain*), 29, 32–33
Martin, Trayvon, 119, 249
Marx, Nick, 177n31
Mary Sue, 86
masculinity as excuse for rape culture, 63
masochistic passivity, 208. *See also* queering of "straight" games
Mass Effect (BioWare), 111–112, 117, 199, 226n6, 228
masses, 42, 52, 200
The Matrix trilogy (films), 116
Mattes, Eva and Franco, 181, 184, 191
Matthews, Dennis, 109
Max Payne 2 (Remedy Entertainment), 20, 24–28, *26*, *28*
McMillen, Edmund, 213
Mendes, Sam, 148
Men Going Their Own Way forum, 59
meritocratic play, 246–247
Metafilter (blog), 87
Metal Gear Solid (Konami), 226n5
Miami, 166
microflow, 46–47
Middle-earth: Shadow of Mordor (Monolith Productions), 111
Middle Eastern tropes, 132, 133, 139. *See also* *Journey* (thatgamecompany)
Mika, Mike, 104n4
Milestone, Lewis, 22
"militainment," 160
military shooter games, 132, 133–134, 153–156. *See also Spec Ops: The Line* (Yager Development)
Miller, Kiri, 175
Mirror's Edge (Digital Illusions CE), 111
"Misogyny, Racism, and Homophobia" (Heir), 109–110

Mitchell, William J. T., 143
MMORPGs (massively multiplayer online role-playing games), 98
modernism as Eurocentric, 152
Modleski, Tania, 47
Moleva, Anna, 85–86
Moore, Alan, 110
"Morojo," 74, 77–78
Morpheus (in *The Matrix*), 116
Morris, Errol, 187
Morrison, Toni, x–xi
Motion Picture Production Code (Hays Code), 36n4, 235, 243n28
Mourningstar (in *Firefall*), 85
Moylan, Tom, 110–111, 114, 116, 125–126
Mullich, David, 64
multitasking by women, 44–47, 53
Mulvey, Laura, 1, 36n3

Nama, Adilifu, 117
Native American "savage," 129–130
nature, 139–140, *140*, 152
Nava, Matt, 137
Need for Speed (Criterion Games), 205, 209
Neff, Walter (in *Double Indemnity*), 22
neoliberalism, 7, 157–158
neo-noir, 20, 23, 26
networked warfare, 141–142
Neville, Robert (in *I Am Legend*), 116
Nidhogg (Messhof), 205, 209
Night of the Living Dead (film), 114–116, 125
Nigri, Jessica, 84
1984 (Orwell), 110
Ninja Ninja (in *Afro Samurai*), 117
Nintendo, 41, 72n56. *See also Super Mario Bros.* (Nintendo)
nondiscrimination policies, success of, 68
Norris, Michelle, xi
Nothing to Hide (NCase), 111
Not in the Kitchen Anymore (website), 62

Obama, Barack, x, xi
Olatunji, Olajide, 62
#1reasonwhy hashtag, 57–58, 62, 64–66
Operation Desert Storm, 134
O'Reilly, Bill, 163n11
Orientalism, 169–171, 173, 221
Origami Killer (in *Heavy Rain*), 29–30, 32
Orwell, George, 110
the "other," 39, 135, 138, 166

Paco (in *Heavy Rain*), 30, *31*
Paglen, Trevor, 136
paidea versus ludus, 167, 173–175
Paige, Madison (in *Heavy Rain*), 29, 32–33, 37nn26–27
Papers, Please (Lucas Pope), 111
Paris Spleen (Baudelaire), 38
parody, 90–92, 96–103, *100*, *103*
Parry, David, 174
Passage (Jason Rohrer), 204
Patapon (Pyramid), 201
PAX conventions, 63, 78, 80, 83–84
Payne, Matthew, 160
PBS Game/Show, xiv
Peacock, Joe, 81, 87
Penn, Chris, 165
Penny Arcade Expo, 62–63, 68
permadeath, 223
Petit, Carolyn, 61
Phantasmal Media (Harrell), 6
"phantasms" of culture, 7
Pixelles, 64
Place, Janey, 21–23
Plant, Sadie, 139
Platoon (film), 148
playable characters (PCs), xii, 20, 25–26, 164
player-character relations, nature of, 215–216
Playing the Race Card (Williams), 113
polymorphic poetics, 7
popular culture, feminization of, 52
pornotopia, 58
Portal (Valve), 111, 199–200
Potanin, Robin, 66
Prescott, Julie, 67
Prey (Human Head Studios), 112
Princess Peach (in *Super Mario Bros.*), 92–98, *95*, *96*, 104n12
"Princess Peach and Daisy vs. Michael Jackson" (anonymous), 94, *95*
princess-rescue plot device, 92–93
PS3 controller, 41
Pursued (film), 22

QTEs (quick time events), 29
Quake (id Software), 246
The Queer Art of Failure (Halberstam), 197, 202–203
queering of normative space-time, 218–219, 223
queering of "straight" games, 198–203, 208–210, 228, 232, 235–237
queer logic of becoming, 216–218, 221–225
Quinn, Zoë, xii, xiii, 60, 68, 249

race/ethnicity: in *Alter Ego*, 190–191; anti-Semitic humor, 177n31; of avatars in *Second Life*, 185; and Barack Obama, x, xi; black female playable characters (PCs), xii; blackness

race/ethnicity (*continued*)
as signifier for suffering and survival, 110; in *Diner Dash*, 56n38; in dystopias, 110, 112–113; of game players versus avatars, 181, 190–191; in *GTA: San Andreas*, 164, 169, 172–174; and imperial violence, 139; in *Journey*, 137–138; performing, 189; in *Second Life*, 186; in *The Simpsons*, 177n26; in *South Park*, 177n31; in *Spec Ops: The Line*, 148–153, *149*; in *13 Most Beautiful Avatars*, 185–186; and video game playing time, 176n10; white male developers depicting, 166; whites experiencing racial profiling, 175
Raina (in *Law and Order: SVU*), xiii–xiv
Rand, Ayn, 231–232
"Ran Fa Li" mission (in *GTA: San Andreas*), 171
rape culture, 61–64, 66
Rapp, Alison, 72n56
Red Dead Redemption (Rockstar San Diego), 157
Red 5 Studios, 85
religious fanaticism, 222–223
Remember Me (Dontnod Entertainment), 112
Reparaz, Mikel, 43
representation, 3–4, 48–52, 180–181
Resident Evil (Capcom), xii, 112, 166
Resogun (Housemarque), 111
Revolt, 72n56
rigging of games, 33
Right Said Fred, 102
Riley (in *The Last of Us: Left Behind*), 112–113, 117
"The Roast of Mario" (College Humor), 94
Rockstar North, 166
Rodriguez, Hector, 236
romance options within games, 214
Romero, George, 114–116, 127n9
RTX convention, 62
Rutter, Jason, 6
Ryan, Andrew, 232

sacrificial blackness, 110–113, *113*
Salen, Katie, 230–231
salary survey, 65, *65*, 67
"sales fallacy," 109
sand, 135, 152–153
San Diego Comic-Con, 80
Santiago, Kellee, 131, 135
Sarkeesian, Anita, xii–xiii, 36n7, 58, 60, 68, 92, 94, 249
Sartres, John-Paul, 91
Satchbag's Goods, xiv
Sax, Mona (in *Max Payne 2*), 24–28, *26*, *28*
Sayles, John, 115
Scalzi, John, 86, 247
scholarship on cosplay, 75–77
scholarship on gaming, ix–xi, 1–7, 36n7, 48, 175, 181, 198
scholarship on queerness in classic movies, 200
School House Shuffle (Sarbakan), 43
Schulzke, Marcus, 111–112
Scott, Ridley, 148
Scott, Suzanne, 75
Scraps of the Untainted Sky (Moylan), 110–111
screen tests, Warhol's. *See Thirteen Most Beautiful* (Warhol)
Second Life, xiii, 181, 184–186, 191
Second Skin (film), 230
Sedgwick, Eve Kosofsky, 236–237
selective blindness, 137
self-doubt, discrimination leading to, 66
Seltzer, Mark, 138
semiliving mesh of on- and off-screen bodies, 219–220
September 11 attacks, 141
sexist parody versus parody of sexism, 91, 96–98
sexual aggression: against children, 69; against femmes fatales, 30–31, *31*; in gaming, 61–64
sexual politics of video games, 213. *See also* women
Shaun (in *Heavy Rain*), 29–30, 33
Shaw, Adrienne, 2, 6–7, 31, 59, 180, 213, 242
"sheroes," xii
Shildrick, Margrit, 224–225
ShrineNI, 67
Siebers, Tobin, 173
Sienkiewicz, Matt, 177n31
Silk Fox (in *Jade Empire*), 215–216
The Simpsons, 177n26
The Sims (Maxis), 228
16-bit Sirens, 86, 87
Sky (in *Jade Empire*), 215
Skyrim (Bethesda), 111
slut shaming, xiii
Smith, Ryan, 119–120
Smith, Will, 116
"snake mother" costume, 77
Snow White, 93
soap opera narratives, 47
Sobchack, Vivian, 218–219
Sontag, Susan, 161
SoulCalibur IV (Namco), 204–205
South Park, humor in, 177n31
Spec Ops: The Line (Yager Development), 147–149, *149*; as antiwar military shooter game, 111–112, 160–162; and *Apocalypse Now*, 12, 148, 150, 152, 162n5; bantering dialogue in, 155; degeneration of Captain Walker in, 158–160; goal of, 149–150; and *Heart of Darkness*, 148, 150, 152; moral ambiguity in, 149–150, 153–156,

154; murder of civilians in, 158–160, *160*; rogue soldiers in, 150–151; role of women in, 157, *158*; ruined Dubai as backdrop for, 149, 151–153; Walt Williams on, 155
Spider (film), 148
Stabile, Carol, 246
Stables, Kate, 23
Stair Dismount (tAAt), 204
Stallabrass, Julian, 230
Star, Annie Laurie, 26
Starling, Juliet (in *Lollipop Chainsaw*), 84
Star Trek (TV series), 116
Star Wars: Battlefront (Pandemic Studios), 190–191
Star Wars: Knights of the Old Republic (BioWare), 215
Steam Greenlight, 60
Stern, D'arci, xii
stillies, 182
Stone, Oliver, 148
"Straight White Male" (Scalzi), 247
The Strange Love of Martha Ivers (film), 21–22
"strange temporalities," 216
struggle for meaning, 136
suicide, failing by, 205, 207. *See also* queering of "straight" games
Suits, Bernard, 217, 224
Sundén, Jenny, 219–220
Super Mario Bros. (Nintendo), 91–98, *95*, *96*, 226n5
Sweden rating system, xiv
Sweet (in *GTA: San Andreas*), 168

Takahashi, Nobuyuki, 74
The Taxidermist (Quantic Dream), 29
technologies of gender, games as, 90
"Technology's Making Queers of Us All" (Carrico), 229
techno-primitivism in *Journey*, 138–141, *140*
Tekken: Dark Resurrection (Namco), 188
temporalities, queer versus heteronormative, 217–218, 222–225
Tenenbaum, Brigid (in *BioShock*), 239, 242
Tenpenny, Frank, 168
Terminator 2 (film), 116
Terry, Jennifer, 157
Thacker, Eugene, 141
Think Progress, 86
third shift, 46
Thirteen Most Beautiful (Warhol), 181–184, *183*
13 Most Beautiful Avatars (Mattes), 181, 184–186, 191
This Bridge Called My Back (Moraga, Anzaldua, and Bambara), 249
Thompson, E. P., 53
time, 40, 43, 45, 53, 174–175
"Time, Work-Discipline, and Industrial Capitalism" (Thompson), 53
The Time Bind (Hochschild), 53
Toffler, Alvin, 75
Toledano, Gabrielle, 64
Tomb Raider (Eidos; Crystal Dynamics), 31, 36n7, 85, 98
trading system, patriarchical, 92
"traditional America," 153–154, 163n11
Tropes vs Women in Video Games (Sarkeesian), 249
True Lies (film), 206
Tumblr, 83, 86
Turner, Emily, 63
28 Days Later (film), 116
Twitter, 3, 57–58, 62, 64–66, 249

"ugly nerd" label, 82–84
"upskirt" pictures, 86
Urban Chaos (Mucky Foot Productions), xii

Vamp (in *Metal Gear Solid*), 226n5
Vanderhoef, John, 42
Van Dyke, John C., 129–131, 136, 138
V for Vendetta (Moore), 110
Vialpando, Cesar (in *GTA: San Andreas*), 169
victim blaming, 63
Victorian-era separate spheres, 60
video game industry: failure of, to address stereotyping, 2; GIC (gaming industrial complex), ix–xii; lack of women in production in, 57, 66–67; and #1reasonwhy hashtag, 57–58, 62, 64–66; as seeking female customers and employees, 19–20; and threats of sexual violence, 60
Voltaire, 91

Wagner, Kyle, 245
Wajcman, Judy, 46
Walker, Martin (in *Spec Ops: The Line*), 147, 155, 158–160
The Walking Dead (Telltale Games), 109–111, 117–126, *121*, *122*, *124*, 128n27, 128n29
Walsh, Raoul, 22
"Wanted: More Female Game Developers" (Mullich), 64
war and moral culpability, 150
"War Bytes" (Payne), 160
Warhol, Andy, 181–182, 186
Wark, McKenzie, 212–213, 216
War on Terror, 139
Watch Dogs (Ubisoft), 111

Water Dragon (in *Jade Empire*), 212
Watkins, S. Craig, 5, 189
Watts, Evan, 156–157
"we" and "you" in gaming, 199
wearable computers, *140*, 140–141
"We Are Not Heroes" (Williams), 156
weaving and Charles Babbage, 139–140
West, American, 136–139
Whalen, Zach, 167
Whatever (blog), 86
white phosphorous, 159, *160*
white supremacy, 157–158
"who fed" jokes, 83
Wii, 41
"The Wild Bunny" (Cohen), 236
Wilder, Billy, 22
Willard (in *Apocalypse Now*), 148–152
Williams, Linda, 58, 113
Williams, Walt, 148–149, 155–156
Wilson, Darren, 248–249
Winge, Theresa, 75
winning, 224. *See also* queering of "straight" games
Wintory, Austin, 136
Wired, 86
The Wizard of Oz (film), 200
Wolfe, Cary, 229
"The Woman's Labour" (Collier), 53
"woman's picture" genre, 19
women: as associated with domesticity, maternity, 93; and "attention whore" label, 82–84, 87; and beauty, 81, 98–99, 185; as both weak and a threat, 67; and casual gaming, 41–42; and crossplaying characters, 82; discrimination against, and self-doubt, 66; double oppression of women of color, xii; as equated with low culture, 42; idealized depictions of, 82; misogyny in gaming, 34, 41, 59–65, 67, 87; multitasking by, 43–47, 51–53, 55n29; mutual assistance between, 96; myth of favoritism toward, 64–65; need for female developers, 42; as passive victims of war, 157, *158*, 159, *160*; passivity of, in Hollywood film, 36n3; as percentage of gamers, xii, 40, 57, 67; as spoils of war, merchandise, 92–94; weaponry and, *26*, 26–27, 95; weaving as feminine technology, 139–140, *140*
Woods, James, 165
WorldCon, 74, 77
World of Warcraft (Blizzard Entertainment), 45, 91, 98–102, *100*, 219–220, 230–231, 246
Wu, Brianna, xiii
Wu Zi Mu (in *GTA: San Andreas*), 165, 169–174
Wyler, William, 243n28

XOJane, 82

Years of Living Dangerously (TV series), 162n7
Yee, Nick, 231
YouTube, 62, 79–80, 91, 101, 183–184, 203–204

Zimmerman, Eric, 230–231